the **ULTIMATE** chicken

COOKBOOK

Editor: Krista Lanphier
Art Director: Rudy Krochalk
Layout Designer: Kathy Crawford
Content Production Supervisor: Julie Wagner
Proofreader: Linne Bruskewitz
Recipe Asset Management System: Coleen Martin (Manager), Sue A. Jurack (Specialist)
Editorial Assistant: Barb Czysz
Indexer: Jean Duerst

Food Director: Diane Werner
Test Kitchen Manager: Karen Scales
Recipe Editors: Mary King, Christine Rukavena
Studio Photographers: Rob Hagen (Senior), Dan Roberts, Jim Wieland, Lori Foy
Food Stylists: Sarah Thompson (Senior), Kaitlyn Bessi, Tamara Kaufman
Set Stylists: Jenny Bradley Vent (Senior), Stephanie Marchese (Senior), Melissa Haberman, Dee Dee Jacq
Assistant Food Stylists: Alynna Malson, Shannon Roum, Leah Rekau
Photo Studio Coordinator: Kathleen Swaney

Vice President, Executive Editor/Books: Heidi Reuter Lloyd
Senior Editor/Books: Mark Hagen
Creative Director: Ardyth Cope
Creative Director/Creative Marketing: Jim Palmen
Vice President/Book Marketing: Dan Fink
Chief Marketing Officer: Lisa Karpinski
Senior Vice President, Editor in Chief: Catherine Cassidy
President, Food & Entertaining: Suzanne M. Grimes
President and Chief Executive Officer: Mary G. Berner

Cover Photography: Rob Hagen (Photographer), Dee Dee Jacq (Set Stylist)
Jennifer Janz (Food Stylist), Diane Armstrong (Food Stylist)

Taste of Home Books
©2009 Reiman Media Group, Inc.
5400 S. 60th Street
Greendale, WI 53129

International Standard Book Number (10): 0-89821-635-4
International Standard Book Number (13): 978-0-89821-635-6
Library of Congress Control Number: 2008933649

Pictured on front cover: Clockwise from upper left, Chicken Tortilla Soup (p. 55), Broccoli Chicken Cups (p. 35), Moist Drumsticks (p. 219), Chicken Pesto Pizza (p. 194) and Smothered Chicken Breasts (p. 120)

Pictured on title page: Mexican Chicken Soup (p. 220)
Pictured on introduction page: From left to right, Chicken Tostadas with Mango Salsa (p. 258), Slow 'n' Easy Barbecued Chicken (p. 224), Chicken Penne Casserole (p. 146) and Roasted Chicken with Rosemary (p. 179)

"Timeless Recipes from Trusted Home Cooks" is a registered trademark of Reiman Media Group, Inc.

Chicken icon graphic: Neptune/Shutterstock.com

table of CONTENTS

the ULTIMATE
in great chicken recipes

It's no wonder chicken is the basis of countless recipes for home cooks everywhere. In this latest addition to *Taste of Home*'s must-have collection of cookbooks, *The Ultimate Chicken Cookbook,* you'll find all of the appetizing chicken specialties you and your family crave.

Experience the wonderful versatility of poultry, from everyday favorites like Southern Barbecued Chicken to elegant entrees such as Chicken Piccata. No matter what your preference is, you'll find a range of affordable, wholesome dishes for every season. Here's a sample of what's inside.

APPETIZERS
Whether you're having a holiday party or a casual weekend get-together, these tasty bites satisfy every time. In this chapter, you'll find all-time favorites such as Chicken Quesadillas and Honey-Glazed Chicken Wings, as well as recipes with no-fuss flair like Mexican Sopes, Curried Chicken Turnovers and Barbecued Chicken Egg Rolls.

SALADS
Golden chicken and crispy greens go together like salt and pepper. Whether you're looking for a starter to a hearty meal, a side dish or a light chicken entree, there are plenty of dishes to choose from in this chapter like the Bow Tie Lemon Chicken or Spicy Chicken Salad with Mango Salsa.

SOUPS & MORE
You can't go wrong with a soothing bowl of chicken soup on a cold winter day. Warm your bones with chill-chasing recipes like Hearty Sausage-Chicken Chili, Amish Chicken Corn Soup or Roasted Chicken Noodle Soup. There's even a recipe for homemade Chicken Broth.

SANDWICHES
Everyone loves sandwiches, and the variety of choices in this chapter will satisfy even the pickiest eater. Feast your eyes on mouth-watering recipes including Buffalo Chicken Burgers with Tangy Slaw, a Jumbo Greek Sub or the Chicken Salad Panini. From a light lunch to a tailgating party, there's a sandwich for every need.

GRILLED
There's no doubt about it, grilling adds fabulous flavor to almost any cut of meat, and chicken is no exception. Fire up your grill and try tasty recipes like Apple-Butter Barbecue Chicken, Can-Can Chicken and Prosciutto Chicken Kabobs. You won't regret it!

SKILLET & STOVETOP
Stovetop cooking means quick, easy-to-clean meals that come in handy for busy cooks. It's a snap to feed your family with delicious, simple-to-make dishes like Skillet Chicken Cordon Bleu, Chicken Fricassee with Dumplings or Chicken Marsala.

CASSEROLES

Home-Style Chicken Potpie, Chicken Noodle Casserole and Chicken Shepherd's Pie are just a few of the comforting and hearty one-dish meals that never fail to satisfy hungry appetites. Don't wait, whip up one of these meal-in-one wonders tonight!

OVEN

Traditional baked chicken dishes get a refreshing twist with oven-fresh recipes including Creamy Chicken Lasagna, Brined Roasting Chicken and Bacon-Wrapped Chicken. Go ahead and dig in!

SLOW COOKER

The convenience of a slow cooker can't be beat. Just "set it and forget it," and before you know it, your dinner is ready. Cozy up to warm, inviting suppers like Chicken Saltimbocca, Slow Cooker Cacciatore or Chicken Merlot with Mushrooms.

COOKING FOR ONE OR TWO

Perfect for a single portion or a dining duo, everything you need for a deliciously pared-down meal is in this chapter. Savor fantastic dishes like Spiced Chicken with Melon Salsa, Sesame Chicken Stir-Fry or Spinach Chicken Roll. You won't be disappointed.

WEEKNIGHT FAVORITES

Fixing dinner has never been easier for busy cooks. Your family will want seconds of satisfying suppers like Saucy Tarragon Chicken, Barbecue Chicken Burritos or Chicken Pesto Pasta.

A WORLD OF FLAVOR

Flavors from around the world can grace your table with this collection of international favorites. Add some pizzazz to mealtime with any of the fabulous recipes in this chapter such as Chicken Chorizo Lasagna, Stir-Fried Basil Chicken or Spanish-Style Paella.

In this must-have cookbook you'll find a handy Chicken Reference Guide (p. 6) that includes definitions along with purchasing and defrosting information about chicken. Throughout the book, don't miss the dozens of helpful cooking tips from our Test Kitchen. And, for delicious dishes on the lighter side that include Nutrition Facts, just look for this icon:

This chicken recipe is lower in calories, fat or sodium.

With all of these benefits, plus over 450 irresistible recipes, there's no doubt that *The Ultimate Chicken Cookbook* from *Taste of Home* truly is the ultimate!

CHICKEN *reference guide*

There are many ways to roast, bake and cook chicken...in all its forms. Here are some poultry basics to help you get started.

When purchasing chicken, buy before the "sell-by" date for the best quality, making sure the package is cold and has no holes or tears. (The skin color of chicken ranges from white to deep yellow. This is due to the chicken's diet and is not an indication of its freshness or quality.) Place the poultry in its own plastic grocery bag to prevent it from leaking onto other groceries. When you get home, refrigerate or freeze immediately. Use uncooked, refrigerated chicken within 1 to 2 days.

Never defrost frozen poultry at room temperature. Thaw in the refrigerator, in cold water (see defrosting information on the next page), or in the microwave according to the manufacturer's directions. Always wash your hands and anything that has come into contact with uncooked poultry (knives, cutting boards, countertops) with hot, soapy water to avoid contamination to other foods.

Cook chicken breasts to an internal temperature of 170°. Cook whole chicken and dark meat to 180°. Cook ground chicken and stuffing in a whole chicken to 165°. The juice of thoroughly cooked chicken should run clear when pierced with a fork. Regardless of the cut, chicken is fully cooked when the meat is no longer pink.

USEFUL DEFINITIONS

Basted or Self-Basted: Chicken or turkey that has been injected or marinated with a solution of water, broth or stock that contains a fat, such as butter, spices and various flavor enhancers.

Broiler/Fryer: A chicken about 7 weeks old that weighs 2-1/2 to 4-1/2 pounds.

Chicken Leg: The attached drumstick and thigh.

Chicken Quarter: A quarter of the chicken, which may be the leg or breast quarter. The leg quarter contains the drumstick, thigh and portion of the back. The breast quarter contains the breast, wing and portion of the back.

Cut-Up Chicken: A broiler/fryer that has been cut into two breast halves, two thighs, two drumsticks and two wings. It may or may not have the back.

Drummette: The first section of a chicken wing.

Drumstick: The lower portion of the leg.

Free Range or Free Roaming: The poultry was not confined to a chicken house but was allowed outside to forage for food.

Fresh Poultry: Uncooked poultry that has never been commercially stored below 26°.

Giblets: The heart, liver, neck and gizzard.

Roaster: A chicken between 3 and 5 months old that weighs 5 to 7 pounds.

Split Chicken: A broiler/fryer that was cut lengthwise in half.

HOW MUCH TO PURCHASE

The amount of chicken you need to buy depends on the variety, portion and amount of bone.

STYLE OF THE CUT	SERVINGS PER POUND
CHICKEN (whole)	1 to 2
CHICKEN PARTS (bone-in, skin on)	2 to 3
CHICKEN BREASTS (boneless, skinless)	3 to 4

DEFROSTING GUIDELINES

Defrosting times for poultry depend on the weight of the package and the thickness of the meat. When defrosting chicken in the refrigerator, place a plate or tray under the package to catch any liquid. Here are some basic timelines for defrosting poultry in the refrigerator:

- For bone-in parts or a small whole chicken, allow at least 1 to 2 days.
- For a large whole chicken, allow 24 hours for every 4 pounds.

DEFROSTING IN COLD WATER

Cold-water thawing is an option that takes less time than thawing in the refrigerator but requires more attention.

The poultry must be in a leakproof bag such as its original, tightly sealed wrapper. If its package is not leakproof, place it in a heavy-duty resealable storage bag.

Submerge the wrapped chicken in cold tap water. Change the water every 30 minutes until the poultry is thawed. For this method, allow 30 minutes for every pound.

Cutting Up a Whole Chicken

1 Pull the leg and thigh away from the body. With a small sharp knife, cut through the skin to expose the joint.

2 Cut through joint, then cut skin around thigh to free leg. Repeat with other leg.

3 Separate drumstick from thigh by cutting skin at the joint. Bend drumstick to expose joint; cut through joint and skin.

4 Pull wing away from the body. Cut through skin to expose joint. Cut through joint and skin to separate wing from body. Repeat.

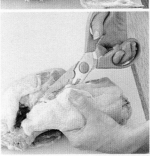

5 Snip along each side of the backbone between rib joints with kitchen or poultry shears.

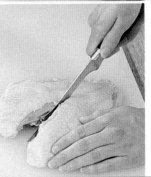

6 Hold chicken breast in both hands (skin side down) and bend it back to snap breastbone. Turn over. With a knife, cut in half along breastbone. Breastbone will remain attached to one of the halves.

APPETIZERS

BAKED CHICKEN NACHOS, P. 29

TEMPURA CHICKEN WINGS

prep 40 minutes | **bake** 25 minutes

susan wuckowitsch

lenexa, kansas

When I moved to Kansas City from Texas, I brought many of my mom's best-loved recipes with me, including these saucy sweet-and-sour wings. This recipe turned a friend of mine, who's not a fan of chicken, into a real wing lover.

15	whole chicken wings (about 3 pounds)
1	cup cornstarch
3	eggs, lightly beaten

Oil for deep-fat frying

1/2	cup sugar
1/2	cup white vinegar
1/2	cup currant jelly
1/4	cup soy sauce
3	tablespoons ketchup
2	tablespoons lemon juice

Cut chicken wings into three sections; discard wing tip section. Place cornstarch in a large resealable plastic bag; add chicken wings, a few at a time, and shake to coat evenly. Dip wings in eggs.

In an electric skillet or deep-fat fryer, heat oil to 375°. Fry wings for 8 minutes or until golden brown and juices run clear, turning occasionally. Drain on paper towels.

In a small saucepan, combine the sugar, white vinegar, currant jelly, soy sauce, ketchup and lemon juice. Bring to a boil. Reduce heat; simmer, un-covered, for 10 minutes.

Place the chicken wings in a greased 15-in. x 10-in. baking pan. Pour half of the sauce over wings. Bake, uncovered, at 350° for 15 minutes. Turn wings; top with remaining sauce. Bake 10-15 minutes longer or until chicken juices run clear and coating is set. **yield:** 2-1/2 dozen.

editor's note: Uncooked chicken wing sections (wingettes) may be substituted for whole chicken wings.

CHICKEN MEATBALL APPETIZERS

prep/total time 30 minutes

3	tablespoons finely chopped onion
3	tablespoons finely chopped celery
2	tablespoons finely chopped carrot
2	tablespoons dry bread crumbs
1	egg white
1/2	teaspoon poultry seasoning

Pinch pepper

2-1/2	cups minced cooked chicken breast

In a large bowl, combine the first seven ingredients; add the cooked chicken and mix well. Shape into 3/4-in. balls.

Place meatballs on a rack that has been coated with cooking spray in a shallow pan. Bake at 400° for 8-10 minutes or until lightly browned; drain. **yield:** about 2-1/2 dozen.

nutrition facts: 3 meatballs equals 42 calories, 1 g fat (0 saturated fat), 21 mg cholesterol, 23 mg sodium, 2 g carbohydrate, 0 fiber, 6 g protein.

diabetic exchange: 1 very lean meat.

This chicken recipe is lower in calories, fat or sodium.

norma snider

chambersburg, pennsylvania

These nicely seasoned chicken meatballs are a crowd-pleasing change of pace on the appetizer tray. They're great plain or dipped in mustard.

HOT CHICKEN SWIRLS

prep 25 minutes | **bake** 10 minutes

This chicken recipe is lower in calories, fat or sodium.

- 2 tubes (8 ounces *each*) refrigerated reduced-fat crescent rolls
- 1 cup shredded cooked chicken breast
- 4 ounces fat-free cream cheese
- 1/4 cup prepared reduced-fat ranch salad dressing
- 1/4 cup shredded reduced-fat cheddar cheese
- 1/4 cup finely chopped sweet red pepper
- 2 green onions, finely chopped
- 2 tablespoons Louisiana-style hot sauce

Separate each tube of crescent dough into four rectangles; gently press perforations to seal. In a small bowl, combine the remaining ingredients; spread evenly over rectangles. Roll up jelly-roll style, starting with a short side; pinch seams to seal.

Cut each into eight slices; place cut side down on ungreased baking sheets. Bake at 375° for 10-12 minutes or until golden brown. Refrigerate leftovers. **yield:** 64 appetizers.

nutrition facts: 1 appetizer equals 34 calories, 2 g fat (trace saturated fat), 2 mg cholesterol, 82 mg sodium, 3 g carbohydrate, trace fiber, 2 g protein.

diabetic exchange: 1/2 starch.

evelyn mcginnis
bay city, michigan

I was trying to use up crescent rolls and leftover chicken breast and came up with this tasty recipe! I lightened it by using reduced-fat dressing and fat-free cream cheese.

SOUTHWEST EGG ROLLS WITH COOL RANCH DIP

prep 35 minutes | **cook** 5 minutes/batch

becky aylor

sisters, oregon

East meets West in these irresistible egg rolls that are chock-full of my favorite Southwestern ingredients. The refreshing dip adds a delicious touch.

2-1/2   cups shredded cooked chicken
1-1/2   cups (6 ounces) shredded Mexican cheese blend
2/3   cup frozen corn, thawed
2/3   cup canned black beans, rinsed and drained
5   green onions, chopped
1/4   cup minced fresh cilantro
1   teaspoon salt
1   teaspoon ground cumin
1   teaspoon grated lime peel
1/4   teaspoon cayenne pepper
1   package (16 ounces) egg roll wrappers
Oil for deep-fat frying
SAUCE
1   cup ranch salad dressing
1   medium ripe avocado, peeled and mashed
1   tablespoon minced fresh cilantro
1   teaspoon grated lime peel

In a large bowl, combine the first 10 ingredients. Place 1/4 cup of chicken mixture in the center of one egg roll wrapper. (Keep remaining wrappers covered with a damp paper towel until ready to use.) Fold bottom corner over filling. Fold sides toward center over filling. Moisten remaining corner with water; roll up tightly to seal. Repeat.

In an electric skillet or deep-fat fryer, heat oil to 375°. Fry egg rolls, a few at a time, for 2 minutes on each side or until golden brown. Drain on paper towels.

Meanwhile, combine the sauce ingredients. Serve the sauce with the egg rolls. **yield:** 20 egg rolls (1-1/2 cups sauce).

ASIAGO CHICKEN SPREAD

prep 25 minutes + chilling

3/4   pound boneless skinless chicken breasts, cut into 1/2-inch cubes
1/4   teaspoon salt
1/8   teaspoon pepper
2   garlic cloves, minced
2   tablespoons butter
1/3   cup salted cashew halves
1/3   cup mayonnaise
1/2   cup chopped onion
1/4   cup shredded Asiago cheese
1/4   cup minced fresh basil
1/2   teaspoon hot pepper sauce
Assorted crackers *or* toasted baguette slices

james korzenowski

fennville, michigan

Rich, flavorful Asiago cheese, fresh basil, onion and garlic add great flavor to this tasty spread.

Season chicken with salt and pepper. In a large skillet, saute chicken and garlic in butter for 5-6 minutes or until chicken is no longer pink. Stir in cashews. Remove from the heat; cool.

In a food processor, combine the mayonnaise, onion, cheese, basil, pepper sauce and chicken mixture; cover and process until blended. Press into a 2-cup bowl; cover and refrigerate for at least 2 hours.

If desired, unmold onto a serving platter; serve with crackers or baguette slices. **yield:** 2 cups.

CHICKEN SALAD CUPS

prep 30 minutes + chilling | **bake** 10 minutes + cooling

lois holdson
millersville, maryland

Pineapple and almonds enhance the creamy chicken salad in these cute tartlets made with convenient refrigerated pie pastry.

- 1 package (15 ounces) refrigerated pie pastry
- 2 cups cubed cooked chicken
- 1 can (8 ounces) unsweetened crushed pineapple, drained
- 1/2 cup slivered almonds
- 1/2 cup chopped celery
- 1/2 cup shredded cheddar cheese
- 1/2 cup mayonnaise
- 1/2 teaspoon salt
- 1/2 teaspoon paprika

TOPPING
- 1/2 cup sour cream
- 1/4 cup mayonnaise
- 1/2 cup shredded cheddar cheese

Cut each sheet of pie pastry into 4-1/2-in. rounds; reroll scraps and cut out additional circles. Press pastry onto the bottom and up the sides of 14 ungreased muffin cups.

Bake at 450° for 6-7 minutes or until golden brown. Cool on a wire rack.

In a large bowl, combine the chicken, pineapple, almonds, celery, cheddar cheese, mayonnaise, salt and paprika; refrigerate until chilled.

Just before serving, spoon two rounded tablespoonfuls of chicken salad into each pastry cup. For the topping, combine sour cream and mayonnaise; spoon over filling. Sprinkle with cheese. **yield:** 14 servings.

CURRIED CHICKEN TURNOVERS

prep 40 minutes | **bake** 20 minutes

- 1/2 cup finely chopped celery
- 1/4 cup finely chopped onion
- 1/4 cup finely chopped carrot
- 2 teaspoons butter
- 1 tablespoon all-purpose flour
- 1-1/2 teaspoons curry powder
- 1/4 teaspoon salt
- 1/2 cup chicken broth
- 1-1/2 cups diced cooked chicken
- 1/4 cup sour cream
- 1/4 cup plain yogurt
- 1 package (17.3 ounces) frozen puff pastry, thawed
- 1 egg yolk
- 1 teaspoon water

In a large skillet, saute the celery, onion and carrot in butter for 4-6 minutes or until tender. Stir in the flour, curry powder and salt until blended. Add broth. Bring to a boil; cook and stir for 1 minute or until thickened. Remove from the heat. Stir in the chicken, sour cream and yogurt.

On a lightly floured surface, roll each pastry sheet into a 12-in. x 10-in. rectangle. With a floured 3-in. round cookie cutter, cut out 12 circles from each rectangle. Place 2 teaspoons chicken mixture on one side of each circle. Moisten edges with water; fold dough over filling. Press edges with a fork to seal.

Place 1 in. apart on a greased baking sheet. In a small bowl, beat egg yolk and water; brush over pastry. Bake at 400° for 17-20 minutes or until golden brown. Serve warm. **yield:** 2 dozen.

mary kisinger
calgary, alberta

You'll want to try these party-perfect turnovers. My guests enjoy the delicious curried chicken. Plus, the puff pastry makes for an elegant snack.

CHICKEN QUESADILLAS

prep/total time 30 minutes

linda miller
klamath falls, oregon

The cheese, olives and chilies taste great in my quesadillas, but it's the tender homemade tortillas that make this savory snack extra-special.

4	cups all-purpose flour
1-1/2	teaspoons salt
1/2	teaspoon baking powder
1	cup shortening
1-1/4	cups warm water
1	cup *each* shredded cheddar, part-skim mozzarella and pepper Jack cheese
2	cups diced cooked chicken
1	cup sliced green onions
1	cup sliced ripe olives
1	can (4 ounces) chopped green chilies, drained

Salsa and sour cream

In a large bowl, combine the flour, salt and baking powder. Cut in the shortening until the mixture is crumbly. Add enough warm water, stirring until mixture forms a ball. Let stand for 10 minutes. Divide into 28 portions.

On a lightly floured surface, roll each portion of dough into a 7-in. circle. Cook on a lightly greased griddle for 1-1/2 to 2 minutes on each side, breaking any bubbles with a toothpick. Keep warm.

In a large bowl, combine the shredded cheeses. For each quesadilla, place a tortilla on the griddle; sprinkle with about 2 tablespoons cheese mixture, 2 tablespoons chicken, 1 tablespoon onions, 1 tablespoon olives and 1 teaspoon chilies. Top with 1 tablespoon cheese mixture and another tortilla. Cook for 30-60 seconds; turn and cook 30 seconds longer or until cheese is melted. Cut into wedges. Serve with salsa and sour cream. **yield:** 14 quesadillas.

SUMMER TEA SANDWICHES

prep 45 minutes | **bake** 20 minutes + cooling

**taste of home
test kitchen**

greendale, wisconsin

*Our home economists
prepared these dainty
finger sandwiches that are
perfect for casual picnics or
ladies' luncheons alike.
Tarragon-seasoned chicken
complements cucumber
and cantaloupe slices.*

1/2 teaspoon dried tarragon
1/2 teaspoon salt, *divided*
1/4 teaspoon pepper
1 pound boneless skinless chicken breasts
1/2 cup reduced-fat mayonnaise
1 tablespoon finely chopped red onion
1 teaspoon dill weed
1/2 teaspoon lemon juice
24 slices soft multigrain bread, crusts removed
1 medium cucumber, thinly sliced
1/4 medium cantaloupe, cut into 12 thin slices

Combine the dried tarragon, 1/4 teaspoon salt and pepper; rub over the chicken. Place on a baking sheet coated with cooking spray. Bake at 350° for 20-25 minutes or until juices run clear. Cool to room temperature; thinly slice.

Combine the mayonnaise, red onion, dill, lemon juice and remaining salt; spread over one side of 12 slices of bread. Top with the cucumber, chicken, cantaloupe and remaining bread. Cut the sandwiches in half diagonally. Serve immediately. **yield:** 12 servings.

JALAPENO CHICKEN WRAPS

prep 15 minutes | **grill** 20 minutes

1 pound boneless skinless chicken breasts
1 tablespoon garlic powder
1 tablespoon onion powder
1 tablespoon pepper
2 teaspoons seasoned salt
1 teaspoon paprika
1 small onion, cut into strips
15 jalapeno peppers, halved and seeded
1 pound sliced bacon, halved widthwise

Blue cheese salad dressing

Cut chicken into 2-in. x 1-1/2-in. strips. In a large resealable plastic bag, combine the garlic powder, onion powder, pepper, seasoned salt and paprika; add chicken and shake to coat. Place a chicken and onion strip in each jalapeno half. Wrap each with a piece of bacon and secure with toothpicks.

Grill, uncovered, over indirect medium heat for 9-10 minutes on each side or until chicken juices run clear and bacon is crisp. Serve with blue cheese dressing. **yield:** 2-1/2 dozen.

editor's note: When cutting hot peppers, disposable gloves are recommended. Avoid touching your face.

leslie buenz

tinley park, illinois

*These easy appetizers are
always a hit at parties!
Zesty strips of chicken and
bits of onion sit in jalapeno
halves that are wrapped in
bacon and grilled. Serve
them with blue cheese or
ranch salad dressing for
effortless dipping.*

GARLIC GINGER CHICKEN STRIPS

prep 5 minutes + marinating | **broil** 10 minutes

candy snyder

salem, oregon

Whether you serve these tender chicken strips as an appetizer or main dish, they're sure to satisfy your hungry bunch. The five-spice powder and red pepper flakes add a bit of zip.

1/4   cup sherry *or* chicken broth
1/4   cup reduced-sodium soy sauce
3   garlic cloves, minced
1   tablespoon honey
1   tablespoon minced fresh basil *or* 1 teaspoon dried basil
1/2   teaspoon ground ginger
1/2   teaspoon Chinese five-spice powder
1/4   teaspoon crushed red pepper flakes, optional
1/4   teaspoon pepper
1   pound boneless skinless chicken breasts, cut into 1-inch strips

In a large resealable plastic bag, combine the first nine ingredients. Remove 3 tablespoons for basting; set aside. Place chicken in bag. Seal and turn to coat. Refrigerate for at least 4 hours. Cover and refrigerate reserved marinade.

Drain and discard marinade. Broil chicken 3-4 in. from the heat for 3 minutes; turn strips over. Baste with reserved marinade. Broil 4-5 minutes longer or until chicken juices run clear, turning occasionally. **yield:** 4 servings.

SPICY CHICKEN APPETIZER PIZZA

prep 25 minutes + marinating | **bake** 15 minutes

michelle martin

waterville, ohio

This flavorful pizza uses marinated chicken and a surprise ingredient, sliced almonds, to pack a crunchy and tasty punch.

1/2   cup rice vinegar
1/4   cup reduced-sodium soy sauce
1   cup chopped green onions, *divided*
4   garlic cloves, minced
3   teaspoons olive oil, *divided*
1/2   teaspoon pepper
1/4   teaspoon cayenne pepper
3/4   pound boneless skinless chicken breasts, cut into 1/2-inch pieces
1   tablespoon cornstarch
1   prebaked thin Italian bread shell crust (10 ounces)
1/4   cup shredded Monterey Jack cheese
1/4   cup shredded part-skim mozzarella cheese
2   tablespoons sliced almonds

Combine the vinegar, soy sauce, 1/2 cup onions, garlic, 1 teaspoon oil, pepper and cayenne. Pour 1/2 cup into a large resealable plastic bag; add chicken. Seal bag and turn to coat; refrigerate for 30 minutes. Cover and refrigerate remaining marinade.

Drain chicken, discarding marinade. In a large nonstick skillet over medium heat, cook chicken in remaining oil until no longer pink. Combine cornstarch and reserved marinade until blended; stir into skillet. Bring to a boil; cook and stir for 2 minutes or until thickened. Remove from the heat.

Place the crust on an ungreased baking sheet; top with chicken mixture. Sprinkle with cheeses. Bake at 400° for 12 minutes. Top with almonds and remaining onions. Bake 2-3 minutes longer or until cheese is golden brown. **yield:** 12 slices.

BARBECUED CHICKEN EGG ROLLS

prep/total time 20 minutes

erin stroud
sterling, illinois

If you like barbecued chicken, you'll really enjoy these filling chicken roll-ups. To round out the meal, I like to serve them with cheesy garlic mashed potatoes.

1   cup shredded cooked chicken
1/2   cup shredded cheddar-Monterey Jack cheese
1/3   cup honey barbecue sauce
4   egg roll wrappers
Canola oil for frying

In a small bowl, combine the chicken, cheese and barbecue sauce. Place about 1/4 cup in the center of each egg roll wrapper. Fold bottom corner over filling; fold sides over filling. Moisten remaining corner with water; roll up tightly to seal.

In an electric skillet, heat 1 in. of canola oil to 375°. Fry the egg rolls, two at a time, for 30 seconds on each side or until golden brown. Drain on paper towels. Serve warm. **yield:** 2 servings.

CHICKEN VEGGIE STRUDEL

prep 30 minutes | **bake** 35 minutes

3   cups cubed cooked chicken
3   cups fresh broccoli florets
3   cups fresh cauliflowerets
3   cups finely chopped carrots
2   cups (8 ounces) shredded cheddar cheese
2   cups (8 ounces) shredded Swiss cheese
1   cup chopped onion
3   eggs
2   garlic cloves, minced
2   tablespoons minced fresh parsley
2   teaspoons *each* dried basil, tarragon and thyme
2   teaspoons pepper
2   tablespoons plus 1-1/2 cups butter, *divided*
2   tablespoons all-purpose flour
1   cup milk
24   sheets phyllo dough (14 inches x 9 inches)
1   package (15 ounces) seasoned bread crumbs

In a large bowl, combine the first seven ingredients. In a small bowl, beat the eggs. Stir in the garlic, parsley, basil, tarragon, thyme and pepper. Add to chicken mixture; toss to coat. In a small saucepan, melt 2 tablespoons butter. Stir in the flour until smooth; gradually stir in milk. Bring to a boil; cook and stir for 2 minutes or until thickened. Pour over chicken mixture; toss to coat.

Melt remaining butter. Place one sheet of phyllo dough on a work surface (keep remaining dough covered with plastic wrap and a damp towel to avoid drying out). Brush with butter; sprinkle with bread crumbs. Repeat layers five times.

Spread about 3-1/3 cups of filling down the center of dough to within 1 in. of edges. Fold short sides 1 in. over filling. Roll up jelly-roll style, starting with a long side. Brush with butter. Place seam side down in an ungreased 15-in. x 10-in. baking pan.

Make three more strudels with the remaining phyllo dough, melted butter and filling. Bake at 375° for 35-40 minutes or until golden brown. **yield:** 4 loaves (6 servings each).

debra mckim
hastings, nebraska

I serve this hearty strudel often as an appetizer at dinner parties. I usually keep a few extra in the freezer in case company unexpectedly shows up.

ULTIMATE KITCHEN TIP

Shredding a block of soft cheese can be difficult. To make grating it easier, freeze the cheese for 10-20 minutes first, then shred it. Place extra shredded cheese in a resealable plastic bag and store it in the freezer. To use, break off what you need and thaw.

CHICKEN HAM PINWHEELS

prep 15 minutes | **bake** 30 minutes

laura mahaffey

annapolis, maryland

*These pretty pinwheels
have been a part of our
annual Christmas Eve
appetizer buffet for many
years. I love them because
they can be made a day in
advance and taste great
alone or served with a
simple citrus spread.*

4   boneless skinless chicken breast
    halves
1/8 teaspoon plus 1/2 teaspoon dried
    basil, *divided*
1/8 teaspoon salt
1/8 teaspoon garlic salt
1/8 teaspoon pepper
4   thin sliced deli ham
2   teaspoons lemon juice
Paprika
ORANGE SPREAD
1/2 cup mayonnaise
1   teaspoon grated orange peel
1   teaspoon orange juice

Flatten chicken to 1/4-in. thickness. Combine 1/8 teaspoon basil, salt, garlic salt and pepper; sprinkle over chicken. Top each with a ham slice.

Roll up jelly-roll style; place seam side down in a greased 11-in. x 7-in. baking dish. Drizzle with lemon juice and sprinkle with paprika. Bake, uncovered, at 350° for 30 minutes or until chicken juices run clear. Cover and refrigerate.

Meanwhile, for orange spread, in a small bowl combine the mayonnaise, orange peel, orange juice and remaining basil. Cover and refrigerate until serving. Cut chicken rolls into 1/2-in. slices. Serve with orange spread. **yield:** 24 servings.

COCONUT CHICKEN BITES

prep 10 minutes + chilling | **cook** 5 minutes

2   cups flaked coconut
1   egg
2   tablespoons milk
1/2 cup all-purpose flour
3/4 pound boneless skinless chicken
    breasts, cut into 3/4-inch pieces
Oil for frying
1   teaspoon celery salt
1/2 teaspoon garlic powder
1/2 teaspoon ground cumin

Place coconut in a blender, cover and process coconut until finely chopped. Transfer to a shallow bowl; set aside. In another shallow bowl, combine egg and milk. Place flour in a third shallow bowl. Coat chicken with flour; dip in egg mixture, then in coconut. Arrange in a single layer on a baking pan. Refrigerate for 30 minutes.

In an electric skillet or deep-fat fryer, heat 2 in. of oil to 375°. Fry chicken, a few pieces at time, for 1-1/2 minutes on each side or until golden brown. Drain on paper towels; place in a bowl. Sprinkle with celery salt, garlic powder and cumin; toss to coat. Serve warm. **yield:** 3 dozen.

linda schwarz

bertrand, nebraska

*These tender nuggets are
great for nibbling, thanks to
the coconut, cumin, celery
salt and garlic powder that
season them. I've served the
bites several times for
parties, and everyone
enjoyed them.*

SOPES

prep 15 minutes | **cook** 35 minutes

2 cups masa harina
1 teaspoon salt
1-1/3 cups warm water
1-1/2 cups shredded cooked chicken breast
1 cup salsa, *divided*
1/4 cup lard
1 cup refried beans
1 cup shredded lettuce
1/2 cup crumbled queso fresco

In a small bowl, combine masa harina and salt; stir in water. Knead until mixture forms a ball. Divide dough into 16 portions; shape into balls and cover with plastic wrap.

Working between two sheets of plastic wrap, press four balls into 3-1/2-in. circles. On an un-greased griddle, cook dough circles over medium-low heat for 1-2 minutes or until the bottoms are lightly set. Turn and cook 2 minutes longer. Remove from the heat; quickly pinch the edge of circles to form a 1/2-in. rim. Return to the griddle; cook 2 minutes longer or until the bottoms are lightly browned. Remove to wire racks; cover. Repeat with the remaining dough.

In a small saucepan, combine chicken and 1/2 cup salsa. Cook over medium-low heat until heated through, stirring occasionally. In a large skillet, melt the lard. Cook sopes over medium-high heat for 2 minutes on each side or until crisp and lightly browned. Remove to paper towels to drain.

To assemble, layer each sope with refried beans, chicken mixture and the remaining salsa. Sprinkle with lettuce and queso fresco. Serve immediately. **yield:** 16 servings.

taste of home test kitchen
greendale, wisconsin

A sope (SOH-peh) is a type of Mexican appetizer that consists of a corn dough base filled with many toppings, such as shredded beef or chicken, tomatoes or lettuce and cheese. Queso fresco is a mild, white Mexican cheese, and can be found with other specialty cheeses at the supermarket.

CHEESY CHICKEN WONTONS

prep 30 minutes | **cook** 20 minutes

taste of home test kitchen

greendale, wisconsin

When hosting an informal get-together with friends, enlist guests to help assemble these savory snacks from our Test Kitchen. As a reward, they get to eat the fruits of their labor!

2	cups (8 ounces) shredded part-skim mozzarella cheese
1-1/2	cups shredded cooked chicken
3	green onions, chopped
1/3	cup chopped fresh tomato
1	tablespoon salt-free garlic and herb seasoning
1/8	teaspoon cayenne pepper
1	package (12 ounces) wonton wrappers
1	egg, lightly beaten

Oil for frying

Pizza *or* spaghetti sauce, warmed

In a large bowl, combine the cheese, chicken, onions, tomato, herb seasoning and cayenne. Place about 2 tablespoons in the center of each wonton wrapper. Brush edges with egg; fold corner over, making a triangle. Seal seams.

In an electric skillet or deep-fat fryer, heat I in. of oil to 375°. Fry wontons, a few at a time, for I to I-1/2 minutes on each side or until golden brown. Drain on paper towels. Serve warm with pizza or spaghetti sauce. **yield:** about 4 dozen.

nutrition facts: 3 wontons (without pizza or spaghetti sauce) equals 129 calories, 4 g fat (2 g saturated fat), 35 mg cholesterol, 203 mg sodium, 13 g carbohydrate, 1 g fiber, 10 g protein.

diabetic exchanges: 1 very lean meat, 1 starch, 1/2 fat.

CHICKEN ENCHILADA DIP

prep/total time 20 minutes

2	cups shredded cooked chicken
1	can (10-3/4 ounces) condensed cream of chicken soup, undiluted
1	cup (4 ounces) shredded cheddar cheese
1	can (5 ounces) evaporated milk
1/2	cup chopped celery
1/3	cup finely chopped onion
1	can (4 ounces) chopped green chilies
1	envelope taco seasoning

Tortilla chips

In a 2-qt. microwave-safe dish, combine the first eight ingredients. Microwave, uncovered, on high for 4-5 minutes; stir. Microwave, uncovered, 3-4 minutes longer or until heated through. Serve with tortilla chips. **yield:** 3 cups.

editor's note: This recipe was tested in a 1,100-watt microwave.

leah davis

morrow, ohio

A friend brought this appetizer to our house for a dinner party. Everyone loved the zesty chicken and cheese dip so much that no one was hungry for supper. My friend graciously shared the recipe, and I've served it many times, always with rave reviews.

ULTIMATE KITCHEN TIP

If you don't have a deep-fat fryer or electric fry pan to prepare the chicken wontons, you can use a Dutch oven and a thermometer. To avoid splattering, carefully place foods into the hot oil and never add any liquids to it. To keep fried foods warm, drain on a paper towel, then place on an ovenproof platter. Cover loosely with foil and place in a 200° oven.

BARBECUE CHICKEN BITS

prep/total time 25 minutes

celena cantrell-richardson
eau claire, michigan

Folks who enjoy the taste of barbecue will gobble up these tender chunks of chicken coated in crushed barbecue potato chips. They're a hit at home and at friendly gatherings.

 1 egg
 2 tablespoons milk
 4 cups barbecue potato chips, crushed
 1/2 pound boneless skinless chicken breasts, cut into 1-1/2-inch cubes

Barbecue sauce

In a shallow bowl, whisk egg and milk. Place potato chips in another shallow bowl. Dip chicken in egg mixture, then roll in chips. Place in a single layer on a greased baking sheet. Bake at 400° for 10-15 minutes or until juices run clear. Serve with barbecue sauce. **yield:** 4 servings.

TENDER CHICKEN NUGGETS

prep/total time 25 minutes

 1/2 cup seasoned bread crumbs
 2 tablespoons grated Parmesan cheese
 1 egg white
 1 pound boneless skinless chicken breasts, cut into 1-inch cubes

In a large resealable plastic bag, combine bread crumbs and cheese. In a shallow bowl, beat the egg white. Dip chicken pieces in egg white, then place in bag and shake to coat.

Place in a 15-in. x 10-in. baking pan coated with cooking spray. Bake, uncovered, at 400° for 12-15 minutes or until no longer pink, turning once. **yield:** 4 servings.

lynne hahn
winchester, california

Four ingredients are all it takes to create these moist golden bites that are healthier than fast food. I serve them with ranch dressing and barbecue sauce for dipping.

CREAMY CHICKEN SPREAD

This chicken recipe is lower in calories, fat or sodium.

charlene barrows
reedley, california

Every time I take this eye-catching log to a party, it's gone in no time. This mild spread smooths easily onto any kind of cracker.

prep/total time 25 minutes

 1 package (8 ounces) cream cheese, softened
 1/4 cup mayonnaise
 2 tablespoons lemon juice
 1/2 teaspoon salt
 1/4 teaspoon ground ginger
 1/8 teaspoon pepper
 1/8 teaspoon hot pepper sauce
 2 cups finely chopped cooked chicken breast
 2 hard-cooked eggs, finely chopped
 1/4 cup sliced green onions

Diced pimientos and additional sliced green onions

Assorted crackers *or* snack rye bread

In a small bowl, beat the first seven ingredients until blended. Stir in the chopped chicken, eggs and green onions.

Shape into an 8-in. x 2-in. log. Garnish with pimientos and onions. Cover and chill. Remove from the refrigerator 15 minutes before serving. Serve with crackers or bread. **yield:** 3 cups.

nutrition facts: 1/4 cup of spread (prepared with reduced-fat cream cheese and fat-free mayonnaise) equals 100 calories, 5 g fat (3 g saturated fat), 67 mg cholesterol, 223 mg sodium, 3 g carbohydrate, trace fiber, 10 g protein.

diabetic exchanges: 1 lean meat, 1 fat.

CURRIED CHICKEN CREAM PUFFS

prep 20 minutes | **bake** 20 minutes

kerry vaughn
kalispell, montana

I've made these fluffy puffs for baby showers as well as holiday parties. The savory appetizers have a wonderful mixture of lightness, creaminess and crunch.

1/2   cup water
1/3   cup butter, cubed
Dash salt
1/2   cup all-purpose flour
2   eggs

FILLING

1   package (8 ounces) cream cheese, softened
1/4   cup milk
1/4   teaspoon salt
1/4   teaspoon curry powder
Dash pepper
1-1/2   cups cubed cooked chicken
1/3   cup slivered almonds, toasted
1   green onion, chopped

In a large saucepan, bring water, butter and salt to a boil. Add flour all at once and stir until a smooth ball forms. Remove from the heat; let stand for 5 minutes. Add eggs, one at a time, beating well after each addition. Continue beating until mixture is smooth and shiny.

Drop by rounded teaspoonfuls 2 in. apart onto greased baking sheets. Bake at 425° for 15-20 minutes or until golden brown. Remove to wire racks. Immediately split puffs open; remove tops and set aside. Reduce heat to 375°.

In a small bowl, beat the cream cheese, milk, salt, curry powder and pepper until smooth. Stir in the chicken, almonds and green onion. Spoon into the bottom half of puffs; replace tops. Place on a baking sheet; bake for 5 minutes or until heated through. **yield:** 2 dozen.

CHICKEN LIVER PATE

prep 30 minutes + chilling

roberta wolff
waltham, massachusetts

My family loves this savory spread on crackers. But I've also put it to use as a sandwich filling with lettuce and tomato.

1	pound chicken livers
1	small onion, chopped
1/3	cup rendered chicken fat *or* canola oil
1/2	pound fresh mushrooms, quartered
2	hard-cooked eggs, quartered
1	to 2 tablespoons sherry *or* chicken broth
3/4	teaspoon salt
1/4	teaspoon pepper

Melba rounds *or* assorted crackers

In a large skillet, saute chicken livers and onion in chicken fat for 10 minutes or until livers are no longer pink. Transfer to a food processor; cover and process until chicken livers are coarsely chopped.

Add the mushrooms, eggs, 1 tablespoon sherry or broth, salt and pepper. Cover and process until smooth, adding more sherry or broth if needed for pate to reach desired consistency.

Transfer to a bowl. Cover and refrigerate for at least 3 hours. Serve with melba rounds or assorted crackers. **yield:** 12 servings.

SESAME CHICKEN BITES

prep/total time 30 minutes

1/2	cup dry bread crumbs
1/4	cup sesame seeds
2	teaspoons minced fresh parsley
1/2	cup mayonnaise
1	teaspoon onion powder
1	teaspoon ground mustard
1/4	teaspoon pepper
1	pound boneless skinless chicken breasts, cut into 1-inch cubes
2	to 4 tablespoons canola oil

HONEY-MUSTARD SAUCE

3/4	cup mayonnaise
4-1/2	teaspoons honey
1-1/2	teaspoons Dijon mustard

In a large resealable plastic bag, combine the bread crumbs, sesame seeds and parsley; set aside. In a small bowl, combine the mayonnaise, onion powder, mustard and pepper. Coat chicken in mayonnaise mixture, then add to crumb mixture, a few pieces at a time; shake to coat.

In a large skillet, saute chicken in oil in batches until juices run clear, adding additional oil as needed. In a small bowl, combine sauce ingredients. Serve with the chicken. **yield:** 8-10 servings.

kathy green
layton, new jersey

So tender and tasty, these chicken appetizers are enhanced by a honey-mustard dipping sauce. I used to spend several days creating hors d'oeuvres for our holiday open house, and these bites were among the favorites.

HONEY-GLAZED WINGS

prep 20 minutes + marinating | **bake** 50 minutes

marlene wahl
baldwin, wisconsin

My family favors chicken wings that are mildly seasoned with honey, ginger, soy sauce and chili sauce. Tasty and tender, they are sure to be a hit at your next get-together. They're a crowd-pleaser!

15   whole chicken wings (about 3 pounds)
1/2   cup honey
1/3   cup soy sauce
2   tablespoons canola oil
2   tablespoons chili sauce
2   teaspoons salt
1   teaspoon garlic powder
1   teaspoon Worcestershire sauce
1/2   teaspoon ground ginger

Cut chicken wings into three sections; discard wing tip section. Set wings aside. In a small saucepan, combine the honey, soy sauce, oil, chili sauce, salt, garlic powder, Worcestershire sauce and ginger. Cook and stir until blended and heated through. Cool to room temperature.

Place the chicken wings in a large resealable plastic bag; add honey mixture. Seal bag and turn to coat. Refrigerate for at least 8 hours or overnight.

Drain and discard marinade. Place wings in a well-greased 15-in. x 10-in. baking pan. Bake, uncovered, at 375° for 30 minutes. Drain; turn wings. Bake 20-25 minutes longer or until chicken juices run clear and glaze is set. **yield:** 2-1/2 dozen.

editor's note: Uncooked chicken wing sections (wingettes) may be substituted for whole chicken wings.

CHICKEN CRESCENT APPETIZER

prep/total time 30 minutes

1   package (12 ounces) frozen spinach souffle
2   cups cubed cooked chicken
1   can (2.8 ounces) french-fried onions
1/2   cup shredded Parmesan cheese
1   tube (8 ounces) refrigerated crescent rolls

Heat spinach souffle according to package directions. Meanwhile, in a small bowl, combine the chicken, onions and Parmesan cheese; set aside.

Unroll crescent dough; separate into eight triangles. Arrange on an ungreased 12-in. round baking pan or pizza pan, forming a ring with pointed ends facing the outer edge of pan and wide ends overlapping.

Stir souffle into chicken mixture; spoon over wide ends of rolls. Fold points over filling and tuck under wide ends (filling will be visible). Bake at 375° for 11-13 minutes or until golden brown. **yield:** 8 servings.

debbie todd
arrington, tennessee

Refrigerated crescent rolls and a savory packaged filling make this yummy hors d'oeuvre swift and easy to fix.

BROCCOLI CHICKEN CUPS

prep 15 minutes | **bake** 25 minutes

2-1/2 cups diced cooked chicken breast
1 can (10-3/4 ounces) reduced-fat reduced-sodium condensed cream of chicken soup, undiluted
1 cup frozen chopped broccoli, thawed and drained
2 small plum tomatoes, seeded and chopped
1 small carrot, grated
1 tablespoon Dijon mustard
1 garlic clove, minced
1/4 teaspoon pepper
1 sheet frozen puff pastry, thawed
1/4 cup grated Parmesan cheese

In a large bowl, combine the first eight ingredients; set aside. On a lightly floured surface, roll pastry into a 12-in. x 9-in. rectangle. Cut lengthwise into four strips and widthwise into three strips. Gently press puff pastry squares into muffin cups coated with cooking spray.

Spoon the chicken mixture into the pastry cups. Sprinkle with Parmesan cheese. Bake at 375° for 25-30 minutes or until golden brown. Serve warm. **yield:** 1 dozen.

marty kingery
point pleasant,
west virginia

Frozen puff pastry makes these rich and creamy appetizers a snap to prepare. Sometimes, instead of chopping the tomatoes, I put a small slice on top of each cup before popping them in the oven.

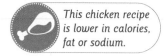

This chicken recipe is lower in calories, fat or sodium.

BAKED EGG ROLLS

prep/total time 30 minutes

barbra annino

galena, illinois

Chinese take-out can be high in sodium, fat and calories, so these crispy appetizers are a nice alternative. Whenever my husband craves a take-out egg roll, I just make these instead.

1-1/3 cups chopped fresh broccoli stir-fry vegetable blend
  1 cup shredded cooked chicken breast
4-1/2 teaspoons reduced-sodium soy sauce
  2 teaspoons sesame oil
  2 garlic cloves, minced
1/2 teaspoon ground ginger
  8 egg roll wrappers

In a small bowl, combine the first six ingredients. Place 1/4 cup chicken mixture in the center of one egg roll wrapper. Fold bottom corner over filling; fold sides toward center. Moisten remaining corner with water; roll up tightly to seal. Repeat with remaining wrappers and filling.

Place seam side down on a baking sheet coated with cooking spray. Spray tops of egg rolls with cooking spray. Bake at 425° for 10-15 minutes or until lightly browned. Serve warm. Refrigerate leftovers. **yield:** 8 egg rolls.

nutrition facts: 1 egg roll equals 140 calories, 2 g fat (trace saturated fat), 16 mg cholesterol, 315 mg sodium, 21 g carbohydrate, 1 g fiber, 9 g protein.

diabetic exchanges: 1 starch, 1 lean meat, 1 vegetable.

CRISPY CHICKEN NIBBLERS

prep/total time 20 minutes

3/4 cup Corn Chex
1/3 cup cornflakes
  1 garlic clove, peeled
  1 teaspoon dried minced onion
  1 teaspoon Italian seasoning
1/8 teaspoon salt
  1 egg
1/2 pound boneless skinless chicken breast, cut into bite-size pieces
  1 cup canola oil
Ranch salad dressing, optional

In a blender, combine the first six ingredients; cover and process until fine crumbs form. Transfer to a resealable plastic bag. In a shallow bowl, beat the egg. Coat chicken pieces with egg, then place in bag and shake to coat.

In a large skillet, heat oil to 375°. Cook chicken pieces in oil for 5-6 minutes or until golden brown, turning occasionally. Drain on paper towels. Serve with ranch dressing for dipping if desired. **yield:** 2 servings.

lora pioli-rohrich

everett, washington

I like foods that are simple, scrumptious and with some Italian flair. That's why we enjoy these chicken nuggets so much. Try them with mashed potatoes and corn.

ULTIMATE KITCHEN TIP

Egg roll and wonton wrappers are made with ingredients that are similar to those used to make pasta. Wonton wrappers are about 3-1/2 inches square and thin. Egg roll wrappers are also square, but larger and thicker than wontons. Because both tend to dry out quickly, while using them, it's important to keep the wrappers covered with plastic or a damp towel.

This chicken recipe is lower in calories, fat or sodium.

CHICKEN TACO CUPS

prep 20 minutes | **bake** 20 minutes

lee ann lowe
gray, maine

For holiday parties and summer picnics, I like to stuff cute wonton cups with an easy Southwest-style chicken filling. You can freeze them, too—just reheat the cups after thawing.

1	pound boneless skinless chicken breasts, cut into 1-inch pieces
1	envelope reduced-sodium taco seasoning
1	small onion, chopped
1	jar (16 ounces) salsa, *divided*
2	cups (8 ounces) shredded reduced-fat cheddar cheese, *divided*
36	wonton wrappers

Sour cream, chopped green onions and chopped ripe olives, optional

Sprinkle chicken with taco seasoning. In a large skillet coated with cooking spray, cook and stir the chicken over medium heat for 5 minutes or until juices run clear. Transfer chicken to a food processor; cover and process until chopped. In a large bowl, combine the chicken, onion, half of the salsa and 1 cup cheese.

Press wonton wrappers into miniature muffin cups coated with cooking spray. Bake at 375° for 5 minutes or until lightly browned.

Spoon rounded tablespoonfuls of chicken mixture into cups; top with remaining salsa and cheese. Bake 15 minutes longer or until heated through. Serve warm. Garnish with sour cream, green onions and olives if desired. **yield:** 3 dozen.

nutrition facts: 2 taco cups (calculated without optional ingredients) equals 124 calories, 3 g fat (2 g saturated fat), 24 mg cholesterol, 408 mg sodium, 12 g carbohydrate, trace fiber, 10 g protein.

diabetic exchanges: 1 starch, 1 very lean meat, 1/2 fat.

WALNUT CHICKEN SPREAD

prep/total time 15 minutes

1-3/4	cups finely chopped cooked chicken
1	cup finely chopped walnuts
2/3	cup mayonnaise
1	celery rib, finely chopped
1	small onion, finely chopped
1	teaspoon salt
1/2	teaspoon garlic powder

Assorted crackers

In a bowl, combine the chicken, walnuts, mayonnaise, celery, onion, salt and garlic powder. Serve with crackers. Refrigerate any leftovers. **yield:** 2-1/2 cups.

joan whelan
green valley, arizona

It's a breeze to stir together this tasty chicken spread. We enjoy the mild yet delicious combination of chicken, crunchy walnuts, onion and celery. It's perfect with crackers or as a sandwich filling.

BUFFALO WING POPPERS

prep 20 minutes | **bake** 20 minutes

barbara nowakowski

mesa, arizona

The taste of buffalo wings and jalapeno pepper poppers are delicious together. They'll disappear fast, so be sure to make a double batch, and always have copies of the recipe handy!

20	jalapeno peppers
1	package (8 ounces) cream cheese, softened
1-1/2	cups (6 ounces) shredded part-skim mozzarella cheese
1	cup diced cooked chicken
1/2	cup blue cheese salad dressing
1/2	cup buffalo wing sauce

Cut the jalepeno peppers in half lengthwise, leaving stems intact; discard seeds. In a small bowl, combine the remaining ingredients. Pipe or stuff into pepper halves.

Place in a greased 15-in. x 10-in. baking pan. Bake, uncovered, at 325° for 20 minutes for spicy flavor, 30 minutes for medium and 40 minutes for mild. **yield:** 40 appetizers.

editor's note: When cutting hot peppers, disposable gloves are recommended. Avoid touching your face.

BAKED CHICKEN NACHOS

prep 20 minutes | **bake** 15 minutes

2   medium sweet red peppers, diced
1   medium green pepper, diced
3   teaspoons canola oil, *divided*
1   can (15 ounces) black beans, rinsed and drained
1   teaspoon minced garlic
1   teaspoon dried oregano
1/4 teaspoon ground cumin
2-1/4 cups shredded cooked rotisserie chicken (skin removed)
4-1/2 teaspoons lime juice
1/8 teaspoon salt
1/8 teaspoon pepper
7-1/2 cups tortilla chips
8   ounces pepper Jack cheese, shredded
1/4 cup thinly sliced green onions

1/2 cup minced fresh cilantro
1   cup (8 ounces) sour cream
2   to 3 teaspoons diced pickled jalapeno peppers, optional

In a large skillet, saute peppers in 1-1/2 teaspoons oil for 3 minutes or until crisp-tender; transfer to a small bowl. In the same skillet, saute the beans, garlic, oregano and cumin in remaining oil for 3 minutes or until heated through.

Meanwhile, combine the chicken, lime juice, salt and pepper. In a greased 13-in. x 9-in. baking dish, layer half of the tortilla chips, pepper mixture, bean mixture, chicken, cheese, onions and cilantro. Repeat layers.

Bake, uncovered, at 350° for 15-20 minutes or until heated through. Serve with sour cream and pickled jalapenos if desired. **yield:** 16 servings.

gail cawsey
fawnskin, california

Here's a colorful, party starter that's delicious and so simple. Rotisserie chicken keeps it quick, and the seasonings and splash of lime juice lend fantastic flavor. My husband likes it so much, he often requests it for dinner!

SALADS

BASIL CHICKEN OVER GREENS, P. 38

MEDITERRANEAN CHICKEN SALAD

prep/total time 25 minutes

amy lewis
carmichael, california

This is a variation on two different salads I enjoy. My family especially likes this when it's warm outside.

3 cups cubed cooked chicken breast
1-1/2 cups chopped tomatoes
1 cup water-packed artichoke hearts, rinsed, drained and quartered
1/2 cup crumbled feta cheese
1/2 cup pitted Greek olives
1/3 cup dried currants
1/4 cup finely chopped red onion

DRESSING
1/4 cup olive oil
2 tablespoons tarragon vinegar

1 tablespoon minced fresh tarragon *or* 1 teaspoon dried tarragon
1-1/2 teaspoons lemon juice
1-1/2 teaspoons Dijon mustard
1/4 teaspoon salt
1/8 teaspoon pepper

In a large bowl, combine the first seven ingredients. In a small bowl, whisk the dressing ingredients. Pour over chicken mixture and toss to coat. Refrigerate until serving. **yield:** 6 servings.

CREAMY CHICKEN SALAD

prep/total time 15 minutes

2 cups cubed cooked chicken breast
1 cup cooked small ring pasta
1 cup halved seedless red grapes
1 can (11 ounces) mandarin oranges, drained
3 celery ribs, chopped
1/2 cup sliced almonds
1 tablespoon grated onion
1 cup reduced-fat mayonnaise
1 cup reduced-fat whipped topping
1/4 teaspoon salt
Lettuce leaves, optional

In a bowl, combine the chicken, cooked pasta, grapes, oranges, celery, almonds and onion.

In another bowl, combine the mayonnaise, whipped topping and salt. Add to the chicken mixture; stir to coat. Serve in a lettuce-lined bowl if desired. **yield:** 6 servings.

kristi abernathy
lewistown, montana

I modified the original recipe for this chicken salad to make it healthier. The ingredients are so flavorful that my changes didn't take away from the taste. This refreshing salad never lasts long at our house. Even if I double the recipe, my husband asks, "Why didn't you make more?"

FIERY CHICKEN SPINACH SALAD

prep/total time 10 minutes

6   frozen breaded spicy chicken breast strips, thawed
1   package (6 ounces) fresh baby spinach
1   medium tomato, cut into 12 wedges
1/2   cup chopped green pepper
1/2   cup fresh baby carrots
1   can (15 ounces) black beans, rinsed and drained
1   can (11 ounces) Mexicorn, drained
3   tablespoons salsa
3   tablespoons barbecue sauce

3   tablespoons prepared ranch salad dressing
2   tablespoons shredded Mexican cheese blend

Heat chicken strips in a microwave according to package directions. Meanwhile, arrange the spinach on individual plates; top with tomato, green pepper, carrots, beans and corn.

In a small bowl, combine the salsa, barbecue sauce and ranch dressing. Place chicken over salads. Drizzle with dressing; sprinkle with cheese. **yield:** 6 servings.

kati spencer
taylorsville, utah

This colorful main-course salad is easy to throw together when I get home from work, because it uses canned black beans, Mexicorn and packaged chicken breast strips. Sometimes I add a can of ripe olives and fresh cherry tomatoes from our garden.

COUSCOUS CHICKEN SALAD

prep/total time 25 minutes

linda baggett
arcata, california

My chicken salad is perfect for a speedy lunch. It's easy to make and you can keep most of the ingredients on hand for a nutritious meal.

1   can (14-1/2 ounces) reduced-sodium chicken broth
1/3   cup water
1-3/4   cups uncooked couscous
3   cups cubed cooked chicken breast
1   can (14 ounces) water-packed artichoke hearts, rinsed, drained and chopped
2   medium tomatoes, chopped
1   medium sweet red pepper, chopped
1   small cucumber, sliced
1/2   cup minced fresh parsley

1/2   cup crumbled feta cheese
3   green onions, sliced
1/4   teaspoon pepper
3/4   cup fat-free Italian salad dressing

In a large saucepan, bring broth and water to a boil. Stir in couscous. Cover and remove from the heat; let stand for 5 minutes. Fluff with a fork.

Stir in the chicken, artichokes, tomatoes, red pepper, cucumber, parsley, cheese, onions and pepper. Drizzle with dressing and toss to coat. Refrigerate until serving. **yield:** 6 servings.

BROWN RICE SALAD WITH GRILLED CHICKEN

prep/total time 20 minutes

glenda harper
cable, ohio

This delightful dish is nutritious, delicious and simple to fix. It brightens up a buffet table, and I think it's a terrific way to use leftover chicken.

3 cups cooked brown rice
2 cups cubed grilled chicken breast
2 medium tart apples, diced
1 medium sweet red pepper, diced
2 celery ribs, finely chopped
2/3 cup chopped green onions
1/2 cup chopped pecans
3 tablespoons minced fresh parsley
1/4 cup cider vinegar
3 tablespoons canola oil
1 tablespoon lemon juice
1 teaspoon salt
1/4 teaspoon pepper
Lettuce leaves, optional

In a large bowl, combine the first eight ingredients. In a jar with a tight-fitting lid, combine the vinegar, oil, lemon juice, salt and pepper; shake well. Pour over the rice mixture and toss to coat. Serve immediately or refrigerate. Serve in a lettuce-lined bowl if desired. **yield:** 9 servings.

CANTALOUPE CHICKEN-ORZO SALAD

prep 25 minutes | **cook** 10 minutes

1/2 cup uncooked orzo pasta
1 snack-size cup (4 ounces) pineapple tidbits
1/2 cup fat-free mayonnaise
1/3 cup fat-free plain yogurt
4 teaspoons lemon juice
1 teaspoon minced fresh mint
1 teaspoon grated lemon peel
1 teaspoon honey
1/4 teaspoon salt
1/8 teaspoon pepper
2 cups cubed cooked chicken breast
1/2 cup chopped celery
1/3 cup chopped sweet red pepper
1/4 cup chopped green onions
1 small cantaloupe, quartered and seeded
1/4 cup unsalted cashews

Cook pasta according to package directions. Meanwhile, drain pineapple, reserving juice; set pineapple aside. In a small bowl, whisk the mayonnaise, yogurt, lemon juice, mint, lemon peel, honey, salt, pepper and pineapple juice until smooth.

Drain pasta and rinse in cold water. Place in a large bowl; add the chicken, celery, red pepper, onions and pineapple. Add mayonnaise mixture and toss to coat. Serve on cantaloupe wedges. Sprinkle with cashews. **yield:** 4 servings.

taste of home test kitchen
greendale, wisconsin

Too hot to cook? Then try a main-dish salad served on cool, refreshing cantaloupe wedges. The salad tastes great served with a grainy muffin or hard roll and a pitcher of iced tea.

CHICKEN BREAD SALAD

prep 15 minutes + chilling

**taste of home
test kitchen**

greendale, wisconsin

Use leftover chicken or cooked chicken from the refrigerated section of your supermarket. This will shorten the preparation time for this hearty entree-salad recipe.

24 slices French bread (3/4 inch thick)
3 cups cubed cooked chicken breast
4 medium tomatoes, cut into chunks
1 can (15-1/2 ounces) great northern beans, rinsed and drained
1 large cucumber, seeded and chopped
1/4 cup chopped fresh basil
1/4 teaspoon salt
1/4 teaspoon pepper
3/4 cup balsamic vinaigrette
1/2 cup shredded Parmesan cheese

Place the slices of bread on a baking sheet. Broil 3-4 in. from the heat for 2-3 minutes or until golden brown, turning once. Cool on a wire rack. Cut bread into 1-in. pieces.

In a large bowl, combine the bread, chicken, tomatoes, beans, cucumber, basil, salt and pepper. Drizzle with vinaigrette and toss to coat. Refrigerate for 30 minutes. Sprinkle with Parmesan cheese and toss. **yield:** 6 servings.

LENTIL CHICKEN SALAD

prep/total time 15 minutes

2 cups shredded iceberg lettuce
1 cup cooked lentils
1 cup diced cooked chicken
1 cup diced celery
1/2 cup shredded carrot
1/2 cup chopped pecans
1 cup mayonnaise
1/4 cup chunky salsa
4 green onions, chopped
1 tablespoon lemon juice

In a large bowl, combine the first six ingredients. In a small bowl, combine the mayonnaise, salsa, green onions and lemon juice. Pour over the salad; toss gently to coat. Serve immediately. **yield:** 4-6 servings.

margaret pache

mesa, arizona

A great way to use lentils is in my satisfying salad, which won a blue ribbon and lots of praise from the tasters at our church fair. The combination of textures and tasty items blends well with the creamy dressing.

RASPBERRY GREEK SALAD

prep/total time 20 minutes

2 packages (6 ounces *each*) ready-to-use grilled chicken breast strips
1 package (6 ounces) fresh baby spinach
1/2 pound sliced fresh mushrooms
1 medium cucumber, peeled and sliced
4 plum tomatoes, seeded and sliced
1/2 cup crumbled feta cheese
1/4 cup chopped Greek olives

1/4 cup dried cranberries
1/4 cup chopped red onion
1/3 cup raspberry vinaigrette
4 whole wheat pita breads (6 inches), cut into quarters and warmed, optional

In a large salad bowl, toss the first nine ingredients. Just before serving, drizzle with the vinaigrette; toss to coat. Serve with whole wheat pita bread if desired. **yield:** 8 servings.

carine nadel
laguna hills, california

An interesting blend of sweet and salty flavors gives this Greek salad a delicious twist. The tart chewiness of the dried cranberries makes a wonderful complement to the salty feta cheese.

BASIL CHICKEN OVER GREENS

prep 40 minutes + marinating | **cook** 15 minutes

marie rizzio
interlochen, michigan

This eye-catching salad entree pairs basil-stuffed chicken breasts with sliced fennel and salad greens. It's one of my favorite ways to serve chicken.

4   boneless skinless chicken breast halves (6 ounces *each*)
1/2 cup plus 1/3 cup Italian salad dressing, *divided*
1   package (10 ounces) Italian-blend salad greens
1   medium fennel bulb, sliced
1/4 cup minced fresh basil
2   plum tomatoes, chopped
1   egg
1   tablespoon water
2/3 cup seasoned bread crumbs
1/2 cup grated Parmesan cheese
2   tablespoons olive oil
Chopped fennel fronds, optional

Flatten chicken to 1/4-in. thickness; place in a large resealable plastic bag. Add 1/2 cup salad dressing; seal bag and turn to coat. Refrigerate for 30 minutes. Arrange salad greens and fennel slices on a serving platter; drizzle with remaining dressing. Cover and refrigerate.

Drain and discard marinade from chicken. Place 1 tablespoon of basil on each piece of chicken; top with tomatoes. Roll up jelly-roll style, starting with a short side; tie with kitchen string. In a shallow bowl, beat the egg and water. In another shallow bowl, combine the bread crumbs with the Parmesan cheese. Dip chicken in egg mixture, then roll in crumb mixture.

In a large nonstick skillet over medium heat, cook chicken in oil on all sides for 15-20 minutes or until juices run clear. Slice and arrange over greens. Garnish with fennel fronds if desired. **yield:** 4 servings.

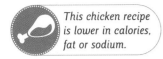

PINEAPPLE CHICKEN PARADISE

prep 25 minutes + chilling

dorothy anderson
ottawa, kansas

You'll think you've traveled to the tropics when you bite into this inviting chicken salad, served in an attractive pineapple "boat." The salad blends a variety of tastes and textures, including coconut, peanuts, mandarin oranges and green grapes.

2	fresh pineapples with tops
1-1/2	cups cubed cooked chicken breast
3/4	cup chopped celery
1/3	cup reduced-fat mayonnaise
1/3	cup fat-free plain yogurt
2	tablespoons chutney
1/2	teaspoon salt
1/4	cup dry roasted peanuts
1/4	cup flaked coconut, toasted
1	can (11 ounces) mandarin oranges, drained
1/2	cup halved green grapes

Cut each pineapple in half lengthwise, then cut in half lengthwise again, making four shells with part of the leaves. Remove fruit; cut into cubes.

Turn pineapple shells cut side down on paper towels to drain; set aside.

In a large bowl, combine the pineapple cubes, chicken and celery; cover and refrigerate. In another bowl, combine the mayonnaise, yogurt, chutney and salt; cover and refrigerate for at least 30 minutes.

Before serving, drain the chicken mixture; toss with mayonnaise mixture and peanuts. Using a slotted spoon, fill pineapple shells. Sprinkle with coconut; top with mandarin oranges and grapes. **yield:** 8 servings.

nutrition facts: 3/4 cup chicken salad equals 203 calories, 8 g fat (2 g saturated fat), 26 mg cholesterol, 300 mg sodium, 25 g carbohydrate, 3 g fiber, 11 g protein.

diabetic exchanges: 2 fruit, 1 lean meat, 1 fat.

APPLE CHICKEN SLAW

prep/total time 10 minutes

1/4	cup poppy seed salad dressing
5	teaspoons mayonnaise
2	cups cubed cooked chicken breast
2	cups coleslaw mix
1	medium apple, chopped

Lettuce leaves, optional

In a small bowl, combine the salad dressing and mayonnaise. In a large bowl, combine the chicken, coleslaw mix and apple. Drizzle with the dressing and toss to coat. Serve on lettuce-lined plates if desired. **yield:** 4 servings.

taste of home test kitchen
greendale, wisconsin

Coleslaw mix and leftover cooked chicken make a quick salad combination for a tasty, busy-day dinner.

ULTIMATE KITCHEN TIP

Warm breadsticks make a delicious accompaniment to the Apple Chicken Slaw. To make your own, unroll and separate 1 (11 ounce) tube of refrigerated breadstick dough. Twist each breadstick two or three times and place on an ungreased baking sheet. Brush the breadsticks with 1 tablespoon of melted butter, then sprinkle with 1 tablespoon of toasted sesame seeds. Bake at 375° for 10-12 minutes or until golden brown. Serve warm.

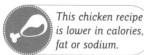 *This chicken recipe is lower in calories, fat or sodium.*

STRAWBERRY CHICKEN SALAD

prep/total time 15 minutes

michelle hallock
warwick, rhode island

This salad is similar to one I loved at a local restaurant. When we moved away, I created my own version. It goes together in minutes and is perfect for picnics. It makes a wonderful main-dish salad anytime.

1	package (5 ounces) spring mix salad greens
1	small red onion, thinly sliced and separated into rings
1/2	cup cubed fresh pineapple
2	packages (6 ounces *each*) ready-to-use grilled chicken breast strips
2	medium tomatoes, seeded and chopped
1	medium cucumber, chopped
1	pint fresh strawberries, sliced
3/4	cup crumbled blue cheese
3/4	cup raspberry vinaigrette

Place the salad greens in a large shallow bowl. In rows, arrange the onion, pineapple, chicken, tomatoes, cucumber and strawberries. Sprinkle with blue cheese. Drizzle with raspberry vinaigrette. **yield:** 10 servings.

nutrition facts: 1-1/2 cups (prepared with fat-free vinaigrette) equals 130 calories, 4 g fat (2 g saturated fat), 30 mg cholesterol, 538 mg sodium, 13 g carbohydrate, 2 g fiber, 11 g protein.

diabetic exchanges: 1 lean meat, 1 vegetable, 1/2 starch.

BARBECUE BLT CHICKEN SALAD

prep 10 minutes + chilling

1/4	cup reduced-fat mayonnaise
1/4	cup barbecue sauce
1	tablespoon lemon juice
1/2	teaspoon pepper
1/4	teaspoon salt
2	cups chopped cooked chicken breast
2	medium tomatoes, chopped
1	celery rib, sliced
5	cups torn salad greens
4	bacon strips, cooked and crumbled

In a small bowl, combine the mayonnaise, barbecue sauce, lemon juice, pepper and salt. Cover and refrigerate for at least 1 hour. Just before serving, combine the chicken, tomatoes and celery; stir in dressing. Serve over salad greens; sprinkle with bacon. **yield:** 5 servings.

kathleen williams
maryville, tennessee

My family requests this satisfying salad often. Barbecue sauce and lemon juice give the dressing an unexpected tang.

AVOCADO CHICKEN SALAD

prep/total time 20 minutes

- 1 medium ripe avocado, peeled and cubed
- 2 tablespoons lemon juice, *divided*
- 2 cups cubed cooked chicken
- 2 cups seedless red grapes, halved
- 1 medium tart apple, chopped
- 1 cup chopped celery
- 3/4 cup mayonnaise
- 1/2 cup chopped walnuts, toasted
- 1/2 teaspoon ground ginger

Lettuce leaves, optional

In a small bowl, toss avocado with 1 tablespoon lemon juice; set aside. In a large bowl, combine the chicken, grapes, apple, celery, mayonnaise, walnuts, ginger and remaining lemon juice. Stir in avocado. Serve on lettuce-lined plates if desired. **yield:** 5 servings.

karlene johnson
mooresville,
north carolina

This is the first time I've ever shared this recipe, but it's one that my family and friends request for every outing we have! I like to serve it with crackers or sometimes in pita bread for a filling grab-and-go lunch.

BALSAMIC CHICKEN SALAD

prep/total time 20 minutes

rebecca lindamood
belfast, new york

This is an easy, elegant and tasty alternative to frozen dinners. My husband fell in love with this main course the first time I served it and regularly requests that I make it again.

6	boneless skinless chicken breast halves (4 ounces *each*), cut into 3-inch strips
1/2	teaspoon minced garlic
4	tablespoons olive oil, *divided*
1/4	cup balsamic vinegar
1-1/2	cups halved cherry tomatoes
1	tablespoon minced fresh basil *or* 1 teaspoon dried basil
1/4	teaspoon salt
1/8	teaspoon pepper
6	cups torn mixed salad greens

In a large skillet, saute the chicken and minced garlic in 1 tablespoon olive oil until chicken juices run clear; remove from pan.

In the same skillet, bring vinegar to a boil. Add chicken, tomatoes, basil, salt, pepper and remaining oil; cook and stir until heated through. Divide salad greens among six plates; top with chicken mixture. **yield:** 6 servings.

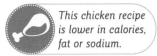
MANGO CHICKEN SALAD

prep/total time 25 minutes

carolyn black
richmond,
british columbia

Come summer, I like to pack this refreshing salad for a picnic lunch. Each of the ingredients can be stored in a separate container in a cooler and assembled at the picnic. It's always a hit.

8   cups torn red leaf lettuce
2   cups torn mixed salad greens
4   medium tomatoes, thinly sliced
1-1/2   cups thinly sliced cucumber
6   boneless skinless chicken breast halves (4 ounces *each*), grilled and thinly sliced

MANGO SALAD DRESSING

2   large ripe mangos *or* 4 medium peaches, peeled and cut into chunks
1/4   cup lime juice
1/4   teaspoon salt
1/8   to 1/4 teaspoon cayenne pepper
1/4   cup sunflower kernels

Divide lettuce and salad greens among six plates. Top with the tomatoes, cucumber and chicken. For the dressing, in a blender, combine the mangos, lime juice, salt and cayenne; cover and process until smooth. Serve with salad. Sprinkle with sunflower kernels. **yield:** 6 servings.

nutrition facts: 1 serving equals 221 calories, 6 g fat (1 g saturated fat), 63 mg cholesterol, 166 mg sodium, 18 g carbohydrate, 3 g fiber, 25 g protein.

diabetic exchanges: 3 lean meat, 1 vegetable, 1 fruit.

CHICKEN CAESAR SALAD

prep/total time 30 minutes

4   boneless skinless chicken breast halves (4 ounces *each*)
1/2   cup shredded Parmesan cheese, *divided*
1   tablespoon lemon juice
1   teaspoon minced garlic
1   teaspoon Worcestershire sauce
1/4   teaspoon ground mustard
1/8   teaspoon pepper
1/4   cup olive oil
8   cups hearts of romaine salad mix
2   hard-cooked eggs, sliced
1   cup Caesar salad croutons

Place chicken on a greased broiler pan. Broil 6 in. from the heat for 7-8 minutes on each side or until juices run clear. Cut chicken into strips; set aside.

Meanwhile, in a blender, combine 1/4 cup Parmesan cheese, lemon juice, garlic, Worcestershire sauce, mustard and pepper. Cover and process until blended. While processing, gradually add oil in a steady stream.

Place romaine in a large salad bowl. Add Parmesan cheese mixture; toss to coat. Top with the chicken strips, eggs, croutons and remaining Parmesan cheese. **yield:** 4 servings.

rebecca porter
yigo, guam

A simple homemade dressing sets this Caesar salad apart from ordinary salads. With lots of Parmesan, romaine and chicken strips, it's a true classic...only better!

CHICKEN SALAD IN TOMATO CUPS

prep/total time 25 minutes

judy robertson
southington, connecticut

Garden-fresh tomatoes make this standout recipe hard to beat. It's fast, delicious, economical…and my family loves it!

4   large tomatoes
2   cups finely chopped cooked chicken
3/4 cup mayonnaise
1/2 cup chopped pecans
1/4 cup chopped celery
1   tablespoon diced pimientos
1   tablespoon lime juice
1/8 teaspoon salt
1/8 teaspoon pepper

Cut a thin slice off the top of each tomato. Scoop out pulp, leaving 1/2-in. thick shells. Invert onto paper towels to drain. In a large bowl, combine the remaining ingredients. Spoon into tomatoes. Serve immediately. **yield:** 4 servings.

LAYERED SOUTHWESTERN CHICKEN SALAD

prep/total time 30 minutes

1/2 cup lime juice
1/2 cup sour cream
1/3 cup fresh cilantro leaves
2   tablespoons sugar
1/2 teaspoon salt
1/2 teaspoon pepper
1/2 cup olive oil
1   package (10 ounces) hearts of romaine salad mix
1   medium tomato, chopped
1   can (15 ounces) black beans, rinsed and drained
1   small red onion, chopped
2   packages (6 ounces *each*) ready-to-use Southwestern chicken strips
2   cups (8 ounces) shredded Mexican cheese blend
1   can (11 ounces) Mexicorn, drained
1   can (6 ounces) sliced ripe olives, drained
2   cups coarsely crushed tortilla chips
Additional fresh cilantro leaves

For the dressing, in a blender, combine the first six ingredients; cover and process until smooth. While processing, gradually add the oil in a steady stream. Transfer to a small bowl; cover and refrigerate until serving.

In a 4-qt. glass salad bowl, layer the remaining ingredients in the order listed; garnish with cilantro. Serve with the dressing. **yield:** 8 servings.

marci dietrich
fairfax station, virginia

This beautiful salad is pretty enough to be a centerpiece, and it comes together in a snap. But don't tell your guests, they'll think you spent hours on it!

SPECIAL SESAME CHICKEN SALAD

prep 30 minutes + chilling

- 1 package (16 ounces) bow tie pasta
- 1 cup canola oil
- 2/3 cup white wine vinegar
- 2/3 cup teriyaki sauce
- 1/3 cup sugar
- 1/2 teaspoon pepper
- 3 cans (11 ounces *each*) mandarin oranges, drained
- 2 cans (8 ounces *each*) sliced water chestnuts, drained
- 2 cups cubed cooked chicken
- 1-1/3 cups honey roasted peanuts
- 1 package (9 ounces) fresh spinach, torn
- 1 package (6 ounces) dried cranberries
- 6 green onions, chopped
- 1/2 cup minced fresh parsley
- 1/4 cup sesame seeds, toasted

Cook pasta according to package directions; drain and place in a very large bowl.

In a small bowl, combine the oil, vinegar, teriyaki sauce, sugar and pepper. Pour over pasta and toss to coat. Cover and refrigerate for 2 hours.

Just before serving, add the remaining ingredients; gently toss to coat. **yield:** 22 servings (1 cup each).

carolee ewell
santaquin, utah

With its delicious mix of crunchy peanuts, tangy dried cranberries and mandarin oranges, this colorful pasta salad is a definite crowd-pleaser. Water chestnuts and a teriyaki dressing give this main dish its Asian flair.

CASHEW-CHICKEN ROTINI SALAD

prep 30 minutes + chilling

kara cook
elk ridge, utah

*I've tried many chicken
salad recipes over the years,
but this is my very favorite.
It's fresh and fruity, and
the cashews add wonderful
crunch. Every time I serve
it at a potluck or picnic,
I get rave reviews…and
always come home with
an empty bowl!*

1	package (16 ounces) spiral *or* rotini pasta
4	cups cubed cooked chicken
1	can (20 ounces) pineapple tidbits, drained
1-1/2	cups sliced celery
3/4	cup thinly sliced green onions
1	cup seedless red grapes
1	cup seedless green grapes
1	package (6 ounces) dried cranberries
1	cup ranch salad dressing
3/4	cup mayonnaise
2	cups salted cashews

Cook the pasta according to package directions. Meanwhile, in a large bowl, combine the chicken, pineapple, celery, onions, grapes and cranberries. Drain the pasta and rinse in cold water; stir into chicken mixture.

In a small bowl, whisk the ranch dressing and mayonnaise. Pour over salad and toss to coat. Cover and refrigerate for at least 1 hour. Just before serving, stir in cashews. **yield:** 12 servings.

BOW TIE LEMON CHICKEN

prep/total time 30 minutes

rebecca snapp
cynthiana, kentucky

The zesty flavor of lemon brightens every bite of this chicken and pasta dish. With two small sons and a farmer husband, it's good to have a collection of speedy recipes.

4-2/3 cups uncooked bow tie pasta
12 ounces boneless skinless chicken breast, cut into 1-inch strips
1/2 teaspoon salt-free lemon-pepper seasoning
2 garlic cloves, minced
1 tablespoon canola oil
1 cup chicken broth
1 cup frozen peas, thawed
2/3 cup shredded carrots
1/4 cup cubed reduced-fat cream cheese
2 teaspoons lemon juice

1/2 teaspoon salt
1/3 cup shredded Parmesan cheese

Cook the pasta according to package directions. Meanwhile, sprinkle the chicken with lemon-pepper. In a large nonstick skillet, stir-fry chicken and garlic in oil until chicken juices run clear. Remove and keep warm.

Add chicken broth, peas, carrots, cream cheese and lemon juice to the skillet; cook and stir until cheese is melted. Drain the pasta. Add pasta, cooked chicken and salt to vegetable mixture; cook until heated through. Sprinkle with Parmesan cheese. **yield:** 4 servings.

CRISPY CHICKEN STRIP SALAD

prep 40 minutes | **cook** 10 minutes

1 tablespoon butter
1/2 cup pecan halves
2 tablespoons sugar
3/4 cup all-purpose flour
2 tablespoons minced fresh tarragon *or* 2 teaspoons dried tarragon
1 tablespoon grated lemon peel
2 eggs
1 pound boneless skinless chicken breast, cut into 1-inch strips
2 tablespoons canola oil
4 cups spring mix salad greens
1 cup torn Bibb *or* Boston lettuce
1/2 cup raspberry vinaigrette
2 cups fresh *or* frozen unsweetened raspberries

In a small skillet, melt butter. Add pecans and cook over medium heat until nuts are toasted, about 4 minutes. Sprinkle with sugar. Cook and stir for 2-4 minutes or until sugar is melted. Transfer to a greased foil-lined baking sheet; cool completely.

In a large resealable bag, combine the flour tarragon and lemon peel. In a shallow bowl, beat the eggs. Add chicken strips to flour mixture in batches; seal and shake to coat. Dip in eggs, then return to bag and coat again.

In a large skillet over medium heat, cook chicken in oil for 6-8 minutes or until no longer pink, turning once.

Break the pecans apart. Toss the greens and lettuce with vinaigrette; arrange on individual plates. Top with raspberries, chicken strips and pecans. **yield:** 4 servings.

lillian julow
gainesville, florida

If you like chicken fingers, you'll love this salad. The crispy chicken strips are delicious with the refreshing lettuce and sweet-and-sour dressing.

ULTIMATE KITCHEN TIP

For 8 ounces of pasta, bring 3 quarts water to a boil and add 1 tablespoon salt if desired. Pasta should be cooked until "al dente," or firm yet tender. Test often while cooking to avoid overcooking, which can result in a soft or mushy texture. After draining, if using in a salad, rinse it with cold water.

GREEK CHICKEN SALAD

prep 15 minutes + chilling

donna smith
palisade, colorado

*I encourage you to use all
of the garlic and oregano
called for in this recipe.
I receive raves reviews when
I serve the flavorful salad.*

3   cups cubed cooked chicken
2   medium cucumbers, peeled,
    seeded and chopped
1   cup crumbled feta cheese
2/3 cup sliced pitted black olives
1/4 cup minced fresh parsley
1   cup mayonnaise
3   garlic cloves, minced

1/2 cup plain yogurt
1   tablespoon dried oregano

In a large bowl, combine the chicken, cucumbers,
cheese, olives and parsley. In a small bowl, combine remaining ingredients. Toss with chicken mixture. Cover and refrigerate for several hours before
serving. **yield:** 7 servings.

CHICKEN PASTA SALAD

prep 35 minutes | **cook** 20 minutes

1   package (12 ounces) tricolor spiral
    pasta
2   cups cubed part-skim mozzarella
    cheese
2   cups cubed cooked chicken
1   large green pepper, chopped
1   large sweet red pepper, chopped
1   cup sliced fresh mushrooms
2   cans (2-1/4 ounces *each*) sliced ripe
    olives, drained
6   green onions, sliced
1   package (3-1/2 ounces) sliced
    pepperoni, halved
1/2 cup canola oil

1/3 cup red wine vinegar
1   teaspoon Italian seasoning
1/2 teaspoon garlic powder
1/2 teaspoon salt
1/4 teaspoon pepper

Cook the pasta according to package directions;
rinse with cold water and drain well. In a large serving bowl, combine the mozzarella cheese, chicken,
peppers, mushrooms, olives, green onions, pepperoni and pasta.

In a small bowl, whisk together the remaining
ingredients. Pour over salad; toss to coat. Cover
and refrigerate until serving. Toss again before serving. **yield:** 14 servings.

megan moore
memphis, tennessee

*Combining the coolness of
a salad and the zesty
seasonings of pizza, this
salad is perfect for a
summer get-together.*

SPICY CHICKEN SALAD WITH MANGO SALSA

prep/total time 30 minutes

2 cups chopped peeled mangoes
1 medium red onion, chopped
1/2 cup chopped sweet red pepper
1/4 cup minced fresh cilantro
1 jalapeno pepper, seeded and chopped
2 tablespoons lime juice
2 packages (9 ounces *each*) ready-to-use grilled chicken breast strips
2 garlic cloves, minced
2 teaspoons ground cumin
1 teaspoon onion powder
1 teaspoon chili powder
1/4 teaspoon cayenne pepper
Dash salt
2 tablespoons olive oil
2 packages (8 ounces *each*) ready-to-serve European blend salad greens

1/3 cup oil and vinegar salad dressing
2 cups (8 ounces) shredded pepper Jack cheese
Tortilla chips

For the salsa, in a large bowl, combine the first six ingredients; chill until serving. In a large skillet, saute the chicken, garlic, cumin, onion powder, chili powder, cayenne and salt in olive oil until heated through.

Toss greens with dressing; divide among seven serving plates. Top with chicken mixture, mango salsa and cheese. Serve immediately with tortilla chips. **yield:** 7 servings.

editor's note: When cutting hot peppers, disposable gloves are recommended. Avoid touching your face.

jan warren-rucker
clemmons, north carolina

When I need a different weeknight meal, I pull out this salad recipe. To make it in record time, I use fully cooked chicken strips, jarred mango slices, bottled vinaigrette and packaged shredded cheese.

SUMMER CHICKEN SALAD

prep 10 minutes | **cook** 25 minutes + chilling

nancy whitford
edwards, new york

I found this recipe many years ago in a church cookbook. It's special enough for a fancy dinner, but easy enough to fix for a light lunch. There's a spicy kick to the tangy citrus dressing, which even my picky son enjoys.

4   boneless skinless chicken breast halves (4 ounces *each*)
1   can (14-1/2 ounces) chicken broth
6   cups torn mixed salad greens
2   cups halved fresh strawberries

CITRUS DRESSING
1/2   cup fresh strawberries, hulled
1/3   cup orange juice
2   tablespoons canola oil
1   tablespoon lemon juice
2   teaspoons grated lemon peel
1   teaspoon sugar
1/2   teaspoon chili powder
1/4   teaspoon salt
1/4   teaspoon pepper
1/4   cup chopped walnuts, toasted

Place chicken in a large skillet; add broth. Bring to a boil. Reduce heat; cover and simmer for 20-25 minutes or until juices run clear. Drain; cover and refrigerate. In a large bowl, combine the greens and sliced strawberries; refrigerate.

For the dressing, in a blender, combine the hulled strawberries, orange juice, canola oil, lemon juice and lemon peel, sugar, chili powder, salt and pepper. Cover and process until smooth. Pour into a small saucepan. Bring to a boil. Reduce heat; simmer for 5-6 minutes until slightly thickened. Cool slightly.

Drizzle half of the dressing over greens and berries; toss to coat. Divide among four plates. Cut chicken into 1/8-in. slices; arrange over salads. Drizzle remaining dressing over chicken; sprinkle with walnuts. **yield:** 4 servings.

GOAL-LINE CHICKEN SALAD

prep/total time 15 minutes

**house of loreto,
sister judith labrozzi**
canton, ohio

*Crisp apples lend autumn
appeal to the chunky
chicken salad made for our
football theme supper. I
sometimes serve it on a bed
of lettuce with a sliced
tomato on top.*

4-1/2   cups diced cooked chicken
1-1/2   cups diced apples
  3/4   cup halved green grapes
    6   tablespoons sweet pickle relish
    6   tablespoons mayonnaise
    6   tablespoons prepared ranch salad dressing
  3/4   teaspoon onion salt
  3/4   teaspoon garlic salt
Lettuce leaves

In a large bowl, combine the chicken, apples and grapes. In a small bowl, combine the pickle relish, mayonnaise, ranch dressing, onion salt and garlic salt. Pour over chicken mixture and toss to coat. Serve in a lettuce-lined bowl. **yield:** 18 servings.

ULTIMATE
KITCHEN TIP

Apples are rich in vitamins A, B1, B2 and C, and they also contain calcium, phosphorous, magnesium and even potassium.

Refrigerate unwashed apples away from other vegetables with strong aromas for up to 6 weeks. One pound (3 medium apples) yields 2-3/4 cups sliced.

GARDEN COBB SALAD

prep 30 minutes + chilling

    1   cup (8 ounces) sour cream
  1/2   cup mayonnaise
  1/4   cup crumbled blue cheese
    2   teaspoons cider vinegar
  1/2   teaspoon salt
  1/4   teaspoon pepper
    8   to 10 romaine leaves
   12   cups torn mixed salad greens
    8   thick-sliced bacon strips, cooked and crumbled
    1   cup diced avocado
    1   cup finely chopped cooked chicken breast
    1   cup chopped seeded tomatoes
    2   hard-cooked eggs, chopped
Edible pansies, optional

For dressing, in a small bowl, combine the sour cream, mayonnaise, blue cheese, vinegar, salt and pepper. Cover and refrigerate for at least 1 hour.

Line an 8-in. decorative flowerpot with plastic wrap or use a serving bowl. Arrange romaine around the edge; fill with mixed greens. Arrange the bacon, avocado, chicken, tomatoes and eggs in a spoke pattern over greens. Garnish with edible pansies if desired. Serve with dressing. **yield:** 6 servings.

editor's note: Verify that flowers are edible and have not been treated with chemicals.

christine panzarella
buena park, california

This sensational salad is my favorite for a ladies' lunch…but men and kids eat it up, too. Presenting it in a flowerpot emphasizes its garden-fresh goodness. Be prepared to serve up more fixings when guests come back for seconds.

SOUPS&MORE
WHITE BEAN CHICKEN CHILI, P. 67

CHICKEN SOUP WITH BEANS

prep 10 minutes | **cook** 6 hours

penny peronia
west memphis, arkansas

I like to place lime-flavored tortilla chips at the bottom of individual bowls, then ladle my Southwestern soup on top. Loaded with chicken, beans, corn, tomatoes and green chilies, it's satisfying and fuss-free.

1   large onion, chopped
2   garlic cloves, minced
1   tablespoon canola oil
1-1/4   pounds boneless skinless chicken breasts, cooked and cubed
2   cans (15-1/2 ounces *each*) great northern beans, rinsed and drained
2   cans (11 ounces *each*) white *or* shoepeg corn, drained
1   can (10 ounces) diced tomatoes with green chilies, undrained
3   cups water
1   can (4 ounces) chopped green chilies

2   tablespoons lime juice
1   teaspoon lemon-pepper seasoning
1   teaspoon ground cumin
1/4   teaspoon salt
1/4   teaspoon pepper

In a small skillet, saute onion and garlic in oil until tender. Transfer to a 5-qt. slow cooker. Stir in the chicken, beans, corn, tomatoes, water, chopped green chilies, lime juice and seasonings. Cover and cook on low for 6-7 hours or until heated through. **yield:** 12 servings (3 quarts).

CHICKEN BROTH

prep 15 minutes | **cook** 1-1/2 hours

1   broiler/fryer chicken (3 to 4 pounds), cut up
10   cups water
1   large carrot, sliced
1   large onion, sliced
1   celery rib, sliced
1   garlic clove, minced
1   bay leaf
1   teaspoon dried thyme
1   teaspoon salt
1/4   teaspoon pepper

In a large soup kettle or Dutch oven, combine all the ingredients. Slowly bring to a boil over low heat. Cover and simmer for 45-60 minutes or until the chicken is tender, skimming the surface as foam rises.

Remove chicken and set aside until cool enough to handle. Remove and discard skin and bones. Chop chicken; save for another use. Strain broth through a cheesecloth-lined colander, discarding vegetables and bay leaf. If using immediately, skim fat or refrigerate for 8 hours or overnight; remove fat from surface. Broth can be covered and refrigerated for up to 3 days or frozen for 4 to 6 months. **yield:** 8 servings (about 2 quarts).

nila grahl
gurnee, illinois

Whether you're making chicken soup or just a broth to use in other dishes, this recipe makes a tasty base for almost any soup.

CHICKEN TORTILLA SOUP

prep 30 minutes | **cook** 25 minutes

- 2 medium tomatoes
- 1 small onion, cut into wedges
- 1 garlic clove, peeled
- 4 teaspoons canola oil, *divided*
- 1 boneless skinless chicken breast half (6 ounces)
- 1/4 teaspoon lemon-pepper seasoning
- 1/8 teaspoon salt
- 2 corn tortillas (6 inches)
- 1/2 cup diced zucchini
- 2 tablespoons chopped carrot
- 1 tablespoon minced fresh cilantro
- 3/4 teaspoon ground cumin
- 1/2 teaspoon chili powder
- 1 cup reduced-sodium chicken broth
- 1/2 cup spicy hot V8 juice
- 1/3 cup frozen corn
- 2 tablespoons tomato puree
- 1-1/2 teaspoons chopped seeded jalapeno pepper
- 1 bay leaf
- 1/4 cup cubed *or* sliced avocado
- 1/4 cup shredded Mexican cheese blend

Brush tomatoes, onion and garlic with 1 teaspoon oil. Broil 4 in. from the heat for 6-8 minutes or until tender, turning tomatoes once. Peel and discard charred skin from tomatoes; place in a blender. Add onion and garlic; cover and process for 1-2 minutes or until smooth.

Sprinkle chicken with lemon-pepper and salt; broil for 5-6 minutes on each side or until juices run clear. Cut one tortilla into 1/4-in. strips; coarsely chop remaining tortilla. In a large saucepan, heat remaining oil. Fry tortilla strips until crisp and browned; remove with a slotted spoon.

In the same pan, cook the zucchini, carrot, cilantro, cumin, chili powder and chopped tortilla over medium heat for 4 minutes. Stir in the tomato mixture, broth, V8 juice, corn, tomato puree, jalapeno and bay leaf. Bring to a boil. Reduce heat; simmer, uncovered, for 20 minutes.

Cut chicken into strips and add to the soup; simmer 5 minutes longer. Discard bay leaf. Garnish with avocado, shredded cheese and tortilla strips. **yield:** 3-1/2 cups.

editor's note: When cutting hot peppers, disposable gloves are recommended. Avoid touching your face.

kathy averbeck
dousman, wisconsin

Chock-full of veggies and autumn color, this soup is ideal for using up fresh garden bounty. I add richness by first grilling the chicken and vegetables.

HEARTY SAUSAGE-CHICKEN CHILI

prep 20 minutes | **cook** 4 hours

carolyn etzler
thurmont, maryland

The company I work for has an annual chili cook-off, and this unusual recipe of mine was a winner. It combines two other recipes and includes a special touch or two of my own.

1 pound Italian turkey sausage links, casings removed
3/4 pound boneless skinless chicken thighs, cut into 3/4-inch pieces
1 medium onion, chopped
2 cans (14-1/2 ounces *each*) diced tomatoes with mild green chilies, undrained
2 cans (8 ounces *each*) tomato sauce
1 can (16 ounces) kidney beans, rinsed and drained
1 can (15 ounces) white kidney *or* cannellini beans, rinsed and drained
1 can (15 ounces) pinto beans, rinsed and drained
1 can (15 ounces) black beans, rinsed and drained
1 teaspoon chili powder
1/2 teaspoon garlic powder
1/8 teaspoon pepper

Crumble sausage into a large nonstick skillet coated with cooking spray. Add chicken and onion; cook and stir over medium heat until meat is no longer pink. Drain.

Transfer to a 5-qt. slow cooker. Stir in the remaining ingredients. Cover and cook on low for 4 hours. **yield:** 11 servings (2-3/4 quarts).

FLORENTINE CHICKEN SOUP

prep/total time 30 minutes

1 cup uncooked penne pasta
1 package (6 ounces) ready-to-use chicken breast cuts
4 cups chopped fresh spinach
1 jar (7 ounces) roasted sweet red peppers, drained and sliced
3 fresh rosemary sprigs, chopped
1/2 teaspoon garlic powder
1/4 teaspoon pepper
1 tablespoon butter
1-1/2 cups reduced-sodium chicken broth
3/4 cup Alfredo sauce
3 tablespoons prepared pesto
2 tablespoons pine nuts, toasted
1 tablespoon shredded Parmesan cheese

cindie henf
sebastian, florida

My husband loves Alfredo sauce, so I'm always looking for new variations. This easy-to-make soup is wonderful with crusty Italian bread and a tomato, mozzarella and basil salad. Best of all, it's the perfect amount for small households.

Cook the pasta according to package directions. Meanwhile, in a large saucepan, saute the chicken, spinach, red peppers, rosemary, garlic powder and pepper in butter until spinach is wilted. Stir in the broth, Alfredo sauce and pesto; cook for 4-5 minutes or until heated through. Drain pasta and add to the soup. Sprinkle with toasted pine nuts and Parmesan cheese. **yield:** 5 servings.

This chicken recipe is lower in calories, fat or sodium.

CREAMY CHICKEN POTATO SOUP

prep/total time 30 minutes

carla reid
charlottetown,
prince edward island

Any time I serve this hearty, comforting soup, I'm asked for the recipe. Because it is loaded with chunks of potatoes and chicken, no one ever suspects that it's low in fat and calories.

1	medium onion, chopped
2	tablespoons butter
3	cups reduced-sodium chicken broth
1	pound potatoes, (about 2 medium), cut into 1/2-inch cubes
1-1/2	cups diced cooked chicken breast
1/2	teaspoon salt
1/4	teaspoon pepper
1/4	cup all-purpose flour
1	cup fat-free milk
1	cup reduced-fat evaporated milk
1	teaspoon minced fresh parsley
1	teaspoon minced chives

In a large saucepan, saute onion in butter until tender. Stir in broth and potatoes. Bring to a boil. Reduce heat; cover and simmer for 10-15 minutes or until potatoes are tender. Stir in the chicken, salt and pepper.

Combine flour and fat-free milk until smooth; stir into saucepan. Add evaporated milk. Bring to a boil; cook and stir for 2 minutes or until thickened. Sprinkle with parsley and chives. **yield:** 6 servings.

nutrition facts: 1-1/3 cups equals 232 calories, 5 g fat (3 g saturated fat), 43 mg cholesterol, 646 mg sodium, 27 g carbohydrate, 2 g fiber, 19 g protein.

diabetic exchanges: 2 very lean meat, 1-1/2 starch, 1/2 fat-free milk.

SAUSAGE CHICKEN SOUP

prep/total time 30 minutes

3/4	pound boneless skinless chicken breasts
2	medium potatoes, peeled and cut into 1/4-inch cubes
1	can (14-1/2 ounces) chicken broth
1	medium onion, diced
1	medium sweet red pepper, diced
1	medium green pepper, diced
1	garlic clove, minced
3/4	cup picante sauce
3	tablespoons all-purpose flour
3	tablespoons water
1/2	pound smoked sausage, diced

Sliced habanero peppers, optional

Place chicken in a greased microwave-safe dish. Cover and microwave on high for 3-6 minutes or until juices run clear, turning every 2 minutes. Cut into cubes; set aside.

Place potatoes and broth in a 2-1/2-qt. microwave-safe bowl. Cover and microwave on high for 3-1/2 minutes. Add the onions, peppers and garlic; cook 3-1/2 minutes longer or until potatoes are tender. Stir in the picante sauce.

In a small bowl, combine the flour and water until smooth. Add to the potato mixture. Cover and cook on high for 2-3 minutes or until thickened. Add chicken and sausage; cook 1-2 minutes longer or until heated through. Sprinkle with habaneros if desired. **yield:** 6 servings.

editor's note: This recipe was tested in a 1,100-watt microwave. When cutting hot peppers, disposable gloves are recommended. Avoid touching your face.

helen macdonald
lazo, british columbia

I've been making this satisfying soup for years, but my husband is still thrilled whenever I put it on the table. It's loaded with slices of smoked sausage, chunks of chicken, fresh peppers and chunky potatoes. Spice it up or tone it down with your family's favorite picante sauce.

CHICKEN ASPARAGUS SOUP

prep 1 hour | **cook** 45 minutes

sandy clayton
visalia, california

Asparagus is the star in this flavorful soup, a favorite recipe from my Italian grandmother. I have fond memories of chopping veggies and cooking with her as a child.

- 2 pounds thin fresh asparagus
- 2 large potatoes, peeled and diced
- 1 large onion, chopped
- 2 celery ribs, chopped
- 1 medium carrot, chopped
- 2 teaspoons dried parsley flakes
- 1 garlic clove, minced
- 2 tablespoons canola oil
- 2 cans (14-1/2 ounces *each*) chicken broth
- 1 teaspoon salt
- 1/2 teaspoon pepper, *divided*
- 1 bay leaf
- 2 cups cubed cooked chicken
- 2 cups half-and-half cream

Shaved Parmesan cheese, optional

Cut tips from asparagus spears; set aside. Place stalks in a large skillet; cover with water. Bring to a boil. Reduce heat; cover and simmer for 40 minutes. Strain, reserving 4 cups cooking liquid. Discard stalks.

In a Dutch oven, saute the potatoes, onion, celery, carrot, parsley and garlic in oil until vegetables are tender. Stir in the broth, salt, 1/4 teaspoon pepper, bay leaf and reserved cooking liquid. Bring to a boil. Reduce heat; simmer, uncovered, for 30 minutes. Discard bay leaf. Cool slightly.

In a blender, cover and puree the soup in batches until smooth. Return to the pan. Add the chicken, cream, remaining pepper and reserved asparagus tips. Bring to a boil. Reduce heat; simmer, uncovered, for 5 minutes or until the asparagus is tender. Garnish with Parmesan cheese if desired.
yield: 10 servings (about 2 quarts).

CURRIED CHICKEN CORN CHOWDER

prep 15 minutes | **cook** 30 minutes

kendra doss

smithville, missouri

This recipe is close to one my mom used to make for us kids when the weather turned cold. Her's called for heavy cream, but I came up with a slimmer version that is pretty true to the original!

- 2 medium onions, chopped
- 2 celery ribs, chopped
- 1 tablespoon butter
- 3 cans (14-1/2 ounces *each*) reduced-sodium chicken broth
- 5 cups frozen corn
- 2 teaspoons curry powder
- 1/4 teaspoon salt
- 1/4 teaspoon pepper
- Dash cayenne pepper
- 1/2 cup all-purpose flour
- 1/2 cup 2% milk
- 3 cups cubed cooked chicken breast
- 1/3 cup minced fresh cilantro

In a Dutch oven, saute onions and celery in butter until tender. Stir in the broth, corn, curry, salt, pepper and cayenne. Bring to a boil. Reduce heat; cover and simmer for 15 minutes.

In a small bowl, whisk flour and milk until smooth. Whisk into the pan. Bring to a boil; cook and stir for 2 minutes or until thickened. Add chicken and cilantro; heat through. **yield:** 9 servings (2-1/4 quarts).

nutrition facts: 1 cup equals 221 calories, 4 g fat (1 g saturated fat), 40 mg cholesterol, 517 mg sodium, 29 g carbohydrate, 3 g fiber, 20 g protein.

diabetic exchanges: 2 starch, 2 very lean meat.

AMISH CHICKEN CORN SOUP

prep 15 minutes | **cook** 40 minutes

- 12 cups water
- 2 pounds boneless skinless chicken breasts, cubed
- 1 cup chopped onion
- 1 cup chopped celery
- 1 cup shredded carrots
- 3 chicken bouillon cubes
- 2 cans (14-3/4 ounces *each*) cream-style corn
- 2 cups uncooked egg noodles
- 1/4 cup butter
- 1 teaspoon salt
- 1/4 teaspoon pepper

In a Dutch oven or soup kettle, combine the water, chicken, onion, celery, carrots and bouillon. Bring to a boil. Reduce heat; simmer, uncovered, for 30 minutes or until chicken is no longer pink and vegetables are tender.

Stir in the corn, noodles and butter; cook 10 minutes longer or until noodles are tender. Season with salt and pepper. **yield:** 16 servings (about 4 quarts).

beverly hoffman

sandy lake, pennsylvania

Cream-style corn and butter add richness to this homey chicken noodle soup. It makes a big batch, but freezes well for future meals (which is one reason soups are my favorite thing to make).

ENCHILADA CHICKEN SOUP

prep/total time 10 minutes

cristin fischer
bellevue, nebraska

Canned soups, bottled enchilada sauce and a few other convenience items make this recipe one of my fast-to-fix favorites.

1 can (11 ounces) condensed fiesta nacho cheese soup, undiluted
1 can (10-3/4 ounces) condensed cream of chicken soup, undiluted
2-2/3 cups milk
1 can (10 ounces) chunk white chicken, drained
1 can (10 ounces) enchilada sauce

1 can (4 ounces) chopped green chilies
Sour cream

In a large saucepan, combine the soups, milk, chicken, enchilada sauce and green chilies. Cook until heated through. Serve with sour cream.
yield: 7 servings.

SOOTHING CHICKEN SOUP

prep/total time 20 minutes

2 cups sliced celery
3 quarts chicken broth
4 cups cubed cooked chicken
1 can (10-3/4 ounces) condensed cream of mushroom soup, undiluted
1 cup uncooked instant rice
1 envelope onion soup mix
1 teaspoon poultry seasoning

1/2 teaspoon seasoned salt
1/2 teaspoon dried thyme
1/2 teaspoon pepper

In a Dutch oven or soup kettle, simmer the celery in broth until tender. Stir in the remaining ingredients. Bring to a boil. Reduce heat; cover and simmer for 6-8 minutes or until the rice is tender.
yield: 16 servings (4 quarts).

kris countryman
joliet, illinois

I made a few improvements to a quick and easy recipe to create this comforting soup. It's easy to stir up with broth, soup mix, instant rice and seasonings.

ROASTED CHICKEN NOODLE SOUP

prep 10 minutes | **cook** 30 minutes

This chicken recipe is lower in calories, fat or sodium.

- 1 cup chopped onion
- 1 cup chopped carrots
- 1 cup chopped celery
- 1 garlic clove, minced
- 2 teaspoons olive oil
- 1/4 cup all-purpose flour
- 1/2 teaspoon dried oregano
- 1/4 teaspoon dried thyme
- 1/4 teaspoon poultry seasoning
- 6 cups reduced-sodium chicken broth
- 4 cups cubed peeled potatoes
- 1 teaspoon salt
- 2 cups cubed cooked chicken breast
- 2 cups uncooked yolk-free wide noodles
- 1 cup fat-free evaporated milk

In a Dutch oven or soup kettle, saute the onion, carrots, celery and garlic in oil for 5 minutes or until tender. Stir in the flour, oregano, thyme and poultry seasoning until blended; saute 1 minute longer. Gradually add broth, potatoes and salt; bring to a boil. Reduce heat; cover and simmer for 15-20 minutes or until potatoes are tender.

Stir in the chicken and noodles; simmer for 10 minutes or until noodles are tender. Reduce heat. Stir in the milk; heat through (do not boil). **yield:** 8 servings.

nutrition facts: One serving (1-1/2 cups) equals 235 calories, 3 g fat (1 g saturated fat), 31 mg cholesterol, 851 mg sodium, 33 g carbohydrate, 3 g fiber, 20 g protein.

diabetic exchanges: 2 very lean meat, 1-1/2 starch, 1 vegetable, 1/2 fat.

julee wallberg
salt lake city, utah

When the weather turns chilly, I stock up my soup pot with this warmer-upper. The creamy, nicely seasoned broth is chock-full of tender chicken, potatoes, carrots and celery. There's old-fashioned goodness in every spoonful of this thick, hearty soup!

WEDDING SOUP

prep 20 minutes | **cook** 25 minutes

kimberly parker
elyria, ohio

My family loves this quick and easy version of Italian wedding soup. They ask for it frequently, and my son begs me to put any leftovers in his lunch box.

1 egg, lightly beaten
3/4 cup chopped onion, *divided*
1/3 cup dry bread crumbs
1/2 pound ground turkey
1-1/2 teaspoons canola oil
2 cups sliced fresh carrots
1-1/2 cups chopped celery
1 tablespoon butter
4 cups fresh baby spinach
3 cans (14-1/2 ounces *each*) chicken broth
1 cup cubed cooked chicken breast
2 tablespoons minced fresh parsley
1/2 teaspoon dried thyme
1/8 teaspoon salt
1/8 teaspoon pepper
1-1/4 cups acini di pepe pasta *or* small pasta shells

In a large bowl, combine the egg, 1/4 cup onion and bread crumbs. Crumble turkey over mixture and mix well. Shape into 1-in. balls. In a large skillet, brown meatballs in oil until no longer pink; drain and set aside.

Meanwhile, in a large saucepan, saute the carrots, celery and remaining onion in butter until crisp-tender. Add the baby spinach, broth, chicken, fresh parsley, thyme, salt, pepper and reserved meatballs. Cook, uncovered, over medium heat for 10 minutes.

Bring to a boil. Add pasta; cook, uncovered, for 6-7 minutes or until pasta is tender, stirring occasionally. **yield:** 6 servings.

CREAM CHEESE CHICKEN SOUP

prep/total time 30 minutes

1 small onion, chopped
1 tablespoon butter
3 cups chicken broth
3 medium carrots, cut into 1/4-inch slices
2 medium potatoes, peeled and cubed
2 cups cubed cooked chicken
2 tablespoons minced fresh parsley
Salt and pepper to taste
1/4 cup all-purpose flour
1 cup milk
1 package (8 ounces) cream cheese, cubed

kathleen rappleye
mesa, arizona

After tasting a similar soup in a restaurant, I went home and cooked up my own version. It's so soothing on a winter evening served with crusty French bread. For a change of pace, try substituting ham or turkey for the chicken.

In a large saucepan, saute the onion in butter. Add broth, carrots and potatoes. Bring to a boil. Reduce heat; cover and simmer for 15 minutes or until vegetables are tender. Add the chicken, parsley, salt and pepper; heat through.

Combine flour and milk until smooth; add to the vegetable mixture. Bring to a boil; cook and stir for 2 minutes or until thickened. Reduce heat. Add the cream cheese; cook and stir until melted. **yield:** 8 servings.

LEMONY CHICKEN SOUP

prep 5 minutes | **cook** 30 minutes

brenda tollett

san antonio, texas

While living in California, I enjoyed a delicious chicken-lemon soup at a local restaurant. When I returned to Texas, I longed for it but never came across a recipe. I experimented with many versions before creating this one.

1/3 cup butter, cubed
3/4 cup all-purpose flour
6 cups chicken broth, *divided*
1 cup milk
1 cup half-and-half cream
1-1/2 cups cubed cooked chicken
1 tablespoon lemon juice
1/2 teaspoon salt
1/8 teaspoon pepper
Dash ground nutmeg
8 lemon slices

In a soup kettle or large saucepan, melt butter. Stir in flour until smooth; gradually add 2 cups broth, milk and cream. Bring to a boil; cook and stir for 2 minutes or until thickened.

Stir in the chicken, lemon juice, salt, pepper, nutmeg and remaining broth. Cook over medium heat until heated through, stirring occasionally. Garnish each serving with a lemon slice. **yield:** 8 servings (2 quarts).

LIME CHICKEN CHILI

prep 25 minutes | **cook** 40 minutes

1 medium onion, chopped
1 *each* medium sweet yellow, red and green pepper, chopped
3 garlic cloves, minced
2 tablespoons olive oil
1 pound ground chicken
1 tablespoon all-purpose flour
1 tablespoon baking cocoa
1 tablespoon ground cumin
1 tablespoon chili powder
2 teaspoons ground coriander
1/2 teaspoon salt
1/2 teaspoon garlic pepper blend
1/4 teaspoon pepper
2 cans (14-1/2 ounces *each*) diced tomatoes, undrained
1/4 cup lime juice
1 teaspoon grated lime peel
1 can (15 ounces) white kidney *or* cannellini beans, rinsed and drained
2 flour tortillas (8 inches), cut into 1/4-inch strips
6 tablespoons reduced-fat sour cream

In a large saucepan, saute the onion, peppers and garlic in oil for 7-8 minutes or until crisp-tender. Add chicken; cook and stir over medium heat for 8-9 minutes or until no longer pink.

Stir in the flour, cocoa and seasonings. Add tomatoes, lime juice and lime peel. Bring to a boil. Reduce heat; simmer, uncovered, for 20-25 minutes or until thickened, stirring frequently. Stir in beans; heat through.

Meanwhile, place tortilla strips on a baking sheet coated with cooking spray. Bake at 400° for 8-10 minutes or until crisp. Serve chili with sour cream and tortilla strips. **yield:** 6 servings.

diane randazzo

sinking spring, pennsylvania

Lime juice gives this chili a zesty twist, while canned tomatoes and beans make preparation a snap. For extra flair, I top the chili with toasted tortilla strips.

BARLEY CHICKEN CHILI

prep/total time 25 minutes

kayleen grew
essexville, michigan

I was looking for a new recipe for chicken when I discovered a dish I thought my husband might like. After making a few changes and additions, I came up with a zesty chili. It was great! Leftovers store well in the freezer.

1	cup chopped onion
1/2	cup chopped green pepper
1	teaspoon olive oil
2-1/4	cups water
1	can (15 ounces) tomato sauce
1	can (14-1/2 ounces) chicken broth
1	can (10 ounces) diced tomatoes and green chilies, undrained
1	cup quick-cooking barley
1	tablespoon chili powder
1/2	teaspoon ground cumin
1/4	teaspoon garlic powder
3	cups cubed cooked chicken

In a large saucepan, saute onion and green pepper in oil until tender. Add the water, tomato sauce, broth, tomatoes, barley, chili powder, cumin and garlic powder; bring to a boil. Reduce heat; cover and simmer for 10 minutes. Add chicken. Cover and simmer for 5 minutes longer or until barley is tender. **yield:** 9 servings (about 2 quarts).

CHICKEN WILD RICE SOUP

prep 10 minutes | **cook** 40 minutes

virginia montmarquet
riverside, california

This savory soup has a lot of substance, especially for the hearty eaters of the family. We enjoy eating brimming bowls of it all winter long.

2 quarts chicken broth
1/2 pound fresh mushrooms, chopped
1 cup finely chopped celery
1 cup shredded carrots
1/2 cup finely chopped onion
1 teaspoon chicken bouillon granules
1 teaspoon dried parsley flakes
1/4 teaspoon garlic powder
1/4 teaspoon dried thyme
1/4 cup butter, cubed
1/4 cup all-purpose flour
1 can (10-3/4 ounces) condensed cream of mushroom soup, undiluted
1/2 cup dry white wine *or* additional chicken broth
3 cups cooked wild rice
2 cups cubed cooked chicken

In a large saucepan, combine the first nine ingredients. Bring to a boil. Reduce heat; cover and simmer for 30 minutes.

In a soup kettle or Dutch oven, melt butter. Stir in flour until smooth. Gradually whisk in broth mixture. Bring to a boil; cook and stir for 2 minutes or until thickened. Whisk in soup and wine or broth. Add the cooked wild rice and chicken; heat through. **yield:** 14 servings (3-1/2 quarts).

COMFORTING CHICKEN NOODLE SOUP

prep/total time 25 minutes

2 quarts water
8 chicken bouillon cubes
6-1/2 cups uncooked wide egg noodles
2 cans (10-3/4 ounces *each*) condensed cream of chicken soup, undiluted
3 cups cubed cooked chicken
1 cup (8 ounces) sour cream
Minced fresh parsley

In a large saucepan, bring water and bouillon to a boil. Add noodles; cook, uncovered, until tender, about 10 minutes. Do not drain. Add soup and chicken; heat through.

Remove from heat; stir in sour cream. Sprinkle with minced parsley. **yield:** 10-12 servings (about 2-1/2 quarts).

joanna sargent
sandy, utah

This rich, comforting soup is so simple to fix. I like to give a pot of it, along with the recipe, to new mothers so they don't have to worry about dinner.

CHINESE CHICKEN SOUP

prep/total time 25 minutes

taste of home test kitchen

greendale, wisconsin

This attractive, simple soup begins with frozen stir-fry vegetables. Convenient refrigerated and minced gingerroot adds to the Asian flavor.

3 cans (14-1/2 ounces *each*) chicken broth
1 package (16 ounces) frozen stir-fry vegetable blend
2 cups cubed cooked chicken
1 teaspoon minced fresh gingerroot
1 teaspoon soy sauce
1/4 teaspoon sesame oil

In a large saucepan, combine all of the ingredients. Bring to a boil. Reduce the heat; cover and simmer for 15 minutes or until heated through. **yield:** 6 servings.

HAM AND CHICKEN GUMBO

prep 10 minutes | **cook** 45 minutes

3 bacon strips, cut into 1/2-inch pieces
1/3 cup chopped onion
1 garlic clove, minced
1/2 cup cubed fully cooked ham
1/4 cup cubed cooked chicken
1 cup frozen sliced okra
1 can (8 ounces) diced tomatoes, undrained
1 cup chicken broth
1/2 teaspoon Worcestershire sauce

1/8 teaspoon salt
4 drops hot pepper sauce
Hot cooked rice

In a large skillet, cook bacon just until crisp. Add onion and cook, stirring constantly, until bacon is crisp and onion is soft. Add garlic, ham and chicken; cook for 2 minutes, stirring constantly. Stir in okra, tomatoes and broth; bring to a boil. Reduce heat; cover and simmer for 30 minutes. Add Worcestershire sauce, salt and hot pepper sauce. Serve over rice. **yield:** 2 servings.

jean leonard

houston, texas

This is one of my favorite soups, and it is super easy to make. Bacon gives it a nice smoky flavor.

WHITE BEAN CHICKEN CHILI

prep 35 minutes | **cook** 3 hours

3/4   pound boneless skinless chicken breasts, cubed
1/2   teaspoon salt
1/4   teaspoon pepper
2   tablespoons olive oil
1   medium onion, chopped
4   garlic cloves, minced
1   jalapeno pepper, seeded and chopped
2   teaspoons dried oregano
1   teaspoon ground cumin
2   cans (15 ounces *each*) white kidney *or* cannellini beans, rinsed and drained, *divided*
3   cups chicken broth, *divided*
1-1/2   cups (6 ounces) shredded cheddar cheese
Sour cream and minced fresh cilantro, optional

Sprinkle chicken with salt and pepper. In a large skillet over medium heat, cook the chicken in olive oil for 2 minutes.

Stir in the onion, garlic and jalapeno; cook 2 minutes longer. Sprinkle with oregano and cumin; cook 1 minute longer or until the chicken is browned and vegetables are tender. Transfer to a 3-qt. slow cooker.

In a small bowl, mash 1 cup of beans. Add 1/2 cup broth; stir until blended. Add to the slow cooker with the remaining beans and broth.

Cover and cook on low for 3 to 3-1/2 hours or until chicken juices run clear. Stir before serving. Sprinkle with cheese. Garnish with sour cream and cilantro if desired. **yield:** 6 servings.

editor's note: When cutting hot peppers, disposable gloves are recommended. Avoid touching your face.

kristine bowles
albuquerque, new mexico

My sister shared this chili recipe with me. I usually double it and add one extra can of beans, then serve it with cheddar biscuits or warmed tortillas. The jalapeno adds just enough heat to notice but not too much for my children.

COLORFUL CHICKEN 'N' SQUASH SOUP

prep 25 minutes | **cook** 1-1/2 hours

trina bigham
fairhaven, massachusetts

I try to make food that pleases my preference for fresh ingredients and my family's tastes. I make this soup every week, and everyone loves it.

1   broiler/fryer chicken (4 pounds), cut up
13   cups water
5   pounds butternut squash, peeled and cubed (about 10 cups)
1-1/4   pounds fresh kale, chopped
6   medium carrots, chopped
2   large onions, chopped
3   teaspoons salt

Place chicken and water in a soup kettle. Bring to a boil. Reduce heat; cover and simmer for 1 hour or until chicken is tender.

Remove chicken from broth. Strain broth and skim fat. Return broth to the pan; add the squash, kale, carrots and onions. Bring to a boil. Reduce heat; cover and simmer for 25-30 minutes or until vegetables are tender.

When chicken is cool enough to handle, remove meat from bones and cut into bite-size pieces. Discard bones and skin. Add chicken and salt to soup; heat through. **yield:** 14 servings (5-1/2 quarts).

CHICKEN DUMPLING SOUP

prep 15 minutes | **cook** 50 minutes

1   pound boneless skinless chicken breasts, cut into 1-1/2-inch cubes
3   cans (14-1/2 ounces *each*) reduced-sodium chicken broth
3   cups water
4   medium carrots, chopped
1   medium onion, chopped
1   celery rib, chopped
1   teaspoon minced fresh parsley
1/2   teaspoon salt
1/4   teaspoon garlic powder
1/4   teaspoon poultry seasoning
1/4   teaspoon pepper

DUMPLINGS
3   egg whites
1/2   cup 1% cottage cheese
2   tablespoons water
1/4   teaspoon salt
1   cup all-purpose flour

brenda white
morrison, illinois

My husband was fooled and pleasantly surprised with this chicken soup. I'm sure your family will be, too! A savory broth, hearty chunks of chicken and thick, chewy dumplings provide plenty of comforting flavor.

In a large nonstick skillet coated with cooking spray, brown chicken. Add the broth, water, vegetables and seasonings. Bring to a boil. Reduce heat simmer, uncovered, for 30 minutes.

Meanwhile, for the dumplings, in a large bowl, beat the egg whites and cottage cheese until blended. Add water and salt. Stir in the flour and mix well.

Bring soup to a boil. Drop dumplings by tablespoonfuls onto the boiling soup. Reduce heat; cover and simmer for 15 minutes or until a toothpick inserted in dumplings comes out clean (do not lift cover while simmering). Serve immediately. **yield:** 4 servings.

SPICY CHICKEN RICE SOUP

prep/total time 25 minutes

mary shaver
jonesboro, arkansas

Arkansas is the top rice-producing state in the country, so this quick and delicious recipe definitely represents our region.

2   cans (14-1/2 ounces *each*) chicken broth
3   cups cooked rice
2   cups cubed cooked chicken
1   can (15-1/4 ounces) whole kernel corn, undrained
1   can (11-1/2 ounces) V8 juice
1   cup salsa
1   can (4 ounces) chopped green chilies, drained
1/2 cup chopped green onions
2   tablespoons minced fresh cilantro
1/2 cup shredded Monterey Jack cheese, optional

In a large saucepan, combine the first nine ingredients. Bring to a boil. Reduce heat; cover and simmer for 15 minutes or until heated through. Sprinkle with shredded cheese if desired. **yield:** 8 servings.

SUNDAY CHICKEN STEW

prep 30 minutes | **cook** 6-1/2 hours

1/2 cup all-purpose flour
1   teaspoon salt
1/2 teaspoon white pepper
1   broiler/fryer chicken (3 pounds), cut up and skin removed
2   tablespoons canola oil
3   cups chicken broth
6   large carrots, cut into 1-inch pieces
2   celery ribs, cut into 1/2-inch pieces
1   large sweet onion, thinly sliced
1   teaspoon dried rosemary, crushed
1-1/2 cups frozen peas

DUMPLINGS

1   cup all-purpose flour
2   teaspoons baking powder
1/2 teaspoon salt
1/2 teaspoon dried rosemary, crushed
1   egg, beaten
1/2 cup milk

In a large resealable plastic bag, combine the flour, salt and pepper; add chicken, a few pieces at a time, and shake to coat. In a large skillet, brown chicken in oil; remove and keep warm. Gradually add broth to the skillet; bring to a boil.

In a 5-qt. slow cooker, layer the carrots, celery and onion; sprinkle with rosemary. Add the chicken and hot broth. Cover and cook on low for 6-7 hours or until chicken juices run clear, vegetables are tender and stew is bubbling. Stir in peas.

For the dumplings, in a small bowl, combine the flour, baking powder, salt and rosemary. Combine the egg and milk; stir into dry ingredients. Drop by heaping teaspoonfuls onto simmering chicken mixture. Cover and cook on high for 25-30 minutes or until a toothpick inserted in a dumpling comes out clean (do not lift the cover while simmering). **yield:** 6 servings.

diane halferty
corpus christi, texas

I love this recipe because I can prepare the veggies the night before and, in the morning, brown the chicken and assemble everything in the slow cooker before I go to church. I can spend time with my family while Sunday dinner cooks.

CHICKEN SOUP WITH POTATO DUMPLINGS

prep 25 minutes | **cook** 40 minutes

marie mcconnell
shelbyville, illinois

Our family calls this comforting, old-fashioned soup our "Sunday dinner soup", because it's almost a complete dinner in a bowl. You'll love the flavor!

1/4	cup chopped onion
2	garlic cloves, minced
1	tablespoon canola oil
6	cups chicken broth
2	cups cubed cooked chicken
2	celery ribs, chopped
2	medium carrots, sliced
1/4	teaspoon dried sage leaves

DUMPLINGS

1-1/2	cups biscuit/baking mix
1	cup cold mashed potatoes (with added milk)
1/4	cup milk
1	tablespoon chopped green onion
1/8	teaspoon pepper

In a large saucepan, saute onion and garlic in oil for 3-4 minutes or until onion is tender. Stir in the broth, chicken, celery, carrots and sage. Bring to a boil. Reduce heat; cover and simmer for 10-15 minutes or until vegetables are tender.

In a small bowl, combine the dumpling ingredients. Drop heaping tablespoonfuls of batter onto simmering soup. Cover and simmer for 20 minutes or until a toothpick inserted in a dumpling comes out clean (do not lift cover while simmering). **yield:** 5 servings.

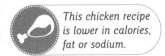

This chicken recipe is lower in calories, fat or sodium.

MUSHROOM CHICKEN SOUP

prep/total time 30 minutes

joan anderson
west covina, california

Tarragon really brightens the flavor of this creamy soup featuring leftover cooked chicken. I serve it as a main dish with crusty bread. It's fabulous!

1/4 cup chopped onion
1/4 cup sliced carrot
1 tablespoon canola oil
2 tablespoons all-purpose flour
1/4 teaspoon dried tarragon
1/4 teaspoon pepper
4 cups chicken broth
1-1/2 cups diced cooked chicken
1 can (8 ounces) mushroom stems and pieces, drained
1 cup evaporated milk

In a large saucepan, saute onion and carrot in oil until tender. Stir in the flour, tarragon and pepper until blended. Gradually add broth. Bring to a boil over medium heat; cook and stir for 2 minutes or until slightly thickened.

Reduce heat; stir in the chicken, mushrooms and evaporated milk. Cover and simmer for 10-15 minutes or until heated through (do not boil). **yield:** 5 servings.

nutrition facts: 1 cup (made with reduced-sodium broth and fat-free evaporated milk) equals 185 calories, 6 g fat (1 g saturated fat), 39 mg cholesterol, 760 mg sodium, 12 g carbohydrate, 1 g fiber, 20 g protein.

diabetic exchanges: 2 lean meat, 1 starch.

ITALIAN PEASANT SOUP

prep/total time 25 minutes

1 pound Italian sausage links, casings removed and cut into 1-inch slices
2 medium onions, chopped
6 garlic cloves, chopped
1 pound boneless skinless chicken breasts, cut into 1-inch cubes
2 cans (15 ounces *each*) cannellini *or* white kidney beans, rinsed and drained
2 cans (14-1/2 ounces *each*) chicken broth
2 cans (14-1/2 ounces *each*) diced tomatoes
1 teaspoon dried basil

1 teaspoon dried oregano
6 cups fresh spinach leaves, chopped
Shredded Parmesan cheese, optional

In a Dutch oven or soup kettle, cook sausage over medium heat until no longer pink; drain. Add onions and garlic; saute until tender. Add chicken; cook and stir until no longer pink.

Stir in the beans, broth, tomatoes, basil and oregano. Cook, uncovered, for 10 minutes. Add the spinach and heat just until wilted. Serve with shredded Parmesan cheese if desired. **yield:** 11 servings (2-3/4 quarts).

kim knight
hamburg, pennsylvania

My father shared this recipe with me, and I use it when I need a hearty, healthy meal. Loaded with sausage, chicken, beans and spinach, the quick soup is nice for special occasions. It also happens to be my sons' favorite!

SANDWICHES

ROASTED PEPPER CHICKEN SANDWICHES, P. 84

PINEAPPLE CHICKEN FAJITAS

prep 25 minutes | **cook** 15 minutes

raymonde bourgeois

swastika, ontario

Honey and pineapple add a sweet twist to these fajitas that my family loves. I like to serve them with coleslaw and baked or fried potatoes. For a special touch, offer sour cream, shredded cheese, salsa and toasted almonds alongside.

2   pounds boneless skinless chicken breasts, cut into strips
1   tablespoon olive oil
1   *each* medium green, sweet red and yellow pepper, julienned
1   medium onion, cut into thin wedges
2   tablespoons fajita seasoning mix
1/4   cup water
2   tablespoons honey
1   tablespoon dried parsley flakes
1   teaspoon garlic powder
1/2   teaspoon salt
1/2   cup unsweetened pineapple chunks, drained
8   flour tortillas (10 inches), warmed

In a large nonstick skillet, cook chicken in oil for 4-5 minutes. Add peppers and onion; cook and stir 4-5 minutes longer.

In a small bowl, combine seasoning mix and water; stir in the honey, parsley, garlic powder and salt. Stir into skillet. Add pineapple. Cook and stir for 1-2 minutes or until chicken juices run clear and vegetables are tender.

Place chicken mixture on one side of each tortilla; fold tortillas over filling. **yield:** 8 fajitas.

BACON-CHICKEN CRESCENT RING

prep 25 minutes | **bake** 20 minutes

2   tubes (8 ounces *each*) refrigerated crescent rolls
1   can (10 ounces) chunk white chicken, drained and flaked
1-1/2   cups (6 ounces) shredded Swiss cheese
3/4   cup mayonnaise
1/2   cup finely chopped sweet red pepper
1/4   cup finely chopped onion
6   bacon strips, cooked and crumbled
2   tablespoons Dijon mustard
1   tablespoon Italian salad dressing mix

Grease a 14-in. pizza pan. Unroll the crescent roll dough; separate into 16 triangles. Place wide end of one triangle 3 in. from edge of prepared pan with point overhanging edge of pan. Repeat with the remaining triangles along outer edge of pan, overlapping the wide ends (dough will look like a sun when complete). Lightly press the wide ends together.

In a small bowl, combine the remaining ingredients. Spoon over the wide ends of dough. Fold the points of triangles over filling and tuck under wide ends (filling will be visible). Bake at 375° for 20-25 minutes or until golden brown. **yield:** 8 servings.

michele mcwhorter

jacksonville, north carolina

This stuffed and baked ring is really easy to assemble. It's so good that people always ask for the recipe.

BUFFALO CHICKEN BURGERS WITH TANGY SLAW

prep 25 minutes | **broil** 10 minutes

This chicken recipe is lower in calories, fat or sodium.

SLAW
- 1/4 cup thinly sliced celery
- 1/4 cup shredded apple
- 2 tablespoons prepared fat-free blue cheese salad dressing
- 1 teaspoon finely chopped walnuts

SAUCE
- 3 tablespoons Louisiana-style hot sauce
- 2 teaspoons ketchup
- 2 teaspoons reduced-fat butter, melted

BURGERS
- 2 tablespoons chopped sweet red pepper
- 2 tablespoons plus 4 teaspoons thinly sliced green onions, *divided*
- 1 tablespoon unsweetened applesauce
- 1/4 teaspoon salt
- 1/4 teaspoon garlic salt
- 1/4 teaspoon pepper
- 1 pound ground chicken
- 4 lettuce leaves
- 4 hamburger buns, split

For the slaw, in a small bowl, combine the celery, apple, salad dressing and walnuts. For the sauce, in another small bowl, combine the hot sauce, ketchup and butter; set aside.

For the burgers, in a large bowl, combine the red pepper, 2 tablespoons green onion, applesauce, salt, garlic salt and pepper. Crumble chicken over mixture and mix well. Shape into four burgers.

Broil 6 in. from the heat for 5-7 minutes on each side or until a meat thermometer reads 165° and juices run clear, basting occasionally with reserved sauce. Serve on lettuce-lined buns; top each with 2 tablespoons slaw and sprinkle with remaining green onion. **yield:** 4 servings.

nutrition facts: 1 burger equals 312 calories, 12 g fat (4 g saturated fat), 78 mg cholesterol, 682 mg sodium, 29 g carbohydrate, 2 g fiber, 23 g protein.

diabetic exchanges: 3 lean meat, 2 starch.

editor's note: This recipe was tested with Land O'Lakes light stick butter.

jeanne holt
mendota heights, minnesota

These burgers are my way of enjoying the flavors of buffalo chicken wings while avoiding some of the fat and calories.

MAKEOVER CHICKEN 'N' BROCCOLI BRAID

prep 25 minutes | **bake** 15 minutes

dana rabe
west richland,
washington

*A beautiful chicken and
pastry braid delivers both
on taste and presentation.
It's rich, creamy, full of
chicken and veggies, and
surrounded with a crispy,
flaky crust.*

2 cups cubed cooked chicken breast
1 cup chopped fresh broccoli
1 cup (4 ounces) shredded
  reduced-fat cheddar cheese
1/2 cup chopped sweet red pepper
2 teaspoons dill weed
2 garlic cloves, minced
1/4 teaspoon salt
1/4 cup reduced-fat mayonnaise
1/4 cup reduced-fat plain yogurt
2 tubes (8 ounces *each*)
  refrigerated reduced-fat crescent
  rolls
1 egg white, lightly beaten
1 tablespoon slivered almonds

In a large bowl, combine the first seven ingredients. Stir in mayonnaise and yogurt. Unroll both tubes of crescent dough onto an ungreased baking sheet; press together, forming a 15-in. x 12-in. rectangle. Seal seams and perforations. Spoon filling lengthwise down the center third of dough.

On each long side, cut dough 3 in. toward the center at 1-1/2-in. intervals, forming strips. Bring one strip from each side over filling; pinch ends to seal. Repeat. Pinch ends of loaf to seal.

Brush with egg white; sprinkle with slivered almonds. Bake at 375° for 15-20 minutes or until the crust is golden brown and filling is heated through. **yield:** 8 servings.

DILLED CAJUN CHICKEN SANDWICHES

prep/total time 25 minutes

4 boneless skinless chicken breast
  halves (4 ounces *each*)
3 tablespoons olive oil
2 tablespoons Cajun seasoning
1/4 cup mayonnaise
2 teaspoons dill weed
1 teaspoon minced garlic
4 sandwich rolls, split
4 lettuce leaves
4 slices tomato
4 slices provolone cheese

abby teel
boise, idaho

*I came up with this recipe
when my husband and I
were looking for something
quick. We both love Cajun
seasoning, and the same
goes for garlic and dill. We
combined them for these
sandwiches that even my
four-year-old loves!*

Flatten chicken to 1/4-in. thickness. In a large skillet, combine olive oil and Cajun seasoning; add chicken and turn to coat. Cook, uncovered, over medium heat for 5-6 minutes on each side or until juices run clear.

Meanwhile, in a small bowl, combine the mayonnaise, dill and garlic. Spread over cut sides of rolls. On roll bottoms, layer the lettuce, tomato, cheese and chicken; replace roll tops. **yield:** 4 servings.

**ULTIMATE
KITCHEN TIP**

Look for Cajun seasoning in the spice section of your grocery store. You can also make your own Cajun seasoning. Although there are many different blends, a typical mix includes salt, onion powder, garlic powder, cayenne pepper, ground mustard, celery seed and pepper. Be mindful of the amount of cayenne pepper you use, and adjust according to your preference.

ULTIMATE CHICKEN SANDWICHES

prep 10 minutes + marinating | **bake** 20 minutes

gregg voss
emerson, nebraska

After making these sandwiches, you'll never order the fast-food kind again. Marinating the chicken overnight in buttermilk gives it a wonderful tenderness. The golden, crispy breading adds a zippy touch.

6	boneless skinless chicken breast halves (4 ounces *each*)
1	cup 1% buttermilk
1/2	cup reduced-fat biscuit/baking mix
1/2	cup cornmeal
1-1/2	teaspoons paprika
3/4	teaspoon salt
3/4	teaspoon poultry seasoning
1/2	teaspoon garlic powder
1/2	teaspoon pepper
1/4	teaspoon cayenne pepper
6	onion *or* kaiser rolls, split
6	lettuce leaves
12	tomato slices

Flatten chicken to 1/2-in. thickness. Pour buttermilk into a large resealable plastic bag; add chicken. Seal bag and turn to coat; refrigerate for 8 hours or overnight.

In a shallow bowl, combine the biscuit mix, cornmeal, paprika, salt, poultry seasoning, garlic powder, pepper and cayenne. Remove chicken one piece at a time, allowing excess buttermilk to drain off. Discard buttermilk. Coat chicken with cornmeal mixture; place in a 13-in. x 9-in. baking dish coated with cooking spray.

Bake, uncovered, at 400° for 8-12 minutes on each side or until a meat thermometer reaches 170° and the coating is lightly browned. Serve on split rolls with lettuce leaves and tomato. **yield:** 6 servings.

NACHO CHICKEN PITAS

prep 20 minutes | **bake** 20 minutes

1	egg
1	cup crushed nacho tortilla chips
1	pound boneless skinless chicken breasts, cut into 1-inch strips
1/2	cup mayonnaise
4	pita breads (6 inches), halved
8	lettuce leaves
1	large tomato, sliced
1/2	cup shredded part-skim mozzarella cheese

In a shallow bowl, beat the egg. Place crushed chips in another shallow bowl. Dip chicken in egg, then coat with chips. Place in a single layer in a greased 11-in. x 7-in. baking dish. Bake at 400° for 20-25 minutes or until juices run clear.

Spread mayonnaise inside pita halves; line with lettuce. Fill with chicken and tomato; sprinkle with cheese. **yield:** 4 servings.

taste of home test kitchen
greendale, wisconsin

Chicken breasts strips are coated with tortilla chips and baked for a sandwich that is super yummy. Lettuce, tomato and cheese seal the deal.

SPICY CHICKEN BUNDLES

prep 25 minutes | **bake** 15 minutes

vicki bluemner
collinsville, illinois

A friend introduced me to these popovers, and I enhanced the recipe a bit by adding jalapeno peppers. My family has enjoyed these for almost 18 years. Hope yours does, too.

1 package (3 ounces) cream cheese, softened
2 tablespoons milk
1 tablespoon pickled jalapeno slices, chopped
1/4 teaspoon pepper
2 cups cubed cooked chicken
1/2 cup chopped onion
2 tubes (8 ounces *each*) refrigerated crescent rolls
1 tablespoon butter, melted
4 teaspoons seasoned bread crumbs

MUSHROOM SAUCE

1 can (10-3/4 ounces) condensed cream of mushroom soup, undiluted
1/2 cup milk

In a large bowl, beat the cream cheese, milk, jalapenos and pepper until blended. Stir in the chicken and onion.

Separate crescent dough into eight rectangles; seal perforations. Spoon 1/4 cup chicken mixture onto the center of each rectangle; bring corners up to the center and pinch edges to seal.

Place on an ungreased baking sheet. Brush with butter; sprinkle with bread crumbs. Bake at 375° for 15-20 minutes or until golden brown.

For the sauce, in a small saucepan, combine the soup and milk. Cook and stir over medium heat until heated through. Serve with the bundles. **yield:** 8 servings.

editor's note: When cutting hot peppers, disposable gloves are recommended. Avoid touching your face.

TERIYAKI CHICKEN SANDWICHES

prep/total time 20 minutes

pam may
auburn, alabama

I turn lemon juice, soy sauce, garlic, ginger and a little brown sugar into a lip-smacking sauce that seasons cooked and shredded chicken.

2-1/2 cups shredded cooked chicken
1/4 cup lemon juice
1/4 cup soy sauce
2 tablespoons sugar
1 tablespoon brown sugar
3/4 teaspoon minced garlic
1/2 teaspoon ground ginger
4 sandwich buns, split

In a large saucepan, combine the first seven ingredients. Bring to a boil. Reduce heat; simmer, uncovered, for 3-4 minutes or until heated through. Spoon the chicken mixture onto each bun bottom; replace tops. **yield:** 4 servings.

MEXICAN CHICKEN SANDWICHES

prep/total time 25 minutes

3 tablespoons olive oil
4 teaspoons chili powder
1/2 teaspoon garlic powder
1/4 to 1/2 teaspoon cayenne pepper
4 boneless skinless chicken breast halves (4 ounces *each*)
1-1/2 cups (6 ounces) shredded taco *or* Mexican cheese blend, *divided*
1/3 cup mayonnaise
8 slices sourdough bread
1/2 cup salsa

In a small bowl, combine the oil and seasonings. Rub over both sides of chicken. Grill, covered, over medium heat for 6-8 minutes on each side or a meat thermometer reaches 170°.

Meanwhile, combine 1 cup cheese and mayonnaise; set aside. Grill bread slices on one side until lightly browned. Spread with cheese mixture; grill until cheese is melted.

Place chicken on four slices of bread; top with salsa, remaining cheese and remaining bread, cheese side down. **yield:** 4 servings.

editor's note: Reduced-fat or fat-free mayonnaise is not recommended for this recipe.

samantha anhalt
redford township, michigan

These lively sandwiches look extra special with grilled bread and savory melted cheese, but they come together in less than 30 minutes!

JUMBO GREEK SUB

prep 20 minutes + marinating | **cook** 15 minutes + chilling

taste of home test kitchen

greendale, wisconsin

It's nice to make just one sandwich that generously feeds six people. This meal is easy to transport to a tailgate party or potluck.

2 boneless skinless chicken breast halves (6 ounces *each*)

1 cup olive oil vinaigrette salad dressing, *divided*

1 tablespoon olive oil

1 loaf (1 pound) unsliced Italian bread

1/4 cup crumbled tomato and basil feta cheese *or* plain feta cheese

1/4 cup sliced ripe olives

1 jar (7 ounces) roasted sweet red peppers, drained

15 to 20 cucumber slices (1/8 inch thick)

Flatten chicken to 1/4-in. thickness. Place in a large resealable plastic bag. Add 3/4 cup salad dressing; seal and turn to coat. Refrigerate for 3 hours.

Drain and discard marinade. In a large skillet, cook chicken in oil for 5 minutes on each side or until juices run clear. Cool.

Cut the top third off the loaf of bread. Carefully hollow out top and bottom, leaving a 1/2-in. shell (discard removed bread or save for another use).

Brush remaining salad dressing on cut sides of bread. Sprinkle feta and olives in bottom half of bread. Top with chicken, red peppers and cucumber. Replace bread top. Wrap tightly in plastic wrap; refrigerate for at least 2 hours. **yield:** 6-8 servings.

CHEESY CHICKEN SUBS

prep/total time 25 minutes

12 ounces boneless skinless chicken breasts, cut into strips

1 envelope Parmesan Italian *or* Caesar salad dressing mix

1 cup sliced fresh mushrooms

1/2 cup sliced red onion

1/4 cup olive oil

4 submarine buns, split and toasted

4 slices Swiss cheese

Place chicken in a bowl; sprinkle with salad dressing mix. In a skillet, saute mushrooms and onion in oil for 3 minutes. Add chicken; saute for 6 minutes or until chicken juices run clear.

Spoon the mixture onto roll bottoms; top with Swiss cheese. Broil 4 in. from the heat for 4 minutes or until the cheese is melted. Replace tops. **yield:** 4 servings.

jane hollar

vilas, north carolina

As part of the food service staff at the Appalachian State University for 33 years, thousands of students have enjoyed this flavorful sandwich that combines seasoned grilled chicken, Swiss cheese and sauteed mushrooms and onions.

ITALIAN CHICKEN WRAPS

prep/total time 25 minutes

- 1 package (16 ounces) frozen stir-fry vegetable blend
- 2 packages (6 ounces *each*) ready-to-use grilled chicken breast strips
- 1/2 cup fat-free Italian salad dressing
- 3 tablespoons shredded Parmesan cheese
- 6 flour tortillas (8 inches), room temperature

In a large saucepan, cook vegetables according to package directions; drain. Stir in the chicken, salad dressing and cheese. Simmer, uncovered, for 3-4 minutes or until heated through. Spoon about 3/4 cup down the center of each tortilla; roll up tightly. **yield:** 6 servings.

cathy hofflander
adrian, michigan

After enjoying a chicken wrap at a restaurant, I experimented at home to create something similar. This delicious version is as fast as it is delicious.

 ULTIMATE **KITCHEN TIP**

If your flour tortillas are a little too stiff to roll up for burritos and enchiladas, wrap them in a damp microwave-safe paper towel and gently warm in the microwave for a few seconds until they are soft and pliable. If you have leftover tortillas, brush them with melted butter and sprinkle with herbs or cinnamon-sugar. Bake on a cookie sheet until crisp.

BACON-PROVOLONE CHICKEN SANDWICHES

prep/total time 30 minutes

taste of home test kitchen
greendale, wisconsin

Bacon and provolone take this hearty chicken sandwich over the top. Add a little Dijon mustard to spice things up a bit.

4	boneless skinless chicken breast halves (6 ounces *each*)
1	teaspoon poultry seasoning
1	tablespoon olive oil
4	kaiser rolls, split
8	strips ready-to-serve fully cooked bacon
4	slices provolone cheese
8	romaine leaves
1	small onion, sliced
1/4	cup mayonnaise

Flatten chicken to 1/4-in. thickness; sprinkle with poultry seasoning. In a large skillet, cook chicken in oil over medium heat for 4-5 minutes on each side or until juices run clear; drain.

On roll bottoms, layer the bacon, chicken and cheese. Broil 4-6 in. from the heat for 1-2 minutes or until cheese is melted. Top with romaine and onion. Spread mayonnaise over cut side of roll tops; replace tops. **yield:** 4 servings.

BBQ CHICKEN SANDWICHES

prep 20 minutes | **cook** 15 minutes

This chicken recipe is lower in calories, fat or sodium.

1/2	cup chopped onion
1/2	cup diced celery
1	garlic clove, minced
1	tablespoon butter
1/2	cup salsa
1/2	cup ketchup
2	tablespoons brown sugar
2	tablespoons cider vinegar
1	tablespoon Worcestershire sauce
1/2	teaspoon chili powder
1/4	teaspoon salt
1/8	teaspoon pepper
2	cups shredded cooked chicken
6	hamburger buns, split and toasted

leticia lewis
kennewick, washington

These are great sandwiches and are a cinch to make. For a spicier taste, eliminate the ketchup and increase the salsa to 1 cup.

In a large saucepan, saute the onion, celery and garlic in butter until tender. Stir in the salsa, ketchup, brown sugar, vinegar, Worcestershire sauce, chili powder, salt and pepper. Stir in chicken. Bring to a boil. Reduce heat; cover and simmer for 15 minutes. Serve about 1/3 cup chicken mixture on each bun. **yield:** 6 servings.

nutrition facts: 1 sandwich equals 284 calories, 8 g fat (3 g saturated fat), 47 mg cholesterol, 770 mg sodium, 35 g carbohydrate, 3 g fiber, 18 g protein.

diabetic exchanges: 2 starch, 2 lean meat.

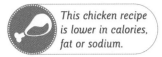
This chicken recipe is lower in calories, fat or sodium.

COLORFUL CHICKEN CROISSANTS

prep/total time 15 minutes

shelia lammers

englewood, colorado

A friend of mine invented this fruity chicken salad. I've made it many times, and guests are always surprised at the pleasant blend of tastes and textures. It's handy to store the components of the salad in a cooler for a picnic, where you can assemble the croissants on site.

- 1/4 cup diced celery
- 1/4 cup golden raisins
- 1/4 cup dried cranberries
- 1/4 cup sliced almonds
- 3/4 cup mayonnaise
- 2 tablespoons chopped red onion
- 1/4 teaspoon pepper
- 1/4 teaspoon salt, optional
- 2 cups cubed cooked chicken breast
- 4 croissants, split

In a large bowl, combine the first seven ingredients and salt if desired. Stir in the chicken. Spoon about 1/2 cup into each croissant. **yield:** 4 servings.

nutrition facts: 1 chicken croissant equals 184 calories, 5 g fat (0 saturated fat), 43 mg cholesterol, 331 mg sodium, 20 g carbohydrate, 2 g fiber, 13 g protein.

diabetic exchanges: 2 lean meat, 1 vegetable, 1 fruit.

MARINATED CHICKEN SANDWICHES

prep 20 minutes + marinating | **grill** 10 minutes

- 1/2 cup reduced-sodium soy sauce
- 1/4 cup packed brown sugar
- 1/4 cup ketchup
- 1 tablespoon canola oil
- 1 tablespoon molasses
- 1 teaspoon garlic powder
- 1 teaspoon minced fresh gingerroot
- 1 teaspoon prepared mustard
- 6 boneless skinless chicken breast halves (6 ounces *each*)
- 3 tablespoons reduced-fat mayonnaise
- 6 kaiser rolls, split and toasted
- 6 lettuce leaves
- 6 slices (1/2 ounce *each*) reduced-fat Swiss cheese

In a large resealable plastic bag, combine the first eight ingredients; add the chicken. Seal bag and turn to coat; refrigerate for at least 1 hour.

Coat grill rack with cooking spray before starting the grill. Drain and discard marinade. Grill chicken, covered, over medium heat for 4-6 minutes on each side or until juices run clear. Spread mayonnaise over bottom of rolls; top with chicken, lettuce and cheese. Replace roll tops. **yield:** 6 servings.

ruth lee

troy, ontario

Every bite of this grilled chicken is packed with flavor. The sweet brown sugar combines well with zesty mustard and fresh ginger. You can top the sandwich with any kind of cheese you like.

ULTIMATE KITCHEN TIP

Molasses is the byproduct of the process of refining sugarcane into table sugar. Made from the third boiling of sugar syrup, blackstrap molasses is stronger, darker and more bitter than light or dark molasses. While light and dark molasses can be used interchangeably, use blackstrap molasses with caution. The intense flavor can be overwhelming.

ROASTED PEPPER CHICKEN SANDWICHES

prep 30 minutes + marinating | **grill** 10 minutes

laura merkle
dover, delaware

This is such a wonderful, flavorful sandwich that it is perfect for a casual dinner, special lunch or when hosting a luncheon. It's sure to get rave reviews.

1	tablespoon lemon juice
1	tablespoon Dijon mustard
2	teaspoons olive oil
1	garlic clove, minced
1/4	teaspoon dried thyme
1/4	teaspoon dried marjoram
4	boneless skinless chicken breast halves (4 ounces *each*)

PEPPER MIXTURE

1	large onion, thinly sliced
4	garlic cloves, minced
1	teaspoon sugar
3/4	teaspoon fennel seed, crushed
1/4	teaspoon crushed red pepper flakes
1/8	teaspoon salt
1/8	teaspoon pepper
1	jar (7 ounces) roasted sweet red peppers, drained and sliced
1	tablespoon red wine vinegar

SANDWICHES

1	loaf (8 ounces) focaccia bread
4	teaspoons fat-free mayonnaise
4	slices reduced-fat Swiss cheese

In a large resealable plastic bag, combine the first six ingredients; add chicken. Seal bag and turn to coat; refrigerate for 1 hour.

For the pepper mixture, in a large nonstick skillet coated with cooking spray, cook and stir the onion, garlic, sugar and seasonings over medium heat until tender. Stir in roasted peppers and vinegar; cook 2 minutes longer. Remove from the heat; keep warm.

Coat grill rack with cooking spray before starting the grill. Drain chicken if necessary, discarding any excess marinade. Grill chicken, covered, over medium heat for 4-7 minutes on each side or until juices run clear. Cut into 1/2-in. strips.

For the sandwiches, cut focaccia bread in half lengthwise; spread mayonnaise over cut side of bread bottom. Layer with cheese, chicken strips and pepper mixture. Replace bread top; lightly press down. Grill, covered, for 2-3 minutes or until cheese is melted. Cut into four sandwiches. **yield:** 4 servings.

APRICOT-PISTACHIO CHICKEN SALAD SANDWICHES

prep/total time 20 minutes

lesley pew
lynn, massachusetts

I ordered an entree similar to this at the local museum cafe and liked it so much I decided to make something similar. I tend to serve it as a salad during the summer. It's really good on a hot day.

1-1/2   cups shredded rotisserie chicken (skin removed)
1/3   cup chopped dried apricots
2   tablespoons mayonnaise
2   tablespoons sour cream
4   teaspoons coarsely chopped pistachios
1   teaspoon prepared horseradish
1   teaspoon whole grain mustard
1   teaspoon honey
Dash salt

Dash white pepper
Dash hot pepper sauce
4   slices sourdough bread
2   Bibb lettuce leaves
2   slices tomato
2   slices sweet onion

In a small bowl, combine the first 11 ingredients. Spread over two slices of bread; top with the lettuce, tomato, sweet onion and remaining bread. **yield:** 2 servings.

CURRY CHICKEN SALAD WRAPS

prep/total time 25 minutes

1/2   cup mayonnaise
1/2   cup sour cream
1/4   cup finely chopped green onions
2   tablespoons curry powder
1   tablespoon mango chutney
1/2   teaspoon salt
1/2   teaspoon pepper
1   package (10 ounces) ready-to-serve roasted chicken breast strips
1   cup seedless red grapes, halved
1/2   cup julienned carrot
6   tablespoons chopped pecans, toasted

1/4   cup thinly sliced onion
6   lettuce leaves
6   flour tortillas (10 inches), room temperature
3/4   cup fresh mint (about 24 leaves)

For dressing, in a small bowl, combine the first seven ingredients. Set aside 1-1/2 cups for serving. In a large bowl, combine the chicken, grapes, carrot, pecans and onion. Stir in the remaining dressing.

Place a lettuce leaf on each tortilla; top with 2/3 cup chicken salad and mint leaves. Roll up. Serve with reserved dressing. **yield:** 6 servings.

robyn cavallaro
easton, pennsylvania

With curry powder and mango chutney, these scrumptious sandwiches offer a twist on traditional chicken salad. The fresh mint leaves and creamy from-scratch dressing make them ideal for a summer dinner or special lunch.

BUFFALO CHICKEN LETTUCE WRAPS

prep/total time 25 minutes

priscilla gilbert
indian harbour beach,
florida

These homemade buffalo chicken wraps are excellent. Honey and lime juice help tone down the hot wing sauce for a refreshing zip. They're perfect for lunch or a light summer meal with a tall glass of ice-cold lemonade.

- 1/3 cup crumbled blue cheese
- 1/4 cup mayonnaise
- 2 tablespoons milk
- 4-1/2 teaspoons lemon juice
- 1 tablespoon minced fresh parsley
- 1 teaspoon Worcestershire sauce
- 1 pound boneless skinless chicken breasts, cubed
- 1 teaspoon salt
- 1 tablespoon canola oil
- 1/4 cup lime juice
- 1/4 cup Louisiana-style hot sauce
- 1/4 cup honey
- 1 small cucumber, halved lengthwise, seeded and thinly sliced
- 1 celery rib, thinly sliced
- 3/4 cup julienned carrots
- 8 Bibb *or* Boston lettuce leaves

For dressing, in a small bowl, combine the first six ingredients. Cover and refrigerate until serving.

Sprinkle chicken with salt. In a large skillet, cook chicken in oil until no longer pink. Combine the lime juice, hot sauce and honey; pour over the chicken. Bring to a boil. Reduce heat; simmer, uncovered, for 2-3 minutes or until heated through. Remove from the heat; stir in the cucumber, celery and carrots.

Spoon 1/2 cup chicken mixture onto each lettuce leaf; fold sides over filling and secure with a toothpick. Serve with the blue cheese dressing. **yield:** 8 servings.

WALDORF CHICKEN SALAD SANDWICHES

prep/total time 15 minutes

- 3 cups cubed cooked chicken
- 1 medium tart apple, chopped
- 3/4 cup mayonnaise
- 1/4 cup raisins
- 1/4 cup chopped pecans, toasted
- 1 tablespoon apple juice
- 1/2 teaspoon salt

- 1/4 teaspoon ground nutmeg
- 8 slices pumpernickel bread

Lettuce leaves, optional

In a large bowl, combine the first eight ingredients. Spread about 1 cup chicken salad over four slices of bread. Top with lettuce if desired and remaining bread. **yield:** 4 servings.

karen small
maple shade, new jersey

Autumn is apple-picking time here in New Jersey, so with such an abundance of that delicious fruit, it just seemed natural to toss a chopped apple into my chicken salad.

CHICKEN SALAD PANINI

prep/total time 25 minutes

1/4   cup mayonnaise
1-1/2   teaspoons honey
3/4   teaspoon snipped fresh dill
3/4   teaspoon Dijon mustard
Dash salt
Dash pepper
1   cup cubed cooked chicken breast
3/4   cup shredded cheddar cheese
1/2   cup chopped peeled apple
1/4   cup chopped pecans, toasted
6   slices white bread
4   teaspoons butter, softened

In a small bowl, combine the first six ingredients. In another bowl, combine the chicken, cheese, apple and pecans; add dressing and toss to coat.

Spread half of the chicken salad on two slices of bread. Top each with another slice of bread, remaining chicken salad and remaining bread. Spread butter on both sides of sandwiches. Cook on a panini maker or indoor grill until bread is toasted and cheese is melted. **yield:** 2 servings.

lisa huff
birmingham, alabama

This delightful sandwich is great during the summer, but can be enjoyed any time of year. The honey mustard dressing gives the chicken plenty of pizzazz, and the apples and pecans lend a lively crunch.

FANCY JOES

prep/total time 30 minutes

linda emery
bearden, arkansas

This yummy recipe is a new twist on an old favorite. I use ground chicken or turkey instead of the usual sloppy joe fixings. English muffins add an extra-special touch.

1 pound ground chicken *or* turkey
1 large onion, chopped
1 medium green pepper, chopped
2 cans (15-1/2 ounces *each*) sloppy joe sauce
3 cups cooked rice
8 English muffins, split and toasted

In a large skillet, cook the chicken, onion and green pepper over medium heat until chicken is no longer pink; drain. Stir in the sloppy joe sauce. Bring to a boil. Reduce heat; cover and simmer for 10 minutes. Stir in rice; cook 5 minutes longer or until heated through. Spoon 1 cup onto each English muffin. **yield:** 8 servings.

CAESAR CHICKEN WRAPS

prep/total time 30 minutes

1/2 cup Caesar salad dressing
1/2 cup grated Parmesan cheese, *divided*
1 teaspoon lemon juice
1 garlic clove, minced
1/4 teaspoon pepper
1 package (8 ounces) cream cheese, softened
3 cups shredded romaine
1/2 cup diced sweet red pepper
1 can (2-1/4 ounces) sliced ripe olives, drained
5 flour tortillas (10 inches)
1-3/4 cups cubed cooked chicken

christi martin
elko, nevada

When we have chicken for dinner, I cook a little extra for these full-flavored roll-ups. Featuring Caesar salad dressing, cream cheese, red pepper, black olives and a hint of lemon and garlic, the wraps are perfect alongside corn on the cob and a green vegetable.

In a small bowl, combine the salad dressing, 1/4 cup Parmesan cheese, lemon juice, garlic and pepper. In a small mixing bowl, beat cream cheese until smooth. Add half of the salad dressing mixture and mix well; set aside.

In a large bowl, combine the romaine, red pepper and olives. Add the remaining salad dressing mixture; toss to coat. Spread about 1/4 cup cream cheese mixture on each tortilla. Top with the romaine mixture and chicken; sprinkle with remaining Parmesan cheese. Roll up; cut in half. **yield:** 5 servings.

BUFFALO CHICKEN SANDWICHES

prep/total time 10 minutes

dawn onuffer
crestview, florida

This is a simple and quick way to dress up breaded chicken patties. We like these sandwiches with additional blue cheese dressing for dipping. Or try them with Monterey Jack cheese and ranch dressing instead.

2 refrigerated breaded chicken patties
1/4 cup Louisiana-style hot sauce
2 teaspoons canola oil
2 tablespoons butter, softened
2 sandwich buns, split
2 slices provolone cheese
2 tablespoons blue cheese salad dressing
Lettuce, tomato and red onion slices
Additional hot sauce

Place chicken patties in a large resealable plastic bag; add hot sauce. Seal bag and turn to coat. In a large skillet, brown patties in oil over medium heat for 1-2 minutes on each side or until heated through. Remove and keep warm.

Spread butter over cut sides of buns. In the same skillet, toast buns, buttered side down, over medium heat for 1-2 minutes or until lightly browned. Top with a chicken patty, provolone cheese, salad dressing, lettuce, tomato and onion. Serve with additional hot sauce. **yield:** 2 servings.

editor's note: This recipe was prepared with Frank's Hot Pepper Sauce.

OPEN-FACED CHICKEN SANDWICHES

prep/total time 30 minutes

This chicken recipe is lower in calories, fat or sodium.

1 loaf (8 ounces and 8 inches long) French bread
1 pound fresh mushrooms, sliced
1 large sweet onion, sliced
1 cup fat-free mayonnaise
1/2 cup crumbled blue cheese
1/4 teaspoon pepper
1 pound boneless skinless chicken breasts, grilled and sliced
1 cup (4 ounces) shredded part-skim mozzarella cheese

Cut bread into eight 1-in. slices and toast slices. Meanwhile, in a large nonstick skillet coated with cooking spray, saute the mushrooms and onion for 15-20 minutes or until onion is tender and golden brown; set aside.

In a small bowl, combine the mayonnaise, blue cheese and pepper; mix well. Spread blue cheese mixture over each bread slice. Top with the chicken, mushroom mixture and mozzarella cheese. Place on a broiler pan. Broil 4-6 in. from the heat for 3-4 minutes or until the cheese is melted. **yield:** 8 servings.

nutrition facts: 1 open-faced sandwich equals 276 calories, 8 g fat (4 g saturated fat), 66 mg cholesterol, 618 mg sodium, 23 g carbohydrate, 3 g fiber, 27 g protein.

diabetic exchange: 3 lean meat, 1 starch, 1 vegetable.

lynda clark
spokane, washington

Caramelized onions, mushrooms and cheese make these my favorite sandwiches. I invented them for a last-minute picnic by combining items I had on hand. They've been a hit ever since.

GRILLED

GRILLED BASIL CHICKEN AND TOMATOES, P. 104

GRILLED RASPBERRY CHICKEN

prep 15 minutes + marinating | **grill** 30 minutes

gloria warczak
cedarburg, wisconsin

Raspberry vinaigrette and raspberry jam lend fruity flavor to this moist, easy-to-make chicken dish I created.

1	cup plus 4-1/2 teaspoons raspberry vinaigrette, *divided*
2	tablespoons minced fresh rosemary *or* 2 teaspoons dried rosemary, crushed, *divided*
6	bone-in chicken thighs
6	chicken drumsticks
1/2	cup seedless raspberry jam
1-1/2	teaspoons lime juice
1/2	teaspoon soy sauce
1/8	teaspoon garlic powder

In a large resealable plastic bag, combine 1 cup vinaigrette and half of the rosemary. Add chicken. Seal bag and turn to coat; refrigerate for 1 hour.

In a bowl, combine the jam, lime juice, soy sauce, garlic powder, and remaining vinaigrette and rosemary; set aside.

Drain and discard marinade. Place chicken skin side down on grill rack. Grill, covered, over indirect medium heat for 20 minutes. Turn; grill 10-20 minutes longer or until juices run clear, basting occasionally with raspberry sauce. **yield:** 6 servings.

GRILLED JERK CHICKEN WINGS

prep/total time 30 minutes

1/2	cup Caribbean jerk seasoning
18	fresh chicken wingettes (2 to 3 pounds)
2	cups honey barbecue sauce
1/3	cup packed brown sugar
2	teaspoons prepared mustard
1	teaspoon ground ginger

Coat grill rack with cooking spray before starting the grill. Place the jerk seasoning in a large resealable plastic bag; add the chicken wings, a few at a time, and shake to coat. In a small bowl, combine the barbecue sauce, brown sugar, mustard and ginger; set aside.

Grill chicken wings, covered, over medium heat for 12-16 minutes, turning occasionally. Brush with sauce. Grill, uncovered, 8-10 minutes longer or until juices run clear, basting and turning several times. **yield:** 6 servings.

editor's note: Caribbean jerk seasoning may be found in the spice aisle of your grocery store.

caren adams
fontana, california

I've been making this recipe ever since I can remember. It's so simple to fix, doesn't take a lot of ingredients or time, and is always a favorite with my guests. You can change it up by varying the seasoning from mild to extra-spicy.

CHICKEN AND ASPARAGUS KABOBS

prep 25 minutes + marinating | **grill** 10 minutes

DIPPING SAUCE

2	cups mayonnaise
1/4	cup sugar
1/4	cup soy sauce
2	tablespoons sesame seeds, toasted
1	tablespoon sesame oil
1/2	teaspoon white pepper

KABOBS

1/4	cup soy sauce
2	tablespoons brown sugar
2	tablespoons water
1	tablespoon sesame oil
1	teaspoon crushed red pepper flakes
1	teaspoon minced fresh gingerroot
1-1/2	pounds boneless skinless chicken breasts, cut into 1-1/2-inch pieces
1	pound fresh asparagus, trimmed and cut into 2-inch pieces
2	tablespoons olive oil
1/2	teaspoon salt

In a small bowl, combine the sauce ingredients. Cover and refrigerate for 2-4 hours.

For the kabobs, in a large resealable plastic bag, combine the soy sauce, brown sugar, water, sesame oil, pepper flakes and ginger. Add the chicken; seal bag and turn to coat. Refrigerate for 2 hours, turning occasionally.

Drain and discard marinade. In a large bowl, toss the asparagus with olive oil and salt. On six metal or soaked wooden skewers, alternately thread one chicken piece and two asparagus pieces.

Grill, covered, over medium heat for 4-5 minutes on each side or until chicken juices run clear and asparagus is crisp-tender. Serve with dipping sauce. **yield:** 6 servings.

kelly townsend
syracuse, nebraska

These Asian-flavored kabobs, served with a tasty dipping sauce, are special enough to make for guests at your next backyard get-together. Sometimes I substitute fresh salmon for the chicken.

MAYONNAISE LOVER'S CHICKEN

prep 15 minutes + marinating | **grill** 10 minutes

jennifer rytting
west jordan, utah

My father-in-law was looking for a good chicken marinade when a friend suggested mayonnaise with Italian dressing. He added the ham and cheese on his own, and we can't get enough of it! You'd never guess this recipe is so easy and fast!

1/2 cup Italian salad dressing
1-1/4 cups mayonnaise, *divided*
6 boneless skinless chicken breast halves (4 ounces *each*)
6 slices deli ham
6 slices Swiss cheese
1-1/2 teaspoons prepared mustard
1-1/2 teaspoons honey

In a small bowl, combine salad dressing and 1/2 cup mayonnaise. Pour 3/4 cup into a large resealable plastic bag; add chicken. Seal bag and turn to coat; refrigerate for at least 30 minutes. Cover and refrigerate remaining marinade for basting.

Drain and discard marinade. Grill the chicken, covered, over medium heat or broil 4 in. from the heat for 4-6 minutes on each side or until juices run clear, basting frequently with reserved marinade. Top each piece of chicken with a slice of ham and cheese. Grill, covered, 1-2 minutes longer or until cheese is melted.

In a small bowl, combine the mustard, honey and remaining mayonnaise. Serve with chicken. **yield:** 6 servings.

FAJITA PITAS

prep 40 minutes | **bake** 10 minutes

6 boneless skinless chicken breast halves (4 ounces *each*)
1 large onion, sliced
1 large green pepper, thinly sliced
1 tablespoon canola oil
2 cups (8 ounces) shredded Mexican cheese blend *or* cheddar cheese
8 pita breads (6 inches), halved

SAUCE

1 medium onion, finely chopped
1 medium tomato, finely chopped
1/2 jalapeno pepper, finely chopped
1 tablespoon minced fresh cilantro
1 tablespoon canola oil
Guacamole and sour cream, optional

Grill chicken, covered, over medium heat for 6-8 minutes on each side or until juices run clear. Cut into strips.

In a large skillet, saute onion and green pepper in oil until crisp-tender. Add chicken and cheese.

Stuff into pita halves; place on an ungreased baking sheet. Bake at 325° for 10 minutes or until cheese is melted.

Meanwhile, for sauce, combine the onion, tomato, jalapeno, cilantro and oil in a bowl. Serve sauce, guacamole and sour cream if desired with pitas. **yield:** 8 servings.

editor's note: When cutting hot peppers, disposable gloves are recommended. Avoid touching your face.

diana jones
springtown, texas

I was late coming home one evening and forgot to pick up tortillas for the fajitas we planned for dinner. So we used pita bread that I had in the freezer instead. The warm chicken-filled pockets, with a homemade sauce and other tasty toppings, are often requested when we're hungry.

BOMBAY CHICKEN

june thomas
chesterton, indiana

prep 10 minutes + marinating | **grill** 25 minutes

This grilled dinner always turns out moist and tender. The marinade has a Middle Eastern flair, giving the dish a zesty flavor. The rich orange color makes a beautiful presentation.

1-1/2 cups (12 ounces) plain yogurt
1/4 cup lemon juice
2 tablespoons chili powder
2 tablespoons paprika
2 tablespoons olive oil
1-1/2 teaspoons salt
1/2 to 1 teaspoon cayenne pepper
1/2 teaspoon garlic powder
1/4 teaspoon ground ginger
1/4 teaspoon ground cardamom
1/8 teaspoon ground cinnamon
4 to 5 pounds bone-in chicken thighs and legs, skin removed

In a large resealable plastic bag, combine the first 11 ingredients. Add the chicken thighs and legs; seal bag and turn to coat. Refrigerate overnight.

Rub grill rack with oil or coat with cooking spray before starting the grill. Drain and discard marinade.

Grill chicken, covered, over medium-hot heat for 10-15 minutes on each side or until a meat thermometer reads 180°.
yield: 8 servings.

CHICKEN PIZZA PACKETS

prep 15 minutes | **grill** 20 minutes

1 pound boneless skinless chicken breasts, cut into 1-inch pieces
2 tablespoons olive oil
1 small zucchini, thinly sliced
16 pepperoni slices
1 small green pepper, julienned
1 small onion, sliced
1/2 teaspoon dried oregano
1/2 teaspoon dried basil
1/4 teaspoon salt
1/4 teaspoon garlic powder
1/4 teaspoon pepper
1 cup halved cherry tomatoes

1/2 cup shredded part-skim mozzarella cheese
1/2 cup shredded Parmesan cheese

In a large bowl, combine the first 11 ingredients. Coat four pieces of heavy-duty foil (about 12 in. square) with cooking spray. Place a quarter of the chicken mixture in the center of each piece. Fold foil round mixture and seal tightly.

Grill, covered, over medium-hot heat for 15-18 minutes or until chicken juices run clear.

Carefully open each packet. Sprinkle with tomatoes and cheeses. Seal loosely; grill 2 minutes longer or until cheese is melted. **yield:** 4 servings.

amber zurbrugg
alliance, ohio

Basil, garlic, pepperoni and mozzarella give plenty of pizza flavor to chicken, green pepper, zucchini and cherry tomatoes in these individual foil dinners. This speedy grilled supper is a tasty way to get little ones to eat their veggies.

ULTIMATE KITCHEN TIP

With its perfumy flavor, cilantro gives a distinctive taste to Mexican, Latin American and Asian dishes. Like all other fresh herbs, cilantro should be used as soon as possible. To store, immerse freshly cut stems in about 2 inches of water. Cover leaves loosely with a plastic bag and refrigerate for several days. Wash just before using.

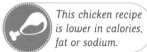 *This chicken recipe is lower in calories, fat or sodium.*

GREEK-STYLE CHICKEN BURGERS

prep 25 minutes + chilling | **grill** 10 minutes

judy puskas
wallaceburg, ontario

The original ingredients for this recipe called for lamb or beef, but I decided to try ground chicken to decrease the fat. The sauce easily doubles as a great dip for veggies and toasted pita.

1/2	cup fat-free plain yogurt
1/4	cup chopped peeled cucumber
1/4	cup crumbled reduced-fat feta cheese
1-1/2	teaspoons snipped fresh dill
1-1/2	teaspoons lemon juice
1	small garlic clove, minced

BURGERS

1	medium onion, finely chopped
1/4	cup dry bread crumbs
1	tablespoon dried oregano
1	tablespoon lemon juice
2	garlic cloves, minced
1/2	teaspoon salt
1/4	teaspoon pepper
1	pound ground chicken
4	hamburger buns, split
4	lettuce leaves
4	tomato slices

Line a strainer with four layers of cheesecloth or one coffee filter and place over a bowl. Place yogurt in strainer; cover yogurt with edges of cheesecloth. Refrigerate for 8 hours or overnight.

Remove yogurt from cheesecloth and discard liquid from bowl. Stir in the cucumber, feta cheese, dill, lemon juice and garlic; set aside.

For the burgers, in a small bowl, combine the onion, bread crumbs, oregano, lemon juice, garlic, salt and pepper. Crumble chicken over mixture and mix well. Shape into four burgers.

Coat grill rack with cooking spray before starting the grill. Grill the burgers, covered, over medium heat for 5-7 minutes on each side or until the meat is no longer pink. Serve each on a bun with lettuce, tomato and 2 tablespoons yogurt sauce.
yield: 4 servings.

nutrition facts: 1 burger equals 350 calories, 12 g fat (4 g saturated fat), 78 mg cholesterol, 732 mg sodium, 35 g carbohydrate, 3 g fiber, 27 g protein.

diabetic exchanges: 3 lean meat, 2 starch, 1 vegetable.

GRILLED CHICKEN WITH PEACH SAUCE

prep/total time 30 minutes

beverly minton
milan, michigan

I've been cooking since I was a young girl growing up on a farm in Indiana. This recipe was adapted from a pie filling. I've served it many times to family and friends, and folks always seem to like it.

1   cup sugar
2   tablespoons cornstarch
1   cup water
2   tablespoons peach *or* orange gelatin
1   medium peach, peeled and finely chopped
4   boneless skinless chicken breast halves (4 ounces *each*)

In a small saucepan, combine the sugar, cornstarch and water until smooth. Bring to a boil over medium heat; cook and stir for 2 minutes. Remove from heat. Stir in the gelatin powder and chopped peach; mix well until gelatin powder is dissolved. Set aside 1 cup for serving.

Grill chicken, uncovered, over medium heat for 3 minutes on each side. Baste with some of the remaining peach sauce. Continue grilling for 6-8 minutes or until meat juices run clear, basting and turning several times. Serve with the reserved peach sauce. **yield:** 4 servings.

GRILLED PINEAPPLE CHICKEN SANDWICHES

prep/total time 30 minutes

2   bacon strips, halved
2   boneless skinless chicken breast halves (5 ounces *each*)
1   tablespoon olive oil
2   tablespoons barbecue sauce
2   pineapple slices
2   kaiser rolls, split
2   lettuce leaves, optional
2   slices provolone cheese

In a small skillet, cook bacon over medium heat until crisp. Remove to paper towels. Flatten chicken to 3/8-in. thickness; brush both sides with oil. Grill, uncovered, over medium heat for 4 minutes. Turn; brush with barbecue sauce. Grill 3-4 minutes longer or until juices run clear.

Meanwhile, place the pineapple and rolls cut side down on grill; cook for 3-4 minutes or until browned, turning the pineapple once. Place lettuce if desired on roll bottoms; top with chicken, cheese, bacon and pineapple. Replace roll tops. **yield:** 2 servings.

sandra fisher
kent, washington

For a fun and hearty handheld summer entree, try these mouth-watering sandwiches. To make a meal, serve them with chips and glasses of iced tea.

RASPBERRY CHICKEN SANDWICHES

prep 25 minutes | **grill** 15 minutes

kelly williams

morganville, new jersey

The raspberry barbecue sauce makes my grilled chicken sandwiches special. I also use this sauce on meatballs, chicken wings and pork chops.

1   cup chili sauce
3/4   cup raspberry preserves
2   tablespoons red wine vinegar
1   tablespoon Dijon mustard
6   boneless skinless chicken breast halves (4 ounces *each*)
2   tablespoons plus 1/2 cup olive oil, *divided*
1/2   teaspoon salt
1/4   teaspoon pepper
24   slices French bread (1/2 inch thick)
12   slices Muenster cheese, halved
Shredded lettuce

Coat grill rack with cooking spray before starting the grill. In a small saucepan, combine the first four ingredients. Bring to a boil. Reduce heat; simmer, uncovered, for 2 minutes. Set aside 1 cup for serving and remaining sauce for basting.

Flatten chicken breasts to 1/4-in. thickness. Cut in half widthwise; place in a large resealable plastic bag. Add 2 tablespoons oil, salt and pepper. Seal bag and turn to coat.

Grill chicken, uncovered, over medium heat for 5-7 minutes on each side or until the juices run clear, basting frequently with raspberry sauce. Remove and keep warm.

Brush remaining oil over both sides of bread. Grill bread, uncovered, for 1-2 minutes or until lightly browned on one side. Turn and top each piece of bread with a slice of cheese. Grill 1-2 minutes longer or until bottom of bread is toasted. Place a piece of chicken, lettuce and reserved raspberry sauce on half of bread slices; top with remaining bread. **yield:** 12 servings.

CHICKEN PEAR MIXED GREENS SALAD

prep/total time 25 minutes

5   boneless skinless chicken breast (4 ounces *each*)
7   cups torn mixed salad greens
2   ounces Brie *or* Camembert cheese, cubed
2   medium pears, chopped
1/4   cup chopped pecans, toasted
1/4   cup apple juice concentrate, thawed
2   tablespoons canola oil
4-1/2 teaspoons cider vinegar
2   teaspoons Dijon mustard
1/4   teaspoon salt
1/8   teaspoon pepper

janet duran

des moines, washington

Apple juice concentrate combined with mustard and vinegar makes a sweet and tangy vinaigrette that pairs well with grilled chicken and Brie.

Coat grill rack with cooking spray before starting the grill. Grill chicken, covered, over medium heat for 6-8 minutes on each side or until juices run clear.

Arrange the salad greens, cheese, pears and pecans on individual plates. Slice chicken; arrange over salad. In a jar with a tight-fitting lid, combine the apple juice concentrate, oil, vinegar, mustard, salt and pepper; shake well. Drizzle over salad and serve immediately. **yield:** 5 servings.

GRILLED THIGHS AND DRUMSTICKS

prep 10 minutes + marinating | **grill** 30 minutes

brenda beachy
belvidere, tennessee

This chicken is juicy, has great barbecue flavor and makes a big batch. It's perfect for summer picnics and family reunions.

2-1/2 cups packed brown sugar
2 cups water
2 cups cider vinegar
2 cups ketchup
1 cup canola oil
4 tablespoons salt
3 tablespoons prepared mustard
4-1/2 teaspoons Worcestershire sauce
1 tablespoon soy sauce
1 teaspoon pepper
1 teaspoon Liquid Smoke, optional
10 pounds bone-in chicken thighs and chicken drumsticks
1/2 teaspoon seasoned salt

In a large bowl, combine the first 11 ingredients. Pour into two large resealable plastic bags; add chicken. Seal bags and turn to coat; refrigerate overnight.

Prepare grill for indirect heat. Drain and discard, marinade. Sprinkle the chicken with seasoned salt. Grill the chicken skin side down, covered, over indirect medium heat for 15 minutes. Turn; grill 15-20 minutes longer or until juices run clear. **yield:** 12-14 servings.

NEW-WORLD CRANBERRY MOLASSES BARBECUE CHICKEN OVER DOUBLE CORN GRITS

prep/total time 30 minutes

1/2 cup molasses
1/2 cup cranberry sauce
1/2 cup balsamic vinegar
1 teaspoon chopped chipotle pepper
1 teaspoon adobo sauce
1 cup barbecue sauce
1 pound boneless skinless chicken breasts
3 cups chicken stock
1 cup instant grits
1 can cream-style corn (14-3/4 ounces)
1 cup coarsely grated cheddar cheese
Salt and pepper to taste

In a small saucepan, combine the molasses, cranberry sauce, vinegar, chipotle pepper, adobo sauce and barbecue sauce. Bring to a boil and simmer for 5 minutes; let cool slightly. Reserve 1/4 cup of the sauce; set aside. Season the chicken with salt and pepper on both sides.

Grill or broil chicken for 6-8 minutes on each side, or until the juices run clear, basting frequently with barbecue sauce. Remove and keep warm.

To prepare grits, bring the chicken stock to a boil and slowly whisk in the instant grits. Add the corn and bring to a boil. Cover, reduce heat and simmer for 6 minutes. Stir in the cheese and season with salt and pepper.

Serve chicken with grits. Drizzle chicken with reserved barbecue sauce. **yield:** 4 servings.

taste of home cooking school
greendale, wisconsin

Molasses, cranberry sauce, balsamic vinegar and spicy chipotle peppers and adobo sauce come together to create a delicious barbecue sauce for grilled chicken breasts.

CHUTNEY-GLAZED CHICKEN

prep 5 minutes | **grill** 30 minutes

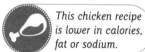
This chicken recipe is lower in calories, fat or sodium.

angie ridgway
fairfield, nebraska

I like to garnish these grilled chicken breasts with fresh chives. They make a really delicious meal when served with a tossed salad and dinner rolls.

    1/2   cup mango chutney
      2   tablespoons sherry *or* apple juice
      2   tablespoons Dijon mustard
      1   teaspoon curry powder
      6   bone-in chicken breast halves
           (8 ounces *each*), skin removed

Coat grill rack with cooking spray before starting the grill for indirect heat. In a small bowl, combine the chutney, sherry or apple juice, mustard and curry powder.

Grill chicken meaty side down over indirect medium heat for 15 minutes. Turn; grill 15-20 minutes longer or until a meat thermometer reads 170°, basting occasionally with chutney mixture. **yield:** 6 servings.

nutrition facts: One serving (1 chicken breast half) equals 243 calories, 5 g fat (1 g saturated fat), 102 mg cholesterol, 220 mg sodium, 10 g carbohydrate, 1 g fiber, 38 g protein.

diabetic exchanges: 2 starch, 1 fat, 1/2 fruit.

ZESTY MUSTARD CHICKEN

prep 10 minutes | **grill** 40 minutes

This chicken recipe is lower in calories, fat or sodium.

michael everidge
morristown, tennessee

Whether you're grilling a broiler chicken or chicken breasts, next time consider using this lip-smacking sauce. It only has four ingredients and can be whipped up in minutes.

    1/2   cup prepared mustard
    1/2   cup honey
      1   tablespoon salt-free seasoning
           blend
      1   tablespoon Worcestershire sauce
      1   broiler/fryer chicken (3 pounds),
           cut in half

In a small bowl, combine the first four ingredients. Carefully loosen the skin of the chicken; spoon some of the mustard sauce under the skin.

Coat grill rack with cooking spray before starting the grill. Place chicken skin side up on grill rack. Grill, covered, over indirect medium heat for 20 minutes on each side or until juices run clear, basting occasionally with remaining mustard sauce. Remove chicken skin; cut into serving-size pieces. **yield:** 6 servings.

nutrition facts: 1 serving equals 261 calories, 7 g fat (2 g saturated fat), 72 mg cholesterol, 334 mg sodium, 25 g carbohydrate, 1 g fiber, 25 g protein.

diabetic exchanges: 3 lean meat, 1-1/2 starch.

GRILLED CHICKEN SATAY

prep 15 minutes + marinating | **grill** 5 minutes

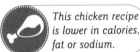

This chicken recipe is lower in calories, fat or sodium.

2	pounds boneless skinless chicken breasts
1/2	cup milk
6	garlic cloves, minced
1	tablespoon brown sugar
1	tablespoon *each* ground coriander, ground turmeric and ground cumin
1	teaspoon salt
1	teaspoon white pepper
1/8	teaspoon coconut extract

PEANUT BUTTER SAUCE

1/3	cup peanut butter
1/3	cup milk
2	green onions, chopped
1	small jalapeno pepper, seeded and finely chopped
2	to 3 tablespoons lime juice
2	tablespoons soy sauce
1	garlic clove, minced
1	teaspoon sugar
1	teaspoon minced fresh cilantro
1	teaspoon minced fresh gingerroot
1/8	teaspoon coconut extract

Flatten chicken to 1/4-in. thickness; cut lengthwise into 1-in.-wide strips. In a large resealable plastic bag, combine the milk, garlic, brown sugar, seasonings and extract. Add chicken; seal bag and turn to coat. Refrigerate for 8 hours or overnight.

In a bowl, whisk the sauce ingredients until blended. Cover and refrigerate until serving. Drain and discard marinade. Thread two chicken strips onto each metal or soaked wooden skewer.

Grill, uncovered, over medium-hot heat for 2-3 minutes on each side or until chicken juices run clear. Serve with the peanut butter sauce. **yield:** 8 servings (1 cup sauce).

nutrition facts: 2 skewers with 2 tablespoons sauce (prepared with reduced-fat peanut butter, fat-free milk and reduced-sodium soy sauce) equals 202 calories, 6 g fat (1 g saturated fat), 63 mg cholesterol, 428 mg sodium, 8 g carbohydrate, 1 g fiber, 27 g protein.

diabetic exchanges: 3 lean meat, 1/2 starch.

editor's note: When cutting hot peppers, disposable gloves are recommended. Avoid touching your face.

sue gronholz
beaver dam, wisconsin

These golden skewered chicken snacks are marinated and grilled, then served with a zesty Thai-style sauce made with peanut butter, lime juice and seasonings.

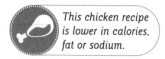

CHICKEN WITH CITRUS SALSA

prep 25 minutes | **grill** 15 minutes

molly slosson
westport, washington

Topped with tart citrus and sweet honey salsa, this tender grilled chicken entree is an attractive change of pace.

- 1 cup pink grapefruit sections
- 2/3 cup orange sections
- 1/2 medium lemon, peeled and cut into sections
- 1 tablespoon minced fresh cilantro
- 1 tablespoon lime juice
- 3/4 teaspoon honey
- 1/4 teaspoon grated lime peel
- 1/8 teaspoon cayenne pepper
- 1/2 teaspoon ground cumin
- 1/2 teaspoon chili powder
- 1/4 teaspoon salt
- Dash onion powder
- Dash garlic powder
- Dash dried oregano
- 2 boneless skinless chicken breast halves (4 ounces *each*)

For salsa, in a small bowl, combine the grapefruit, orange and lemon. Combine the cilantro, lime juice, honey, lime peel and cayenne; stir into fruit mixture. Cover and refrigerate until serving.

In a small bowl, combine the cumin, chili powder, salt, onion powder, garlic powder and oregano; sprinkle over chicken. Coat grill rack with cooking spray before starting the grill. Grill the chicken, covered, over medium heat for 6-8 minutes on each side or until juices run clear. Serve with salsa. **yield:** 2 servings.

nutrition facts: 1 chicken breast half with 1/2 cup salsa equals 206 calories, 3 g fat (1 g saturated fat), 63 mg cholesterol, 359 mg sodium, 21 g carbohydrate, 3 g fiber, 24 g protein.

diabetic exchanges: 3 very lean meat, 1-1/2 fruit.

CAN-CAN CHICKEN

prep 30 minutes + chilling | **grill** 1-1/4 hours

- 1 tablespoon kosher salt
- 1 teaspoon sugar
- 1 teaspoon onion powder
- 1 teaspoon garlic powder
- 1 teaspoon cayenne pepper
- 1 teaspoon paprika
- 1 teaspoon ground mustard
- 1 broiler/fryer chicken (3-1/2 to 4 pounds)
- 1 can (12 ounces) beer

steve bath
lincoln, nebraska

I spray my chicken with a mixture of 2 cups apple cider and 1 tablespoon balsamic vinegar. This adds moisture to the crisp skin, but will require an additional 15 to 30 minutes of cooking time.

In a small bowl, combine the first seven ingredients. Loosen skin from around the chicken breast, thighs and legs. Rub the spice mixture onto and under skin. Tuck wing tips behind the back. Refrigerate for 1 hour.

Prepare the grill for indirect grilling, using a drip pan. Pour out half of the beer, reserving for another use. Poke additional holes in top of the can with a can opener. Holding the chicken with legs pointed down, lower the chicken over the can so it fills the body cavity.

Place chicken over drip pan; grill, covered, over indirect medium heat for 1-1/4 to 1-1/2 hours or until a meat thermometer inserted into a thigh reads 180°. Remove chicken from grill; cover and let stand for 10 minutes. Remove chicken from can. **yield:** 6 servings.

FONTINA-FRUIT CHICKEN BREASTS

prep 30 minutes + marinating | **grill** 10 minutes

lillian julow
gainesville, florida

This is one of my favorite chicken dishes because it's festive enough for a special occasion, but easy enough for an everyday meal.

- 1/3 cup olive oil
- 3 tablespoons cider vinegar
- 2 tablespoons red wine vinegar
- 2 teaspoons honey
- 1 teaspoon Dijon mustard
- 1/2 teaspoon ground mustard
- 8 boneless skinless chicken breast halves (4 ounces *each*)
- 1 large tart apple, peeled and chopped
- 1 teaspoon butter
- 1/2 cup shredded fontina cheese
- 1/2 cup dried cherries, coarsely chopped
- 1/2 teaspoon salt
- 1/2 teaspoon pepper

In a large resealable plastic bag, combine the first six ingredients. Carefully cut a pocket in each chicken breast half; place in bag. Seal and turn to coat; refrigerate for 1 hour.

In a small nonstick skillet, saute apple in butter until tender. Transfer to a small bowl. Stir in the cheese, cherries, salt and pepper. Drain chicken, discarding marinade; stuff with apple mixture. Secure with soaked toothpicks.

Coat grill rack with cooking spray before starting the grill. Grill chicken, covered, over medium heat for 5-8 minutes on each side or until a meat thermometer reads 170°. Discard toothpicks before serving. **yield:** 8 servings.

HONEY-CITRUS CHICKEN KABOBS

prep 15 minutes + marinating | **grill** 10 minutes

- 1/2 cup lime juice
- 1/2 cup lemon juice
- 1/2 cup honey
- 1 garlic clove, minced
- 1 pound boneless skinless chicken breasts, cut into 1-inch cubes
- 1 *each* medium green, sweet red and yellow pepper, cut into 1-inch pieces

In a small bowl, combine the lime juice, lemon juice, honey and garlic. Pour 1-1/4 cups into a large resealable plastic bag; add the chicken. Seal the bag and turn to coat; refrigerate for at least 30 minutes. Cover and refrigerate the remaining marinade for basting.

Coat grill rack with cooking spray before starting the grill. Drain and discard marinade from chicken. On eight metal or soaked wooden skewers, alternately thread the chicken and peppers. Grill, covered, over medium-hot heat for 8-10 minutes or until chicken juices run clear, turning and basting frequently with the reserved marinade. **yield:** 4 servings.

nutrition facts: 2 kabobs equals 194 calories, 3 g fat (1 g saturated fat), 63 mg cholesterol, 57 mg sodium, 19 g carbohydrate, 2 g fiber, 24 g protein.

diabetic exchanges: 3 very lean meat, 1 starch, 1 vegetable.

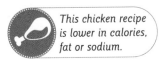
This chicken recipe is lower in calories, fat or sodium.

amanda mills
austin, texas

It only takes 30 minutes to marinate the chicken for these tangy lemon-lime skewers. Not only are they easy to assemble and grill, but they're fun to eat, too!

GRILLED BASIL CHICKEN AND TOMATOES

prep 15 minutes + marinating | **grill** 10 minutes

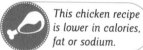
This chicken recipe is lower in calories, fat or sodium.

laura lunardi
exton, pennsylvania

Here's the perfect recipe for a midweek summer barbecue! Relax after work with a cold drink while your savory chicken marinates. Then toss it on the grill and enjoy!

- 8 plum tomatoes, *divided*
- 3/4 cup balsamic vinegar
- 1/4 cup tightly packed fresh basil leaves
- 2 tablespoons olive oil
- 1 garlic clove, minced
- 1/2 teaspoon salt
- 4 boneless skinless chicken breast halves (4 ounces *each*)

Cut four tomatoes into quarters and place in a food processor. Add the vinegar, basil, oil, garlic and salt; cover and process until blended.

Pour 1/2 cup dressing into a small bowl; cover and refrigerate until serving. Pour remaining dressing into a large resealable plastic bag; add chicken. Seal bag and turn to coat; refrigerate for up to 1 hour.

Coat grill rack with cooking spray before starting the grill. Drain and discard marinade. Grill chicken, covered, over medium heat for 4-6 minutes on each side or until juices run clear. Cut remaining tomatoes in half; grill for 2-3 minutes on each side or until tender. Serve with chicken and reserved dressing. **yield**: 4 servings.

nutrition facts: 1 chicken breast half with 1 tomato and 2 tablespoons dressing equals 174 calories, 5 g fat (1 g saturated fat), 63 mg cholesterol, 179 mg sodium, 7 g carbohydrate, 1 g fiber, 24 g protein.

diabetic exchanges: 3 very lean meat, 1 vegetable, 1/2 fat.

TROPICAL ISLAND CHICKEN

prep 10 minutes + marinating | **grill** 45 minutes

sharon hanson
franklin, tennessee

The marinade makes a bold statement in this all-time-favorite chicken recipe that I served at our son's pirate-theme birthday party. It smelled so good on the grill that guests could hardly wait to try a piece!

1/2   cup soy sauce
1/3   cup canola oil
1/4   cup water
2   tablespoons dried minced onion
2   tablespoons sesame seeds
1   tablespoon sugar
4   garlic cloves, minced
1   teaspoon ground ginger
3/4   teaspoon salt
1/8   teaspoon cayenne pepper
2   broiler/fryer chickens (3 to 4 pounds *each*), quartered

In a large resealable plastic bag, combine the first 10 ingredients. Remove 1/3 cup for basting; cover and refrigerate. Add chicken to bag; seal and turn to coat. Refrigerate for 8 hours or overnight.

Drain and discard marinade. Grill chicken, covered, over medium-hot heat for 45-60 minutes or until juices run clear, turning and basting often with reserved marinade. **yield:** 8 servings.

HONEY LEMON CHICKEN

prep 10 minutes + marinating | **grill** 15 minutes

This chicken recipe is lower in calories, fat or sodium.

1/2   cup lemon juice
1/3   cup honey
1/4   cup soy sauce
2   tablespoons finely chopped onion
4   garlic cloves, minced
2   teaspoons dried parsley flakes
2   teaspoons dried basil
1   teaspoon salt-free seasoning blend
1   teaspoon white pepper
1   teaspoon lime juice
6   boneless skinless chicken breast halves

In a large bowl, combine the first 10 ingredients. Pour 2/3 cup marinade into a large resealable plastic bag; add the chicken. Seal bag and turn to coat; refrigerate for at least 4 hours or overnight. Cover and refrigerate the remaining marinade.

Drain and discard marinade from chicken. Coat grill rack with cooking spray before starting the grill. Grill chicken, uncovered, over medium heat for 12-15 minutes or until juices run clear, turning once and basting occasionally with reserved marinade. **yield:** 6 servings.

nutrition facts: 1 serving equals 179 calories, 3 g fat (1 g saturated fat), 63 mg cholesterol, 515 mg sodium, 14 g carbohydrate, trace fiber, 24 g protein.

diabetic exchanges: 3 very lean meat, 1 starch.

tamara mcfarlin
eau claire, wisconsin

When I told our 12-year-old daughter that we were grilling chicken, she asked to make a marinade. Now we use her combination of honey, lemon, garlic and seasonings every time we grill chicken.

CANTONESE CHICKEN BURGERS

prep/total time 30 minutes

betty carr
huntsville, ohio

Ground chicken is perked up with onion, chopped peanuts and carrots for these delectable chicken burgers that can be served year-round. These sandwiches may take a little more work than the regular burger, but the taste is worth it.

1	egg
1	teaspoon sesame oil
1	teaspoon soy sauce
1/3	cup dry bread crumbs
1/4	cup chopped salted peanuts
2	tablespoons sliced green onion
2	tablespoons shredded carrot
1/8	teaspoon garlic powder
1	pound ground chicken
4	hamburger buns, split and toasted
1/2	cup plum sauce
8	spinach leaves, chopped

In a large bowl, whisk the egg, oil and soy sauce. Stir in the bread crumbs, peanuts, onion, carrot and garlic powder. Crumble chicken over mixture and mix well. Shape into four patties.

Grill, uncovered, over medium-hot heat or broil 3-4 in. from the heat for 8-10 minutes on each side or until juices run clear. Serve on buns, topped with plum sauce and spinach. **yield:** 4 servings.

JALAPENO-LIME MARINATED CHICKEN

prep 10 minutes + marinating | **cook** 10 minutes

1	cup orange juice concentrate
2/3	cup chopped onion
1/2	cup lime juice
1/2	cup honey
1	jalapeno pepper, seeded and diced
2	teaspoons ground cumin
2	teaspoons grated lime peel
1/2	teaspoon garlic salt
2	garlic cloves, minced
10	boneless skinless chicken breast halves (4 ounces *each*)

In a 4-cup measuring cup, combine the first nine ingredients. Pour 2 cups into a large resealable plastic bag; add chicken. Seal bag and turn to coat; refrigerate for 2-4 hours. Cover and refrigerate remaining marinade for basting.

Coat grill rack with cooking spray before starting the grill. Drain and discard marinade from chicken. Grill chicken, covered, over medium heat for 4-6 minutes on each side or until juices run clear, basting frequently with the reserved marinade. **yield:** 10 servings.

editor's note: When cutting hot peppers, disposable gloves are recommended. Avoid touching your face.

coleen martin
brookfield, wisconsin

The marinade adds a zesty flavor to the chicken and makes it very tender. Because it's easy to make and travels well, it's the perfect recipe for a summer picnic meal.

GRILLED CHICKEN WITH CHUTNEY

prep 30 minutes + cooling | **grill** 10 minutes

This chicken recipe is lower in calories, fat or sodium.

3 medium plums, chopped
2/3 cup sugar
1/2 cup white wine vinegar
3 tablespoons balsamic vinegar
2 tablespoons dried cranberries
1 garlic clove, minced
1 teaspoon minced fresh gingerroot
1/4 teaspoon ground allspice
1/4 teaspoon crushed red pepper flakes
2 cups chopped peeled peaches
1/4 cup finely chopped red onion
1 teaspoon Dijon mustard
1/2 teaspoon minced seeded jalapeno pepper
6 boneless skinless chicken breast halves (5 ounces *each*)
2 tablespoons olive oil
1 tablespoon Tex-Mex chili seasoning mix
Red leaf lettuce
Additional chopped jalapenos, optional

For the chutney, in a large saucepan, combine the first nine ingredients. Bring to a boil; cook and stir for 6-8 minutes or until thickened. Stir in the peaches, onion, mustard and jalapeno. Cool to room temperature.

Brush chicken with oil; sprinkle with chili seasoning mix. Grill chicken, covered, over medium heat for 5-6 minutes on each side or until a meat thermometer reads 170°. Slice chicken; serve on lettuce leaves with chutney. Sprinkle with additional jalapenos if desired. **yield:** 6 servings.

nutrition facts: 1 chicken breast half with 1/3 cup chutney equals 346 calories, 8 g fat (2 g saturated fat), 78 mg cholesterol, 178 mg sodium, 38 g carbohydrate, 2 g fiber, 30 g protein.

diabetic exchanges: 4 very lean meat, 1-1/2 starch, 1 fruit, 1 fat.

editor's note: When cutting hot peppers, disposable gloves are recommended. Avoid touching your face.

gilda lester
wilmington,
north carolina

My husband didn't like plums until he tasted them cooked with peaches, dried cranberries and spices in this robust chutney recipe. It wakes up just about any kind of meat, whether it's chicken breasts, pork roast or tenderloin.

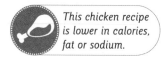

CHILI-HEAD CHICKEN

prep 30 minutes | **cook** 1-1/4 hours

1-1/2 cups dark stout beer, *divided*
2 dried pasilla chilies
2 teaspoons kosher salt
2 teaspoons paprika
1 teaspoon ground cumin
1 teaspoon onion powder
1/2 teaspoon garlic powder
1/2 teaspoon dried oregano
1/2 teaspoon pepper
1/2 teaspoon cayenne pepper
2 teaspoons canola oil
1 jalapeno pepper, chopped
1 broiler/fryer chicken (3-1/2 to 4 pounds)
1 empty 12-ounce beverage can

Place 3/4 cup beer in a microwave-safe bowl; microwave, uncovered, for 1-1/2 minutes or until very hot. Remove stems and seeds from chilies; add chilies to the beer. Let stand for 20 minutes or until softened. Drain, reserving 4 tablespoons seasoned beer. Set chilies aside.

In a small bowl, combine the kosher salt, paprika, cumin, onion powder, garlic powder, oregano, pepper and cayenne; set aside 1 teaspoon of the seasoning mix.

In a blender, combine the oil, 2 tablespoons seasoned beer, jalapeno pepper, reserved chilies, and remaining seasoning mix; cover and process until a smooth thick paste forms, adding additional seasoned beer if necessary.

Loosen skin from around the chicken breast, thighs and legs. Rub the chili paste under the skin. Tuck wing tips behind the back. Rub any remaining paste into the body and neck cavities. Sprinkle chicken with reserved seasoning mix.

Prepare grill for indirect heat, using a drip pan. Poke additional holes in top of the empty can with a can opener. Pour the remaining 3/4 cup beer into the can. Holding the chicken with legs pointed down, lower chicken over the can so it fills the body cavity.

Place chicken over drip pan; grill, covered, over indirect medium heat for 1-1/4 to 1-1/2 hours or until a meat thermometer inserted into a thigh reads 180°. Remove chicken from grill; cover and let stand for 10 minutes. Remove chicken from can. **yield:** 6 servings.

editor's note: This recipe was tested in a 1,100-watt microwave oven. When handling chilies, disposable gloves are recommended. Avoid touching your face.

BARBECUE JACK CHICKEN

prep/total time 25 minutes

4 boneless skinless chicken breast halves (6 ounces *each*)
4 slices pepper Jack cheese
1 cup barbecue sauce

Carefully cut a pocket in each chicken breast half. Fill with cheese; secure with metal or soaked wooden skewers.

Grill chicken, covered, over medium heat or broil 4 in. from the heat for 6-8 minutes on each side or until juices run clear, basting frequently with barbecue sauce. **yield:** 4 servings.

BLACKENED CHICKEN

prep/total time 25 minutes

stephanie kenney
falkville, alabama

This spicy standout packs a one-two punch of flavor. The grilled chicken is basted with a peppery white sauce. Plus there's plenty of extra sauce left over for dipping.

1	tablespoon paprika
4	teaspoons sugar, *divided*
1-1/2	teaspoons salt, *divided*
1	teaspoon garlic powder
1	teaspoon dried thyme
1	teaspoon lemon-pepper seasoning
1	teaspoon cayenne pepper
1-1/2	to 2 teaspoons pepper, *divided*
4	boneless skinless chicken breast halves
1-1/3	cups mayonnaise
2	tablespoons water
2	tablespoons cider vinegar

In a small bowl, combine paprika, I teaspoon sugar, I teaspoon salt, garlic powder, thyme, lemon-pepper, cayenne and 1/2 to I teaspoon pepper; sprinkle over both sides of chicken. Set aside. In another bowl, combine mayonnaise, water, vinegar and remaining sugar, salt and pepper; cover and chill I cup for serving. Save remaining sauce for basting.

Grill the chicken, covered, over indirect medium heat for 4-6 minutes on each side or until juices run clear, basting frequently with remaining sauce. Serve with reserved sauce. **yield:** 4 servings.

APPLE-BUTTER BARBECUED CHICKEN

prep 15 minutes | **grill** 1-1/2 hours + standing

1	teaspoon salt
3/4	teaspoon garlic powder
1/4	teaspoon pepper
1/8	teaspoon cayenne pepper
1	roasting chicken (6 to 7 pounds)
1	can (11-1/2 ounces) unsweetened apple juice
1/2	cup apple butter
1/4	cup barbecue sauce

Combine the salt, garlic powder, pepper and cayenne; sprinkle over chicken.

Prepare grill for indirect heat, using a drip pan.

Pour half of the apple juice into another container and save for another use. With a can opener, poke additional holes in the top of the can. Holding the chicken with legs pointed down, lower chicken over the can so it fills the body cavity. Place chicken on grill rack over drip pan.

Grill, covered, over indirect medium heat for 1-1/2 to 2 hours or until a meat thermometer reads 180°. Combine apple butter and barbecue sauce; baste chicken occasionally during the last 30 minutes. Remove chicken from grill; cover and let stand for 10 minutes. Remove chicken from can before carving. **yield:** 6-8 servings.

holly kilbel
akron, ohio

I love cooking so much I sometimes dream of recipes in my sleep and write them down after I wake up! This dish is my family's favorite way to eat chicken.

ULTIMATE KITCHEN TIP

Grilling over indirect heat is used for foods that cook for a long time over medium or medium-low heat. With a charcoal grill, place a drip pan in the center of your grill's bottom charcoal grate. Arrange hot coals around the drip pan or on both sides of it. Place the food on the grate over the drip pan to catch any drippings, then place the cover on the grill.

PROSCIUTTO CHICKEN KABOBS

prep 30 minutes + marinating | **grill** 10 minutes

elaine sweet
dallas, texas

Everyone will think you spent hours preparing these clever grilled wraps that are served with a guacamole-style dip. Basil gives the chicken a lovely, fresh herb flavor.

3/4 cup five-cheese Italian salad dressing
1/4 cup lime juice
2 teaspoons white Worcestershire sauce for chicken
1/2 pound boneless skinless chicken breasts, cut into 3-inch x 1/2-inch strips
12 thin slices prosciutto
24 fresh basil leaves

AVOCADO DIP
2 medium ripe avocados, peeled
1/4 cup minced fresh cilantro
2 green onions, chopped
2 tablespoons lime juice
2 tablespoons mayonnaise
1-1/2 teaspoons prepared horseradish
1 garlic clove, minced
1/4 teaspoon salt

In a large resealable plastic bag, combine the salad dressing, lime juice and Worcestershire sauce; add the chicken. Seal bag and turn to coat; refrigerate for 1 hour.

Drain and discard marinade. Fold the prosciutto slices in half; top each with two basil leaves and a chicken strip. Roll up jelly-roll style, starting with a short side. Thread onto metal or soaked wooden skewers.

Grill, covered, over medium heat for 5 minutes on each side or until chicken juices run clear.

Meanwhile, for the dip, in a small bowl, mash the avocados. Stir in the cilantro, onions, lime juice, mayonnaise, horseradish, garlic and salt. Serve with kabobs. **yield:** 12 appetizers.

TACO-FLAVORED CHICKEN WINGS

Prep/Total Time: 20 min.

deb keslar
utica, nebraska

I dress up chicken wings with a lively marinade to create a fantastic summertime appetizer. I like these wings hot, so I often add a little extra hot sauce.

1 envelope taco seasoning
3 tablespoons vegetable oil
2 tablespoons red wine vinegar
2 teaspoons hot pepper sauce, *divided*
34 fresh or frozen chicken wingettes (about 4 pounds)
1 cup ranch salad dressing

In a large resealable plastic bag, combine the taco seasoning, oil, vinegar and 1 teaspoon hot pepper sauce; add chicken. Seal bag and turn to coat.

Grill chicken, covered, over medium heat for 5 minutes. Grill 10-15 minutes longer or until juices run clear, turning occasionally. Combine ranch dressing and remaining hot pepper sauce. Serve with chicken. **yield:** about 2-1/2 dozen.

CHIPOTLE CHICKEN FAJITAS

prep 30 minutes + marinating | **grill** 10 minutes

1 bottle (12 ounces) chili sauce
1/4 cup lime juice
4 chipotle peppers in adobo sauce
1 pound boneless skinless chicken breasts, cut into strips
1/2 cup cider vinegar
1/3 cup packed brown sugar
1/3 cup molasses
4 medium green peppers, cut into 1-inch pieces
1 large onion, cut into 1-inch pieces
1 tablespoon olive oil
1/8 teaspoon salt
1/8 teaspoon pepper
10 flour tortillas (8 inches)
1-1/2 cups chopped tomatoes
1 cup (4 ounces) shredded Mexican cheese blend

Place the chili sauce, lime juice and chipotle peppers in a food processor; cover and process until blended. Transfer 1/2 cup to a large resealable plastic bag; add chicken. Seal bag and turn to coat; refrigerate for 1-4 hours.

Pour remaining marinade into a small bowl; add the vinegar, brown sugar and molasses. Cover and refrigerate.

On six metal or soaked wooden skewers, alternately thread chicken, green peppers and onion. Brush with oil; sprinkle with salt and pepper. Grill, covered, over medium heat for 10-16 minutes or until chicken juices run clear, turning occasionally.

Unskewer chicken and vegetables into a large bowl; add 1/2 cup chipotle-molasses mixture and toss to coat. Keep warm.

Grill tortillas, uncovered, over medium heat for 45-55 seconds on each side or until warmed. Top with chicken mixture, tomatoes, cheese and remaining chipotle-molasses mixture. **yield:** 5 servings.

melissa thomeczek
hannibal, missouri

I've had this recipe for three years and my husband and I just love it. Be careful with the chipotle peppers as they can be very hot. You can adjust the amount of heat to suit your preference.

SKILLET& STOVETOP

LEMON CHICKEN WITH PASTA, P. 131

 *This chicken recipe is lower in calories, fat or sodium.*

CHICKEN WITH SPICY FRUIT

prep/total time 30 minutes

kathy rairigh
milford, indiana

This speedy stovetop entree is special enough for company, yet easy enough for an everyday meal. The chicken gets wonderful flavor from a sauce made with strawberry jam, dried cranberries and pineapple juice.

1-1/4	cups unsweetened pineapple juice
1/4	cup dried cranberries
2	garlic cloves, minced
1/8	to 1/4 teaspoon crushed red pepper flakes
4	boneless skinless chicken breast halves (4 ounces *each*)
1/4	cup strawberry spreadable fruit
1	teaspoon cornstarch
2	green onions, thinly sliced

In a large skillet, combine the pineapple juice, cranberries, garlic and red pepper flakes; bring to a boil.

Add chicken. Reduce heat; cover and simmer for 10 minutes or until a meat thermometer reaches 170°. Remove chicken to a platter and keep warm.

Bring cooking liquid to a boil; cook for 5-7 minutes or until liquid is reduced to 3/4 cup. Combine spreadable fruit and cornstarch until blended; add to the skillet. Boil and stir for 1 minute or until thickened. Spoon over chicken. Sprinkle with onions. **yield:** 4 servings.

nutrition facts: 1 chicken breast half equals 248 calories, 3 g fat (0 saturated fat), 73 mg cholesterol, 66 mg sodium, 26 g carbohydrate, 1 g fiber, 27 g protein.

diabetic exchanges: 4 very lean meat, 1-1/2 fruit.

CHICKEN BULGUR SKILLET

prep 15 minutes | **cook** 30 minutes

1	pound boneless skinless chicken breasts, cut into 1-inch cubes
2	teaspoons olive oil
2	medium carrots, chopped
2/3	cup chopped onion
3	tablespoons chopped walnuts
1/2	teaspoon caraway seeds
1/4	teaspoon ground cumin
1-1/2	cups bulgur
2	cups reduced-sodium chicken broth
2	tablespoons raisins

1/4	teaspoon salt
1/8	teaspoon ground cinnamon

In a large nonstick skillet, cook the chicken in oil over medium-high heat until meat is no longer pink. Remove and keep warm. In the same skillet, cook and stir the carrots, onion, walnuts, caraway seeds and cumin for 3-4 minutes or until the onion starts to brown.

Stir in bulgur. Gradually add broth; bring to a boil over medium heat. Reduce heat; add the raisins, salt, cinnamon and cooked chicken. Cover and simmer for 12-15 minutes or until the bulgur is tender. **yield:** 4 servings.

leann hillmer
sylvan grove, kansas

This recipe was passed to me by a friend, and I've altered it slightly to suit our tastes. We enjoy it with a fresh green salad.

CREAMY CHICKEN ANGEL HAIR

prep 15 minutes | **cook** 20 minutes

- 1 package (16 ounces) angel hair pasta
- 1-1/4 pounds boneless skinless chicken breasts, cut into 1-inch cubes
- 1/2 teaspoon salt
- 1/4 teaspoon pepper
- 3 tablespoons olive oil, *divided*
- 1 large carrot, diced
- 2 tablespoons butter
- 1 medium onion, chopped
- 1 celery rib, diced
- 3 large garlic cloves, minced
- 2 cups heavy whipping cream
- 5 bacon strips, cooked and crumbled
- 3 tablespoons lemon juice
- 1 teaspoon Italian seasoning
- 1 cup shredded Parmesan cheese

Cook pasta according to package directions. Meanwhile, in a large skillet, saute the chicken, salt and pepper in 2 tablespoons oil until no longer pink. Remove and keep warm.

In the same skillet, saute carrot in butter and remaining oil for 1 minute. Add the onion, celery and garlic; saute 3-4 minutes longer or until tender.

Stir in the cream, cooked bacon, lemon juice and Italian seasoning. Bring to a boil. Reduce heat; simmer, uncovered, for 2-3 minutes or until slightly thickened, stirring constantly. Return the chicken to the pan.

Drain pasta; toss with chicken mixture. Garnish with Parmesan cheese. **yield:** 6 servings.

vanessa sorenson
isanti, minnesota

Our pasta-loving family often requests this savory recipe featuring chicken, bacon and vegetables. Lemon juice adds a light touch to the sauce, which is well-seasoned with garlic and Italian herbs.

APPLE-STUFFED CHICKEN BREASTS

prep 35 minutes | **cook** 30 minutes

lois gallup edwards
woodland, california

When my family asks me to serve chicken for dinner, I usually prepare these elegant stuffed chicken rolls. I can easily double the recipe for a crowd.

6 boneless skinless chicken breast halves (6 ounces *each*)
1 teaspoon salt, *divided*
1/4 teaspoon pepper
1/2 cup finely chopped onion
2 garlic cloves, minced
3 tablespoons butter, *divided*
1 medium apple, peeled and grated
3/4 cup soft bread crumbs
1/4 teaspoon dried basil
1/4 teaspoon dried rosemary, crushed
1/4 cup all-purpose flour
1/2 cup unsweetened apple juice
1 tablespoon sherry *or* additional unsweetened apple juice

Flatten chicken to 1/4-in. thickness. Combine 1/2 teaspoon salt and pepper; sprinkle over both sides of chicken. Set aside.

In a small nonstick skillet, saute onion and garlic in 1 tablespoon butter until tender. Add apple; saute 1 minute longer. Stir in the bread crumbs, basil, rosemary and remaining salt; heat through.

Top each piece of chicken with 3 tablespoons apple mixture. Roll up and secure with toothpicks; coat with flour. In a large nonstick skillet, cook chicken in 1 tablespoon butter until browned on all sides. Remove and keep warm.

Stir apple juice and sherry or additional juice into pan, stirring to loosen any browned bits. Return chicken to pan. Bring to a boil. Reduce heat; cover and simmer for 15-20 minutes or until chicken juices run clear.

Remove chicken to a serving platter; discard toothpicks. Add the remaining butter to the pan juices; whisk until blended. Serve with chicken. **yield:** 6 servings.

CRANBERRY SALSA CHICKEN

prep/total time 20 minutes

4 boneless skinless chicken breast halves (4 ounces *each*)
1 tablespoon olive oil
1 jar (16 ounces) chunky salsa
1 cup dried cranberries
1/4 cup water
1 tablespoon honey
2 garlic cloves, minced
3/4 teaspoon ground cinnamon
1/2 teaspoon ground cumin
2 cups hot cooked couscous
1/4 cup slivered almonds, toasted

amy vanguilder dik
minneapolis, minnesota

After I made this dish for my fiancé, he absolutely loved it. Now that we're married, I prepare it for our dinner guests. Everyone enjoys it, and no one guesses they're eating healthy food!

In a large nonstick skillet, saute the chicken in oil until browned on both sides.

In a small bowl, combine the salsa, cranberries, water, honey, garlic, cinnamon and cumin; mix well. Pour over chicken. Cover and cook over medium-low heat for 10-15 minutes or until a meat thermometer reads 170°. Serve with couscous. Sprinkle with almonds. **yield:** 4 servings.

COUNTRY FRIED CHICKEN

prep 10 minutes | **cook** 25 minutes

rebekah miller
rocky mountain, virginia

This is one of our favorite meals for Sunday dinner or picnics. Served hot or cold, it's a real treat. To round out the meal, I add potato salad, dinner rolls and refreshing lemonade.

- 1/3 cup all-purpose flour
- 1 teaspoon garlic salt
- 1 teaspoon pepper
- 1/2 teaspoon paprika
- 1/4 teaspoon poultry seasoning
- 1 egg, lightly beaten
- 1/4 cup 2% milk
- 2 bone-in chicken thighs (6 ounces *each*)
- 2 chicken drumsticks (4 ounces *each*)
- 1/3 cup canola oil

In a large resealable plastic bag, combine the first five ingredients. In a shallow bowl, beat the egg and milk. Add chicken to bag, a few pieces at a time, and shake to coat. Dip into egg mixture, then return to flour mixture and shake again. Remove from bag and let stand for 5 minutes.

Fry chicken in oil until golden brown on all sides. Reduce heat to medium and cook about 15 minutes or until a meat thermometer reads 180°. **yield:** 2 servings.

CREAMED CHICKEN IN A BASKET

prep 40 minutes + cooling

- 6 bone-in chicken breast halves (about 4 pounds)
- 1 small onion, quartered
- 2 celery ribs with leaves, cut into chunks
- 2-1/2 cups water
- 2 teaspoons salt, *divided*
- 6 whole peppercorns
- 8 to 10 frozen puff pastry shells
- 1/2 cup butter
- 1/2 cup all-purpose flour
- 1/4 teaspoon ground nutmeg
- 1/8 teaspoon pepper
- 1/2 pound fresh mushrooms, sliced
- 1 can (5 ounces) sliced water chestnuts, drained
- 1 jar (2 ounces) diced pimientos, drained
- 1 tablespoon lemon juice
- 2 cups heavy whipping cream

Place the chicken, onion, celery, water, 1 teaspoon salt and peppercorns in a large saucepan. Bring to a boil; skim foam. Reduce heat; cover and simmer 35-40 minutes or until a meat thermometer reaches 170°. Remove the chicken with a slotted spoon; set aside until cool enough to handle. Bake the puff pastry shells according to package directions.

Remove the chicken from bones; cut into cubes and set aside. Discard the skin and bones. Strain the broth, discarding vegetables and peppercorns. Set aside 2 cups broth and save the remaining broth for another use.

In a large saucepan, melt butter. Stir in flour until smooth. Gradually add reserved broth, nutmeg, pepper and remaining salt. Bring to a boil; cook and stir 2 minutes. Remove from the heat; stir in the mushrooms, water chestnuts, pimientos, lemon juice and chicken. Return to the heat. Gradually stir in cream and heat through (do not boil). Spoon into pastry shells. **yield:** 8-10 servings.

sue bolsinger
anchorange, alaska

Chunks of tender chicken in a creamy sauce are spooned into puff pastry shells in this delicious dish, which has long been one of our family's favorites. I served it to my husband and our five children for years, and it's now a "must" for our Easter brunch.

CHICKEN FRICASSEE WITH DUMPLINGS

prep 20 minutes | **cook** 1 hour 25 minutes

lena hrynyk
sherwood park, alberta

Aromatic herbs and spices give this classic chicken stew great flavor. Topped with dumplings, it's warm and comforting on a chilly autumn or winter day.

1 bay leaf
9 whole peppercorns
4 whole cloves
1/3 cup all-purpose flour
1-1/2 teaspoons salt
1 teaspoon dried marjoram
1 broiler/fryer chicken (3 to 4 pounds), cut up
2 to 4 tablespoons butter
6 large carrots, cut into 1-inch pieces
1-1/2 cups chopped onions
2 celery ribs, cut into 1-inch pieces
1 can (14-1/2 ounces) chicken broth
1 cup water

DUMPLINGS
1-1/2 cups biscuit/baking mix
2 tablespoons minced chives
1 egg, lightly beaten
1/4 cup milk
2 tablespoons all-purpose flour
1/2 cup half-and-half cream

Place the bay leaf, peppercorns and cloves on a double thickness of cheesecloth; bring up corners of cloth and tie with string to form a bag. Set aside. In a large resealable bag, combine flour, salt and marjoram. Add chicken, a few pieces at a time, and shake to coat.

In a Dutch oven, brown chicken in batches in butter. Remove and keep warm. In the drippings, saute the carrots, onions and celery for 5-6 minutes or until onions begin to brown. Stir in the broth, water and spice bag. Bring to a boil; add chicken. Reduce heat; cover and simmer for 40 minutes. Discard spice bag.

For the dumplings, in a small bowl, combine biscuit mix and chives. Combine egg and milk; add to biscuit mix just until moistened. Drop by heaping tablespoonfuls onto simmering chicken mixture. Cook, uncovered, for 10 minutes. Cover and cook 10 minutes longer or until a toothpick inserted into dumplings comes out clean.

Using a slotted spoon, carefully remove chicken and dumplings; keep warm. Combine flour and cream until smooth; stir into cooking juices. Bring to a boil; cook and stir for 2 minutes or until thickened. Serve with chicken and dumplings.
yield: 6-8 servings.

CRISPY CHICKEN CUTLETS

prep/total time 20 minutes

debra smith
brookfield, missouri

These moist and tender cutlets feature a nutty coating and go especially well with egg noodles.

- 4 boneless skinless chicken breast halves (6 ounces *each*)
- 1 egg white
- 3/4 cup finely chopped pecans
- 3 tablespoons all-purpose flour
- 1/4 teaspoon salt
- 1/4 teaspoon pepper
- 1 tablespoon butter
- 1 tablespoon canola oil

Flatten chicken to 1/4-in. thickness. In a shallow bowl, lightly beat egg white. In another shallow bowl, combine the pecans, flour, salt and pepper. Dip chicken in egg white, then coat with pecan mixture. Let stand for 5 minutes.

In a large skillet, brown chicken in butter and oil over medium heat for 4-6 minutes on each side or until juices run clear. **yield:** 4 servings.

CRAB-STUFFED CHICKEN BREASTS

prep 35 minutes | **cook** 25 minutes

- 4 tablespoons butter, *divided*
- 2 teaspoons plus 3 tablespoons all-purpose flour, *divided*
- 1/2 teaspoon salt
- 1/8 teaspoon pepper
- 1/4 cup milk
- 2 cans (6 ounces *each*) lump crabmeat, drained
- 2/3 cup chopped fresh mushrooms
- 1/3 cup grated Parmesan cheese
- 6 boneless skinless chicken breast halves (6 ounces *each*)
- 1/2 teaspoon paprika
- 3/4 cup marsala wine

SAUCE
- 2 teaspoons all-purpose flour
- 1 teaspoon chicken bouillon granules
- 1 tablespoon water

In a small saucepan, melt 2 tablespoons butter. Stir in 2 teaspoons flour, salt and pepper until smooth; gradually add milk. Bring to a boil; cook and stir for 1-2 minutes or until thickened. Stir in the crab, mushrooms and Parmesan cheese.

Flatten chicken to 1/4-in. thickness. Top each piece with 3 tablespoons crab mixture. Roll up jelly-roll style, starting with a short side; tie with kitchen string.

In a shallow bowl, combine paprika and remaining flour. Add chicken rolls, one at a time, and turn to coat. In a large skillet, brown chicken in remaining butter on all sides.

Add the marsala wine. Bring to a boil. Reduce heat; cover and simmer for 15-20 minutes or until a meat thermometer reads 170°. Remove chicken and keep warm.

For the sauce, in a small bowl, combine flour and bouillon; stir in water until blended. Stir into cooking juices. Bring to a boil; cook and stir for 1-2 minutes or until thickened. Remove cut string from chicken rolls; top with sauce. **yield:** 6 servings.

lorna hudson
weott, california

Holiday dinners in my youth meant Mom would be serving these stuffed chicken breasts. They're now part of my own family's custom for special occasions like Christmas Eve.

SMOTHERED CHICKEN BREASTS

prep/total time 30 minutes

brenda carpenter
warrensburg, missouri

After trying this delicious chicken dish in a restaurant, I decided to re-create it at home. Topped with bacon, caramelized onions and zippy shredded cheese, it comes together in no time with ingredients I usually have on hand. Plus, it cooks in one skillet, so it's a cinch to clean up!

4   boneless skinless chicken breast halves (6 ounces *each*)
1/4 teaspoon salt
1/4 teaspoon lemon-pepper seasoning
1   tablespoon canola oil
8   bacon strips
1   medium onion, sliced
1/4 cup packed brown sugar
1/2 cup shredded Colby-Monterey Jack cheese

Sprinkle chicken with salt and lemon-pepper. In a large skillet, cook chicken in oil for 13-15 minutes or until juices run clear; remove and keep warm.

In the same skillet, cook the bacon over medium heat until crisp. Using a slotted spoon, remove to paper towels; drain, reserving 2 tablespoons of the drippings.

In the drippings, saute the onion and brown sugar until onion is golden. Place two bacon strips on each chicken breast half; top with caramelized onions and cheese. **yield:** 4 servings.

FRUITED CHICKEN CURRY

prep 15 minutes | **cook** 45 minutes

4   bone-in chicken breast halves (8 ounces *each*)
1   tablespoon butter
1/4 cup chopped onion
2   teaspoons curry powder
1/2 teaspoon salt
1/8 teaspoon pepper
1   cup dried mixed fruit (such as apples, apricots and prunes)
3/4 cup hot water
1   tablespoon sugar
1   teaspoon lemon juice

Hot cooked rice
    1/4 cup slivered almonds, toasted

In a large skillet, brown the chicken in butter on each side; remove and keep warm. In the drippings, cook the onion, curry powder, salt and pepper until onion is tender. Stir in the dried fruit, water, sugar and lemon juice.

Return chicken to pan. Bring to a boil. Reduce heat; cover and simmer for 25-30 minutes or until a meat thermometer reaches 170°. Serve with rice; sprinkle with almonds. **yield:** 4 servings.

bernadine dirmeyer
harpster, ohio

The curry lovers in your house will certainly take to this juicy chicken that's served over a bed of hot rice. Dried fruit and toasted almonds make it a wonderful change-of-pace entree for any occasion.

CHICKEN MARSALA

prep 25 minutes + marinating | **bake** 25 minutes

This chicken recipe is lower in calories, fat or sodium.

6   boneless skinless chicken breast halves (4 ounces *each*)
1   cup fat-free Italian salad dressing
1   tablespoon all-purpose flour
1   teaspoon Italian seasoning
1/2   teaspoon garlic powder
1/4   teaspoon paprika
1/4   teaspoon pepper
2   tablespoons olive oil, *divided*
1   tablespoon butter
1/2   cup reduced-sodium chicken broth
1/2   cup marsala wine *or* 3 tablespoons unsweetened apple juice plus 5 tablespoons additional reduced-sodium chicken broth
1   pound sliced fresh mushrooms
1/2   cup minced fresh parsley

Flatten the chicken to 1/2-in. thickness. Place in a large resealable plastic bag; add the salad dressing. Seal bag and turn to coat; refrigerate for 8 hours or overnight.

Drain and discard the marinade. Combine the flour, Italian seasoning, garlic powder, paprika and pepper; sprinkle over both sides of chicken. In a large nonstick skillet coated with cooking spray, cook the chicken in 1 tablespoon olive oil and butter for 2 minutes on each side or until browned. Transfer to a 13-in. x 9-in. baking dish coated with cooking spray.

Gradually add broth and wine or apple juice mixture to skillet, stirring to loosen browned bits. Bring to a boil; cook and stir for 2 minutes. Strain sauce; set aside. In the same skillet, cook mushrooms in remaining oil for 2 minutes; drain. Stir sauce into mushrooms; heat through. Pour over chicken; sprinkle with parsley. Bake, uncovered, at 350° for 25-30 minutes or until chicken juices run clear. **yield:** 6 servings.

nutrition facts: 1 chicken breast half with 1/3 cup mushroom mixture equals 247 calories, 9 g fat (3 g saturated fat), 68 mg cholesterol, 348 mg sodium, 9 g carbohydrate, 1 g fiber, 26 g protein.

diabetic exchanges: 3 very lean meat, 1-1/2 fat, 1/2 starch.

nancy granaman
burlington, iowa

Chicken marsala is usually high in fat and calories. But in this version, I eliminated the extra oil. But don't worry, I deglaze the skillet with broth and wine so the flavor isn't lost.

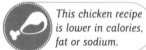
CHICKEN PATTIES WITH ROASTED TOMATO SALSA

prep 30 minutes | **cook** 45 minutes

mary relyea
canastota, new york

Bold and zesty tomato salsa perks up these moist and tender chicken patties. Great for lunch or dinner, this recipe ranks high among my Southwestern specialties no matter when I serve it.

6   plum tomatoes
3   teaspoons olive oil, *divided*
3/4 teaspoon salt, *divided*
1-1/2 cups fresh cilantro leaves, *divided*
1   teaspoon adobo sauce
2   cups cubed cooked chicken breast, *divided*
1   small zucchini, cut into 3/4-inch chunks
1/3 cup dry bread crumbs
1/3 cup reduced-fat mayonnaise
1/4 teaspoon pepper

Core tomatoes and cut in half lengthwise. Place cut side up on a broiler pan coated with cooking spray; brush with 2 teaspoons olive oil and sprinkle with 1/4 teaspoon salt. Turn tomatoes cut side down. Bake at 425° for 30-40 minutes or until the edges are well browned. Cool slightly. Remove and discard tomato peels.

Place cilantro in a food processor; cover and process until coarsely chopped. Set aside 1/4 cup cilantro for chicken patties. Add the roasted tomatoes, adobo sauce and 1/4 teaspoon salt to the food processor; cover and process just until chunky. Place salsa in a small bowl; set aside.

For chicken patties, in same food processor, combine 1-1/2 cups chicken and zucchini. Cover and process just until chicken is coarsely chopped. Add the bread crumbs, mayonnaise, pepper, reserved cilantro and remaining chicken and salt. Cover and process just until mixture is chunky.

Shape into eight 3-in. patties. In a large nonstick skillet coated with cooking spray, cook the patties in remaining olive oil for 4 minutes on each side or until lightly browned. Serve with salsa. **yield:** 8 servings.

nutrition facts: 1 chicken patty with 1-1/2 tablespoons salsa equals 134 calories, 7 g fat (1 g saturated fat), 30 mg cholesterol, 373 mg sodium, 7 g carbohydrate, 1 g fiber, 12 g protein.

diabetic exchanges: 2 very lean meat, 1 fat, 1/2 starch.

BACON CHICKEN ALFREDO

prep 35 minutes | **cook** 10 minutes

dana simmons
lancaster, ohio

I had a rich pasta dish similar to this one at a restaurant. It was so unique that I tried to duplicate it at home a few days later. This is remarkably close, but not as fussy because it uses ready-made ingredients.

1	package (16 ounces) fettuccine
1	pound sliced bacon, diced
1-1/4	pounds boneless skinless chicken breast, cubed
1/4	teaspoon salt
1/4	teaspoon pepper
1	jar (16 ounces) prepared Alfredo sauce
1	package (10 ounces) frozen chopped spinach, thawed and squeezed dry
1/2	teaspoon Italian seasoning
1/4	cup grated Parmesan cheese

Cook fettuccine according to package directions. Meanwhile, in a large skillet, cook bacon over medium heat until crisp. Using a slotted spoon, remove to paper towels; drain, reserving 3 tablespoons drippings.

Sprinkle the chicken with salt and pepper. Cook chicken in the drippings over medium-high heat until the juices run clear.

Drain fettuccine; stir into a skillet. Add the Alfredo sauce, spinach, Italian seasoning and bacon. Cook and stir until heat through. Sprinkle with Parmesan cheese. **yield:** 6-8 servings.

CHICKEN SAUSAGE SKILLET

prep/total time 30 minutes

1	medium onion, thinly sliced
1	medium green pepper, thinly sliced
1	cup sliced fresh mushrooms
1	cup sliced zucchini
2	tablespoons olive oil
1/2	to 3/4 pound boneless skinless chicken breasts, thinly sliced
1/2	to 3/4 pound Italian sausage links, cut into 1/2-inch pieces
2	cans (14-1/2 ounces *each*) diced tomatoes, undrained
1	garlic clove, minced
3/4	teaspoon dried basil
3/4	teaspoon dried oregano

Hot cooked rice

In a large skillet, saute the onion, green pepper, mushrooms and zucchini in oil until tender. Remove vegetables with a slotted spoon; set aside.

Add chicken and sausage to skillet; cook until no longer pink. Drain. Stir in tomatoes, garlic, basil and oregano.

Return the vegetables to the pan. Bring to a boil. Reduce the heat; cover and simmer for 10 minutes or until heated through. Serve over rice. **yield:** 6-8 servings.

connie dowell
orlando, florida

My sister, an excellent cook, shared this wonderful recipe with me. I've always loved its tantalizing blend of flavors.

ULTIMATE KITCHEN TIP

One medium (1/3 pound) zucchini yields about 2 cups sliced or 1-1/2 cups shredded zucchini. Refrigerate in a plastic bag up to 5 days. To freeze, first, steam the shredded zucchini 1 to 2 minutes until translucent, then drain well. Pack in measured amounts into freezer containers, leaving 1/2 inch of space at the top. Cool, seal and freeze.

CHICKEN & TOMATO RISOTTO

prep 25 minutes | **cook** 25 minutes

lorraine caland
thunder bay, ontario

If you're looking for Italian comfort food, this is it! By using store-bought spaghetti sauce, you save time when preparing this creamy dish. You'll enjoy every bite!

3 cups chicken broth
1 pound boneless skinless chicken breasts, cut into 1-inch cubes
1 tablespoon olive oil
1-1/2 cups sliced fresh mushrooms
1 medium onion, chopped
1 garlic clove, minced
2 tablespoons butter
1 cup uncooked arborio rice
1 cup meatless spaghetti sauce
1/4 cup grated Parmesan cheese

In a small saucepan, heat broth and keep warm. In a large skillet, saute chicken in oil until no longer pink. Remove and keep warm.

In the same skillet, saute the mushrooms, onion and minced garlic in butter until crisp-tender. Add arborio rice; cook and stir for 3 minutes. Carefully stir in 1 cup warm broth. Cook and stir until all of the liquid is absorbed.

Add remaining broth, 1/2 cup at a time, stirring constantly. Allow the liquid to absorb between additions. Cook until risotto is creamy and rice is almost tender. (Cooking time is about 20 minutes.)

Stir in the spaghetti sauce, cheese and reserved chicken; cook and stir until thickened. Serve immediately. **yield:** 4 servings.

CHICKEN WITH MUSHROOM SAUCE

prep 15 minutes | **cook** 35 minutes

8 bone-in chicken breast halves (8 ounces *each*)
2 tablespoons olive oil
2 cups sliced fresh mushrooms
2 green onions, chopped
1 cup white wine *or* chicken broth
3 tablespoons butter
1/2 teaspoon salt
1/4 teaspoon pepper
1 tablespoon cornstarch
2 tablespoons cold water

In a large skillet, brown chicken over medium heat in oil. Cover and cook for about 20 minutes or until a meat thermometer reaches 170°. Remove chicken; keep warm. In the same skillet, saute mushrooms and onions until tender. Stir in the wine or broth, butter, salt and pepper.

In a small bowl, combine cornstarch and water until smooth; add to skillet. Bring to a boil; cook and stir for 2 minutes or until thickened. Return chicken to skillet; heat through. **yield:** 8 servings.

patsy jenkins
tallahassee, florida

This is a fast but special way to cook chicken. First, chicken breasts are browned to juicy perfection. Then they're topped with a buttery sauce made with fresh mushrooms and green onions.

ROASTED PEPPER CHICKEN PENNE

prep/total time 30 minutes

1   pound boneless skinless chicken breasts, cut into 1-inch strips
1/4   cup balsamic vinegar
1   package (16 ounces) penne pasta
1   medium onion, sliced
3   garlic cloves, sliced
1/4   cup olive oil
1   can (28 ounces) crushed tomatoes
1   cup roasted sweet red peppers, drained and sliced
1   cup chicken broth
3   teaspoons Italian seasoning
1/4   teaspoon salt
1   cup shredded Parmesan cheese

Place the chicken in a large resealable plastic bag; add balsamic vinegar. Seal bag and turn to coat; refrigerate for 15 minutes.

Cook pasta according to package directions. Meanwhile, in a large skillet, saute onion and garlic in oil for 1 minute. Drain and discard vinegar. Add chicken to skillet; cook for 4-5 minutes or until juices run clear.

Stir in the tomatoes, red peppers, broth, Italian seasoning and salt. Bring to a boil over medium heat; cook and stir for 4-5 minutes or until heated through. Drain pasta; toss with chicken mixture. Sprinkle with Parmesan cheese. **yield:** 8 servings.

regina cowles
boulder, colorado

My husband calls me an aerobic cook because I can make this Italian dish in just 30 minutes. No one will accuse you of cutting corners, because it tastes like it's been simmering deliciously for hours.

SUNDAY FRIED CHICKEN

prep 20 minutes | **bake** 45 minutes

audrey read

fraser lake,
british columbia

The spicy coating for this chicken is one I've put together over the years. My recipe got a workout when our four children (now married) were young and we competed in the rodeo circuit. Whenever the word spread I'd brought along fried chicken, the cowboys would crowd around!

2	cups all-purpose flour
1/2	cup cornmeal
2	tablespoons salt
2	tablespoons ground mustard
2	tablespoons paprika
2	tablespoons garlic salt
1	tablespoon celery salt
1	tablespoon pepper
1	teaspoon ground ginger
1/2	teaspoon dried thyme
1/2	teaspoon oregano
1	broiler/fryer chicken (2-1/2 to 3-1/2 pounds), cut up

Oil for deep-fat frying

In a small bowl, combine the first 11 ingredients. Place about 1 cup flour mixture in a large resealable plastic bag; add the chicken, a few pieces at a time. Seal the bag and shake to coat. Store the remaining mixture in an airtight container and save for another use.

In a large skillet, brown the chicken on medium-high heat in 1/2 in. of oil on all sides; remove to a large shallow baking pan.

Bake, uncovered, at 350° for 45-60 minutes or until chicken juices run clear. **yield:** 4-6 servings.

CHICKEN CARROT FRIED RICE

prep 15 minutes | **cook** 20 minutes

3/4	pound boneless skinless chicken breasts, cubed
4	tablespoons soy sauce, *divided*
2	garlic cloves, minced
1-1/2	cups chopped fresh broccoli
3	green onions, sliced
2	tablespoons canola oil, *divided*
3	large carrots, shredded
4	cups cold cooked rice
1/4	teaspoon pepper

peggy spieckermann

joplin, missouri

A dear friend shared this colorful stir-fry when my children were small. It quickly won over those picky eaters! To cut down on prep time, I make the rice ahead and often marinate the chicken.

In a large bowl, combine the chicken, 1 tablespoon soy sauce and garlic; set aside. In a large skillet or wok, stir-fry broccoli and green onions in 1 tablespoon oil for 5 minutes. Add carrots; stir-fry 4 minutes longer or until crisp-tender. Remove and set aside.

In the same skillet, stir-fry chicken in remaining oil until no longer pink and juices run clear. Add the rice, pepper, vegetables and remaining soy sauce. Stir-fry until heated through. **yield:** 4-6 servings.

TERIYAKI GLAZED CHICKEN

prep/total time 30 minutes

kelly brenneman
riverdale, california

I love to experiment with food. For this recipe, I took advantage of the sweet onions grown on Maui. My whole family just loves this quick main dish.

4   boneless skinless chicken breast halves, cut into strips
3   tablespoons canola oil, *divided*
4   medium carrots, julienned
1   medium sweet onion, julienned
1/2   cup soy sauce
1/4   cup packed brown sugar
Hot cooked rice
Sesame seeds, toasted, optional
Sliced green onions, optional

In a large skillet or wok, stir-fry chicken in 2 tablespoons oil for 6-8 minutes or until juices run clear. Remove chicken and set aside. In the same skillet, stir-fry carrots in remaining oil for 2 minutes. Add onion; stir-fry about 2-4 minutes longer or until vegetables are tender.

Combine soy sauce and brown sugar; add to skillet. Bring to a boil. Return chicken to skillet. Boil for 5 minutes or until sauce is slightly thickened. Serve with rice. Sprinkle with sesame seeds and green onions if desired. **yield:** 4 servings.

CREAMY CHICKEN WITH NOODLES

prep/total time 30 minutes

8   ounces uncooked egg noodles
6   boneless skinless chicken breast halves (4 ounces *each*)
1/2   teaspoon salt
1/4   teaspoon pepper
3   to 4 tablespoons olive oil, *divided*
2   cups sliced fresh mushrooms
1   teaspoon minced garlic
1   can (10-3/4 ounces) condensed cream of chicken soup, undiluted
1   can (10-3/4 ounces) condensed cream of mushroom soup, undiluted
3/4   cup half-and-half cream
1/4   cup marsala wine *or* chicken broth
1/4   teaspoon chili powder
1/2   cup minced fresh parsley, *divided*

Cook noodles according to package directions. Meanwhile, flatten chicken to 1/4-in. thickness. Sprinkle with salt and pepper. In a large skillet, cook chicken in 2 tablespoons oil in batches for 5-7 minutes on each side or until golden brown and a meat thermometer reaches 170°; keep warm.

In the same skillet, saute mushrooms and garlic in remaining oil until tender. Stir in the soups, cream, wine or broth and chili powder until blended; heat through. Stir in 1/4 cup parsley.

Drain noodles; serve with chicken and sauce. Sprinkle with remaining parsley. **yield:** 6 servings.

donna akerley
woodridge, new york

One night I had a few chicken breasts thawed and a limited amount of time. I started tossing things together and was pleasantly surprised by this comforting combination. My family was thrilled and dinner was served in minutes.

ULTIMATE KITCHEN TIP

So vegetables cook evenly when stir-frying, cut them all the same size, then add at intervals. Start with longer-cooking vegetables, such as carrots and broccoli, and end with quicker-cooking ones, like mushrooms. Select a wok or skillet large enough to hold the food you'll be stir-frying. If it's crowded in the pan, it will steam. If necessary, stir-fry the food in batches.

SWEET-AND-SOUR POPCORN CHICKEN

prep/total time 25 minutes

amy corlew-sherlock
lapeer, michigan

Pre-cooked and frozen popcorn chicken simmered in a thick, homemade sweet-and-sour sauce is the secret to this fast and fabulous entree. It's a great way to dress up frozen chicken nuggets!

1   medium green pepper, cut into 1-inch pieces
1   small onion, thinly sliced
1   tablespoon canola oil
1   can (20 ounces) unsweetened pineapple chunks
3   tablespoons white vinegar
2   tablespoons soy sauce
2   tablespoons ketchup
1/3   cup packed brown sugar
2   tablespoons cornstarch
1   package (12 ounces) frozen popcorn chicken

In a large skillet or wok, stir-fry green pepper and onion in oil for 3-4 minutes or until crisp-tender. Drain pineapple, reserving the juice in a 2-cup measuring cup; set pineapple aside. Add enough water to the juice to measure 1-1/3 cups; stir in the vinegar, soy sauce and ketchup.

In a large bowl, combine brown sugar and cornstarch. Stir in pineapple juice mixture until smooth. Gradually add to the skillet. Bring to a boil; cook and stir for 2 minutes or until thickened. Add pineapple. Reduce heat; simmer, uncovered, for 4-5 minutes or until heated through.

Meanwhile, microwave chicken according to package directions. Stir into pineapple mixture. Serve immediately. **yield:** 4 servings.

PINEAPPLE CHICKEN LO MEIN

prep/total time 30 minutes

linda stevens

madison, alabama

The perfect supper to serve on busy weeknights, this speedy lo mein combines tender chicken and colorful veggies with a tangy sauce. Quick-cooking spaghetti and canned pineapple make it a cinch to throw together when time is short.

1 can (20 ounces) unsweetened pineapple chunks
1 pound boneless skinless chicken breasts, cut into 1-inch cubes
2 garlic cloves, minced
3/4 teaspoon ground ginger *or* 1 tablespoon minced fresh gingerroot
3 tablespoons canola oil, *divided*
2 medium carrots, julienned
1 medium green pepper, julienned
4 ounces spaghetti, cooked and drained
3 green onions, sliced
1 tablespoon cornstarch
1/3 cup soy sauce

Drain pineapple, reserving 1/3 cup juice (discarding remaining juice or save for another use); set pineapple aside.

In a large skillet, cook the chicken, garlic and ginger over medium heat in 2 tablespoons oil for 6 minutes or until the chicken juices run clean. Stir in the carrots, green pepper and pineapple. Cover and cook for 2-3 minutes or until vegetables are crisp-tender. Stir in spaghetti and onions.

In a small bowl, combine the cornstarch, soy sauce, reserved pineapple juice and remaining oil until smooth. Gradually add to chicken mixture. Bring to a boil; cook and stir for 2 minutes or until thickened. **yield:** 4 servings.

CHICKEN ARTICHOKE PASTA

prep/total time 25 minutes

8 ounces uncooked bow tie pasta
1-1/2 pounds boneless skinless chicken breasts, cubed
1/2 teaspoon dried oregano
1/4 teaspoon salt
1/4 teaspoon pepper
3 tablespoons olive oil
1 to 2 tablespoons minced garlic
2 cans (14 ounces *each*) water-packed artichoke hearts, rinsed, drained and quartered

1 jar (8-1/2 ounces) oil-packed sun-dried tomatoes, quartered
1 can (2-1/4 ounces) sliced ripe olives, drained
Shredded Parmesan cheese

Cook pasta according to package directions. Meanwhile, sprinkle chicken with the oregano, salt and pepper. In a large skillet, saute chicken in oil until no longer pink. Add garlic; saute 1 minute longer. Stir in the artichokes, tomatoes and olives; heat through. Drain pasta; toss with chicken mixture. Sprinkle with Parmesan cheese. **yield:** 6 servings.

beth washington

ayer, massachusetts

Here's a main course my whole family likes, including the kids! Similar to a restaurant favorite, it uses canned artichokes and olives and a jar of sun-dried tomatoes. It's so simple, I often leave the ingredients on the counter for someone else to fix.

CREAMY MUSHROOM CHICKEN

prep/total time 30 minutes

sharon mcmillen
park city, montana

I call this meal "easy chicken fixins" because the leftovers are equally delicious heated up in the microwave.

6   boneless skinless chicken breast halves (4 ounces *each*)
1/4   teaspoon pepper
2   tablespoons canola oil
1   cup sliced fresh mushrooms
1/4   cup butter
4-1/2   teaspoons all-purpose flour
1   cup milk
3/4   cup grated Parmesan cheese, *divided*
Minced fresh parsley
Hot cooked pasta

Sprinkle chicken with pepper. In a large skillet over medium heat, brown chicken in oil until a meat thermometer reaches 170°. Remove to a serving platter and keep warm.

In the same skillet, saute mushrooms in butter until tender. Sprinkle with flour and stir until coated. Gradually add milk. Bring to a boil; cook and stir for 2 minutes or until thickened.

Remove from the heat; stir in 1/2 cup Parmesan cheese. Pour over the chicken. Sprinkle with fresh parsley and remaining cheese. Serve with pasta. **yield:** 6 servings.

CHICKEN IN PEAR SAUCE

prep/total time 30 minutes

4   boneless skinless chicken breast halves (4 ounces *each*)
1/2   teaspoon salt
1/8   teaspoon white pepper
2   tablespoons canola oil
5   thick-cut bacon strips, diced
1   can (14-1/2 ounces) chicken broth
2   to 3 medium ripe pears, peeled and diced
2   tablespoons cornstarch
2   tablespoons cold water
1/4   cup snipped chives

Sprinkle chicken with salt and pepper. In a large skillet over medium heat, cook chicken in oil 5-6 minutes on both sides or until a meat thermometer reaches 170°.

Meanwhile, in a saucepan, cook bacon until crisp. Drain, reserving 1 tablespoon drippings; set bacon aside. Gradually stir broth into the drippings, scraping pan to loosen browned bits. Bring to a boil. Boil, uncovered, for 5 minutes. Add pears; return to a boil. Boil, uncovered, for 5 minutes or until pears are tender.

Combine cornstarch and water until smooth; add the chives. Gradually stir into pear sauce; bring to a boil. Cook and stir for 2 minutes or until thickened and bubbly. Stir in bacon. Serve with the chicken. **yield:** 4 servings.

andrea lunsford
spokane, washington

Pairing poultry with juicy pears brought applause from my husband and four growing children. Simple enough for everyday meals and ideal for company, this dish is one of our year-round standouts.

LEMON CHICKEN WITH PASTA

prep 20 minutes | **cook** 20 minutes

1-1/2	cups uncooked medium pasta shells
1/4	cup dry bread crumbs
1	teaspoon garlic powder
1/2	teaspoon salt
1/2	teaspoon pepper
1	pound boneless skinless chicken breasts, cubed
6	teaspoons canola oil, *divided*
1	medium onion, chopped
2	tablespoons all-purpose flour
1	cup reduced-sodium chicken broth
1/4	cup lemon juice
1/4	cup shredded Parmesan cheese

Cook pasta shells according to package directions. Meanwhile, in a large resealable plastic bag, combine the bread crumbs, garlic powder, salt and pepper. Add the chicken, a few pieces at a time, and shake to coat.

In a large nonstick skillet coated with cooking spray, saute chicken in 4 teaspoons oil until juices run clear. Remove and keep warm.

In the same skillet, cook onion in remaining oil over medium heat until tender. Sprinkle with flour; stir until blended. Gradually stir in broth and lemon juice. Bring to a boil; cook and stir for 2 minutes or until thickened.

Drain pasta; toss with lemon sauce. Serve with chicken; sprinkle with Parmesan cheese. **yield:** 4 servings.

karen hall
south hamilton, massachusetts

By adding chicken to a few pantry staples, I have a wonderful warm entree in minutes. Guests always ask for the recipe, and my friends and pasta-hating husband ask for seconds!

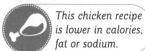 *This chicken recipe is lower in calories, fat or sodium.*

CHICKEN BROCCOLI FETTUCCINE

prep/total time 25 minutes

debbie maier
lynden, washington

My family loves pasta, but often the sauces are loaded with calories. So I came up with a creamy sauce made with reduced-fat soup, milk and cheese. It's much lighter, yet tastes just as rich. I often make it on busy days, and it's always a hit.

6   ounces uncooked fettuccine
3   cups fresh broccoli florets
1   pound boneless skinless chicken breasts, cut into strips
1/4 teaspoon salt
1/4 teaspoon pepper
1   medium onion, chopped
1   cup sliced fresh mushrooms
2   teaspoons olive oil
1   can (10-3/4 ounces) reduced-fat reduced-sodium condensed cream of mushroom soup, undiluted
2/3 cup fat-free milk
1/4 cup shredded Parmesan cheese

In a Dutch oven, cook fettuccine according to package directions, adding the broccoli during the last 5 minutes of cooking.

Meanwhile, sprinkle chicken with salt and pepper. In a large nonstick skillet, saute the chicken, onion and mushrooms in oil until chicken is no longer pink. Remove from the heat; set aside.

Drain fettuccine; stir in the soup, milk and reserved chicken mixture. Cook and stir over low heat until heated through. Sprinkle with Parmesan cheese. **yield:** 4 servings.

nutrition facts: 1-1/4 cups equals 398 calories, 9 g fat (3 g saturated fat), 74 mg cholesterol, 637 mg sodium, 44 g carbohydrate, 4 g fiber, 35 g protein.

diabetic exchanges: 3 very lean meat, 2-1/2 starch, 1 vegetable, 1 fat.

PECAN CHICKEN WITH CHUTNEY

prep 15 minutes | **cook** 20 minutes

carisa bravoco
furlong, pennsylvania

These zippy, pecan-crusted chicken breasts are super tender and the easy-fix peach chutney offers a sweet-and-sour flavor. I usually serve the chicken with rice on the side.

3/4 cup all-purpose flour
1/8 teaspoon salt
1/8 teaspoon pepper
2 eggs
1/3 cup buttermilk
1/8 teaspoon hot pepper sauce
1 cup finely chopped pecans
3/4 cup dry bread crumbs
6 boneless skinless chicken breast halves (6 ounces *each*)
2 tablespoons butter
2 tablespoons canola oil

PEACH MANGO CHUTNEY

2 cups sliced peeled fresh *or* frozen peaches, thawed
1 cup mango chutney

In a shallow bowl, combine the flour, salt and pepper. In another shallow bowl, whisk the eggs, buttermilk and hot pepper sauce. In a third bowl, combine pecans and bread crumbs.

Flatten chicken to 1/4-in. thickness. Coat chicken with flour mixture, then dip in egg mixture and coat with pecan mixture.

In a large skillet over medium heat, cook chicken in butter and oil for 8-10 minutes on each side or until juices run clear.

Meanwhile, for the chutney, in a small saucepan, combine the peaches and chutney. Bring to a boil. Reduce heat; simmer, uncovered, for 15-20 minutes or until heated through. Serve with chicken. **yield:** 6 servings (1-3/4 cups chutney).

HONEY BARBECUE CHICKEN

prep/total time 30 minutes

1 can (20 ounces) pineapple chunks
4 boneless skinless chicken breast halves (4 ounces *each*)
1 teaspoon curry powder
1 tablespoon canola oil
1/2 cup chopped onion
1/2 cup chopped green pepper
1 bottle (18 ounces) honey barbecue sauce
Hot cooked rice

Drain pineapple, reserving juice; set fruit and juice aside. Sprinkle chicken with curry powder. In a large skillet, brown chicken on both sides over medium-high heat in oil. Remove and keep warm.

In the same skillet, saute the onion, green pepper and pineapple until vegetables are tender and pineapple is golden brown. Stir in barbecue sauce and reserved pineapple juice. Return chicken to the pan. Cover and simmer for 15 minutes or until chicken juices run clear. Serve with rice. **yield:** 4 servings.

carrie price
uneeda, west virginia

I love chicken with pineapple, yet I wanted to try something different. So I came up with this sweet and tangy chicken that doesn't take long to prepare and only uses one pan.

SKILLET CHICKEN CORDON BLEU

prep 10 minutes | **cook** 35 minutes

nancy zimmerer

medina, ohio

A dear friend from my high school days shared this recipe with me. You might think it sounds complicated to make, but it's quite easy once you've tried it.

4   boneless skinless chicken breast halves (4 ounces *each*)
4   thin slices fully cooked ham
4   thin slices Swiss cheese
3   tablespoons all-purpose flour
1   teaspoon paprika
1/3 cup butter
1/2 cup white grape juice
1   chicken bouillon cube
1   cup heavy whipping cream
1   tablespoon cornstarch

Flatten chicken to 1/4-in. thickness. Top each with a slice of ham and cheese; fold to fit. Roll up tightly and secure with toothpicks. In a shallow bowl, combine the flour and paprika. Coat chicken with flour mixture.

In a large skillet over medium heat, melt butter. Cook chicken for 5 minutes on each side or until browned. Add grape juice and bouillon. Reduce heat; cover and simmer for 30 minutes or until chicken is tender.

Remove chicken and keep warm. In a small bowl, combine cream and cornstarch until smooth. Gradually stir into pan juices. Bring to a boil; cook and stir for 2 minutes or until thickened. Serve with chicken. **yield:** 4 servings.

CREAMY CHICKEN AND BROCCOLI

prep/total time 30 minutes

1   pound boneless skinless chicken breasts, cut into 1-inch cubes
1   small onion, chopped
2   tablespoons butter
1   can (10-3/4 ounces) condensed cream of mushroom soup, undiluted
2/3 cup mayonnaise
1/2 cup sour cream
2   tablespoons white wine *or* chicken broth
1/8 teaspoon garlic powder
Salt and pepper to taste
1   cup cubed fully cooked ham
1   package (10 ounces) frozen broccoli florets, thawed

3   bacon strips, cooked and crumbled
Hot cooked pasta *or* rice
1   cup (4 ounces) shredded Swiss cheese, optional

In a large skillet, saute chicken and onion in butter until meat is no longer pink.

Meanwhile, in a large bowl, combine the cream of mushroom soup, mayonnaise, sour cream, wine or broth, garlic powder, salt and pepper. Add to the chicken mixture.

Stir in the ham, broccoli and bacon; cover and cook until heated through. Serve with pasta; sprinkle with cheese if desired. **yield:** 4 servings.

editor's note: Reduced-fat or fat-free mayonnaise is not recommended for this recipe.

tamara kalsbeek

grand rapids, michigan

My gang likes the taste of chicken cordon bleu, but I don't like the time required to make it. This skillet sensation, with the addition of broccoli, gives my family the flavors they crave with only a fraction of the work.

BREADED CHICKEN WITH ORANGE SAUCE

prep/total time 30 minutes

1/4	cup milk
3/4	cup seasoned bread crumbs
4-1/2	teaspoons grated Parmesan cheese
3/4	teaspoon Italian seasoning, *divided*
1/2	teaspoon garlic powder
4	boneless skinless chicken breast halves (5 ounces *each*)
3	tablespoons canola oil
3/4	cup orange juice

Hot cooked rice

Place the milk in a shallow bowl. In another shallow bowl, combine the bread crumbs, Parmesan cheese, 1/2 teaspoon Italian seasoning and garlic powder. Dip the chicken in milk, then coat with crumb mixture.

In a large skillet, cook chicken in oil over medium heat for 6-8 minutes on each side or until juices run clear. Remove and keep warm.

Add the orange juice and remaining Italian seasoning to skillet, stirring to loosen browned bits. Bring to a boil; cook until the sauce is reduced to about 1/4 cup. Serve with the chicken and rice.
yield: 4 servings.

soraida angie cannestra
milwaukee, wisconsin

After cooking the chicken in its coating, orange juice and Italian seasoning are added to the brown bits in the pan for a delightful sauce. This moist, tasty chicken is ready in about 30 minutes. I like to garnish it with orange segments.

ULTIMATE KITCHEN TIP

When a recipe calls for a clove of garlic and you have no fresh bulbs, substitute 1/4 teaspoon of garlic powder for each clove. There's really no substitute for garlic, which has a distinctive flavor. If you don't like garlic, leave it out altogether or enhance the recipe with other herbs. In most cases, onion or chives add nice flavor to dishes that call for garlic.

CHINESE CHICKEN SPAGHETTI

prep/total time 30 minutes

jenna noel
glendale, arizona

It's hard to believe that something that comes together this easily could be so tasty, yet low in fat. This dish is pretty zippy, but if you like extra spice, increase the red pepper flakes a bit.

8	ounces uncooked spaghetti
1	tablespoon cornstarch
4	tablespoons reduced-sodium soy sauce, *divided*
2	tablespoons sesame oil, *divided*
1	pound boneless skinless chicken breasts, cut into 2-inch pieces
2	tablespoons white vinegar
1	tablespoon sugar
1	tablespoon canola oil
2	cups fresh snow peas
2	cups shredded carrots
3	green onions, chopped
3/8	teaspoon ground ginger *or* 1-1/2 teaspoons minced fresh gingerroot
1/2	teaspoon crushed red pepper flakes

Cook the pasta according to package directions. In a small bowl, whisk cornstarch and 1 tablespoon soy sauce until smooth; stir in 1 tablespoon sesame oil. Transfer to a large resealable plastic bag. Add the chicken; seal bag and turn to coat. Let stand for 10 minutes. In a small bowl, combine the vinegar, sugar, and the remaining soy sauce and sesame oil; set aside.

In a large nonstick skillet or wok, stir-fry chicken in canola oil until juices run clear. Remove to a platter and keep warm. In the same skillet, stir-fry peas and carrots for 5 minutes. Add the green onions, ginger and pepper flakes. Cook and stir until vegetables are crisp-tender. Return the chicken to the pan. Add the soy sauce mixture; mix well. Drain pasta; add to skillet. Toss until combined. **yield:** 6 servings.

nutrition facts: 1 cup equals 329 calories, 9 g fat (1 g saturated fat), 44 mg cholesterol, 465 mg sodium, 37 g carbohydrate, 3 g fiber, 24 g protein.

diabetic exchanges: 3 lean meat, 2 starch, 1 vegetable.

SAVORY APPLE-CHICKEN SAUSAGE

prep/total time 25 minutes

1	large tart apple, peeled and diced
2	teaspoons poultry seasoning
1	teaspoon salt
1/4	teaspoon pepper
1	pound ground chicken

In a large bowl, combine the apple, poultry seasoning, salt and pepper. Crumble chicken over mixture and mix well. Shape into eight 3-in. patties.

In a large skillet coated with cooking spray, cook patties over medium heat for 5-6 minutes on each side or until no longer pink. Drain if necessary. **yield:** 8 patties.

nutrition facts: 1 patty equals 92 calories, 5 g fat (1 g saturated fat), 38 mg cholesterol, 328 mg sodium, 4 g carbohydrate, 1 g fiber, 9 g protein.

diabetic exchanges: 1 lean meat, 1/2 fruit.

angela buchanan
longmont, colorado

These easy, healthy sausages taste great and make an elegant brunch side dish. The recipe is also very versatile—it can be doubled or tripled for a crowd, and the sausage freezes well whether cooked or uncooked.

DOWN-HOME CHICKEN

prep 30 minutes | **cook** 40 minutes

donna sasser hinds
milwaukie, oregon

This is my mom's recipe, and she served the thick, tangy sauce that coats this tender chicken as a gravy over rice or mashed potatoes. It makes a welcome centerpiece for any meal.

1/2 cup all-purpose flour
1 teaspoon salt
1/2 teaspoon pepper
1 broiler/fryer chicken (3 to 4 pounds), cut up
1/4 cup canola oil

SAUCE
2/3 cup lemon juice
2/3 cup ketchup
2/3 cup molasses
1/3 cup canola oil
1/4 cup Worcestershire sauce
1 teaspoon ground cloves
1/2 teaspoon salt
1/4 teaspoon pepper
Hot cooked rice

In a large resealable plastic bag, combine the flour, salt and pepper. Add chicken, a few pieces at a time, and shake to coat.

In a large skillet, heat the oil. Brown the chicken in oil on all sides; remove to paper towels. Drain drippings and return the chicken to the pan.

For the sauce, in a bowl, combine the lemon juice, ketchup, molasses, oil, Worcestershire sauce, cloves, salt and pepper. Pour over chicken. Bring to a boil. Reduce heat; simmer, uncovered, for 35-40 minutes or until chicken juices run clear. Serve with rice. **yield:** 6 servings.

TOMATO-BASIL CHICKEN SPIRALS

prep 5 minutes | **cook** 35 minutes

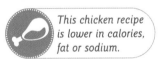

This chicken recipe is lower in calories, fat or sodium.

2 cups finely chopped sweet onion
1 cup chopped fresh basil
4 garlic cloves, minced
1 tablespoon olive oil
5 cups chopped seeded tomatoes
1 can (6 ounces) tomato paste
1/2 teaspoon crushed red pepper flakes
1/2 teaspoon salt
1/4 teaspoon pepper
1 package (16 ounces) spiral pasta
3 cups cubed cooked chicken
1/2 cup shredded Parmesan cheese

In a large saucepan or Dutch oven, saute the onion, basil and garlic in oil until onion is tender. Stir in the tomatoes, tomato paste, red pepper flakes, salt and pepper. Bring to a boil. Reduce heat; cover and simmer for 30-45 minutes.

Meanwhile, cook pasta according to package directions. Add chicken to the tomato mixture; heat through. Drain pasta. Top with chicken mixture; sprinkle with Parmesan cheese. **yield:** 8 servings.

nutrition facts: 1 cup equals 373 calories, 6 g fat (2 g saturated fat), 44 mg cholesterol, 291 mg sodium, 53 g carbohydrate, 5 g fiber, 27 g protein.

diabetic exchanges: 3 vegetable, 2-1/2 starch, 2 lean meat.

sandra giguere
bremen, maine

After tasting a wonderful pasta dish at an Italian restaurant, I experimented until I came up with this recipe. It's become one of our favorite low-fat meals. The riper the tomatoes, the better it is!

PEPPER JACK CHICKEN PASTA

prep/total time 25 minutes

mike kirsch
baumcary, north carolina

My wife, Jennie, is a wonderful cook who's generally skeptical about my kitchen experiments. But she likes this recipe well enough to give me temporary kitchen privileges, and has even encouraged me to enter contests! If you can't find the soup called for here, nacho cheese soup is a good substitution.

3	cups uncooked mostaccioli
1/4	cup chopped onion
1/4	cup chopped sweet red pepper
1/2	teaspoon minced garlic
1	tablespoon canola oil
1	can (10-3/4 ounces) condensed Southwest style pepper Jack soup, undiluted
1	package (9 ounces) ready-to-use Southwestern chicken strips
3/4	cup water
1	can (15 ounces) black beans, rinsed and drained
1/4	cup shredded Monterey Jack cheese, optional

Cook mostaccioli according to package directions. Meanwhile, in a large skillet, saute the onion, red pepper and garlic in oil until tender. Stir in the soup, chicken and water. Bring to a boil. Reduce heat; cover and simmer for 8 minutes.

Stir in beans; heat through. Drain mostaccioli; transfer to a serving bowl; top with chicken mixture. Sprinkle with cheese if desired. **yield:** 6 servings.

HERBED CRANBERRY CHICKEN

prep 20 minutes | **cook** 15 minutes

margee berry

trout lake, washington

Even though it has no added salt, this dish is full of flavor. The zippy cranberry sauce makes the quick entree special.

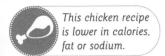

This chicken recipe is lower in calories, fat or sodium.

6 boneless skinless chicken breast halves (4 ounces *each*)
1 tablespoon salt-free herb seasoning blend
2 tablespoons olive oil, *divided*
2/3 cup chopped green onions
1/2 cup dried cranberries
1/2 cup reduced-sodium chicken broth
1/3 cup cranberry juice
4-1/2 teaspoons maple syrup
1 tablespoon balsamic vinegar
1/3 cup chopped pecans, toasted

Rub chicken with seasoning blend. In a large non-stick skillet, cook chicken in 1 tablespoon oil over medium heat for 4-5 minutes on each side or until a meat thermometer reaches 170°. Remove and keep warm.

In the same skillet, saute onions in remaining oil. Stir in the cranberries, broth, cranberry juice, syrup and vinegar; bring to a boil. Reduce heat; cook and stir for 2 minutes. Return chicken to the pan; cook for 1 minute or until heated through. Sprinkle with pecans. **yield:** 6 servings.

nutrition facts: 1 chicken breast half with 2 table-spoons cranberry mixture equals 263 calories, 12 g fat (2 g saturated fat), 63 mg cholesterol, 109 mg sodium, 16 g carbohydrate, 1 g fiber, 24 g protein.

diabetic exchanges: 3 very lean meat, 2 fat, 1/2 starch, 1/2 fruit.

CHICKEN DIANE

prep/total time 5 minutes

This chicken recipe is lower in calories, fat or sodium.

elissa armbruster

medford, new jersey

I've reinvented the famous steak dish of the same name but used chicken instead. It's quick, easy and delicious. You can't go wrong with this recipe!

4 boneless skinless chicken breast halves (4 ounces *each*)
1/2 teaspoon salt
1/2 teaspoon pepper
2 teaspoons olive oil
2 teaspoons butter
1 tablespoon lemon juice
1 tablespoon minced fresh parsley
2 teaspoons Dijon mustard
1/4 cup reduced-sodium chicken broth
3 tablespoons chopped green onions

Flatten chicken to 1/4-in. thickness; sprinkle both sides with salt and pepper. In a large nonstick skillet, brown chicken in oil and butter over medium heat for 3-5 minutes on each side or until a meat thermometer reaches 170°.

In the same skillet, whisk the lemon juice, parsley and mustard until blended. Whisk in broth and green onions; heat through. Serve with chicken. **yield:** 4 servings.

nutrition facts: 1 chicken breast half with 4-1/2 in. teaspoons sauce equals 169 calories, 6 g fat (2 g saturated fat), 71 mg cholesterol, 490 mg sodium, 1 g carbohydrate, trace fiber, 27 g protein.

diabetic exchange: 3 lean meat.

CASSEROLES

BISCUIT-TOPPED LEMON CHICKEN; P. 153

SCALLOPED CHICKEN SUPPER

prep 10 minutes | **bake** 45 minutes

cheryl maczko

eglon, west virginia

Canned soup and a package of scalloped potato mix hurry along this creamy and comforting casserole. You can use either leftover chicken or turkey.

1 package (4.9 ounces) scalloped potatoes
1-3/4 cups boiling water
1 can (10-3/4 ounces) condensed cream of chicken soup, undiluted
1/8 teaspoon poultry seasoning
2 cups cubed cooked chicken
1 cup shredded carrots
1/2 cup chopped celery
1/4 cup finely chopped onion

Place the contents of the sauce mix (from the package of scalloped potatoes) in a large bowl; set the potatoes aside. Whisk in the water, soup and poultry seasoning. Stir in the chicken, carrots, celery, onion and reserved potatoes.

Transfer to a greased 2-qt. baking dish. Bake, uncovered, at 400° for 45-50 minutes or until vegetables are tender. **yield:** 4 servings.

BARBECUE CHICKEN CASSEROLE

prep 25 minutes | **bake** 50 minutes

1 cup all-purpose flour
1 broiler/fryer chicken (3 to 4 pounds), cut up
2 tablespoons canola oil
1 cup chopped onion
1 cup chopped green pepper
1 cup thinly sliced celery
1 cup ketchup
1/2 cup water
3 tablespoons brown sugar
3 tablespoons Worcestershire sauce
1/2 teaspoon salt
1/4 teaspoon pepper
1 package (16 ounces) frozen corn, thawed

Place flour in a large resealable plastic bag. Add chicken, a few pieces at a time, and shake to coat. In a large skillet, brown the chicken in oil; transfer to an ungreased 13-in. x 9-in. baking dish.

Drain skillet, reserving 2 tablespoons drippings. In the drippings, saute onion, green pepper and celery until tender. In a small bowl, combine the ketchup, water, brown sugar, Worcestershire sauce, salt and pepper; add to vegetables. Bring to a boil. Pour over the chicken.

Cover and bake at 350° for 30 minutes. Sprinkle with the corn. Bake 18-20 minutes longer or until the chicken juices run clear and corn is tender. **yield:** 4-6 servings.

gail rector

belle, missouri

I am a minister's wife and have cooked for countless fellowships, funeral dinners and other church activities. This is a recipe I've used often for those occasions.

CHICKEN 'N' CORN BREAD BAKE

prep 25 minutes | **bake** 25 minutes

2-1/2   cups reduced-sodium chicken broth
1   small onion, chopped
1   celery rib, chopped
1/8   teaspoon pepper
4-1/2   cups corn bread stuffing mix, *divided*
4   cups cubed cooked chicken
1-1/2   cups (12 ounces) sour cream
1   can (10-3/4 ounces) condensed cream of chicken soup, undiluted
3   green onions, thinly sliced
1/4   cup butter, cubed

In a large saucepan, combine the broth, onion, celery and pepper. Bring to a boil. Reduce heat; cover and simmer for 5-6 minutes or until vegetables are tender. Stir in 4 cups stuffing mix.

Transfer to a greased 13-in. x 9-in. baking dish. Top with the chicken. In a small bowl, combine the sour cream, soup and green onions. Spread over the chicken. Sprinkle with the remaining stuffing mix; dot with butter.

Bake, uncovered, for 325° for 25-30 minutes or until heated through. **yield:** 8 servings.

ann hillmeyer
sandia park, new mexico

Here's southern comfort food at its best! This casserole is delicious made with chicken or turkey. It's often on the menu when I cook for my husband, our four children and their spouses and our 10 grandkids.

ASPARAGUS CHICKEN DIVAN

prep 20 minutes | **bake** 20 minutes

jeanne koelsch
san rafael, california

I first came across this recipe at a restaurant while living in New York City many years ago. This makes a delectable dish for lunch or dinner served with a simple tossed salad.

1 pound boneless skinless chicken breasts
2 pounds fresh asparagus, trimmed
1 can (10-3/4 ounces) condensed cream of chicken soup, undiluted
1 teaspoon Worcestershire sauce
1/4 teaspoon ground nutmeg
1 cup grated Parmesan cheese, *divided*
1/2 cup heavy whipping cream, whipped
3/4 cup mayonnaise

Broil chicken 4-6 in. from the heat for 6-8 minutes on both sides or until juices run clear. Meanwhile, in a large skillet, bring 1/2 in. of water to a boil. Add asparagus. Reduce heat; cover and simmer for 3-5 minutes or until crisp-tender. Drain and place in a greased shallow 2-1/2-qt. baking dish. Cut chicken into thin slices.

In a small bowl, combine the soup, Worcestershire sauce and nutmeg. Spread half over asparagus. Sprinkle with 1/3 cup Parmesan cheese. Top with chicken. Spread remaining soup mixture over chicken; sprinkle with 1/3 cup Parmesan cheese.

Bake, uncovered, at 400° for 20 minutes. Fold whipped cream into mayonnaise; spread over top. Sprinkle with remaining Parmesan cheese. Broil 4-6 in. from the heat for about 2 minutes or until golden brown. **yield:** 6-8 servings.

editor's note: Reduced-fat or fat-free mayonnaise is not recommended for this recipe.

CHICKEN VEGETABLE CASSEROLE

prep 20 minutes | **bake** 35 minutes

1/2 cup butter, softened
1 cup (8 ounces) sour cream
1 egg
1 cup all-purpose flour
1 teaspoon baking powder
1 teaspoon salt
1/2 teaspoon rubbed sage
1 package (16 ounces) frozen mixed vegetables, thawed
2 cups cubed cooked chicken *or* turkey
1 can (10-3/4 ounces) condensed cream of mushroom soup, undiluted
1/2 cup chopped onion
1/2 cup shredded cheddar cheese

genia mcclinchey
lakeview, michigan

This recipe works wonders with leftover turkey or chicken. It's a great quick-and-easy entree to make when company pops in unexpectedly. I always get lots of compliments when I serve it!

In a small bowl, cream butter and sour cream until smooth. Beat in egg. Combine the flour, baking powder, salt and sage; add to creamed mixture. Spread into a greased 3-qt. baking dish.

In a large bowl, combine the vegetables, chicken, soup and onion. Pour over crust; sprinkle with the shredded cheese. Bake, uncovered, at 400° for 35-40 minutes or until heated through. **yield:** 6 servings.

BROCCOLI CHICKEN CASSEROLE

prep 15 minutes | **bake** 30 minutes

jenn schlachter
big rock, illinois

All ages really seem to go for this comforting, scrumptious meal-in-one. It takes just a handful of ingredients and a few minutes to put together. I've found that adding dried cranberries to the stuffing mix also adds flavor and color!

- 1-1/2 cups water
- 1 package (6 ounces) chicken stuffing mix
- 2 cups cubed cooked chicken
- 1 cup frozen broccoli florets, thawed
- 1 can (10-3/4 ounces) condensed broccoli cheese soup, undiluted
- 1 cup (4 ounces) shredded cheddar cheese

In a small saucepan, bring water to a boil. Stir in stuffing mix. Remove from the heat; cover and let stand for 5 minutes.

Meanwhile, layer chicken and broccoli in a greased 11-in. x 7-in. baking dish. Top with soup. Fluff stuffing with a fork; spoon over soup. Sprinkle with cheese.

Bake, uncovered, at 350° for 30-35 minutes or until heated through. **yield:** 6 servings.

FOUR-CHEESE CHICKEN FETTUCCINE

prep 15 minutes | **bake** 35 minutes

- 8 ounces uncooked fettuccine
- 1 can (10-3/4 ounces) condensed cream of mushroom soup, undiluted
- 1 package (8 ounces) cream cheese, cubed
- 1 jar (4-1/2 ounces) sliced mushrooms, drained
- 1 cup heavy whipping cream
- 1/2 cup butter
- 1/4 teaspoon garlic powder
- 3/4 cup grated Parmesan cheese
- 1/2 cup shredded part-skim mozzarella cheese
- 1/2 cup shredded Swiss cheese
- 2-1/2 cups cubed cooked chicken

TOPPING
- 1/3 cup seasoned bread crumbs
- 2 tablespoons butter, melted
- 1 to 2 tablespoons grated Parmesan cheese

Cook fettuccine according to package directions. Meanwhile, in a Dutch oven or large soup kettle, combine the soup, cream cheese, mushrooms, cream, butter and garlic powder. Cook and stir over medium heat until blended. Reduce heat to low; add cheeses and stir until melted. Add chicken; heat through. Drain fettuccine. Add to the chicken mixture; toss to coat.

Transfer to a greased shallow 2-1/2-qt. baking dish. Combine topping ingredients; sprinkle over the chicken mixture.

Cover and bake at 350° for 30 minutes. Uncover; bake 5-10 minutes longer or until golden brown. **yield:** 8 servings.

rochelle brownlee
big timber, montana

As a cattle rancher, my husband's a big fan of beef. For him to comment positively on a poultry dish is rare. But he always tells me, "I love this casserole!"

ULTIMATE KITCHEN TIP

Heavy cream lends a rich flavor and creamy texture to many foods. But at 100 calories and 11 grams of fat per 2 tablespoons, it's a real calorie and fat buster! Substituting an equal amount of half-and-half for the heavy cream works quite well. Half-and-half has a little more than half the calories of cream, but keeps much of a dish's flavor and creaminess.

CHICKEN PENNE CASSEROLE

prep 35 minutes | **bake** 45 minutes

carmen vanosch
vernon, british columbia

*This is my family's No. 1
favorite casserole recipe.
I make it every week or two,
and we never tire of it.
I usually prepare it in the
early afternoon, so that
I can clean my kitchen and
then relax while it bakes. It
won't disappoint!*

1-1/2 cups uncooked penne pasta
1 pound boneless skinless chicken thighs, cut into 1-inch pieces
1/2 cup *each* chopped onion, green pepper and sweet red pepper
1-1/2 teaspoons minced garlic
1 teaspoon *each* dried basil, oregano and parsley flakes
1/2 teaspoon salt
1/2 teaspoon crushed red pepper flakes
1 tablespoon canola oil
1 can (14-1/2 ounces) diced tomatoes, undrained
3 tablespoons tomato paste
3/4 cup chicken broth
2 cups (8 ounces) shredded part-skim mozzarella cheese
1/2 cup grated Romano cheese

Cook pasta according to package directions. Meanwhile, in a large saucepan, saute the chicken, onion, peppers, garlic and seasonings in oil until chicken is no longer pink.

In a blender, combine tomatoes and tomato paste; cover and process until blended. Add to chicken mixture. Stir in broth. Bring to a boil. Reduce heat; cover and simmer for 10-15 minutes or until slightly thickened.

Drain pasta; toss with chicken mixture. Spoon half of the mixture into a greased 2 qt. baking dish. Sprinkle with half of the mozzarella and Romano cheeses. Repeat layers.

Cover and bake at 350° for 30 minutes. Uncover; bake 15-20 minutes longer or until heated through. **yield:** 4 servings.

MEXICAN CHICKEN BAKE

prep 15 minutes | **bake** 30 minutes

linda humphrey
buchanan, michigan

My kids, grandkids and guests of all ages request this casserole often. Since it takes only about 30 minutes to make, I have it at least once every other month!

1   medium onion, chopped
1   small green pepper, chopped
2   large jalapeno peppers, seeded and chopped
1/4 cup butter
2   cans (10-3/4 ounces *each*) condensed cream of chicken soup, undiluted
1   can (12 ounces) evaporated milk
4   cups cooked long grain rice
3   to 4 cups cubed cooked chicken
3   cups (12 ounces) Colby-Monterey Jack cheese, *divided*

In a large skillet, saute the onion, green pepper and jalapeno peppers in butter until tender. In a large bowl, combine soup and milk. Stir in the rice, chicken, 2 cups cheese and onion mixture.

Transfer to a greased 13-in. x 9-in. baking dish. Bake, uncovered, at 350° for 25 minutes. Sprinkle with the remaining cheese. Bake 5-10 minutes longer or until heated through and the cheese is melted. **yield:** 8-10 servings.

editor's note: When cutting hot peppers, disposable gloves are recommended. Avoid touching your face.

MAKEOVER CHICKEN A LA KING CASSEROLE

prep 10 minutes | **bake** 30 minutes

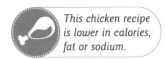
This chicken recipe is lower in calories, fat or sodium.

8   ounces uncooked wide egg noodles
1   can (10-3/4 ounces) reduced-fat reduced-sodium condensed cream of chicken soup, undiluted
2/3 cup fat-free evaporated milk
6   ounces cubed reduced-fat process cheese (Velveeta)
2   cups cubed cooked chicken breast
1   cup sliced celery
1/4 cup chopped green pepper
1   jar (2 ounces) diced pimientos, drained
1/3 cup dry bread crumbs
1   tablespoon butter, melted
1/4 cup slivered almonds

Cook the noodles according to the package directions. Meanwhile, in a large saucepan, combine the soup and milk. Cook and stir over medium heat for 2 minutes. Reduce heat; stir in the cheese until melted. Add the chicken, celery, green pepper and pimientos.

Drain noodles; add to the chicken mixture and mix well. Transfer to a shallow 2-qt. baking dish coated with cooking spray. Cover and bake at 400° for 20 minutes.

Toss bread crumbs and butter; sprinkle over the top. Sprinkle with almonds. Bake, uncovered, for 10-15 minutes or until heated through and golden. **yield:** 8 servings.

nutrition facts: 1 cup equals 306 calories, 9 g fat (3 g saturated fat), 72 mg cholesterol, 405 mg sodium, 31 g carbohydrate, 2 g fiber, 24 g protein.

diabetic exchanges: 2 starch, 2 lean meat, 1 fat.

taste of home test kitchen
greendale, wisconsin

Chicken a la King is a hearty crowd-pleaser that serves up a lot of fat and calories. Our home economists dish up this version with over 50% less fat and sodium, more than 75% less saturated fat and with all the comfort of the classic dish.

SPANISH CHICKEN

prep 25 minutes | **bake** 40 minutes

mrs. robert trygg
duluth, minnesota

I'm always on the lookout for fast recipes that taste great. This one is easy to prepare, and kids love it.

16 ounces boneless skinless chicken breast halves (4 ounces *each*)
2 tablespoons canola oil
1 medium onion, chopped
1/4 cup chopped green pepper
1 garlic clove, minced
1 can (14-1/2 ounces) diced tomatoes, undrained
1 cup water
3/4 cup uncooked long grain rice
2 teaspoons chicken bouillon granules
1 to 3 teaspoons chili powder
1/8 teaspoon ground cinnamon
1/8 teaspoon ground cumin
1/8 teaspoon pepper

1/2 cup picante sauce
1/2 cup shredded cheddar cheese
1 can (2-1/4 ounces) sliced ripe olives, drained

In a large skillet, brown chicken in oil for 2-3 minutes on each side. Remove and keep warm. In the same skillet, saute the onion, green pepper and garlic until tender. Stir in the tomatoes, water, rice, bouillon and seasonings. Bring to a boil.

Pour into a greased 11-in. x 7-in. baking dish; top with the chicken. Cover and bake at 350° for 35-40 minutes or until rice is tender.

Uncover; spoon the picante sauce over the chicken and sprinkle with cheese. Bake 5 minutes longer or until the cheese is melted. Garnish with olives. **yield:** 4 servings.

CHICKEN TORTILLA CASSEROLE

prep 15 minutes | **bake** 45 minutes + standing

5 to 6 corn tortillas (6 inches), cut into strips
8 cups cubed cooked chicken breast
1 can (4 ounces) diced green chilies
1 can (10-3/4 ounces) condensed cream of mushroom soup, undiluted
1 can (10-3/4 ounces) condensed cream of chicken soup, undiluted
1 cup (8 ounces) sour cream
3 cups (12 ounces) shredded Monterey Jack cheese

In a greased 13-in. x 9-in. baking dish, layer half the tortilla strips, half the chicken and half the chilies. In a large bowl, combine the soups and sour cream; spread half over the chicken. Top with half the cheese. Repeat layers.

Bake, uncovered, at 350° for 45 minutes or until bubbly and golden brown. Let stand for 10 minutes before serving. **yield:** 8-10 servings.

sarah thompson
milwaukee, wisconsin

My aunt in California shared this zesty chicken casserole recipe with me. It's simple, filling and easily feeds a big group.

HOME-STYLE CHICKEN POTPIE

prep 1 hour | **bake** 25 minutes + standing

- 3/4 cup cold butter
- 2 cups all-purpose flour
- 1 cup (4 ounces) shredded cheddar cheese
- 1/4 cup cold water

FILLING

- 2-1/2 cups halved baby carrots
- 3 celery ribs, sliced
- 6 tablespoons butter, cubed
- 7 tablespoons all-purpose flour
- 1 teaspoon salt
- 1/4 teaspoon coarsely ground pepper
- 2-1/2 cups chicken broth
- 1 cup heavy whipping cream
- 4 cups cubed cooked chicken
- 1 cup frozen pearl onions, thawed
- 1 cup frozen peas, thawed
- 3 tablespoons minced chives
- 3 tablespoons minced fresh parsley
- 2 teaspoons minced fresh thyme
- 1 egg, lightly beaten

In a large bowl, cut butter into flour until crumbly. Stir in cheese. Gradually add water, tossing with a fork until dough forms a ball. Cover and refrigerate for at least 1 hour.

For the filling, in a large saucepan, cook carrots and celery in a small amount of water until crisp-tender; drain and set aside.

In another saucepan, melt butter. Whisk in the flour, salt and pepper until smooth. Gradually whisk in broth and cream. Bring to a boil; cook and stir for 2 minutes or until thickened. Stir in the carrot mixture, chicken, onions, peas, chives, parsley and thyme; heat through. Transfer to a greased 13-in. x 9-in. baking dish.

On a floured surface, roll out dough to fit top of dish; cut out vents. Place dough over filling; trim and flute edges. Brush with egg. Bake at 400° for 25-30 minutes or until bubbly and crust is golden brown. Let stand for 10 minutes before serving. **yield:** 10-12 servings.

darlene claxton
brighton, michigan

I served this potpie along with chili on Super Bowl Sunday. No one ate the chili. In fact, one of my husband's single friends called the next day and asked for the leftover pie.

CHICKEN CHILI LASAGNA

prep 35 minutes | **bake** 40 minutes

cindee rolston
st. marys, west virginia

This saucy lasagna is my adaptation of a chicken enchilada recipe. My husband and I enjoy the mild blend of seasonings, cheeses and tender chicken. The dish has become very popular with my co-workers after I shared leftovers one day for lunch.

2 packages (3 ounces *each*) cream cheese, softened
1 medium onion, chopped
8 green onions, chopped
2 cups (8 ounces) shredded Mexican cheese blend, *divided*
2 garlic cloves, minced
3/4 teaspoon ground cumin, *divided*
1/2 teaspoon minced fresh cilantro
3 cups cubed cooked chicken
1/4 cup butter
1/4 cup all-purpose flour
1-1/2 cups chicken broth
1 cup (4 ounces) shredded Monterey Jack cheese
1 cup (8 ounces) sour cream
1 can (4 ounces) chopped green chilies, drained
1/8 teaspoon dried thyme
1/8 teaspoon salt
1/8 teaspoon pepper
12 flour tortillas (6 inches), halved

In a large bowl, beat the cream cheese, onions, 1-1/2 cups Mexican-cheese blend, garlic, 1/4 teaspoon cumin and cilantro until blended. Stir in chicken; set aside.

In a large saucepan, melt the butter. Stir in the flour until smooth; gradually add the broth. Bring to a boil; cook and stir for 2 minutes or until thickened. Remove from the heat. Stir in the Monterey Jack cheese, sour cream, chilies, thyme, salt, pepper and remaining cumin.

Spread 1/2 cup of the cheese sauce in a greased 13-in. x 9-in. baking dish. Top with six tortilla halves, a third of the chicken mixture and a fourth of the cheese sauce. Repeat tortilla, chicken and cheese sauce layers twice. Top with remaining tortillas, cheese sauce and Mexican cheese.

Cover and bake at 350° for 30 minutes. Uncover; bake 10 minutes longer or until heated through. Let stand 5 minutes before cutting. **yield**: 12 servings.

COLORFUL CHICKEN AND RICE

prep 20 minutes | **bake** 25 minutes

dana wise

quinter, kansas

Topped with crushed corn chips, shredded lettuce and chopped tomatoes, this marvelous meal-in-one is as pretty as it is tasty. I serve it to company along with bread and dessert, and it always gets compliments.

1   can (10-3/4 ounces) condensed cream of chicken soup, undiluted
1   cup (8 ounces) sour cream
1/2   cup 4% cottage cheese
1   package (3 ounces) cream cheese, cubed
3   cups cubed cooked chicken
3   cups cooked rice
1-1/2 cups (6 ounces) shredded Monterey Jack cheese
1   can (4 ounces) chopped green chilies
1   can (2-1/4 ounces) sliced ripe olives, drained
1/8   teaspoon garlic salt

1-1/2 cups crushed corn chips
2   cups shredded lettuce
2   medium tomatoes, chopped

In a blender, combine the soup, sour cream, cottage cheese and cream cheese; cover and process until smooth. Transfer to a large bowl. Stir in the chicken, rice, Monterey Jack cheese, chilies, sliced olives and garlic salt.

Pour into a greased 2-qt. baking dish. Bake, uncovered, at 350° for 25-30 minutes or until heated through. Just before serving, top with corn chips, lettuce and tomatoes. **yield:** 6-8 servings.

CRUNCHY CHICKEN CASSEROLE

prep 25 minutes | **bake** 25 minutes

1   package (6 ounces) instant chicken-flavored stuffing mix
2   cups frozen mixed vegetables, thawed
1   can (10-3/4 ounces) condensed cream of chicken soup, undiluted
1   can (8 ounces) sliced water chestnuts, drained
2   tablespoons water
1   cup shredded cooked chicken *or* turkey

Prepare the stuffing mix according to package directions; set aside. In a large bowl, combine the mixed vegetables, cream of chicken soup, water chestnuts and water.

Transfer to an ungreased 2-qt. baking dish. Top with the chicken and prepared stuffing. Bake, uncovered, at 350° for 25-30 minutes or until heated through. **yield:** 6 servings.

patricia sayers

smyrna, tennessee

We enjoy this fast all-in-one meal often. I usually have chicken on hand, but it's also a great way to use up leftover turkey after Thanksgiving.

CHICKEN HAM CASSEROLE

prep 15 minutes | **bake** 25 minutes

lovetta breshears

nixa, missouri

I am retired and always looking for fast-to-fix foods to serve when my children or grandchildren stop by. Leftover chicken, ham and a wild rice mix make this comforting dish quick to assemble. If you have extra turkey, you can use it instead of the chicken.

1   package (6 ounces) long grain and wild rice mix
2   cups cubed cooked chicken
1   cup cubed fully cooked ham
1   can (10-3/4 ounces) condensed cream of chicken soup, undiluted
1   can (12 ounces) evaporated milk
1   cup (4 ounces) shredded Colby cheese
1/8   teaspoon pepper
1/4   cup grated Parmesan cheese

Cook rice mix according to package directions. Transfer to a greased 2-qt. baking dish. Top with chicken and ham.

In a large bowl, combine the soup, milk, Colby cheese and pepper; pour over chicken mixture. Sprinkle with the Parmesan.

Bake, uncovered, at 350° for 25-30 minutes or until bubbly. **yield:** 6 servings.

RITZY CHICKEN

prep 20 minutes | **bake** 30 minutes

2-1/2   cups uncooked egg noodles
1   can (10-3/4 ounces) condensed cream of chicken soup, undiluted
3/4   cup milk
1/2   cup sour cream
1/2   teaspoon poultry seasoning
1/4   teaspoon salt
Dash pepper
2   cups cubed cooked chicken
1/2   cup crushed butter-flavored crackers (about 12 crackers)
2   tablespoons butter, melted

Cook the noodles according to package directions; drain. Meanwhile, in a large bowl, combine the soup, milk, sour cream, poultry seasoning, salt and pepper until blended. Stir in the cooked noodles and chicken.

Transfer to a greased 1-1/2-qt. baking dish. Combine the cracker crumbs and melted butter; sprinkle over the top. Bake, uncovered, at 350° for 30-35 minutes or until bubbly and golden brown. **yield:** 4 servings.

millie poe

corning, arkansas

When your family is hungry and the clock is ticking closer to dinnertime, you can't go wrong with this creamy chicken and noodle casserole.

BISCUIT-TOPPED LEMON CHICKEN

prep 40 minutes | **bake** 35 minutes

2   large onions, finely chopped
4   celery ribs, finely chopped
2   garlic cloves, minced
1   cup butter, cubed
8   green onions, thinly sliced
2/3 cup all-purpose flour
1/2 gallon milk
12   cups cubed cooked chicken
2   cans (10-3/4 ounces *each*)
    condensed cream of chicken soup,
    undiluted
1/2 cup lemon juice
2   tablespoons grated lemon peel
2   teaspoons pepper
1   teaspoon salt

CHEDDAR BISCUITS
5   cups self-rising flour
2   cups milk
2   cups (8 ounces) shredded cheddar
    cheese
1/4 cup butter, melted

In a Dutch oven, saute the onions, celery and garlic in butter. Add green onions. Stir in flour until blended; gradually add milk. Bring to a boil; cook and stir for 2 minutes or until thickened.

Add the chicken, soup, lemon juice and peel, pepper and salt; heat through. Pour into two greased 13-in. x 9-in. baking dishes; set aside.

For the biscuits, in a large bowl, combine the biscuit ingredients just until moistened. Turn onto a lightly floured surface; knead 8-10 times. Pat or roll out to 3/4-in. thickness. With a floured 2-1/2-in. biscuit cutter, cut out 30 biscuits.

Place over chicken mixture. Bake, uncovered, at 350° for 35-40 minutes or until golden brown.

yield: 15 servings (2 biscuits per serving).

editor's note: As a substitute for each cup of self-rising flour, place 1-1/2 teaspoons baking powder and 1/2 teaspoon salt in a measuring cup. Add all-purpose flour to measure 1 cup.

pattie ishee
stringer, mississippi

This comforting recipe combines two of my favorite things: hot, crusty biscuits and a flavorful lemon-pepper sauce. It's great for potlucks or as a housewarming gift.

GREEN BEAN CHICKEN CASSEROLE

prep 15 minutes | **bake** 25 minutes

delissa mingee
warr acres, oklahoma

My husband, who claims to be strictly a meat-and-potatoes man, asked for seconds the first time I threw together this hearty all-in-one meal. My daughter and several guests raved about it, too.

1 package (6 ounces) long grain and wild rice mix
4 cups cubed cooked chicken
1-3/4 cups frozen French-style green beans
1 can (10-3/4 ounces) condensed cream of mushroom soup, undiluted
1 can (10-3/4 ounces) condensed cream of chicken and broccoli soup, undiluted
1 can (4 ounces) mushroom stems and pieces, drained
2/3 cup chopped onion
2/3 cup chopped green pepper
1 envelope onion soup mix
3/4 cup shredded Colby cheese

ADDITIONAL INGREDIENT
(for each casserole)
2/3 cup french-fried onions

Prepare the wild rice mix according to package directions. Stir in the chicken, beans, soups, mushrooms, onion, green pepper and soup mix. Spoon into two greased 1-1/2-qt. baking dishes. Sprinkle with the cheese.

Cover and freeze one casserole for up to 3 months. Cover and bake the second casserole at 350° for 25-30 minutes or until heated through. Uncover and sprinkle with french-fried onions; bake 5 minutes longer or until onions are golden.

To use the frozen casserole: Completely thaw in the refrigerator. Remove from the refrigerator 30 minutes before baking. Cover and bake at 350° for 60-65 minutes or until heated through. Uncover and sprinkle with the french-fried onions; bake 5 minutes longer. **yield:** 2 casseroles (4-6 servings each).

SPECIAL DELIVERY CHICKEN

prep 10 minutes | **bake** 25 minutes

2 cups (16 ounces) sour cream
1 can (10-3/4 ounces) condensed cream of chicken soup, undiluted
2 teaspoons poppy seeds
2-1/2 cups cubed cooked chicken
1-3/4 cups crushed butter-flavored crackers (about 36 crackers)
1/2 cup butter, melted

In a large bowl, combine the sour cream, soup and poppy seeds. Stir in chicken. Pour into a greased 11-in. x 7-in. baking dish. Combine the cracker crumbs and butter; sprinkle over top.

Bake, uncovered, at 350° for 25-30 minutes or until heated through. **yield:** 4 servings.

ame andrews
little rock, arkansas

To treat a friend who was bringing her new baby home from the hospital, I delivered a "Welcome to the World" theme dinner to her home. This favorite chicken casserole took on a new name for the occasion. It makes for a creamy, comforting main dish.

ULTIMATE KITCHEN TIP

Instead of sour cream, the same amount of plain yogurt can be used for casseroles, dips, sauces and baked goods. Dips and sauces may have a thinner consistency with yogurt, and nonfat yogurt is not recommended for baked goods. To measure, spoon sour cream or yogurt into a measuring cup and level by sweeping the flat side of a knife across the top.

GREEK PASTA BAKE

prep 20 minutes | **bake** 25 minutes

anne taglienti
kennett square,
pennsylvania

I've brought this hot dish to potlucks and it received rave reviews. There's never a crumb left. Best of all, it's a simple, healthy and filling supper made with easy-to-find ingredients.

1 package (12 ounces) whole wheat penne pasta
4 cups cubed cooked chicken breast
1 can (29 ounces) tomato sauce
1 can (14-1/2 ounces) diced tomatoes, drained
1 package (10 ounces) frozen chopped spinach, thawed and squeezed dry
2 cans (2-1/4 ounces *each*) sliced ripe olives, drained
1/4 cup chopped red onion
2 tablespoons chopped green pepper
1 teaspoon dried basil
1 teaspoon dried oregano
1/2 cup shredded part-skim mozzarella cheese
1/2 cup crumbled feta cheese

Cook pasta according to package directions; drain. In a large bowl, combine the pasta, chicken, tomato sauce, tomatoes, spinach, olives, onion, green pepper, basil and oregano.

Transfer to a 13-in. x 9-in. baking dish coated with cooking spray. Sprinkle with the cheeses. Bake, uncovered, at 400° for 25-30 minutes or until heated through and the cheese is melted. **yield:** 8 servings.

SOMBRERO BAKE

prep 10 minutes | **bake** 45 minutes

2-1/2 cups cubed cooked chicken
1 can (4 ounces) chopped green chilies
1 cup (4 ounces) shredded cheddar cheese
1 medium tomato, chopped
1 can (10-3/4 ounces) condensed cream of chicken soup, undiluted
1/2 cup milk
1/2 teaspoon hot pepper sauce

BISCUIT TOPPING
3/4 cup biscuit/baking mix
1/2 cup cornmeal
2/3 cup milk
1 can (2.8 ounces) french-fried onions, *divided*
1/2 cup shredded cheddar cheese

In a greased 13-in. x 9-in. baking dish, layer the chicken, chilies, cheese and tomato. In a small bowl, combine the soup, milk and hot pepper sauce. Pour over chicken mixture. Cover and bake at 375° for 20 minutes.

For the topping, in a small bowl, combine the biscuit mix, cornmeal, milk and 3/4 cup french-fried onions. Drop into eight mounds over casserole. Bake, uncovered, for 20 minutes (topping will spread). Sprinkle with cheese and remaining onions. Bake 5 minutes longer or until cheese is melted. **yield:** 6 servings.

mary tallman
arbor vitae, wisconsin

Green chilies and hot pepper sauce bring a little zip to this Southwestern-style supper that makes great use of leftover cooked chicken.

CHICKEN NOODLE CASSEROLE

prep 20 minutes | **bake** 15 minutes

lori gleason
minneapolis, minnesota

I work at home while caring for our two children, so I have to be creative at mealtimes to fix something quick and nutritious that everyone enjoys. This homey casserole fits all the requirements.

2/3	cup chopped onion
1	garlic clove, minced
1	tablespoon olive oil
1-1/2	pounds boneless skinless chicken breasts, cut into 3/4-inch cubes
1	can (14-1/2 ounces) chicken broth
1-1/2	cups chopped carrots
3	celery ribs, chopped
1/2	teaspoon dried savory
3	tablespoons butter
3	tablespoons all-purpose flour
3/4	teaspoon salt
1/8	teaspoon white pepper
1-1/2	cups 2% milk
1-1/4	cups shredded reduced-fat cheddar cheese
8	ounces wide egg noodles, cooked and drained

In a large nonstick skillet, saute the onion and garlic in oil until tender. Add the chicken; cook and stir until no longer pink. Add the broth, carrots, celery and savory. Bring to a boil. Reduce heat; cover and simmer for 10-15 minutes or until the vegetables are tender.

Meanwhile, in a saucepan, melt the butter. Stir in the flour, salt and pepper until smooth. Gradually add milk. Bring to a boil; cook and stir for 2 minutes or until thickened. Remove from the heat; stir in cheese until melted. Pour over chicken mixture. Add noodles; mix well.

Transfer to a 3-qt. baking dish coated with cooking spray. Bake, uncovered, at 350° for 15-20 minutes or until bubbly. **yield:** 8 servings.

CHICKEN TETRAZZINI

prep 30 minutes | **bake** 20 minutes

helen mcphee
savoy, illinois

This is my revised version of a rich and delicious recipe a friend shared with me more than 35 years ago. It's nice to give it to friends who are unable to cook.

1 package (12 ounces) spaghetti
1/3 cup butter, cubed
1/3 cup all-purpose flour
3/4 teaspoon salt
1/4 teaspoon white pepper
1 can (14-1/2 ounces) chicken broth
1-1/2 cups half-and-half cream
1 cup heavy whipping cream
4 cups cubed cooked chicken
3 cans (4 ounces *each*) mushroom stems and pieces, drained
1 jar (4 ounces) sliced pimientos, drained
1/2 cup grated Parmesan cheese

Cook the spaghetti according to package directions. Meanwhile, in a Dutch oven, melt the butter. Stir in the flour, salt and pepper until smooth. Gradually add the broth, half-and-half and whipping cream. Bring to a boil; cook and stir for 2 minutes or until thickened.

Remove from the heat. Stir in the chicken, mushrooms and pimientos. Drain spaghetti; add to the chicken mixture and toss to coat.

Transfer to two greased 11-in. x 7-in. baking dishes. Sprinkle with Parmesan cheese. Cover and freeze one casserole for up to 2 months. Bake the second casserole, uncovered, at 350° for 20-25 minutes or until heated through.

To use frozen casserole: Thaw in the refrigerator overnight. Cover and bake at 350° for 30 minutes. Uncover; bake 15-20 minutes longer or until heated through. Stir before serving. **yield:** 2 casseroles (3-4 servings each).

CHICKEN AND SHELLS DINNER

prep 15 minutes | **bake** 20 minutes

1 package (12 ounces) shells and cheese dinner mix
1/4 cup chopped onion
4 tablespoons butter, *divided*
2 cups cubed cooked chicken
1 package (10 ounces) frozen peas, thawed
2/3 cup mayonnaise
1/3 cup seasoned bread crumbs

Prepare the dinner mix according to package directions. Meanwhile, in a small skillet, saute the onion in 2 tablespoons butter until tender. Stir the chicken, peas, mayonnaise and sauteed onion into the cooked dinner mix.

Transfer to a greased 1-1/2-qt. baking dish. Melt remaining butter; toss with bread crumbs. Sprinkle over top. Bake, uncovered, at 350° for 20-25 minutes or until bubbly. **yield:** 4-6 servings.

editor's note: Reduced-fat or fat-free mayonnaise is not recommended for this recipe.

leeann mccue
charlotte, north carolina

Like most kids, mine love macaroni and cheese. The addition of chicken and peas makes this a meal-in-one they never refuse.

CHEDDAR CHICKEN PIE

prep 20 minutes | **bake** 30 minutes

betty pierce
slaterville springs, new york

This speedy main dish uses handy biscuit mix, so there's no need to fuss with a crust. Just add fruit salad and crusty hot bread for a delicious meal.

3 cups (12 ounces) shredded cheddar cheese, *divided*
3 cups frozen chopped broccoli, thawed and drained
1-1/2 cups cubed cooked chicken
2/3 cup finely chopped onion
1-1/3 cups milk
3 eggs
3/4 cup biscuit/baking mix
3/4 teaspoon salt
1/4 teaspoon pepper

In a large bowl, combine 2 cups cheese, broccoli, chicken and onion; spread into a greased 10-in. pie plate. In a small bowl, beat the milk, eggs, biscuit mix, salt and pepper until smooth. Pour over broccoli mixture (do not stir).

Bake at 400° for 30-35 minutes or until a knife inserted near the center comes out clean. Sprinkle with the remaining cheese. Let stand for 5 minutes or until cheese is melted. **yield:** 6 servings.

HOT CHICKEN SALAD

prep 15 minutes | **bake** 30 minutes

2-1/2 cups diced cooked chicken
2 cups cooked rice
1 cup diced celery
1 cup sliced fresh mushrooms
1 can (8 ounces) sliced water chestnuts, drained
1 tablespoon finely chopped onion
1 teaspoon lemon juice
1/2 teaspoon dried rosemary, crushed
1/4 teaspoon pepper
3/4 cup mayonnaise
1 can (10-3/4 ounces) condensed cream of chicken soup, undiluted

TOPPING
1/2 cup cornflake crumbs

1/2 cup slivered almonds
3 tablespoons butter

In a large bowl, combine the first nine ingredients. In a small bowl, combine mayonnaise and soup. Pour over chicken mixture; stir gently to coat. Spoon into a greased 2-qt. baking dish.

For the topping, in a small skillet, brown cornflakes and almonds in butter. Sprinkle over casserole. Bake, uncovered, at 350° for 30-35 minutes or until heated through. **yield:** 6 servings.

nutrition facts: 1 cup equals 272 calories, 12 g fat (0 saturated fat), 40 mg cholesterol, 522 mg sodium, 29 g carbohydrate, 0 fiber, 21 g protein.

diabetic exchanges: 2 lean meat, 1-1/2 starch, 1 vegetable, 1 fat.

editor's note: Reduced-fat or fat-free mayonnaise is not recommended for this recipe.

 This chicken recipe is lower in calories, fat or sodium.

michelle wise
spring mills, pennsylvania

I've always been a baker. So, when I got married, I was happy to have this simple yet scrumptious recipe, which originated with my aunt, who passed it on to my mom.

CHICKEN PIE IN A PAN

prep 25 minutes | **bake** 35 minutes

2 celery ribs, diced
2 medium carrots, diced
1 small onion, chopped
3 tablespoons butter
1/4 cup all-purpose flour
1/2 teaspoon salt
1 cup milk
1 cup chicken broth
1 can (10-3/4 ounces) condensed cream of mushroom soup, undiluted
4 cups cubed cooked chicken

CRUST
1-1/2 cups all-purpose flour
3/4 teaspoon baking powder
1 teaspoon salt
3 tablespoons cold butter
1/2 cup milk
2 cups (8 ounces) shredded cheddar cheese

In a large skillet, saute the celery, carrots and onion in butter until tender. Stir in flour and salt until blended; gradually add milk and broth. Bring to a boil; cook and stir for 2 minutes or until thickened. Stir in soup and chicken. Spoon into a greased 13-in. x 9-in. baking dish; set aside.

For the crust, combine the flour baking powder and salt. Cut in butter until crumbly. Add milk, tossing with a fork until mixture forms a soft dough; shape into a ball.

On a lightly floured surface, roll into a 12-in. x 10-in. rectangle. Sprinkle with cheese. Roll up jelly-roll style, starting from a long side. Cut into 12 slices. Place cut side down over the chicken mixture. Bake, uncovered, at 350° for 35-40 minutes or until the crust is lightly browned. **yield:** 6-8 servings.

kristine conway
alliance, ohio

Tasty and filling, this potpie is a perfect way to use up leftover chicken or turkey. It takes some time to prepare, but luckily, I have five children at home to help me. This dish travels well and is ideal to take to a potluck or family reunion.

CHICKEN 'N' DRESSING CASSEROLE

prep 1 hour | **bake** 35 minutes

billie blanton
kingsport, tennessee

*This casserole is a real
favorite in our area and in
my family, too. It's a great
way to use leftover chicken
or turkey, and it's so easy
that even beginner cooks
will have a lot of success
making it.*

4 cups cubed cooked chicken
2 tablespoons all-purpose flour
1/2 cup chicken broth
1/2 cup milk
Salt and pepper to taste
DRESSING
2 celery ribs, chopped
1 small onion, finely chopped
1 tablespoon butter
1 teaspoon rubbed sage
1/2 teaspoon poultry seasoning
1/4 teaspoon salt
1/8 teaspoon pepper
2 cups unseasoned stuffing cubes,
     crushed
2 cups coarsely crumbled corn bread
1/2 cup chicken broth
1 egg, beaten
GRAVY
1/4 cup butter

6 tablespoons all-purpose flour
2 cups chicken broth
1/2 cup milk

Place chicken in a greased 2-qt. baking dish; set aside. In a small saucepan, combine the flour, broth and milk until smooth. Bring to a boil; cook and stir for 2 minutes. Season with salt and pepper. Spoon over chicken.

For the dressing, in a large skillet, saute celery and onion in butter until tender. Stir in seasonings. Remove from the heat; add the stuffing cubes, corn bread, broth and egg. Mix well. Spoon over chicken mixture. Cover and bake at 350° for 35-40 minutes or until a thermometer inserted near the center reads 160°.

For the gravy, melt butter in a small saucepan. Stir in flour until smooth; gradually add broth and milk. Bring to a boil; cook and stir for 2 minutes or until thickened. Serve with the chicken and dressing. **yield:** 8 servings.

HEARTY CHICKEN CASSEROLE

prep 25 minutes | **bake** 10 minutes

janet applin
gladstone, michigan

I found this recipe in a cookbook we received as a wedding gift and altered it to fit my family's tastes. My husband and daughters rush to the table when they know it's on the menu.

2-1/2 cups frozen mixed vegetables
1/2 cup chopped onion
1/2 cup butter, *divided*
1/3 cup all-purpose flour
1/2 teaspoon dried sage leaves
1/2 teaspoon pepper
1/4 teaspoon salt
2 cups chicken broth
3/4 cup milk
3 cups cubed cooked chicken
1 can (14-1/2 ounces) sliced potatoes, drained and quartered
2 cups seasoned stuffing cubes

Cook the mixed vegetables according to package directions; drain.

Meanwhile, in a large saucepan, saute the onion in 1/4 cup butter for 2-3 minutes or until tender. Stir in the flour, sage, pepper and salt until blended. Gradually add broth and milk. Bring to a boil; cook and stir until thickened. Stir in the chicken, potatoes and mixed vegetables; heat through.

Transfer to a greased 13-in. x 9-in. baking dish. Melt the remaining butter; toss with stuffing cubes. Sprinkle over chicken mixture. Bake, uncovered, at 450° for 10-12 minutes or until heated through. **yield:** 6 servings.

CHICKEN 'N' CHIPS

prep 10 minutes | **bake** 25 minutes

1 can (10-3/4 ounces) condensed cream of chicken soup, undiluted
1 cup (8 ounces) sour cream
2 tablespoons taco sauce
1/4 cup chopped green chilies
3 cups cubed cooked chicken
12 slices process American cheese
4 cups broken tortilla chips

In a large bowl, combine the soup, sour cream, taco sauce and chilies. In an ungreased shallow 2-qt. baking dish, layer half of the chicken, soup mixture, cheese and tortilla chips. Repeat layers.

Bake, uncovered, at 350° for 25-30 minutes or until bubbly. **yield:** 4-6 servings.

kendra schneider
grifton, north carolina

My husband, Chad, loves the flavor of this creamy chicken casserole sprinkled with crushed tortilla chips.

CHICKEN HOT DISH

prep 5 minutes | **bake** 70 minutes

amber dudley

new prague, minnesota

When my brother and his wife came over to visit after our third child was born, they brought this comforting, creamy dish for supper. It's become a favorite since then.

1 package (26 ounces) frozen shredded hash brown potatoes, thawed
1 package (24 ounces) frozen California-blend vegetables
3 cups cubed cooked chicken
1 can (10-3/4 ounces) condensed cream of chicken soup, undiluted
1 can (10-3/4 ounces) condensed cream of mushroom soup, undiluted

1 cup chicken broth
3/4 cup french-fried onions

In a greased 13-in. x 9-in. baking dish, layer the hash brown potatoes, vegetables and chicken. In a bowl, combine both soups and broth; pour over chicken (dish will be full).

Cover and bake at 375° for 1 hour. Uncover; sprinkle with onions. Bake 10 minutes longer or until heated through. **yield:** 6 servings.

BAYOU CHICKEN

prep 25 minutes | **bake** 1-1/4 hours

1/2 cup all-purpose flour
1/2 teaspoon salt
1/4 teaspoon pepper
1/4 teaspoon paprika
1 broiler/fryer chicken (3 to 4 pounds), cut up
2 tablespoons butter
2 tablespoons canola oil
1/2 pound sliced fresh mushrooms
1/4 cup chopped onion
3 cans (15-1/2 ounces *each*) black-eyed peas, drained
1/2 teaspoon garlic salt
1/4 teaspoon herbes de Provence
1/2 cup white wine *or* chicken broth
1 medium tomato, chopped

In a large resealable plastic bag, combine the flour, salt, pepper and paprika. Add chicken, a few pieces at a time, and shake to coat. In a large skillet, brown the chicken in butter and oil on all sides. Remove and set aside.

In the same skillet, saute mushrooms and onion until onion is crisp-tender, stirring to loosen browned bits from pan. Stir in the peas, garlic salt and herbes de Provence. Transfer to an ungreased 13-in. x 9-in. baking dish.

Arrange chicken over pea mixture. Pour wine or broth over chicken; sprinkle with tomato. Cover and bake at 325° for 1-1/4 to 1-1/2 hours or until chicken juices run clear. **yield:** 6 servings.

editor's note: Look for herbes de Provence in the spice aisle. It is also available from Penzeys Spices. Call 1-800/741-7787 or visit www.penzeys.com.

fran dell

las vegas, nevada

When I came across this recipe many years ago, I knew I had a newfound family favorite on my hands. The chicken always turns out moist and tender.

CHICKEN SHEPHERD'S PIE

prep 25 minutes | **bake** 25 minutes

2 boneless skinless chicken breast halves (6 ounces *each*), cubed
4 tablespoons butter, *divided*
1 pouch (3.6 ounces) roasted garlic mashed potatoes
3 tablespoons all-purpose flour
2-1/4 cups milk
1 teaspoon rubbed sage
1 teaspoon dried thyme
1/2 teaspoon salt
1/2 teaspoon pepper
1 cup (4 ounces) shredded Swiss cheese, *divided*
1 cup fresh sugar snap peas, trimmed and chopped
1/2 cup frozen corn

In a small skillet, cook the chicken in 1 tablespoon butter until no longer pink; set aside and keep warm. Prepare the mashed potatoes according to package directions.

Meanwhile, in a large saucepan, melt remaining butter over medium heat. Whisk in flour until smooth. Gradually add milk; stir in seasonings. Bring to a boil. Reduce heat; cook and stir for 1-2 minutes or thickened.

Remove from the heat. Stir in 3/4 cup Swiss cheese until melted. Add peas, corn and chicken. Transfer to a 2-qt. baking dish coated with cooking spray. Top with mashed potatoes; sprinkle with remaining cheese.

Bake, uncovered, at 350° for 25-30 minutes or until heated through. Let stand for 5 minutes before serving. **yield:** 6 servings.

taste of home test kitchen
greendale, wisconsin

Warm up your family with this easy mashed-potato-topped casserole featuring tender chicken, sweet corn and sugar snap peas in a homemade cheese sauce.

CASHEW CHICKEN CASSEROLE

prep 15 minutes | **bake** 35 minutes

julie ridlon
solway, minnesota

I especially like this dish because I can get it ready the day before I need it. It's easy to whip up with common pantry items, including macaroni, canned soup and saltine crackers.

2 cups uncooked elbow macaroni
3 cups cubed cooked chicken
1/2 cup process cheese (Velveeta)
1 small onion, chopped
1/2 cup chopped celery
1/2 cup chopped green pepper
1 can (8 ounces) sliced water chestnuts, drained
1 can (10-3/4 ounces) condensed cream of mushroom soup, undiluted
1 can (10-3/4 ounces) condensed cream of chicken soup, undiluted
1-1/3 cups milk

1 can (14-1/2 ounces) chicken broth
1/4 cup butter, melted
2/3 cup crushed saltines (about 20 crackers)
3/4 cup cashew halves

In a greased 13-in. x 9-in. baking dish, layer the first seven ingredients in the order listed. In a large bowl, combine the soups, milk and chicken broth. Pour over the water chestnuts. Cover and refrigerate overnight.

Toss butter and cracker crumbs; sprinkle over casserole. Top with cashews. Bake, uncovered, at 350° for 35-40 minutes or until macaroni is tender. **yield:** 6 servings.

WILD RICE CHICKEN CASSEROLE

prep 15 minutes | **bake** 30 minutes

mrs. darrell plinsky
wichita, kansas

My husband of 51 years loves to eat and I love to cook, so we're both happy when I make this casserole. It's nice and creamy with a little crunch from almonds. The chicken is canned, but you'd never know it.

1	package (6 ounces) long grain and wild rice
1/3	cup chopped onion
3	tablespoons chopped almonds
2	tablespoons dried parsley flakes
1/4	cup butter, cubed
1/3	cup all-purpose flour
2	cups milk
1-1/2	cups chicken broth
1/2	to 1 teaspoon salt
1/4	teaspoon pepper
1	can (10 ounces) chunk white chicken, drained

Prepare the rice according to package directions. Meanwhile, in a small skillet, saute the onion, almonds and parsley flakes in butter for 4-5 minutes or until the onion is tender and the almonds are lightly toasted.

In a large bowl, combine the flour, milk, broth, salt and pepper until smooth. Stir in the chicken, rice and onion mixture.

Pour into a greased 13-in. x 9-in. baking dish (mixture will be thin). Bake, uncovered, at 425° for 30-35 minutes or until bubbly and golden brown. **yield**: 4-6 servings.

LOVE ME TENDER CHICKEN BAKE

prep 25 minutes | **bake** 20 minutes

2	medium onions, chopped
6	celery ribs, chopped
1/2	cup butter, cubed
5	cups cubed cooked chicken
3/4	cup water
2	cans (10-3/4 ounces *each*) condensed cream of mushroom soup, undiluted
1	cup (8 ounces) sour cream
2	cans (8 ounces *each*) sliced water chestnuts, drained
1	cup sliced almonds, toasted
1	cup crushed butter-flavored crackers

In a large skillet, saute onions and celery in butter until tender. Add chicken and water; heat through. Remove from the heat. Stir in the soup, sour cream, water chestnuts and almonds.

Pour into eight greased 1-1/2-cup baking dishes. Sprinkle with cracker crumbs. Bake, uncovered, at 400° for 20-25 minutes or until bubbly. **yield**: 8 servings.

alcy thorne
los molinos, california

This dish lives up to its name. Basking in a rich, creamy broth and topped with buttery cracker crumbs, the chicken breast pieces melt in your mouth. Even Elvis couldn't have resisted this heart-warming dish.

ZESTY CHICKEN CASSEROLE

prep 15 minutes | **bake** 55 minutes

dianne spurlock
dayton, ohio

Broccoli, chicken and rice get a little "zip" from Italian salad dressing. Anyone who favors food with lots of flavor will enjoy it.

2 cups uncooked instant rice
1 package (16 ounces) frozen broccoli cuts, thawed
1 medium onion, chopped
1 celery rib, chopped
2 tablespoons minced fresh parsley
1 teaspoon salt
6 boneless skinless chicken breast halves (4 ounces *each*)
1 can (10-3/4 ounces) condensed cream of celery soup, undiluted
1-1/4 cups water
3/4 cup process cheese sauce
1/2 cup Italian salad dressing
1/2 cup milk
Fresh red currants, optional

Place rice in a greased 13-in. x 9-in. baking dish. Top with the broccoli, onion, celery, parsley and salt. Arrange chicken over vegetables.

In a large saucepan, combine the soup, water, cheese sauce, salad dressing and milk. Cook and stir until cheese sauce is melted and mixture is smooth. Pour over chicken.

Cover and bake at 375° for 45 minutes. Uncover; bake 10-15 minutes longer or until the chicken juices run clear and the rice and vegetables are tender. Garnish with red currants if desired. **yield:** 6 servings.

CHICKEN TATER BAKE

prep 20 minutes | **bake** 40 minutes

2 cans (10-3/4 ounces *each*) condensed cream of chicken soup, undiluted
1/2 cup milk
1/4 cup butter, cubed
3 cups cubed cooked chicken
1 package (16 ounces) frozen peas and carrots, thawed
1-1/2 cups (6 ounces) shredded cheddar cheese, *divided*
1 package (32 ounces) frozen Tater Tots

In a large saucepan, combine the soup, milk and butter. Cook and stir over medium heat until heated through. Remove from the heat; stir in the chicken, peas and carrots, and 1 cup cheese.

Transfer to two greased 8-in. square baking dishes. Top with the Tater Tots; sprinkle with the remaining cheese.

Cover and freeze one casserole for up to 3 months. Cover and bake the remaining casserole at 350° for 35 minutes. Uncover; bake 5-10 minutes longer or until heated through.

To use frozen casserole: Remove from the freezer 30 minutes before baking (do not thaw). Cover and bake at 350° for 1-1/2 to 1-3/4 hours or until heated through. **yield:** 2 casseroles (6 servings each).

fran allen
st. louis, missouri

It's easy to please everyone in the family with this warm and comforting dish that tastes like a chicken potpie with a Tater Tot crust!

CURRIED CHICKEN WITH ASPARAGUS

prep 20 minutes | **bake** 25 minutes

- 1   can (10-3/4 ounces) condensed cream of chicken soup, undiluted
- 1/3 cup mayonnaise
- 1   teaspoon lemon juice
- 1/2 teaspoon curry powder
- 1/8 teaspoon pepper
- 1   package (10 ounces) frozen asparagus spears, thawed
- 1   pound boneless skinless chicken breasts, cut into 1/2-inch pieces
- 2   tablespoons canola oil
- 1/4 cup shredded cheddar cheese

In a large bowl, combine the soup, mayonnaise, lemon juice, curry and pepper; set aside.

Place half of the asparagus spears in a greased 8-in. square baking dish. Spread with half of the soup mixture.

In a large skillet, saute chicken in oil until no longer pink. Place chicken over soup mixture. Top with remaining asparagus and soup mixture.

Cover and bake at 375° for 20 minutes. Uncover; sprinkle with cheese. Bake 5-8 minutes longer or until cheese is melted. **yield**: 4 servings.

editor's note: Reduced-fat or fat-free mayonnaise is not recommended for this recipe.

miriam christophel

battle creek, michigan

A mild curry sauce nicely coats tender chicken and asparagus in this "must-have" recipe. It's a classic dish I've used for years.

CHICKEN AMANDINE

prep 35 minutes | **bake** 30 minutes

kat woolbright
wichita falls, texas

With colorful green beans and pimientos, this attractive casserole is particularly well-suited for the holidays. This is true comfort food at its finest.

1/4 cup chopped onion
1 tablespoon butter
1 package (6 ounces) long grain and wild rice
2-1/4 cups chicken broth
3 cups cubed cooked chicken
2 cups frozen French-style green beans, thawed
1 can (10-3/4 ounces) condensed cream of chicken soup, undiluted
3/4 cup sliced almonds, *divided*
1 jar (4 ounces) diced pimientos, drained
1 teaspoon pepper

1/2 teaspoon garlic powder
1 bacon strip, cooked and crumbled

In a large saucepan, saute onion in butter until tender. Add rice with contents of seasoning packet and broth. Bring to a boil. Reduce heat; cover and simmer for 25 minutes or until liquid is absorbed. Uncover; set aside to cool.

In a large bowl, combine the chicken, green beans, soup, 1/2 cup of almonds, pimientos, pepper and garlic powder. Stir in rice.

Transfer to a greased 2-1/2-qt. baking dish. Sprinkle with bacon and remaining almonds. Cover and bake at 350° for 30-35 minutes or until heated through. **yield:** 8 servings.

CHICKEN STROGANOFF

prep/total time 20 minutes

phyllis brittenham
garwin, iowa

I concocted this recipe for those evenings when I'm running late and everyone is hungry. Even my finicky 4-year-old asks for seconds.

4 cups uncooked egg noodles
2 cups cubed cooked chicken
1-1/2 cups (12 ounces) sour cream
1 can (10-3/4 ounces) condensed cream of mushroom soup, undiluted
1/2 teaspoon seasoned salt
1/4 teaspoon pepper
Minced fresh parsley, optional

Cook noodles according to package directions; drain. In a greased 2-qt. microwave-safe dish, combine the chicken, sour cream, soup, seasoned salt and pepper. Stir in the noodles.

Cover and microwave on high for 3-6 minutes or until heated through. Sprinkle with parsley if desired. Let stand for 5 minutes before serving. **yield:** 4-6 servings.

editor's note: This recipe was tested in a 1,100-watt microwave.

CHICKEN SPAGHETTI CASSEROLE

prep 20 minutes | **bake** 40 minutes

8 ounces uncooked spaghetti
1 cup ricotta cheese
1 cup (4 ounces) shredded part-skim mozzarella cheese, *divided*
2 tablespoons grated Parmesan cheese
1/2 teaspoon Italian seasoning
1/2 teaspoon garlic powder
1 jar (26 ounces) meatless spaghetti sauce
1 can (14-1/2 ounces) Italian diced tomatoes, undrained
1 jar (4-1/2 ounces) sliced mushrooms, drained
4 breaded fully cooked chicken patties (10 to 14 ounces)

Cook the spaghetti according to package directions. Meanwhile, in a large bowl, combine the ricotta, 1/2 cup of mozzarella, Parmesan, Italian seasoning and garlic powder; set aside. In another bowl, combine the spaghetti sauce, diced tomatoes and mushrooms.

Drain the spaghetti; add 2 cups sauce mixture and toss to coat. Transfer to a greased 13-in. x 9-in. baking dish; top with cheese mixture.

Arrange chicken patties over the top; drizzle with the remaining spaghetti sauce mixture. Sprinkle with the remaining mozzarella. Bake, uncovered, at 350° for 40-45 minutes or until bubbly. **yield:** 4 servings.

bernice janowski
stevens point, wisconsin

I first made this hearty meal-in-one when I had unexpected guests. It's popular when I'm in a hurry, because it takes only 20 minutes to assemble.

OVEN

MARVELOUS CHICKEN ENCHILADAS, P. 180

THAI CHICKEN PIZZAS

prep/total time 20 minutes

lynette randleman
buffalo, wyoming

I found a recipe like this in a cookbook and modified it by cutting down on the peanut butter. I added the cilantro for more flavor.

4   whole wheat tortillas (8 inches)
1/4   cup reduced-fat creamy peanut butter
2   tablespoons reduced-sodium soy sauce
4-1/2   teaspoons honey
2-1/4   teaspoons rice vinegar
2   cups shredded cooked chicken breast
2   small carrots, shredded

1/2   cup minced fresh cilantro
1   cup (4 ounces) shredded part-skim mozzarella cheese

Coat both sides of tortillas with cooking spray; place on ungreased baking sheets. In a small bowl, combine the peanut butter, soy sauce, honey and vinegar. Stir in chicken until blended. Spread over tortillas. Top with carrots, cilantro and cheese.

Bake at 400° for 10-12 minutes or until cheese is melted. **yield:** 4 servings.

CHICKEN CORDON BLEU CALZONES

prep 40 minutes | **bake** 15 minutes

4   boneless skinless chicken breasts (4 ounces *each*)
1   cup sliced fresh mushrooms
1/2   medium onion, chopped
2   tablespoons butter
3   tablespoons cornstarch
1-1/4   cups milk
1   tablespoon minced fresh basil *or* 1 teaspoon dried basil
1   teaspoon salt
1/4   teaspoon pepper
1   package (17.3 ounces) frozen puff pastry, thawed
8   thin slices deli ham
4   slices provolone cheese
Additional milk, optional

Place chicken in a greased 2-qt. baking dish; cover with water. Cover and bake at 350° for 30 minutes or until juices run clear.

Meanwhile, in a small skillet, saute mushrooms and onion in butter until tender. Combine cornstarch and milk until smooth; stir into skillet. Add seasonings. Bring to a boil; cook and stir for 2 minutes or until thickened.

Drain the chicken. Cut puff pastry sheets in half widthwise. On one side of each half, place a chicken breast, 1/4 cup mushroom mixture, two ham slices and one cheese slice. Fold the pastry over the filling and seal edges.

Place on a greased baking sheet. Brush tops with milk if desired. Bake at 400° for 15-20 minutes or until puffed and golden. **yield:** 4 servings.

kathy gounaud
warwick, rhode island

This recipe combines two classic recipes. The delicate flavor of chicken cordon bleu with the impressive look of beef Wellington makes a winning meal.

ROASTED CHICKEN WITH GARLIC-SHERRY SAUCE

prep 30 minutes + marinating | **bake** 20 minutes

2 quarts water
1/2 cup salt
4 bone-in chicken breast halves
(12 ounces *each*)
3/4 teaspoon pepper, *divided*
2 teaspoons canola oil
8 garlic cloves, peeled and thinly sliced
1 cup reduced-sodium chicken broth
1/2 cup sherry *or* additional reduced-sodium chicken broth
3 fresh thyme sprigs
1/4 cup butter, cubed
1 teaspoon lemon juice

For brine, in a large saucepan, bring water and salt to a boil. Cook and stir until salt is dissolved. Remove from the heat; cool to room temperature.

Place a large heavy-duty resealable plastic bag inside a second large resealable plastic bag; add the chicken. Carefully pour the cooled brine into the bag. Squeeze out as much air as possible; seal both bags and turn to coat. Refrigerate for 1-2 hours, turning several times.

Drain and discard brine. Rinse chicken with cold water; pat dry. Sprinkle with 1/2 teaspoon pepper. In a large ovenproof skillet, brown chicken in oil over medium heat.

Bake, uncovered, at 400° for 20-25 minutes or until juices run clear. Remove chicken and keep warm. Drain drippings, reserving 1 tablespoon.

In the drippings, saute the garlic until tender. Add the broth, sherry or additional broth and thyme sprigs. Bring to a boil; cook until liquid is reduced to 1 cup. Discard thyme. Stir in the butter, lemon juice and remaining pepper. Serve with the chicken. **yield:** 4 servings.

sheri sidwell
alton, illinois

This garlic-kissed chicken is delicious. It's an elegant entree for guests, and my husband and I love to use the leftovers in rice casseroles and hot, open-faced sandwiches.

CHICKEN WITH CHEESE SAUCE

prep 20 minutes + marinating | **bake** 35 minutes

joyce breeding
falkville, alabama

Dinner guests are always impressed when I serve this appetizing main dish. It's a delicious and pretty way to dress up plain boneless chicken breasts.

4   boneless skinless chicken breast halves (4 ounces *each*)
1/2   cup Italian salad dressing, *divided*
1/4   cup chopped onion
1   cup crushed saltines (about 30 crackers), *divided*
1   package (10 ounces) frozen chopped spinach, thawed and drained
2   tablespoons minced fresh parsley
2   tablespoons butter
1   envelope white sauce mix
2   cups milk
2/3   cup shredded Swiss cheese
Ground nutmeg, optional

Flatten chicken to 1/8-in. thickness. Place in a resealable plastic bag; add 1/4 cup salad dressing. Seal bag and turn to coat; refrigerate for 2 hours.

In a large skillet, saute onion in remaining salad dressing. Add 1/2 cup cracker crumbs, spinach and parsley. Cook for 5 minutes or until heated through. Remove from the heat.

Drain and discard marinade from chicken. Spoon about 1/2 cup spinach mixture on each chicken breast; roll up and overlap ends. Secure with a toothpick. Roll in remaining crumbs.

Place in a greased 9-in. square baking dish. Bake, uncovered, at 375° for 35 minutes or until chicken juices run clear.

Meanwhile, melt butter in a saucepan. Stir in the white sauce mix until smooth; gradually stir in milk. Bring to boil; cook and stir for 2 minutes or until thickened. Reduce heat; stir in cheese until melted. Serve with chicken. Sprinkle with nutmeg if desired. **yield:** 4 servings.

CHICKEN SUPREME

prep 15 minutes | **bake** 30 minutes

This chicken recipe is lower in calories, fat or sodium.

1/2   cup dry bread crumbs
1/2   cup grated Parmesan cheese
2   tablespoons minced fresh parsley
1   garlic clove, minced
1/4   teaspoon pepper
3   egg whites
6   boneless skinless chicken breast halves (4 ounces *each*)
1/4   cup sliced almonds
Refrigerated butter-flavored spray

candace black
durham, north carolina

I received this wonderful recipe from a friend at church. A light breading seals in the juices of tender chicken breasts, making them special enough to serve company. Sliced almonds top off the eye-catching entree.

In a shallow bowl, combine the first five ingredients. In another shallow bowl, beat the egg whites. Dip chicken in egg whites, then coat with crumb mixture. Place in a 13-in. x 9-in. baking dish coated with cooking spray.

Sprinkle almonds over chicken. Spritz with butter-flavored spray. Bake, uncovered, at 350° for 30 minutes or until chicken juices run clear. **yield:** 6 servings.

nutrition facts: 1 serving equals 224 calories, 6 g fat (2 g saturated fat), 71 mg cholesterol, 304 mg sodium, 8 g carbohydrate, 1 g fiber, 33 g protein.

diabetic exchanges: 3-1/2 lean meat, 1/2 starch.

INDIVIDUAL CHICKEN POTPIES

prep 40 minutes | **bake** 25 minutes

vickie wicks

saint joseph, missouri

These little pies look so appetizing with their paprika-sprinkled crust and colorful veggies in a saucy filling. Always well-received by guests, they taste elegantly rich. Sometimes, I adapt the recipe to make one large casserole.

1/4 cup chopped onion
2 tablespoons chopped green pepper
1/4 cup butter, cubed
1/3 cup all-purpose flour
1 can (14-1/2 ounces) chicken broth
1 cup milk
1 cup fresh broccoli florets
1/2 cup fresh cauliflowerets
1/2 cup thinly sliced celery
1/2 cup thinly sliced carrot
1 cup (4 ounces) shredded Swiss cheese
2 cups cubed cooked chicken

PASTRY
1-1/3 cups all-purpose flour
1/2 teaspoon salt
1/2 teaspoon paprika
1/2 cup shortening
3 to 4 tablespoons cold water

In a large saucepan, saute the onion and green pepper in butter until onion is tender. Add flour until blended. Stir in the broth, milk, broccoli, cauliflower, celery and carrot. Bring to a boil; cook and stir for 2 minutes or until thickened. Remove from the heat. Stir in cheese. Divide chicken among four ungreased 1-1/2-cup baking dishes. Top with the vegetable mixture.

For the pastry, combine the flour, salt and paprika in a bowl; cut in shortening until crumbly. Gradually add water, tossing with a fork until dough forms a ball. Divide into four portions; roll out each to 1/8-in. thickness. Place the pastry over the vegetable mixture. Trim the pastry to 1/2 in. beyond edge of dish; flute edges. Cut slits in top. Bake at 350° for 30-40 minutes or until golden brown. **yield:** 4 servings.

GARLIC-ROASTED CHICKEN

prep 10 minutes | **bake** 1 hour

6 medium chicken drumsticks
6 medium bone-in chicken thighs
6 medium potatoes, peeled and quartered
12 extra-large unpeeled garlic cloves
1/4 cup butter, melted
1 teaspoon salt
1/4 cup honey

Place the chicken drumsticks and thighs, potatoes and garlic in a large roasting pan. Pour butter over all and sprinkle with salt.

Bake at 400° for 40 minutes or until a meat thermometer reaches 170°, basting frequently with the pan juices. Heat honey; drizzle over chicken. Remove the chicken, potatoes and garlic to a serving platter; keep warm. Pour drippings and loosened brown bits into a measuring cup; skim fat. Serve with the chicken, potatoes and garlic. **yield:** 6 servings.

editor's note: Each person can cut through the garlic cloves and spread the soft roasted garlic pulp over chicken and potatoes.

michelle bouchard

st. jean-baptiste, manitoba

While growing up on a farm, I helped out with the meals. I wasn't the greatest cook when I started, but after 10 years of marriage, I've improved! I serve this roasted chicken as a "treat" on weekends. Everyone loves it, and there are rarely leftovers.

PESTO CHICKEN LASAGNA

prep 30 minutes | **bake** 55 minutes + standing

michelle larson
eveleth, minnesota

Pesto really perks up this scrumptious chicken lasagna. Plus, the marinara sauce adds a touch of sweetness. To complete the meal, serve it with warm bread and a salad.

1	large sweet red pepper, diced
1/4	cup diced onion
4	garlic cloves, minced
1	tablespoon butter
1/4	cup all-purpose flour
2	cups milk
1/4	cup chicken broth
1-1/2	teaspoons dried basil
1	teaspoon dried oregano
2	cups cubed cooked chicken
1/2	cup prepared pesto
1	can (3.8 ounces) sliced ripe olives, drained
1	egg, lightly beaten
1	carton (15 ounces) ricotta cheese
1	package (4 ounces) crumbled feta cheese
2	cups marinara sauce
12	no-cook lasagna noodles
1	package (6 ounces) fresh baby spinach, chopped
2	cups (8 ounces) shredded part-skim mozzarella cheese

In a large saucepan, saute red pepper, onion and garlic in butter until tender. Stir in flour until blended. Gradually stir in milk, broth, basil and oregano. Bring to a boil over medium heat; cook and stir for 2 minutes or until thickened. Stir in the chicken, pesto and olives. Remove from heat. In a large bowl, combine egg, ricotta and feta.

Spread 1 cup marinara sauce in a greased 13-in. x 9-in. baking dish. Layer with four noodles, half of the ricotta mixture, half of the spinach, half of the pesto mixture and 2/3 cup mozzarella cheese. Repeat layers. Top with the remaining noodles, sauce and mozzarella.

Cover and bake at 375° for 45 minutes. Uncover; bake 10 minutes more or until bubbly. Let stand 15 minutes before serving. **yield:** 12 servings.

CIDER-ROASTED CHICKEN

prep 15 minutes | **bake** 3-3/4 hours + standing

mary dunphy

stephenville,
newfoundland and labrador

*I've never shared this recipe
before, even with members
of my own family. I use it
only for special occasions
such as Christmas. My six
children love it, and its
also won several
cooking contests.*

1	whole roasting chicken (5 to 7 pounds)
1/4	cup butter
2-1/2	cups apple cider
6	to 8 small unpeeled red potatoes, quartered
6	to 8 small onions, peeled and quartered
1	to 2 medium green peppers, cut into strips
6	to 8 bacon strips
2	to 4 small tomatoes, quartered

Place the chicken, breast side up, on a rack in a roasting pan; dot with butter. Bake, uncovered, at 375° for 15 minutes. Reduce the heat to 325°; bake for 2 hours.

Pour cider over chicken. Add the potatoes, onions and peppers to the pan; place bacon over chicken breast. Bake 1 hour longer, basting often.

Add the tomatoes to the pan. Bake 30 minutes longer or until a meat thermometer reads 180°. Cover and let stand 10 minutes before carving. Thicken the pan juices for gravy if desired. **yield:** 6 servings.

CHICKEN-STUFFED CUBANELLE PEPPERS

prep 20 minutes | **bake** 55 minutes

This chicken recipe is lower in calories, fat or sodium.

6	Cubanelle peppers *or* mild banana peppers
2	eggs
1	cup salsa
3	cups shredded cooked chicken breast
3/4	cup soft bread crumbs
1/2	cup cooked long grain rice
2	cups meatless spaghetti sauce, *divided*

Cut the tops off peppers and remove the seeds. In a bowl, combine the eggs, salsa, shredded chicken breast, bread crumbs and cooked rice. Spoon into hollowed out peppers.

Coat 13-in. x 9-in. baking dish and an 8-in. square baking dish with cooking spray. Spread 1 cup sauce in larger pan and 1/2 cup sauce in smaller pan. Place peppers over sauce. Spoon remaining spaghetti sauce over peppers. Cover; bake at 350° for 55-60 minutes or until peppers are tender. **yield:** 6 servings.

nutrition facts: 1 stuffed pepper equals 230 calories, 4 g fat (1 g saturated fat), 125 mg cholesterol, 661 mg sodium, 20 g carbohydrate, 5 g fiber, 26 g protein.

diabetic exchanges: 3 very lean meat, 2 vegetable, 1 starch.

bev burlingame

canton, ohio

*Here's a new take on
traditional stuffed peppers.
I use chicken instead of beef
and Cubanelle peppers
in place of the usual
green peppers.*

POTATO-CRUST CHICKEN QUICHE

prep 10 minutes | **bake** 40 minutes

halina d'arienzo

murrells inlet,
south carolina

*Shredded hash browns
form the golden crust in
this comforting quiche.
Sometimes I'll substitute
diced cooked ham, flaked
tuna or sliced mushrooms
for the chicken in this
favorite recipe of mine.*

4   cups frozen shredded hash brown
     potatoes, thawed
3   tablespoons butter, melted
1   cup (4 ounces) shredded pepper
     Jack cheese
1   cup diced cooked chicken
4   eggs
1   cup half-and-half cream *or* milk
1/2 teaspoon salt

Pat the hash browns with paper towels to remove excess moisture. Press into a well-greased 9-in. pie plate; brush with melted butter. Bake at 425° for 20-25 minutes or until lightly browned. Reduce the heat to 350°.

Sprinkle cheese and chicken into the crust. In a bowl, beat the eggs, cream and salt; pour over chicken. Bake for 20-25 minutes or until a knife inserted near the center comes out clean. Let stand for 5 minutes before cutting. **yield:** 6-8 servings.

CUMIN CHICKEN WITH APPLES

prep 20 minutes | **bake** 1 hour

4   chicken legs with thighs
2   tablespoons butter
2   medium apples, chopped
2   small onions, halved and sliced
1   can (4-1/2 ounces) mushroom
     stems and pieces, drained
1   tablespoon all-purpose flour
1   can (10-3/4 ounces) condensed
     cream of mushroom soup,
     undiluted
1/2 cup water
1   tablespoon ground cumin
1   teaspoon Worcestershire sauce
3/4 teaspoon salt

1/4 teaspoon pepper
1/4 teaspoon chili powder
Hot cooked rice

In a large skillet, brown the chicken in butter. Transfer to a greased 13-in. x 9-in. baking dish. In the drippings, saute apples, onions and mushrooms until apples are crisp-tender. Stir in the flour, soup, water, cumin, Worcestershire sauce, salt and pepper. Pour over the chicken.

Cover and bake at 350° for 1 hour or until a meat thermometer reads 180° Sprinkle with chili powder. Serve with rice. **yield:** 4 servings.

raymonde bourgeois

swastika, ontario

*A mixture of onions, apples
and mushrooms seasoned
with cumin and
Worcestershire sauce
further enhances the
already excellent flavor of
this tender chicken dish.*

ROASTED CHICKEN WITH ROSEMARY

prep 20 minutes | **bake** 2 hours + standing

- 1/2 cup butter
- 4 tablespoons minced fresh *or* 2 tablespoons dried rosemary, crushed
- 2 tablespoons minced fresh parsley
- 3 garlic cloves, minced
- 1 teaspoon salt
- 1/2 teaspoon pepper
- 1 whole roasting chicken (5 to 6 pounds)
- 6 small red potatoes, halved
- 6 medium carrots, halved lengthwise and cut into 2-inch pieces
- 2 medium onions, quartered

In a small saucepan, melt the butter and stir in the seasonings. Place the chicken, breast side up, on a rack in a roasting pan; tie the drumsticks together with kitchen string. Spoon half of the butter mixture over the chicken. Place potatoes, carrots and onions around chicken. Drizzle the remaining butter mixture over the vegetables.

Cover and bake at 350° for 1-1/2 hours, basting every 30 minutes. Uncover; bake 30-60 minutes more or until a meat thermometer reads 180° and vegetables are tender, basting occasionally.

Cover with aluminum foil and let stand for 10-15 minutes before carving. Serve the vegetables with roast. **yield:** 9 servings.

isabel zienkosky
salt lake city, utah

This is a lot like pot roast, only it uses chicken instead of beef. Rosemary provides an herby, aromatic flavor that blends well with the garlic, butter and parsley.

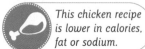

This chicken recipe is lower in calories, fat or sodium.

MARVELOUS CHICKEN ENCHILADAS

prep 30 minutes | **bake** 25 minutes

rebekah sabo
rochester, new york

I love Mexican food, and this is one of my favorite dishes. For a milder flavor, try using Monterey Jack cheese in place of the cheddar.

1	pound boneless skinless chicken breasts, cut into thin strips
4	teaspoons chili powder
2	teaspoons olive oil
2	tablespoons all-purpose flour
1-1/2	teaspoons ground coriander
1	teaspoon baking cocoa
1	cup fat-free milk
1	cup frozen corn, thawed
4	green onions, chopped
1	can (4 ounces) chopped green chilies, drained
1/2	teaspoon salt
1/2	cup minced fresh cilantro, *divided*
6	whole wheat tortillas (8 inches)
1/2	cup salsa
1/2	cup tomato sauce
1/2	cup shredded reduced-fat cheddar cheese

Sprinkle the chicken with chili powder. In a large nonstick skillet coated with cooking spray, cook the chicken in olive oil over medium heat until the juices run clear. Sprinkle with flour, coriander and cocoa; stir until blended.

Gradually stir in milk. Bring to a boil; cook and stir for 2 minutes or until thickened. Add the corn, onions, chilies and salt; cook and stir 2 minutes longer or until heated through. Remove from the heat. Stir in 1/4 cup cilantro.

Spread 2/3 cup filling down center of each tortilla. Roll up and place seam side down in a 13-in. x 9-in. baking dish coated with cooking spray.

In a small bowl, combine the salsa, tomato sauce and remaining cilantro; pour over the enchiladas. Sprinkle with the cheese. Cover and bake at 375° for 25 minutes or until heated through. **yield:** 6 enchiladas.

nutrition facts: 1 enchilada equals 270 calories, 7 g fat (2 g saturated fat), 49 mg cholesterol, 768 mg sodium, 35 g carbohydrate, 4 g fiber, 24 g protein.

diabetic exchanges: 2 starch, 2 very lean meat, 1 fat.

SPINACH CRAB CHICKEN

prep 45 minutes | **cook** 40 minutes

vicki melies

elkhorn, nebraska

I altered a friend's recipe for crab-stuffed chicken to include one of my favorite vegetables, spinach. Now my husband requests this elegant entree all the time. Served over rice, it's special enough for company.

1/2	cup finely chopped onion
1/4	cup chopped fresh mushrooms
1/4	cup finely chopped celery
3	tablespoons butter
3	tablespoons all-purpose flour
1/2	teaspoon salt, *divided*
1	cup chicken broth
1/2	cup milk
4	boneless skinless chicken breast halves (6 ounces *each*)
1/8	teaspoon white pepper
1/2	cup dry bread crumbs
1	can (6 ounces) crabmeat, drained, flaked and cartilage removed
12	fresh spinach leaves, chopped
1	tablespoon minced fresh parsley
1	cup (4 ounces) shredded Swiss cheese
	Hot cooked rice

For the sauce, in a large skillet, saute the onion, mushrooms and celery in butter until tender. Stir in the flour and 1/4 teaspoon salt until blended. Gradually add the broth and milk. Bring to a boil; cook and stir for 1-2 minutes or until thickened. Remove from the heat.

Flatten chicken to 1/4-in. thickness; sprinkle with the pepper and remaining salt. In a large bowl, combine the bread crumbs, crab, spinach and parsley; stir in 1/2 cup sauce. Spoon 1/4 cup down the center of each chicken breast half. Roll up; secure with toothpicks. Place seam side down in a greased 13-in. x 9-in. baking dish. Top with the remaining sauce.

Cover and bake at 375° for 35-45 minutes or until juices run clear. Sprinkle with cheese. Broil 4-6 in. from the heat for 5 minutes or until lightly browned. Discard toothpicks. Serve with rice. **yield:** 4 servings.

PRETZEL-CRUSTED DRUMSTICKS

prep 10 minutes | **bake** 50 minutes

1/2	cup butter, melted
1	teaspoon cayenne pepper
1/8	teaspoon garlic powder
1	cup finely crushed pretzels
1/4	cup chopped pecans
1/2	teaspoon pepper
1-1/2	to 2 pounds chicken drumsticks

In a shallow bowl, combine the butter, cayenne and garlic powder. In another shallow bowl, combine the pretzels, pecans and pepper. Dip chicken in butter mixture, then roll in pretzel mixture.

Place in a greased 13-in. x 9-in. baking dish. Bake, uncovered, at 350° for 50-55 minutes or until a meat thermometer reads 180°, turning once. **yield:** 5 servings.

joann frazier hensley

mcgaheysville, virginia

Crushed salty pretzels make the perfect coating for chicken drumsticks. With this baked recipe, you won't miss traditional fried chicken one bit.

ORANGE CHICKEN KIEV

prep 50 minutes | **bake** 35 minutes

arlene kay butler
ogden, utah

My favorite meal features these golden crumb-coated chicken rolls with a savory chive filling. They have a lovely orange flavor that isn't overwhelming. To round out the meal for Sunday dinner or a party, serve with rice or potatoes.

1/2 cup butter, softened
2 tablespoons minced chives
2 tablespoons minced fresh parsley
1/4 teaspoon salt
1/8 teaspoon pepper
6 boneless skinless chicken breast halves (6 ounces *each*)
1/4 cup all-purpose flour
1 egg
1/4 cup orange juice
1 cup dry bread crumbs
1/2 teaspoon grated orange peel

In a large bowl, combine the butter, chives, parsley, salt and pepper. Shape into a 6-in. x 2-in. rectangle; place on waxed paper. Freeze until firm, about 30 minutes.

Flatten chicken to 1/4-in. thickness. Cut butter mixture into six strips; place one strip in the center of each chicken breast half. Roll up and tuck in ends; secure with a toothpick.

Place the flour in a shallow bowl. In another bowl, beat egg and orange juice. In a third bowl, combine bread crumbs and orange peel. Coat chicken with flour, dip in egg mixture, then roll in crumb mixture. Place seam side down in a greased 13-in. x 9-in. baking dish.

Bake, uncovered, at 375° for 35-40 minutes or until chicken juices run clear. Discard toothpicks before serving. **yield:** 6 servings.

GOLDEN BAKED CHICKEN

prep 20 minutes | **bake** 50 minutes

2 cups mashed potato flakes
3/4 cup grated Parmesan cheese
2 tablespoons dried parsley flakes
1 tablespoon paprika
3/4 teaspoon garlic salt
3/4 teaspoon onion powder
1/2 teaspoon pepper
1 cup butter, melted
3 broiler/fryer chickens (3 to 4 pounds *each*), cut up and skin removed

In a shallow bowl, combine the potato flakes, Parmesan cheese, parsley, paprika, garlic salt, onion powder and pepper. In another shallow bowl, add the butter. Dip the chicken into butter, then into the potato flake mixture.

Place on two greased 15-in. x 10-in. baking pans. Bake at 375° for 50-60 minutes or until chicken juices run clear. **yield:** 12 servings.

harriet stichter
milford, indiana

This recipe makes a delicious crispy chicken without frying it in oil. The paprika gives the chicken pieces a pleasant punch and a pretty color.

CREAMY CHICKEN LASAGNA

prep 40 minutes | **bake** 45 minutes + standing

12 uncooked lasagna noodles
2 tablespoons cornstarch
1 can (12 ounces) evaporated milk
2 cups chicken broth
1 can (8 ounces) tomato sauce
1/2 cup grated Parmesan cheese
2 garlic cloves, minced
2 teaspoons Dijon mustard
1/2 teaspoon dried basil
1/4 teaspoon ground nutmeg
1/8 teaspoon cayenne pepper
2 cups cooked chicken strips (12 ounces)
24 cherry tomatoes, thinly sliced
1 cup (4 ounces) shredded cheddar cheese
Paprika and minced fresh parsley

Cook noodles according to package directions. Meanwhile, in a large saucepan, combine the cornstarch and milk until smooth. Whisk in the broth, tomato sauce, Parmesan cheese, garlic, mustard, basil, nutmeg and cayenne. Bring to a boil over medium heat; cook and stir for 2 minutes or until thickened. Remove from the heat.

Drain noodles. Spread 1/4 cup sauce into a greased 13-in. x 9-in. baking dish. Set aside 1 cup sauce. Stir chicken and tomatoes into the remaining sauce. Layer four noodles and half of the chicken mixture in baking dish. Repeat layers. Top with remaining noodles; spread with reserved sauce. Sprinkle with cheddar cheese and paprika.

Cover and bake at 350° for 45-50 minutes or until bubbly. Let stand for 15 minutes before cutting. Sprinkle with parsley. **yield:** 9-12 servings.

janice christofferson
eagle river, wisconsin

As a girl, I spent summers on my grandparents' farm and helped harvest bushels of fresh vegetables. To this day, I enjoy making recipes like this lasagna, laden with juicy tomatoes and herbs fresh from my own garden.

PHYLLO CHICKEN PACKETS

prep 20 minutes | **bake** 25 minutes

kristin arnett
elkhorn, wisconsin

I used to make this special recipe when I ran my own catering company years ago. It was often requested.

3/4 cup chopped green onions
3/4 cup mayonnaise
3 tablespoons lemon juice
1-1/2 teaspoons minced garlic, *divided*
1/2 teaspoon dried tarragon
2/3 cup butter, melted
12 sheets sheets phyllo dough (14 inches x 9 inches)
6 boneless skinless chicken breast halves (4 ounces *each*)
Salt and pepper to taste
2 tablespoons grated Parmesan cheese

In a small bowl, combine the onions, mayonnaise, lemon juice, 1 teaspoon garlic and tarragon; set aside. in another small bowl, combine the butter and remaining garlic.

Place one sheet of phyllo dough on a work surface with a short edge facing you. Brush with 2 teaspoons butter mixture; brush to distribute evenly. Repeat with one more sheet of phyllo, brushing with another 2 teaspoons of butter mixture. (Keep remaining phyllo dough covered with plastic wrap to avoid drying out.)

Lightly sprinkle chicken breasts with salt and pepper. Center one chicken breast on the lower third of phyllo. Spread about 3 tablespoons of mayonnaise mixture over chicken breast. Fold bottom edge over chicken, then fold in sides. Roll up jelly-roll style; cover with plastic wrap and set aside. Make five more chicken packets.

Place the packets in an ungreased 15-in. x 10-in. baking pan. Brush the tops with the remaining garlic butter; sprinkle with the cheese. Bake uncovered, at 375° for 25-30 minutes or until a meat thermometer reads 170°. Serve warm. **yield:** 6 servings.

editor's note: Reduced-fat or fat-free mayonnaise is not recommended for this recipe.

CHICKEN IN POTATO BASKETS

prep 20 minutes | **bake** 30 minutes

4-1/2 cups frozen shredded hash brown potatoes, thawed
6 tablespoons butter, melted
1-1/2 teaspoons salt
1/4 teaspoon pepper
FILLING
1/2 cup chopped onion
1/4 cup butter
1/4 cup all-purpose flour
2 teaspoons chicken bouillon granules
1 teaspoon Worcestershire sauce
1/2 teaspoon dried basil
2 cups milk
3 cups cubed cooked chicken
1 cup frozen peas, thawed

In a bowl, combine the potatoes, butter, salt and pepper. Press into six greased 10-oz. custard cups; set aside.

For the filling, in a saucepan, saute the onion in butter. Add the flour, bouillon, Worcestershire sauce and basil. Stir in the milk. Bring to a boil; cook and stir for 2 minutes or until thickened. Add chicken and peas. Spoon into prepared crusts.

Bake, uncovered, at 375° for 30-35 minutes or until crust is golden brown. **yield:** 6 servings.

helen lamison
carnegie, pennsylvania

These petite casseroles with their hash brown crusts are so pretty that I like to serve them for special luncheons. Chock-full of meat and vegetables in a creamy sauce, they're a meal-in-one, and a great way to use up leftover chicken or turkey.

CRESCENT-WRAPPED DRUMSTICKS

prep 50 minutes | **bake** 15 minutes

paula plating
colorado springs,
colorado

*Looking for a different way
to do drumsticks? A friend
shared this recipe with me.
The drums are simmered in
barbecue sauce and then
wrapped in crescent roll
dough that's sprinkled with
Parmesan cheese and
Italian seasoning.*

8   chicken drumsticks
1/4 cup butter
1/2 cup barbecue sauce
1   tube (8 ounces) refrigerated crescent rolls
1   egg, lightly beaten
2   teaspoons grated Parmesan cheese
2   teaspoons Italian seasoning
2   teaspoons sesame seeds, toasted

Remove and discard skin from drumsticks. In a large skillet, melt butter over medium heat; stir in the barbecue sauce. Add drumsticks. Bring to a boil. Reduce heat; cover and simmer for 30 minutes or until a meat thermometer reads 170°, turning occasionally. Remove chicken from pan; cool slightly.

Separate crescent dough into eight triangles; place in a lightly greased 15-in. x 10-in. baking pan. Brush dough with some of the beaten egg; sprinkle with Parmesan cheese and Italian seasoning. Place meaty portion of each drumstick at the tip of each triangle, with bony portion extended beyond one long side of triangle. Wrap drumstick in dough; place seam side down. Brush with remaining egg; sprinkle with sesame seeds.

Bake the wrapped drumsticks at 375° for 13-15 minutes or until golden brown and a meat thermometer reads 180°. **yield:** 4 servings (2 drumsticks each).

BAKED CHICKEN

prep 15 minutes + cooling | **bake** 50 minutes

1   broiler/fryer chicken (3 pounds), cut up
1   tablespoon all-purpose flour
1/4 cup water
1/4 cup packed brown sugar
1/4 cup ketchup
2   tablespoons white vinegar
2   tablespoons lemon juice
2   tablespoons Worcestershire sauce
1   small onion, chopped
1   teaspoon ground mustard
1   teaspoon paprika
1   teaspoon chili powder
1/2 teaspoon salt
1/8 teaspoon pepper

Place the chicken in a greased 13-in. x 9-in. baking dish. In a large saucepan, whisk the flour and water until smooth. Stir in the brown sugar, ketchup, vinegar, lemon juice and Worcestershire sauce. Bring to a boil; cook and stir for 2 minutes or until thickened. Cool.

Stir in the remaining ingredients. Pour over chicken. Cover and refrigerate for 2-4 hours.

Remove the chicken from the refrigerator 30 minutes before baking. Bake, uncovered, at 350° for 50-60 minutes or until the chicken juices run clear. **yield:** 4 servings.

barbara wheeler
sparks glencoe, maryland

*A tangy from-scratch sauce
makes this tender chicken
extra flavorful. My mom is
an excellent cook who has
fixed delicious dishes like
this one for years. If you're
in a hurry, just prepare it
ahead and pop it in the
oven when you get home.*

CHICKEN BISCUIT STEW

prep 30 minutes | **bake** 25 minutes

elmeda johnson
williston, north dakota

A hint of curry powder gives this hearty stew its special flavor. Topped with tasty moist biscuits, it's a favorite with my family.

1 cup julienned carrots
1 cup thinly sliced onion
2 garlic cloves, minced
2 teaspoons olive oil
1 pound boneless skinless chicken breast, cut into 1-inch cubes
1 tablespoon all-purpose flour
1/4 cup water
3 tablespoons white wine *or* chicken broth
1 cup (8 ounces) fat-free plain yogurt
1 cup fresh *or* frozen peas
1/4 teaspoon *each* curry powder, salt, pepper, ground cumin and ginger

BISCUITS

1 cup all-purpose flour
1 teaspoon baking powder
1/4 teaspoon baking soda
1/4 teaspoon salt
4-1/2 teaspoons cold butter
1/2 cup fat-free plain yogurt
1-1/2 teaspoons dried parsley flakes

In a large nonstick skillet, saute the carrots, onion and garlic in oil until tender. Add chicken; cook and stir for 5 minutes. Combine the flour, water and wine or broth until smooth; add to the skillet. Bring to a boil; cook and stir for 2 minutes or until thickened. Reduce heat; stir in yogurt, peas and seasonings. Transfer to a shallow 1-1/2-qt. baking dish coated with cooking spray; keep warm.

For biscuits, combine flour, baking powder, baking soda and salt in a bowl. Cut in butter until crumbly. Stir in yogurt and parsley. Drop eight mounds over warm chicken mixture.

Bake, uncovered, at 350° for 25-35 minutes or until biscuits are golden brown and stew bubbles around the edges. **yield:** 4 servings.

BRUSCHETTA CHICKEN

prep 10 minutes | **bake** 30 minutes

carolin cattoi-demkiw
lethbridge, alberta

My husband and I enjoy serving this tasty chicken to company as well as family. It looks like we fussed, but it's really fast and easy to fix. I have made this dish many times and it usually prompts requests for the recipe.

1/2 cup all-purpose flour
1/2 cup egg substitute
4 boneless skinless chicken breast halves (4 ounces *each*)
1/4 cup grated Parmesan cheese
1/4 cup dry bread crumbs
1 tablespoon butter, melted
2 large tomatoes, seeded and chopped
3 tablespoons minced fresh basil
2 garlic cloves, minced
1 tablespoon olive oil
1/2 teaspoon salt
1/4 teaspoon pepper

Place the flour and eggs in separate shallow bowls. Dip the chicken in flour, then in eggs; place in a greased 13-in. x 9-in. baking dish. Combine the Parmesan cheese, bread crumbs and melted butter; sprinkle over the chicken.

Loosely cover baking dish with foil. Bake at 375° for 20 minutes. Uncover; bake 5-10 minutes longer or until top is browned.

Meanwhile, in a small bowl, combine the remaining ingredients. Spoon over the chicken. Return to the oven for 3-5 minutes or until tomato mixture is heated through. **yield:** 4 servings.

PIZZA CHICKEN ROLL-UPS

prep 10 minutes | **bake** 40 minutes

4 boneless skinless chicken breast halves
12 pepperoni slices
8 slices slices part-skim mozzarella cheese
1 can (15 ounces) pizza sauce

Flatten the chicken to 1/4-in. thickness. Place three slices of pepperoni and one slice of cheese on each. Roll up tightly; secure with toothpicks. Place in a greased 11-in. x 7-in. baking dish. Spoon the pizza sauce over top.

Cover and bake at 350° for 35-40 minutes or until chicken juices run clear. Uncover; top with the remaining cheese. Bake 5 minutes longer or until cheese is melted. **yield:** 4 servings.

tanja penquite
oregon, ohio

I love the chicken roll-ups my mom made, filled with spinach and cream cheese, but my kids wouldn't eat those. So I came up with this pizza-flavored variety.

SAVORY CHICKEN DINNER

prep 10 minutes | **bake** 45 minutes

leslie adams
springfield, missouri

No one would guess that these moist chicken breasts and tender potatoes are seasoned with herb- and garlic-flavored soup mix. The meal-in-one is simple to assemble. And because it all bakes in one dish, there's little cleanup.

2 envelopes savory herb with garlic soup mix
6 tablespoons water
4 boneless skinless chicken breast halves (6 to 8 ounces *each*)
2 large red potatoes, cubed
1 large onion, halved and cut into small wedges

In a small bowl, combine soup mix and water; pour half in a large resealable plastic bag. Add chicken. Seal bag and toss to coat. Pour the remaining soup mix in another large resealable plastic bag. Add potatoes and onion. Seal bag and toss to coat.

Drain and discard marinade from chicken. Transfer to a greased 13-in. x 9-in. baking dish. Pour potato mixture and marinade over chicken.

Bake, uncovered, at 350° for 40-45 minutes or until the vegetables are tender and the chicken juices run clear, stirring vegetables occasionally. **yield:** 4 servings.

CRISPY ONION CHICKEN

prep 10 minutes | **bake** 30 minutes

1/2 cup butter, melted
1 tablespoon Worcestershire sauce
1 teaspoon ground mustard
1/2 teaspoon garlic salt
1/4 teaspoon pepper
1 can (6 ounces) cheddar *or* original french-fried onions, crushed
4 boneless skinless chicken breast halves

In a shallow bowl, combine the melted butter, Worcestershire sauce, mustard, garlic salt and pepper. In another shallow bowl, add 1/2 cup french-fried onions. Dip the chicken in the butter mixture, then coat with onions.

Place in a greased 9-in. square baking pan. Top with remaining onions; drizzle with any remaining butter mixture. Bake, uncovered, at 350° for 30-35 minutes or until the chicken juices run clear. **yield:** 4 servings.

charlotte smith
mcdonald, pennsylvania

My family loves chicken...and I'm always trying new ways to prepare it. This golden brown chicken with its crunchy french-fried onion coating is great with rice, baked potatoes, macaroni salad or potato salad.

WHITE CHICKEN ENCHILADAS

prep 15 minutes | **bake** 35 minutes

12	white *or* yellow corn tortillas (6 inches)
4	ounces reduced-fat cream cheese
1	tablespoon plus 1 cup fat-free milk, *divided*
1	teaspoon ground cumin
4	cups cubed cooked chicken breast
1/2	cup chopped green onions
1/2	cup chopped sweet red pepper
1	can (10-3/4 ounces) reduced-fat reduced-sodium condensed cream of chicken soup, undiluted
1	cup (8 ounces) fat-free sour cream
2	jalapeno peppers, seeded and chopped
1/4	teaspoon cayenne pepper
1/2	cup shredded reduced-fat cheddar cheese

Wrap tortillas in foil. Bake at 350° for 10 minutes or until softened. Meanwhile, in a large bowl, combine the cream cheese, 1 tablespoon milk and cumin until smooth. Stir in chicken. In a nonstick skillet coated with cooking spray, saute onions and red pepper until softened. Stir into chicken mixture.

In another bowl, combine the soup, sour cream, jalapenos, cayenne and remaining milk. Stir 2 tablespoons soup mixture into chicken mixture. Place 1/3 cup of chicken mixture down the center of each tortilla; roll up.

Place seam side down in a 13-in. x 9-in. baking dish coated with cooking spray. Top with remaining soup mixture. Cover and bake at 350° for 30 minutes or until heated through. Uncover; sprinkle with cheese. Bake 5 minutes longer or until cheese is melted. **yield:** 6 servings.

editor's note: When cutting hot peppers, disposable gloves are recommended. Avoid touching your face.

sharon welsh
onsted, michigan

A thick and creamy sauce covers these corn tortillas that are filled with tender chunks of chicken. To suit our family's taste, I usually leave out the red peppers and cumin.

TOMATO GARLIC CHICKEN

prep 10 minutes + standing | **bake** 1-1/4 hours

barbara hasanat
tucson, arizona

I came up with this recipe many years ago as a way to warm up my family during cool winter weather. The appealing aroma of garlic and basil wafts through the house as it bakes.

3 to 4 garlic cloves, minced
1 teaspoon salt
5 medium red potatoes, cut into 1/4-inch slices
5 tablespoons olive oil, *divided*
1 large onion, thinly sliced
1 broiler/fryer chicken (3 to 4 pounds), cut up
2 medium tomatoes, chopped
1 tablespoon minced fresh basil

In a large bowl, combine garlic and salt; let stand for 15-20 minutes. Add potatoes and 2 tablespoons oil. In a greased 13-in. x 9-in. baking dish, layer the potato mixture, onion, chicken and tomatoes. Sprinkle with basil. Drizzle with remaining oil.

Cover and bake at 350° for 1 hour. Uncover; bake 15-20 minutes longer or until the chicken juices run clear and the potatoes are tender. **yield:** 4 servings.

ZUCCHINI-STUFFED CHICKEN

prep 20 minutes | **bake** 25 minutes

1 medium onion, chopped
3 garlic cloves, minced
2 tablespoons olive oil, *divided*
2 cups diced zucchini
1 cup diced sweet red pepper
1/3 cup grated Parmesan cheese
1 tablespoon minced fresh basil *or* 1 teaspoon dried basil
1/2 teaspoon salt
1/4 teaspoon pepper
4 bone-in chicken breast halves (8 ounces *each*)

In a large ovenproof skillet, saute the onion and the garlic in 1 tablespoon olive oil for 3 minutes or until crisp-tender. Add the zucchini and red pepper; saute for 3 minutes or until crisp-tender. Remove from the heat; stir in the Parmesan cheese, basil, salt and pepper.

Carefully loosen the skin on one side of each chicken breast to form a pocket; stuff with vegetable mixture.

In the same skillet, brown the chicken, skin side down, in remaining olive oil. Turn the chicken. Bake, uncovered, at 375° for 25-30 minutes or until a meat thermometer reads 170°. **yield:** 4 servings.

lynda postnikoff
beausejour, manitoba

Now that we're empty nesters, my husband is the brave one who gets to test my new recipes. This tasty one always receives an enthusiastic thumbs-up.

CHICKEN CUTLETS

prep 15 minutes | **bake** 20 minutes

cathy kierstead
easton, maine

I keep baked chicken moist and juicy with a golden coating of bread crumbs, wheat germ and Parmesan. If you like a crunchier coating, use cornflake crumbs.

- 6 boneless skinless chicken breast halves (4 ounces *each*)
- 1-1/4 cups dry bread crumbs
- 1/2 cup nonfat Parmesan cheese topping
- 2 tablespoons toasted wheat germ
- 1 teaspoon dried basil
- 1/2 teaspoon garlic powder
- 1 cup plain yogurt
- Refrigerated butter-flavored spray

Flatten chicken to 1/2-in. thickness. In a shallow dish, combine the bread crumbs, Parmesan topping, wheat germ, basil and garlic powder. Place the yogurt in another shallow dish. Dip chicken in yogurt, then coat with the crumb mixture.

Place in a 15-in. x 10-in. baking pan coated with cooking spray. Spritz chicken with the butter-flavored spray. Bake, uncovered, at 350° for 20-25 minutes or until the juices run clear. **yield:** 6 servings.

PICNIC CHICKEN

prep 20 minutes | **bake** 1 hour + chilling

- 3 eggs
- 3 tablespoons water
- 1-1/2 cups dry bread crumbs
- 2 teaspoons paprika
- 1 teaspoon salt
- 1/2 teaspoon *each* dried marjoram, thyme and rosemary, crushed
- 1/2 teaspoon pepper
- 1 cup butter, melted
- 12 chicken drumsticks
- 12 bone-in chicken thighs

CREAMY LEEK DIP
- 1 cup heavy whipping cream
- 1-1/2 cups plain yogurt
- 1 envelope leek soup mix
- 1 cup (4 ounces) shredded Colby cheese

In a shallow bowl, whisk the eggs and water. In another shallow bowl, combine the bread crumbs and seasonings. Divide the melted butter between two 13-in. x 9-in. baking dishes.

Dip chicken pieces in egg mixture, then coat with crumb mixture. Place in prepared pans. Bake, uncovered, at 375° for 1 hour or until juices run clear, turning once. Cool for 30 minutes; refrigerate until chilled.

For the dip, in a small bowl, beat the heavy cream until stiff peaks form. In another bowl, combine the yogurt, soup mix and Colby cheese; fold in the whipped cream. Cover and refrigerate until serving. Serve with the cold chicken. **yield:** 24 servings (4 cups dip).

ami okasinski
memphis, tennessee

I made this well-seasoned chicken one evening for dinner and served it hot from the oven. While raiding the fridge the next day, I discovered how delicious it was cold and created the creamy yogurt dip to go with it.

ULTIMATE **KITCHEN TIP**

Soft bread crumbs are made from fresh or slightly stale bread. Tear the bread apart with a fork or use a blender or food processor to break it into fluffy crumbs. Pile gently into a measuring cup and do not pack. Dry bread crumbs may be purchased or made from very dry bread or Zwieback crackers. Place in a plastic bag and crush with a rolling pin.

SPINACH CHICKEN CREPES

prep 40 minutes + chilling | **bake** 20 minutes

nina de witt
aurora, ohio

I made this dish at a cooking class several years ago. The spinach- and chicken-filled crepes are topped with a tasty mushroom sauce.

1   egg, lightly beaten
1   cup milk
3/4   cup all-purpose flour
1/8   teaspoon salt

SAUCE

2   cups sliced fresh mushrooms
1/2   cup sliced leek (white portion only)
1   medium carrot, shredded
1/2   cup water
2   tablespoons cornstarch
3/4   cup evaporated milk
1/4   teaspoon salt
1/8   teaspoon pepper
1/2   cup shredded cheddar cheese
2   tablespoons sherry *or* chicken broth

FILLING

1   package (10 ounces) frozen chopped spinach, thawed and squeezed dry
2   cups cubed cooked chicken

Combine egg and milk. Add flour and salt until blended. Cover and refrigerate for 1 hour.

Heat lightly greased 6-in. nonstick skillet; pour 2 tablespoons batter into center of skillet. Lift and tilt pan to coat bottom evenly. Cook until top appears dry; turn and cook 15-20 seconds more. Remove to wire rack. Repeat with remaining batter, greasing skillet as needed. When cool, stack crepes with waxed paper or paper towels in between.

For the sauce, in a large saucepan, bring vegetables and water to a boil. Reduce heat; cover and simmer for 5 minutes or until tender.

In a small bowl, combine the cornstarch, evaporated milk, salt and pepper until smooth; stir into vegetables. Bring to a boil; cook and stir for 2 minutes or until thickened. Reduce heat to low. Add cheese and sherry or broth; stir until cheese is melted. Remove from the heat.

For the filling, combine spinach, chicken and 1 cup sauce; spread 1/4 cupful down the center of each crepe. Roll up and place in a greased 13-in. x 9-in. baking dish. Spoon remaining sauce over crepes. Cover and bake at 375° for 20-25 minutes or until heated through. **yield:** 6 servings.

BAKED CHICKEN AND ACORN SQUASH

prep 20 minutes | **bake** 1 hour

connie svoboda
elko, minnesota

With colorful acorn squash and peaches, this main dish is ideal for harvesttime. The fragrance of the rosemary-seasoned chicken while it's baking is heavenly.

2 small acorn squash (1-1/4 pounds)
2 to 4 garlic cloves, minced
2 tablespoons canola oil, *divided*
4 chicken drumsticks (4 ounces *each*)
4 bone-in chicken thighs (4 ounces *each*)
1/4 cup packed brown sugar
1 tablespoon minced fresh rosemary *or* 1 teaspoon dried rosemary, crushed
1 teaspoon salt
1 can (15-1/4 ounces) sliced peaches, undrained

Cut squash in half lengthwise; discard seeds. Cut each half widthwise into 1/2-in. slices; discard ends. Place slices in an ungreased 13-in. x 9-in. baking dish. Sprinkle with garlic and drizzle with 1 tablespoon oil.

In a large skillet, brown chicken in remaining oil. Arrange chicken over squash. Combine the brown sugar, rosemary and salt; sprinkle over chicken. Bake, uncovered, at 350° for 45 minutes, basting with pan juices twice.

Pour peaches over chicken and squash. Bake, uncovered, 15 minutes longer or until chicken juices run clear and peaches are heated through. **yield:** 4 servings.

PECAN-CRUSTED CHICKEN

prep 10 minutes | **bake** 25 minutes

3 egg whites
1 package (4.2 ounces) seasoned coating mix
1/2 cup chopped pecans
1/8 teaspoon Chinese five-spice powder
6 boneless skinless chicken breast halves (4 ounces *each*)

In a shallow bowl, lightly beat the egg whites. In another shallow bowl, combine the coating mix, pecans and five-spice powder. Dip chicken into egg whites, then roll into coating mixture.

Place in a greased 15-in. x 10-in. baking pan. Bake, uncovered, at 400° for 25 minutes or until the chicken is no longer pink and a meat thermometer reaches 170°. **yield:** 6 servings.

ramona parris
marietta, georgia

After trying something similar at a restaurant, I created this impressive baked chicken with a pecan coating. I recommend them with mashed sweet potatoes and stewed cherries.

CHICKEN PESTO PIZZA

prep/total time 30 minutes

paul piantek
middletown, connecticut

I love pizza, and pesto is one of my favorite things with pasta or bread. Here I combine the two for a delicious result!

1   loaf (1 pound) frozen bread dough, thawed
1   egg, lightly beaten
1/2   pound boneless skinless chicken breasts, cut into 1/2-inch pieces
1   small onion, sliced
1   small sweet yellow pepper, julienned
1/4   teaspoon lemon-pepper seasoning
1   tablespoon olive oil
1/4   cup prepared pesto sauce
3   plum tomatoes, thinly sliced
1   cup (4 ounces) shredded part-skim mozzarella cheese

Spread dough into an ungreased 12-in. pizza pan. Prick dough with a fork. Brush with egg. Bake at 400° for 12-15 minutes or until lightly browned.

In a large skillet, saute the chicken, onion, yellow pepper and lemon-pepper in oil until chicken is no longer pink; drain.

Spread the pesto sauce over the crust. Top with the chicken mixture, tomatoes and cheese. Bake for 12-15 minutes or until lightly browned. **yield:** 6 slices.

COUNTRY ROASTED CHICKEN

prep 10 minutes | **bake** 65 minutes

1   broiler/fryer chicken (3 pounds)
1/2   teaspoon dried thyme
2   teaspoons salt, *divided*
1   large onion, cut into eighths
2   celery ribs with leaves, cut into 4-inch pieces
4   fresh parsley sprigs
8   small red potatoes
1/4   cup chicken broth
1/4   cup minced fresh parsley

Sprinkle the inside of the chicken with thyme and 1 teaspoon salt; stuff with the onion, celery and parsley sprigs. Place in a greased Dutch oven.

Cover and bake at 375° for 30 minutes. Sprinkle remaining salt over chicken. Add potatoes and broth to pan. Cover and bake 25 minutes longer.

Increase oven temperature to 400°. Bake, uncovered, for 10-15 minutes or until potatoes are tender and a meat thermometer inserted into the chicken thighs reads 180°. Sprinkle with minced parsley. **yield:** 4 servings.

judy page
edenville, michigan

There's nothing complicated about this recipe, but it turns out a juicy, flavorful roast chicken every time.

BRINED ROASTING CHICKEN

prep 30 minutes + marinating | **bake** 1 hour 20 minutes

8	cups warm water
1/2	cup kosher salt
1/4	cup packed brown sugar
3	tablespoons molasses
1	tablespoon whole peppercorns, crushed
1	tablespoon whole allspice, crushed
2	teaspoons ground ginger
1	roasting chicken
4	cups cold water
1	teaspoon canola oil
3/4	to 1 cup chicken broth
1	tablespoon all-purpose flour

For the brine, combine the first seven ingredients in a large kettle. Bring to a boil; cook and stir until the salt is dissolved. Remove from the heat. Cool to room temperature.

Remove giblets from chicken; discard. Place cold water in a 2-gal. resealable plastic bag; add chicken. Place in a roasting pan. Carefully pour cooled brine into the bag. Squeeze out as much air as possible; seal bag and turn to coat. Refrigerate for 3-4 hours, turning several times.

Discard brine. Rinse chicken with water; pat dry. Skewer chicken openings; tie drumsticks together. Brush with oil. Place chicken in a roasting pan. Bake, uncovered, at 350° for 80-90 minutes or until a meat thermometer reads 180°, basting occasionally with pan drippings (cover loosely with foil if chicken browns too quickly).

Remove chicken to a serving platter and keep warm. Pour drippings and loosened browned bits into a measuring cup; skim fat and discard. Add enough broth to measure 1 cup. In a small saucepan, combine the flour and broth mixture until smooth. Bring to a boil; cook and stir for 2 minutes or until thickened. Serve with the chicken. **yield:** 4-6 servings.

julie noyes
louisville, kentucky

I discovered the art of brining turkey a few years ago and transferred the technique to a whole chicken. I guarantee you will have a moist bird and rich flavorful gravy from the pan drippings.

PLUM-GLAZED CHICKEN KABOBS

prep 20 minutes + marinating | **broil** 10 minutes

nancy morrison
midlothian, virginia

These creative kabobs make a great first impression. I brought them to a neighborhood dinner when we moved to our new home, and people started snatching them up as soon as I walked in the door. They couldn't resist the tantalizing aroma.

2 cups plum jam
6 tablespoons reduced-sodium soy sauce
2 tablespoons sherry *or* chicken broth
1/2 teaspoon garlic powder
1/2 teaspoon ground ginger
1 pound boneless skinless chicken breasts, cubed
1 can (20 ounces) pineapple chunks, drained
1 large green pepper, cut into 1-inch pieces
1 teaspoon cornstarch
3 cups cooked rice

In a small saucepan, combine the first five ingredients; heat on low until jam is melted. Reserve half of the plum mixture; refrigerate. Pour half the remaining plum mixture into a large resealable plastic bag; add the chicken. Seal bag and turn to coat. In another large resealable plastic bag, add the other half of plum mixture. Add pineapple and green pepper. Seal bag and turn to coat; refrigerate both bags for at least 2 hours.

Place cornstarch in a small saucepan; Gradually add reserved plum mixture into saucepan. Stir until smooth. Bring to a boil over medium heat; cook and stir for 1 minute or until thickened. Remove from the heat; set aside.

Drain and discard the marinade from the chicken and vegetables. On 12 metal or soaked wooden skewers, alternately thread the chicken, pineapple and green pepper.

Place skewers on a broiler pan 3-4 in. from the heat. Broil for 1-2 minutes on each side. Baste with plum glaze. Broil 4-6 minutes longer or until chicken juices run clear, turning and basting frequently. Serve over rice with any remaining glaze. **yield:** 4 servings.

PUFF PASTRY CHICKEN BUNDLES

prep 30 minutes | **bake** 25 minutes

brad moritz
limerick, pennsylvania

Inside these golden puff pastry packages are chicken breasts rolled with spinach, herbed cream cheese and walnuts. I like to serve this elegant entree when we have guests or are celebrating a holiday or special occasion.

8 boneless skinless chicken breast halves (about 6 ounces *each*)
1 teaspoon salt
1/2 teaspoon pepper
40 large spinach leaves
2 cartons (8 ounces *each*) spreadable chive and onion cream cheese
1/2 cup chopped walnuts, toasted
2 sheets frozen puff pastry, thawed
1 egg
1/2 teaspoon cold water

Cut a lengthwise slit in each chicken breast to within 1/2 in. of the other side; open the meat so that it lies flat. Cover with plastic wrap; pound the chicken, flattening to 1/8-in. thickness. Remove the plastic wrap. Sprinkle the salt and pepper over the chicken.

In a small saucepan, bring 1 in. of water to a boil; add spinach. Cover and cook for 1-2 minutes or until wilted; drain. Place five spinach leaves on each chicken breast. Spoon 2 tablespoons of cream cheese down center of each chicken breast; sprinkle with walnuts. Roll up chicken and tuck in ends.

Unroll the puff pastry; cut into eight portions. Roll each into an 8-in. x 7-in. rectangle. Combine the egg and cold water; brush over the edges of pastry. Place the chicken at one short end; roll up tightly, tucking in ends.

Place on a greased 15-in. x 10-in. baking sheet. Bake at 350° for 25-30 minutes or until golden brown. **yield:** 8 servings.

BACON-WRAPPED CHICKEN

prep 25 minutes | **bake** 35 minutes

6 boneless skinless chicken breast halves (4 ounces *each*)
1 carton (8 ounces) spreadable chive and onion cream cheese
1 tablespoon butter
Salt to taste
6 bacon strips

Flatten the chicken to 1/2-in. thickness. Spread 3 tablespoons cream cheese over each. Dot with butter and sprinkle with salt; roll up. Wrap each with a bacon strip.

Place the chicken, seam side down in a greased 13-in. x 9-in. baking pan. Bake, uncovered, at 400° for 35-40 minutes or until juices run clear. Broil 6 in. from the heat for 5 minutes or until bacon is crisp. **yield:** 6 servings.

marlakaye skinner
tucson, arizona

Tender chicken gets a special treatment when spread with a creamy filling and wrapped with tasty bacon strips. This easy entree is frequently requested by my bunch.

ULTIMATE KITCHEN TIP

Flattening meat provides more even cooking and an attractive appearance. When pounding out boneless chicken, it's best to place inside a heavy-duty resealable plastic bag or between two sheets of heavy plastic wrap to prevent messy splatters. Use only the smooth side of a meat mallet to gently pound them to the desired thickness. This will prevent the meat from shredding.

HONEY GARLIC CHICKEN

prep/total time 30 minutes

taste of home test kitchen

greendale, wisconsin

The mellow flavor of chicken pairs well with honey, orange juice and garlic. Broiling the chicken for a few minutes gives it a slight golden color.

4   boneless skinless chicken breast halves (4 ounces *each*)
2   tablespoons honey
2   tablespoons orange *or* lemon juice
1   tablespoon canola oil
1/2   teaspoon salt
Dash pepper
1   to 2 garlic cloves, minced

Place chicken in a greased 13-in. x 9-in. baking pan. In a small bowl, combine the remaining ingredients; pour over chicken.

Bake, uncovered, at 400° for 15 minutes. Broil 4 to 6 in. from the heat for 5-7 minutes or until juices run clear, basting occasionally with sauce. **yield:** 4 servings.

FLAVORFUL CHICKEN ROLL-UPS

prep 20 minutes | **bake** 40 minutes

6   boneless skinless chicken breast halves (4 ounces *each*)
1   package (10 ounces) sliced part-skim mozzarella cheese
1/2   cup all-purpose flour
2   eggs, lightly beaten
2/3   cup seasoned bread crumbs
1/2   cup butter, melted
1/2   teaspoon dried oregano

Flatten chicken to 1/3-in. thickness. Place one cheese slice on each piece of chicken; roll up tightly. Secure with a toothpick.

Place flour, beaten eggs and bread crumbs in separate shallow bowls. Coat chicken with flour. Dip in beaten eggs, then coat with bread crumbs.

Place seam side down in an ungreased 2-1/2-qt. baking dish. Combine the butter and oregano; drizzle over the chicken. Bake, uncovered, at 350° for 40-50 minutes or until chicken juices run clear. Discard toothpicks. **yield:** 6 servings.

margaret potten

glendale, new york

These chicken roll-ups taste as though they came from a fancy French restaurant, but they're very simple to make in your own kitchen.

TROPICAL LIME CHICKEN

prep 20 minutes + marinating | **cook** 10 minutes

SALSA
- 1/2 cup pineapple tidbits
- 1 medium kiwifruit, peeled and chopped
- 1/4 cup chopped sweet red pepper
- 1 tablespoon lime juice
- 1 tablespoon white wine vinegar
- 1 tablespoon honey
- 1 teaspoon crushed red pepper flakes

CHICKEN
- 3 tablespoons plus 1-1/2 teaspoons lime juice
- 1 tablespoon canola oil
- 1 teaspoon grated lime peel
- 1/8 teaspoon salt
- 1/8 teaspoon pepper
- 4 boneless skinless chicken breast halves (4 ounces *each*)
- 1 cup uncooked couscous

In a small bowl, combine the salsa ingredients; cover and refrigerate until serving.

For the chicken, in a large resealable plastic bag, combine the lime juice, oil, lime peel, salt and pepper; add chicken. Seal bag and turn to coat; refrigerate for 2-4 hours.

Drain and discard marinade. Place chicken on a broiler pan coated with cooking spray. Broil 3 in. from the heat for 5-6 minutes on each side or until juices run clear. Meanwhile, cook couscous according to package directions. Serve with chicken and salsa. **yield:** 4 servings (1 cup salsa).

jennifer eilts
lincoln, nebraska

This recipe has long been a favorite of my family. I found it many years ago in a recipe book and altered it to please our taste buds. You can add papaya, green pepper or any other healthy ingredient you prefer to the chuncky salsa.

This chicken recipe is lower in calories, fat or sodium.

OVEN BARBECUED CHICKEN

prep 20 minutes | **bake** 45 minutes

marge wagner

roselle, illinois

A friend made this moist chicken for us when we had our first child. I pared down the recipe to make it lower in fat and calories. It is now a family favorite, and even the kids ask for it!

6	bone-in chicken breast halves (8 ounces *each*)
1/3	cup chopped onion
3/4	cup ketchup
1/2	cup water
1/3	cup white vinegar
3	tablespoons brown sugar
1	tablespoon Worcestershire sauce
1	teaspoon ground mustard
1/4	teaspoon salt
1/8	teaspoon pepper

In a nonstick skillet coated with cooking spray, brown chicken over medium heat. Transfer to a 13-in. x 9-in. baking dish coated with cooking spray.

Recoat skillet with cooking spray; cook onion over medium heat until tender. Stir in the remaining ingredients. Bring to a boil. Reduce heat; simmer, uncovered, for 15 minutes. Pour over chicken.

Bake, uncovered, at 350° for 45-55 minutes or until the chicken juices run clear and a meat thermometer reads 170°. **yield:** 6 servings.

nutrition facts: 1 chicken breast half equals 241 calories, 4 g fat (1 g saturated fat), 90 mg cholesterol, 563 mg sodium, 17 g carbohydrate, 1 g fiber, 34 g protein.

diabetic exchanges: 4 very lean meat, 1 starch.

WILD RICE CHICKEN BAKE

prep 10 minutes | **bake** 35 minutes

1	package (6 ounces) long grain and wild rice mix
2	medium carrots, shredded
3/4	cup frozen peas
1	can (8 ounces) sliced water chestnuts, drained
1-1/4	cups water
1	can (10-3/4 ounces) reduced-fat reduced-sodium condensed cream of mushroom soup, undiluted
6	boneless skinless chicken breast halves (4 ounces *each*)
1/8	teaspoon paprika
1/8	teaspoon pepper
1	garlic clove, minced
1	tablespoon olive oil

joyce unruh

shepshewana, indiana

This homey combination is one of my most requested chicken recipes. It's a snap to assemble using a boxed rice mix. Plus, it's low in calories.

In a bowl, combine rice mix with contents of seasoning packet, carrots, peas and water chestnuts. Combine water and soup; pour over rice mixture and mix well. Transfer to a shallow 3-qt. baking dish coated with cooking spray. Cover and bake at 350° for 25 minutes.

Meanwhile, sprinkle chicken with paprika and pepper. In a large nonstick skillet, cook chicken and garlic in oil for 5-6 minutes on each side or until lightly browned. Arrange chicken over rice mixture. Cover and bake 10-15 minutes longer or until a meat thermometer reaches 170° and rice is tender. **yield:** 6 servings.

NUTTY OVEN-FRIED CHICKEN

prep 10 minutes | **bake** 1 hour

diane hixon
niceville, florida

The pecans that give this dish its unique nutty flavor are plentiful in the South. I love to make and serve this easy dish because the chicken comes out moist, tasty and crispy.

1/2 cup evaporated milk
1 cup biscuit/baking mix
1/3 cup finely chopped pecans
2 teaspoons paprika
1/2 teaspoon salt
1/2 teaspoon poultry seasoning
1/2 teaspoon rubbed sage
1 broiler/fryer chicken (3 to 4 pounds), cut up
1/3 cup butter, melted

Place milk in a shallow bowl. In another shallow bowl, combine the baking mix, pecans and seasonings. Dip chicken pieces in milk, then coat generously with pecan mixture.

Place in a lightly greased 13-in. x 9-in. baking dish. Drizzle with butter. Bake, uncovered, at 350° for 1 hour or until chicken juices run clear. **yield:** 6-8 servings.

OLD-FASHIONED CHICKEN POTPIE

prep 1-1/2 hours | **bake** 40 minutes + standing

3 to 4 pounds bone-in chicken breast halves
1-1/2 quarts water
1 small onion, peeled
1 celery rib
1 large carrot
1-1/2 teaspoons salt, *divided*
Pastry for double-crust pie (9 inches)
1/2 cup all-purpose flour
1/2 teaspoon onion salt
1/2 teaspoon celery salt
1/4 teaspoon pepper

In a large kettle, bring the chicken, water, onion, celery, carrot and 1/2 teaspoon salt to a boil. Reduce heat; cover and simmer for 50-60 minutes or until chicken is tender.

Remove chicken and vegetables from broth. Set aside until cool enough to handle. Meanwhile, line a 9-in. deep-dish pie plate with bottom pastry; trim even with edge of plate. Set aside.

Remove chicken from bones; discard skin and bones and cut chicken into cubes. Set aside. Chop the onion, celery and carrot. Strain broth and skim fat; set broth aside.

In a small bowl, combine the flour, onion salt, celery salt, pepper and remaining salt. Add 1/2 cup broth; whisk until smooth. In a large saucepan, bring 3 cups of broth to a boil; whisk in the flour mixture. Cook and stir for 2 minutes or until thickened. Remove from the heat; add chicken and vegetables. Pour into crust.

Roll out remaining pastry to fit top of pie; place over filling. Trim, seal and flute edges. Cut slits in top. Cover edges loosely with foil. Bake at 400° for 40-45 minutes or until golden brown and filling is bubbly. Let stand for 15 minutes before cutting. **yield:** 8 servings.

sue davis
wausau, wisconsin

This buttery, double-crust pie is stuffed with tender chicken pieces, vegetables, seasonings and a creamy sauce.

ULTIMATE **KITCHEN TIP**

To flute the edge of a double-crust pie, trim the pastry beyond the rim of the pie plate to one inch. Turn this overhang under to form a built-up edge. Position your index finger on the edge of the crust, pointing out. Using your other hand's thumb and index finger, pinch dough around your other index finger to form a V-shape. Continue around the edge.

CHICKEN ROLL-UPS WITH CHERRY SAUCE

prep 30 minutes | **bake** 20 minutes

margaret scott
traverse city, michigan

Since I grew up on a cherry farm, I have many recipes featuring the delightful fruit. This one is a delicious way to use chicken.

8 boneless skinless chicken breast halves (4 ounces *each*)
8 slices Swiss *or* Brie cheese
1 egg
1 tablespoon water
1 tablespoon Dijon mustard
3/4 cup dry bread crumbs
1/2 teaspoon dried thyme
1/4 teaspoon salt
Dash pepper
1/4 cup all-purpose flour
1/4 cup canola oil

CHERRY SAUCE
2 cups canned pitted tart red cherries
3/4 cup sugar
2 tablespoons cornstarch
1 teaspoon lemon juice
1/4 teaspoon almond extract
3 drops red food coloring, optional

Flatten chicken breasts to 1/4-in. thickness. Place a slice of cheese on each; roll up and secure with toothpicks. In a shallow bowl, beat egg, water and mustard. In another shallow bowl, combine the bread crumbs, thyme, salt and pepper. Place flour in a third shallow bowl. Lightly coat chicken with flour, then dip in egg mixture and roll in bread crumb mixture.

In a large skillet, brown roll-ups in oil until golden brown, turning often. Transfer to an ungreased 13-in. x 9-in. baking dish. Bake, uncovered, at 350° for 20-25 minutes or until chicken juices run clear.

Meanwhile, for the sauce, drain the cherries, reserving juice. Add enough water to juice to measure 1 cup. In a large saucepan, combine sugar and cornstarch. Stir in cherry juice until smooth. Add cherries. Bring to a boil; cook and stir for 2 minutes or until thickened. Remove from heat. Stir in lemon juice, extract and food coloring if desired. Remove toothpicks from chicken; serve with cherry sauce. **yield:** 8 servings.

PARMESAN CHICKEN

prep 15 minutes | **bake** 50 minutes

sharon crider
st. robert, missouri

This oven-fried chicken is the perfect dish to prepare in advance and take on a picnic because it tastes just as good cold as it does warm. It's been a family favorite for years.

- 1 cup all-purpose flour
- 2 teaspoons salt
- 2 teaspoons paprika
- 1/4 teaspoon pepper
- 2 eggs
- 3 tablespoons milk
- 2/3 cup grated Parmesan cheese
- 1/3 cup dry bread crumbs
- 1 broiler/fryer chicken (3 to 4 pounds), cut up

In a shallow bowl, combine the flour, salt, paprika and pepper. In another shallow bowl, beat the eggs and milk. In a third bowl, combine the Parmesan cheese and bread crumbs. Coat the chicken pieces with the flour mixture, dip in the egg mixture, then roll in the crumb mixture.

Place in a well-greased 15-in. x 10-in. baking pan. Bake at 400° for 50-55 minutes or until chicken juices run clear. **yield:** 4 servings.

MEXICAN CHICKEN MANICOTTI

prep 25 minutes | **bake** 40 minutes

- 1 package (8 ounces) manicotti shells
- 2 cups cubed cooked chicken
- 2 cups (8 ounces) shredded Monterey Jack cheese, *divided*
- 1-1/2 cups (6 ounces) shredded cheddar cheese
- 1 cup (8 ounces) sour cream
- 1 small onion, diced, *divided*
- 1 can (4 ounces) chopped green chilies, *divided*
- 1 can (10-3/4 ounces) condensed cream of chicken soup, undiluted
- 1 cup salsa
- 2/3 cup milk

Cook the manicotti according to package directions. Meanwhile, in a large bowl, combine the chicken, 1-1/2 cups Monterey Jack cheese, cheddar cheese, sour cream, half of the diced onion and 6 tablespoons chilies.

In another bowl, combine the soup, salsa, milk and remaining onion and chilies. Spread 1/2 cup in a greased 13-in. x 9-in. baking dish.

Drain manicotti and rinse in cold water; stuff each with about 1/4 cupful chicken mixture. Arrange over sauce in baking dish. Pour remaining sauce over shells.

Cover and bake at 350° for 30 minutes. Uncover; sprinkle with remaining Monterey Jack cheese. Bake 10 minutes longer or until cheese is melted. **yield:** 7 servings.

keely jankunas
corvallis, montana

Our family of five enjoys trying different ethnic cuisines, so I added a little Mexican zip to this Italian specialty. Be careful not to overcook the manicotti, and if the filled shells happen to break, just place them in the pan seam-side down.

BAKED CHIMICHANGAS

prep/total time 30 minutes

angela oelschlaeger
tonganoxie, kansas

Usually chimichangas are deep-fried, but my baked version is healthier as well as delicious. You can omit the chilies for less heat.

2-1/2 cups shredded cooked chicken breast
  1 cup salsa
  1 small onion, chopped
3/4 teaspoon ground cumin
1/2 teaspoon dried oregano
  6 flour tortillas (10 inches), warmed
3/4 cup shredded reduced-fat cheddar cheese
  1 cup reduced-sodium chicken broth
  2 teaspoons chicken bouillon granules
1/8 teaspoon pepper
1/4 cup all-purpose flour
  1 cup fat-free half-and-half
  1 can (4 ounces) chopped green chilies

In a nonstick skillet, simmer the chicken, salsa, onion, cumin and oregano until heated through and most of the liquid has evaporated.

Place 1/2 cup chicken mixture down the center of each tortilla; top with 2 tablespoons cheese. Fold sides and ends over filling and roll up.

Place the chimichangas seam side down in a 13-in. x 9-in. baking dish coated with cooking spray. Bake, uncovered, at 425° for 15 minutes or until lightly browned.

Meanwhile, in a small saucepan, combine the broth, bouillon and pepper. Cook until bouillon is dissolved. In a small bowl, combine flour and cream until smooth; gradually stir into broth. Bring to a boil; cook and stir for 2 minutes or until thickened. Stir in chilies; cook until heated through. To serve, cut chimichangas in half; top with sauce. **yield:** 6 servings.

HONEY ROSEMARY CHICKEN

prep 5 minutes + marinating | **bake** 55 minutes

This chicken recipe is lower in calories, fat or sodium.

1/4 cup honey
1/4 cup balsamic vinegar
1/4 cup minced fresh rosemary
  2 tablespoons olive oil
  6 bone-in skinless chicken breast halves (7 ounces *each*)
  1 teaspoon salt
1/4 teaspoon pepper

Combine honey, vinegar, rosemary and oil. Pour half of marinade into a large resealable plastic bag; add chicken. Seal bag and turn to coat; re-

frigerate 2 hours. Cover and refrigerate remaining marinade.

Drain and discard marinade from chicken. Place chicken bone side down in a 13-in. x 9-in. baking pan. Sprinkle with salt and pepper. Bake, uncovered, at 350° for 55-65 minutes or until a meat thermometer reaches 170°, basting occasionally with reserved marinade. **yield:** 6 servings.

nutrition facts: 1 serving equals 200 calories, 6 g fat (1 g saturated fat), 79 mg cholesterol, 462 mg sodium, 7 g carbohydrate, trace fiber, 29 g protein.

diabetic exchanges: 4 very lean meat, 1/2 starch, 1/2 fat.

elsie barton
hoover, alabama

I never get tired of finding new ways to cook with herbs! A rosemary marinade sweetened with honey gives this moist chicken wonderful flavor and a pretty golden sheen.

SPINACH CHICKEN MANICOTTI

prep 1 hour | **bake** 35 minutes

  1   large onion, chopped
  1   garlic clove, minced
  1   teaspoon olive oil
2-1/2 cups diced cooked chicken breast
  1   package (10 ounces) frozen
       chopped spinach, thawed and
       squeezed dry
 3/4   cup diced fully cooked lean ham
 1/4   cup grated Parmesan cheese
  2   egg whites
 1/2   teaspoon dried basil
 1/8   teaspoon pepper
Dash ground nutmeg
 12   uncooked manicotti shells

SAUCE

 3/4   cup all-purpose flour
  3   cups reduced-sodium chicken
       broth
  1   cup fat-free milk
 1/4   teaspoon salt
 1/8   teaspoon ground nutmeg
 1/8   teaspoon pepper
Dash cayenne pepper
 1/4   cup grated Parmesan cheese

In a small skillet, saute onion and garlic in oil until tender. In a large bowl, combine the onion mixture, chicken, spinach, ham, Parmesan cheese, egg whites, basil, pepper and nutmeg; set aside.

Cook manicotti shells according to package directions. Meanwhile, for the sauce, combine flour and broth in a large saucepan until smooth. Stir in the milk, salt, nutmeg, pepper and cayenne. Bring to a boil over medium heat; cook and stir for 2 minutes or until thickened. Spoon 1 cup into chicken mixture. Add Parmesan cheese to remaining sauce.

Spread 1 cup sauce into a 13-in. x 9-in. baking dish coated with cooking spray. Drain shells; stuff with chicken mixture. Arrange over sauce. Drizzle with remaining sauce. Cover and bake at 375° for 35-40 minutes or until bubbly and heated through.

yield: 6 servings.

nutrition facts: 2 manicotti equals 372 calories, 7 g fat (2 g saturated fat), 58 mg cholesterol, 866 mg sodium, 43 g carbohydrate, 3 g fiber, 35 g protein.

diabetic exchange: 4 very lean meat, 2 starch, 2 vegetable, 1/2 fat.

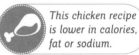
This chicken recipe is lower in calories, fat or sodium.

amy luce
dallas, texas

Pepper and nutmeg spice up the rich sauce in this hearty pasta dish. I made this for my husband many years ago on our first Valentine's Day when we were dating. It was as big of a success then as it is today.

SLOW COOKER

CREAMY TARRAGON CHICKEN, P. 217

CHICKEN SALTIMBOCCA

prep 25 minutes + chilling | **cook** 4 hours

carol mccollough
missoula, montana

White wine dresses up cream of chicken soup to make a lovely sauce for chicken, ham and Swiss cheese roll-ups. The tried-and-true recipe comes from my mother.

6   boneless skinless chicken breast halves (4 ounces *each*)
6   thin slices deli ham
6   slices Swiss cheese
1/4   cup all-purpose flour
1/4   cup grated Parmesan cheese
1/2   teaspoon salt
1/4   teaspoon pepper
2   tablespoons canola oil
1   can (10-3/4 ounces) condensed cream of chicken soup, undiluted
1/2   cup dry white wine *or* chicken broth
Hot cooked rice

Flatten the chicken breast halves to 1/4-in. thickness. Top each piece with a slice of ham and cheese. Roll up tightly; secure with toothpicks. In a shallow bowl, combine the flour, Parmesan cheese, salt and pepper. Roll chicken in flour mixture; refrigerate for 1 hour.

In a large skillet, brown roll-ups in oil on all sides; transfer to a 3-qt. slow cooker. Combine the soup and wine or broth; pour over chicken.

Cover and cook on low for 4-5 hours or until a meat thermometer reads 170°. Remove roll-ups and stir sauce. Discard toothpicks. Serve with rice. **yield:** 6 servings.

SAVORY CHICKEN SANDWICHES

prep 25 minutes | **cook** 8 hours

4   bone-in chicken breast halves
4   bone-in chicken thighs
1   envelope onion soup mix
1/4   teaspoon garlic salt
1/4   cup prepared Italian salad dressing
1/4   cup water
14   to 16 hamburger buns, split

Remove the skin from chicken if desired. Place chicken in a 5-qt. slow cooker. Sprinkle with the soup mix and garlic salt. Pour prepared dressing and water over chicken.

Cover and cook on low for 8-9 hours. Remove chicken; cool slightly. Skim fat from cooking juices. Remove chicken from bones; cut into bite-size pieces and return to slow cooker. Serve with a slotted spoon on buns. **yield:** 14-16 servings.

joan parker
gastonia, north carolina

With eight children under the age of 12, I've learned how to make family-pleasing meals. This tender chicken tastes like you fussed, but requires few ingredients. You can also thicken the juices and serve it over rice.

SLOW-COOKED ITALIAN CHICKEN

prep 10 minutes | **cook** 4 hours 10 minutes

4   boneless skinless chicken breast halves (4 ounces *each*)
1   can (14-1/2 ounces) chicken broth
1   can (14-1/2 ounces) stewed tomatoes, cut up
1   can (8 ounces) tomato sauce
1   medium green pepper, chopped
1   green onion, chopped
1   garlic clove, minced
3   teaspoons chili powder
1   teaspoon ground mustard
1/2 teaspoon garlic salt *or* garlic powder
1/2 teaspoon onion salt *or* onion powder
1/2 teaspoon pepper
1/3 cup all-purpose flour
1/2 cup cold water
Hot cooked pasta

Place chicken in a 3-qt. slow cooker. In a bowl, combine the broth, tomatoes, tomato sauce, green pepper, onion, garlic and seasonings; pour over chicken. Cover and cook on low for 4-5 hours or until a meat thermometer reads 170°.

Remove the chicken and keep warm. Pour cooking juice into a large saucepan; skim fat. Combine the flour and cold water until smooth; stir into juices. Bring to a boil; cook and stir for 2 minutes or until thickened. Serve over chicken and pasta.
yield: 4 servings.

deanna d'auria
banning, california

With its nicely seasoned tomato sauce, this enticing chicken entree is especially good over pasta or rice. My father loved it when I made this.

HARVEST CHICKEN WITH WALNUT GREMOLATA

prep 25 minutes | **cook** 5-1/4 hours

patricia harmon
baden, pennsylvania

This original recipe is based on a classic veal or lamb dish but made more simply in the slow cooker. To lighten up the recipe, use fat-free chicken broth and remove the skin and excess fat from the chicken legs. It's an elegant, complete dinner that always gets compliments.

1 medium butternut squash (about 3 pounds), peeled and cubed
1 can (14-1/2 ounces) diced tomatoes, drained
1 medium onion, chopped
1 celery rib, chopped
1/2 cup reduced-sodium chicken broth
1/4 cup white wine *or* additional reduced-sodium chicken broth
1 garlic clove, minced
1 teaspoon Italian seasoning
1/4 teaspoon coarsely ground pepper, *divided*
1/4 cup all-purpose flour
1 teaspoon seasoned salt
6 chicken drumsticks, skin removed
1 cup uncooked orzo pasta

GREMOLATA
2 tablespoons finely chopped walnuts
2 tablespoons minced fresh parsley
1 garlic clove, minced
1 teaspoon grated lemon peel

In a 5-qt. slow cooker, combine the squash, tomatoes, onion, celery, broth, wine, garlic, Italian seasoning and 1/8 teaspoon pepper.

In a large resealable plastic bag, combine the flour, seasoned salt and remaining pepper. Add chicken, a few pieces at a time, and shake to coat. Place chicken on top of vegetables. Cover and cook on low for 5 hours or until chicken juices run clear. Remove chicken and keep warm.

Stir orzo into vegetable mixture; cover and cook 15-20 minutes longer or until orzo is tender. Meanwhile, combine gremolata ingredients.

Transfer vegetable mixture to a serving platter; top with the chicken. Sprinkle with the gremolata. **yield:** 6 servings.

SOUTHWESTERN CHICKEN

prep 10 minutes | **cook** 3 hours

2 cans (15-1/4 ounces *each*) whole kernel corn, drained
1 can (15 ounces) black beans, rinsed and drained
1 jar (16 ounces) chunky salsa, *divided*
6 boneless skinless chicken breast halves (4 ounces *each*)
1 cup (4 ounces) shredded cheddar cheese

In a 5-qt. slow cooker, combine the corn, black beans and 1/2 cup of salsa. Top with the chicken; pour the remaining salsa over the chicken.

Cover and cook on high for 3-4 hours or on low for 7-8 hours or until meat juices run clear. Sprinkle with cheese; cover until cheese is melted, about 5 minutes. **yield:** 6 servings.

karen waters
laurel, maryland

Prepared salsa and convenient canned corn and beans add fun color, texture and flavor to my tender chicken dish. I usually serve it with salad and white rice. Our children love it.

BUSY MOM'S CHICKEN FAJITAS

prep 15 minutes | **cook** 5 hours

sarah newman
brooklyn center,
minnesota

Staying at home with a little one makes preparing dinner a challenge, but a slow cooker provides an easy way to make a low-fat meal. The tender meat in these fajitas is a hit, and the veggies and beans provide a dose of fiber!

1 pound boneless skinless chicken breast halves
1 can (16 ounces) kidney beans, rinsed and drained
1 can (14-1/2 ounces) diced tomatoes with mild green chilies, drained
1 *each* medium green, sweet red and yellow pepper, julienned
1 medium onion, halved and sliced
2 teaspoons ground cumin
2 teaspoons chili powder
1 garlic clove, minced
1/4 teaspoon salt
6 flour tortillas (8 inches), warmed
Shredded lettuce and chopped tomatoes, optional

In a 3-qt. slow cooker, combine the chicken, beans, tomatoes, peppers, onion and seasonings. Cover and cook on low for 5-6 hours or until chicken is tender.

Remove chicken; cool slightly. Shred chicken and return to the slow cooker; stir to combine. Spoon about 3/4 cup chicken mixture down the center of each tortilla. Top with lettuce and tomatoes if desired. **yield:** 6 servings.

SATISFYING CHICKEN AND VEGGIES

prep 20 minutes | **cook** 4 hours

2 medium potatoes, peeled and cut into 1-inch pieces (about 1-1/2 cups)
1 cup thickly sliced onion
1/2 cup sliced celery
1 medium carrot, cut into 1-inch pieces
1 medium sweet yellow pepper, cut into 1-inch pieces
1 broiler/fryer chicken (3 to 4 pounds), cut up and skin removed
1 jar (26 ounces) meatless spaghetti sauce
1 cup water

1-1/2 teaspoons minced garlic
1/4 teaspoon salt
1/4 teaspoon dried oregano
1/4 teaspoon dried basil
1/4 teaspoon pepper

Place the potatoes, onion, celery, carrot and yellow pepper in a 5-qt. slow cooker. Top with the chicken. Combine the remaining ingredients; pour over the chicken.

Cover and cook on low for 4 to 4-1/2 hours or until chicken juices run clear and vegetables are tender. **yield:** 6 servings.

kat sadi
san luis obispo, california

I'm happy to share the recipe for this tasty meal-in-one supper that's made with chicken, vegetables and herbs. The nice thing about this delicious dish is that you have only one pot to clean.

ULTIMATE
KITCHEN TIP

Generally, three medium russet potatoes or eight to 10 small new white potatoes equal one pound. If you usually purchase the same type of potatoes, weigh them in the produce section of your store so you know just what one pound of your favorite variety is. When working with lots of potatoes, peel and place in cold water to prevent discoloration.

SWEET 'N' TANGY CHICKEN

prep 15 minutes | **cook** 4-1/2 hours

joan airey
rivers, manitoba

My slow cooker comes in so handy during the haying and harvest seasons. We're so busy that if supper isn't prepared before I serve lunch, it doesn't seem to get done on time. This recipe is hearty, delicious and fuss-free.

1	medium onion, chopped
1-1/2	teaspoons minced garlic
1	broiler/fryer chicken (3 pounds), cut up and skin removed
2/3	cup ketchup
1/3	cup packed brown sugar
1	tablespoon chili powder
1	tablespoon lemon juice
1	teaspoon dried basil
1/2	teaspoon salt
1/4	teaspoon pepper
1/8	teaspoon hot pepper sauce
2	tablespoons cornstarch
3	tablespoons cold water

In a 3-qt. slow cooker, combine the onion and garlic; top with chicken. In a small bowl, combine the ketchup, brown sugar, chili powder, lemon juice, basil, salt, pepper and pepper sauce; pour over the chicken.

Cover and cook on low for 4-1/2 to 5 hours or until chicken juices run clear. Remove chicken and keep warm.

Transfer cooking juices to a saucepan. Combine cornstarch and water until smooth; stir into juices. Bring to a boil; cook and stir for 2 minutes or until thickened. Serve with chicken. **yield:** 4 servings.

EASY PEPPER JACK CHICKEN

This chicken recipe is lower in calories, fat or sodium.

prep 20 minutes | **cook** 5 hours

linda foreman
locust grove, oklahoma

Simmer up a low-fat, delicious meal with just a few basic ingredients. Your family is sure to love this colorful medley with tender chicken and a zippy cheese sauce.

6 boneless skinless chicken breast halves (5 ounces *each*), cut into chunks
1 *each* small green, sweet red and orange pepper, cut into thin strips
1 can (10-3/4 ounces) condensed Southwest-style pepper Jack soup, undiluted
1/2 cup chunky salsa
1/8 teaspoon chili powder
4-1/2 cups hot cooked rice

In a 3-qt. slow cooker, combine the chicken, peppers, soup, salsa and chili powder. Cover and cook on low for 5-6 hours or until chicken juices run clear. Serve with rice. **yield:** 6 servings.

nutrition facts: 1 cup chicken mixture with 3/4 cup rice equals 360 calories, 7 g fat (2 g saturated fat), 84 mg cholesterol, 553 mg sodium, 41 g carbohydrate, 2 g fiber, 34 g protein.

diabetic exchanges: 4 very lean meat, 2-1/2 starch, 1/2 fat.

HERBED CHICKEN AND SHRIMP

prep 15 minutes | **cook** 4 hours 20 minutes

1 teaspoon salt
1 teaspoon pepper
1 broiler/fryer chicken (3 to 4 pounds), cut up and skin removed
1/4 cup butter
1 large onion, chopped
1 can (8 ounces) tomato sauce
1/2 cup white wine *or* chicken broth
1 garlic clove, minced
1 teaspoon dried basil
1 pound uncooked medium shrimp, peeled and deveined

Combine salt and pepper; rub over the chicken pieces. In a skillet, brown chicken on all sides in butter. Transfer to an ungreased 5-qt. slow cooker. In a bowl, combine the onion, tomato sauce, wine or broth, garlic and basil; pour over chicken.

Cover and cook on low for 4-5 hours or until a meat thermometer reads 170° in the breast meat and 180° in the thighs and drumsticks. Stir in the shrimp. Cover and cook on high for 20-30 minutes or until shrimp turn pink. **yield:** 4 servings.

diana knight
reno, nevada

Tender chicken and shrimp make a flavorful combination that's easy to prepare, yet elegant enough to serve at a dinner party. While I clean the house, it practically cooks itself. I serve it over hot cooked rice or pasta with crusty bread and a green salad.

ULTIMATE KITCHEN TIP

To peel and devein shrimp, start on the underside by the head. Use the legs to pull the shell to one side. Continue pulling shell up around the top and to the other side. Pull off shell by the tail if desired. Remove the black vein running down the back of shrimp by making a shallow slit with a paring knife along the back from head area to tail. Rinse shrimp under cold water to remove the vein.

This chicken recipe is lower in calories, fat or sodium.

SPICY LEMON CHICKEN

prep 20 minutes | **cook** 4 hours

nancy rambo

riverside, california

I took a favorite recipe and modified it to work in our slow cooker. We enjoy this tender lemony chicken with rice or buttered noodles.

1 medium onion, chopped
1/3 cup water
1/4 cup lemon juice
1 tablespoon canola oil
1/2 to 1 teaspoon salt
1/2 teaspoon *each* garlic powder, chili powder and paprika
1/2 teaspoon ground ginger
1/4 teaspoon pepper
4 boneless skinless chicken breast halves (4 ounces *each*)
4-1/2 teaspoons cornstarch
4-1/2 teaspoons cold water
Hot cooked noodles
Chopped fresh parsley, optional

In a greased 3-qt. slow cooker, combine the onion, water, lemon juice, oil and seasonings. Add chicken; turn to coat. Cover and cook on low for 4-5 hours or until a meat thermometer reads 170°. Remove chicken and keep warm.

In a saucepan, combine the cornstarch and cold water until smooth. Gradually add the cooking juices. Bring to a boil; cook and stir for 2 minutes or until thickened. Serve with the chicken over noodles. Sprinkle with parsley if desired. **yield:** 4 servings.

nutrition facts: 1 chicken breast with 1/4 cup sauce (prepared with 1/2 teaspoon salt; calculated without noodles) equals 190 calories, 5 g fat (1 g saturated fat), 66 mg cholesterol, 372 mg sodium, 8 g carbohydrate, 1 g fiber, 27 g protein.

diabetic exchanges: 3 lean meat, 1/2 starch.

ROSEMARY CHICKEN WITH WHITE BEANS

prep 15 minutes | **cook** 3 hours

6 boneless skinless chicken breast halves (6 ounces *each*)
1 tablespoon canola oil
2 cans (15-1/2 ounces *each*) great northern beans, rinsed and drained
1 cup sliced fresh carrots
1/2 cup sliced celery
2/3 cup Italian salad dressing
2 teaspoons dried rosemary, crushed
1/2 teaspoon salt
1 teaspoon pepper

In a large skillet, brown chicken in oil in batches on both sides. Place the beans, carrots and celery in a 5-qt. slow cooker; top with chicken.

Combine the salad dressing, rosemary, salt and pepper; pour over chicken. Cover and cook on low for 3-4 hours or until chicken juices run clear. **yield:** 6 servings.

sharon johannes,

ashley, illinois

With a full-time job and active child, I'm known as the "slow cooker queen" in my family. I use my slow cookers at least twice a week...sometimes I have two or three going at once with different dishes. I've made this recipe for years and, after making a few tweaks, it's become a treasured favorite.

ULTIMATE KITCHEN TIP

Choose the correct size slow cooker for your recipe. A slow cooker should be from half to three-quarters full. Unless the recipe instructs you to, refrain from lifting the lid as the food cooks. The loss of steam can add 15 to 30 minutes of cooking each time you lift the lid. Be sure the lid is sealed properly, and not tilted or askew because the steam creates a seal.

CHICKEN IN SOUR CREAM SAUCE

prep 15 minutes | **cook** 6 hours

jane carlovsky
sebring, florida

Tender chicken is deliciously dressed up in a flavorful cream sauce with fresh mushrooms. This is an excellent entree for your family or guests.

1-1/2 teaspoons salt
1/4 teaspoon pepper
1/4 teaspoon paprika
1/4 teaspoon lemon-pepper seasoning
6 bone-in chicken breast halves, skin removed
1 can (10-3/4 ounces) condensed cream of mushroom soup, undiluted
1 cup (8 ounces) sour cream
1/2 cup dry white wine *or* chicken broth
1/2 pound fresh mushrooms, sliced

Combine the first four ingredients; rub over chicken. Place in a 3-qt. slow cooker. In a bowl, combine the soup, sour cream, and wine or broth; stir in mushrooms. Pour over chicken. Cover and cook on low for 6-8 hours or until a meat thermometer reads 170°. Thicken the sauce if desired. **yield:** 6 servings.

PROSCIUTTO CHICKEN CACCIATORE

prep 30 minutes | **cook** 4 hours

8 boneless skinless chicken thighs (3 ounces *each*)
1-1/2 pounds boneless skinless chicken breast halves
1/2 cup all-purpose flour
1 teaspoon salt
1/4 teaspoon pepper
3 tablespoons olive oil
1 can (14-1/2 ounces) chicken broth
1 can (14-1/2 ounces) diced tomatoes, undrained
1 cup sliced fresh mushrooms
1 medium onion, chopped
1 package (3 ounces) thinly sliced prosciutto *or* deli ham, coarsely chopped
1 tablespoon diced pimientos
1 teaspoon minced garlic
1/2 teaspoon Italian seasoning
Hot cooked linguine
Grated Parmesan cheese

Cut chicken into serving size pieces. In a large resealable plastic bag, combine the flour, salt and pepper. Add chicken, a few pieces at a time, and shake to coat.

In a large skillet, brown chicken in oil in batches. Transfer to a 5-qt. slow cooker.

Stir in the broth, tomatoes, mushrooms, onion, prosciutto, pimientos, garlic and Italian seasoning. Cover and cook on low for 4 to 4-1/2 hours or until chicken is no longer pink. Serve with a slotted spoon over linguine; sprinkle with Parmesan cheese. **yield:** 6-8 servings.

sandra putnam
corvallis, montana

I tailored my mother's hearty entree recipe to the convenience of a slow cooker. It's great for busy weeknights.

ORANGE CHICKEN WITH SWEET POTATOES

prep 25 minutes | **cook** 3-1/2 hours

vicki smith
okeechobee, florida

Orange peel and pineapple juice lend a fruity flavor to this super chicken and sweet potato combo. Served over rice, this appealing entree is bound to win you compliments.

3   medium sweet potatoes, peeled and sliced
2/3 cup plus 3 tablespoons all-purpose flour, *divided*
1   teaspoon salt
1   teaspoon onion powder
1   teaspoon ground nutmeg
1   teaspoon ground cinnamon
1   teaspoon pepper
4   boneless skinless chicken breast halves (5 ounces *each*)
2   tablespoons butter
1   can (10-3/4 ounces) condensed cream of chicken soup, undiluted
3/4 cup unsweetened pineapple juice
2   teaspoons brown sugar
1   teaspoon grated orange peel
1/2 pound sliced fresh mushrooms
Hot cooked rice

Layer sweet potatoes in a 3-qt. slow cooker. In a large resealable plastic bag, combine 2/3 cup flour and seasonings; add chicken, one piece at a time, and shake to coat.

In a large skillet over medium heat, cook the chicken in butter for 3 minutes on each side or until lightly browned. Arrange the chicken over the sweet potatoes.

Place remaining flour in a small bowl. Stir in the soup, pineapple juice, brown sugar and orange peel until blended. Add mushrooms; pour over chicken.

Cover and cook on low for 3-1/2 to 4 hours or until a meat thermometer reads 170° and potatoes are tender. Serve with rice. **yield:** 4 servings.

SAUCY CHICKEN THIGHS

prep 20 minutes | **cook** 4 hours

9   bone-in chicken thighs (6 ounces *each*)
1/2 teaspoon salt
1/4 teaspoon pepper
1-1/2 cups barbecue sauce
1/2 cup honey
2   teaspoons prepared mustard
2   teaspoons Worcestershire sauce
1/8 to 1/2 teaspoon hot pepper sauce

Sprinkle chicken with salt and pepper. Place on a broiler pan. Broil 4-5 in. from the heat for 6-8 minutes on each side or until juices run clear. Transfer to a 5-qt. slow cooker.

In a small bowl, combine the barbecue sauce, honey, mustard, Worcestershire sauce and pepper sauce. Pour over chicken; stir to coat. Cover and cook on low for 4-5 hours or until heated through. **yield:** 9 servings.

kim puckett
reagan, tennessee

Everyone raves about how sweet the sauce is for these slow-cooked chicken thighs. They're a breeze to make because they simmer away while you do other things. They're ideal appetizers or added to your favorite side dish for a nice meal.

CREAMY TARRAGON CHICKEN

prep 10 minutes | **cook** 6-1/4 hours

- 7 boneless skinless chicken breast halves (6 ounces *each*)
- 1 cup chopped onion
- 1 cup water
- 2 ounces prosciutto *or* deli ham, chopped
- 3 tablespoons quick-cooking tapioca
- 2 teaspoons chicken bouillon granules
- 2 teaspoons dried tarragon
- 1 teaspoon minced garlic
- 1/4 teaspoon salt
- 1/4 teaspoon pepper
- 3 cups frozen broccoli-cauliflower blend, thawed
- 1/2 cup half-and-half cream
- 1-1/2 cups uncooked orzo pasta

In a 5-qt. slow cooker, combine the first 10 ingredients. Cover and cook on low for 6-7 hours or until chicken juices run clear.

Remove three chicken breast halves; cool. Cover and refrigerate for another use.

Stir vegetables and cream into the slow cooker. Cover and cook 15 minutes longer or until vegetables are heated through. Meanwhile, cook orzo according to package directions. Serve with chicken and vegetables. **yield:** 4 servings.

**taste of home
test kitchen**
greendale, wisconsin

Break out the slow cooker to start your busy week with an easy note by making this all-in-one recipe. A cup of chicken broth may be substituted for the water and chicken bouillon granules.

SOFT CHICKEN TACOS

prep 30 minutes | **cook** 5 hours

cheryl newendorp
pella, iowa

My family loves these tacos. It's convenient to throw the ingredients together for the filling in the slow cooker before I leave for work. At the end of the day, I roll the chicken in a tortilla with the remaining items and dinner's ready in minutes. The chicken also makes a great topping for salad.

1 broiler/fryer chicken (3-1/2 pounds), cut up and skin removed
1 can (8 ounces) tomato sauce
1 can (4 ounces) chopped green chilies
1/3 cup chopped onion
2 tablespoons chili powder
2 tablespoons Worcestershire sauce
1/4 teaspoon garlic powder
10 flour tortillas (8 inches), warmed
1-1/4 cups shredded cheddar cheese
1-1/4 cups salsa
1-1/4 cups shredded lettuce

1 large tomato, chopped
3/4 cup sour cream, optional

Place the chicken in a 3-qt. slow cooker. In a small bowl, combine the tomato sauce, chilies, onion, chili powder, Worcestershire sauce and garlic powder; pour over chicken. Cover and cook on low for 5-6 hours or until chicken is tender and juices run clear.

Remove the chicken. Shred meat with two forks and return to the slow cooker; heat through. Spoon 1/2 cup chicken mixture down the center of each tortilla. Top with cheese, salsa, lettuce, tomato and sour cream if desired; roll up. **yield:** 5 servings.

SWEET-AND-SOUR CHICKEN

prep 15 minutes | **cook** 3 hours 20 minutes

1-1/4 pounds boneless skinless chicken breasts, cut into 1-inch strips
1 tablespoon canola oil
Salt and pepper to taste
1 can (8 ounces) pineapple chunks
1 can (8 ounces) sliced water chestnuts, drained
2 medium carrots, sliced
2 tablespoons soy sauce
4 teaspoons cornstarch
1 cup sweet-and-sour sauce
1/4 cup water
1-1/2 teaspoons ground ginger
3 green onions, cut into 1-inch pieces
1-1/2 cups fresh *or* frozen snow peas
Hot cooked rice

dorothy hess
hartwell, georgia

Who would believe that this stir-fry like supper was cooked in a slow cooker? Adding onions, pineapple and snow peas later in the process prevents them from overcooking.

In a large skillet, saute the chicken in oil for 4-5 minutes; drain. Sprinkle with salt and pepper. Drain the pineapple chunks, reserving the juice; set pineapple aside. In a 5-qt. slow cooker, combine the chicken, water chestnuts, sliced carrots, soy sauce and pineapple juice. Cover and cook on low for 3 hours or until the chicken juices run clear.

In a small bowl, combine the cornstarch, sweet-and-sour sauce, water and ginger until smooth. Stir into the slow cooker. Add onions and reserved pineapple; cover and cook on high for 15 minutes or until thickened. Add peas; cook 5 minutes longer. Serve with rice. **yield:** 5 servings.

MOIST DRUMSTICKS

prep 10 minutes | **cook** 5 hours

lianne felton
riverside, california

I found this in my mom's recipe box years ago. It's very quick to prepare and makes the house smell wonderful. My daughter just loves it.

3 pounds chicken drumsticks, skin removed
1 can (8 ounces) tomato sauce
1/2 cup soy sauce
1/4 cup packed brown sugar
1 teaspoon minced garlic
3 tablespoons cornstarch
1/4 cup cold water

Place drumsticks in a 5-qt. slow cooker. In a small bowl, combine the tomato sauce, soy sauce, brown sugar and garlic; pour over chicken. Cover and cook on low for 5-6 hours or until chicken juices run clear.

Remove the chicken and keep warm. Strain cooking juices. In a small saucepan, combine the cornstarch and cold water until smooth; stir in juices. Bring to a boil; cook and stir for 2 minutes or until thickened. Serve with the chicken. **yield:** 6 servings.

CURRIED CHICKEN WITH PEACHES

prep 15 minutes | **cook** 3-1/4 hours

1 broiler/fryer chicken (3 pounds), cut up
1/8 teaspoon salt
1/8 teaspoon pepper
1 can (29 ounces) sliced peaches
1/2 cup chicken broth
2 tablespoons butter, melted
1 tablespoon dried minced onion
2 teaspoons curry powder
2 garlic cloves, minced
1/4 teaspoon ground ginger
3 tablespoons cornstarch
3 tablespoons cold water
1/4 cup raisins
Toasted flaked coconut, optional

Place chicken in a 5-qt. slow cooker; sprinkle with salt and pepper. Drain peaches, reserving 1/2 cup juice; set peaches aside. In a small bowl, combine the broth, butter, onion, curry, garlic, ginger and reserved juice; pour over chicken. Cover and cook on low for 3-4 hours or until chicken juices run clear.

Remove the chicken and keep warm. In a small bowl, combine the cornstarch and water until smooth; stir into the cooking juices. Add raisins. Cover and cook on high for 10-15 minutes or until thickened. Stir in peaches; heat through. Serve over chicken. Garnish with coconut if desired. **yield:** 4 servings.

heidi martinez
colorado springs, colorado

I'm always looking for recipes I can prepare ahead of time. The chicken chunks bask for hours in snappy spices and seasonings, giving this recipe a lot of pizzazz. The peaches round out the amazing flavors.

ULTIMATE KITCHEN TIP

In India, curry powder is traditionally made from up to 20 whole herbs and spices that have been pulverized and blended. The flavor, color and spiciness varies widely. Curry powders that are available at the supermarket are usually mustard yellow in color and mildly spicy. Hot curry powder is labeled as such, and may be a different color, such as red or orange.

MEXICAN CHICKEN SOUP

prep 10 minutes | **cook** 3 hours

marlene kane
lainesburg, michigan

As a busy mom, I'm always looking for dinner recipes that can be prepared in the morning. This zesty soup is loaded with chicken, corn and black beans in a mildly spicy broth. The kids love its taco-like taste.

1-1/2 pounds boneless skinless chicken breasts, cubed
2 teaspoons canola oil
1/2 cup water
1 envelope reduced-sodium taco seasoning
1 can (32 ounces) V8 juice
1 jar (16 ounces) salsa
1 can (15 ounces) black beans, rinsed and drained
1 package (10 ounces) frozen corn, thawed
6 tablespoons shredded reduced-fat cheddar cheese

6 tablespoons reduced-fat sour cream
2 tablespoons minced fresh cilantro

In a large nonstick skillet, saute chicken in oil until no longer pink. Add water and taco seasoning; simmer until chicken is well coated.

Transfer to a 5-qt. slow cooker. Stir in the V8 juice, salsa, black beans and corn. Cover and cook on low for 3-4 hours or until heated through. Serve with shredded cheese, sour cream and cilantro. **yield:** 6 servings.

FRUITED CHICKEN

prep 10 minutes | **cook** 4 hours

mirien church
aurora, colorado

I've worked full-time for more than 30 years, and this super slow cooker recipe has been a lifesaver. It cooks while I'm away and smells heavenly as soon as I walk in the door in the evening after a day's work.

1 large onion, sliced
6 boneless skinless chicken breast halves (6 ounces *each*)
1/3 cup orange juice
2 tablespoons soy sauce
2 tablespoons Worcestershire sauce
2 tablespoons Dijon mustard
1 tablespoon grated orange peel
2 garlic cloves, minced
1/2 cup chopped dried apricots
1/2 cup dried cranberries
Hot cooked rice

Place onion and chicken in a 5-qt. slow cooker. Combine the orange juice, soy sauce, Worcestershire sauce, mustard, orange peel and garlic; pour over chicken. Sprinkle with apricots and cranberries. Cover and cook on low for 4-5 hours or until a meat thermometer reads 170°. Serve with rice. **yield:** 6 servings.

TANGY BARBECUE WINGS

prep 1-1/2 hours | **cook** 3 hours

25 whole chicken wings (about 5 pounds)
2-1/2 cups hot and spicy ketchup
2/3 cup white vinegar
1/2 cup plus 2 tablespoons honey
1/2 cup molasses
1 teaspoon salt
1 teaspoon Worcestershire sauce
1/2 teaspoon onion powder
1/2 teaspoon chili powder
1/2 to 1 teaspoon Liquid Smoke, optional

Cut chicken wings into three sections; discard wing tip sections. Place chicken wings in two greased 15-in. x 10-in. baking pans. Bake, uncovered, at 375° for 30 minutes; drain. Turn wings; bake 20-25 minutes longer or until juices run clear.

Meanwhile, in a large saucepan, combine the ketchup, vinegar, honey, molasses, salt, Worcestershire sauce, onion powder and chili powder. Add Liquid Smoke if desired. Bring to a boil. Reduce heat; simmer, uncovered, for 25-30 minutes. Drain wings; place a third of them in a 5-qt. slow cooker. Top with about 1 cup sauce. Repeat layers twice. Cover and cook on low for 3-4 hours. Stir before serving. **yield:** about 4 dozen.

editor's note: Uncooked chicken wing sections (wingettes) may be substituted for whole chicken wings.

sherry pitzer
troy, missouri

When I took these savory, slow-cooked appetizers to work, they were gone before I even got a bite! Spicy ketchup, vinegar, molasses and honey blend together in a tangy sauce that makes the wings lip-smacking good.

TENDER CHICKEN DINNER

prep 10 minutes | **cook** 5-1/4 hours

wanda sanner
amarillo, texas

This all-in-one poultry dinner provides lots of family appeal. It can be put together very quickly before you leave for school or work.

4 boneless skinless chicken breast halves (4 ounces *each*)
1 can (14-1/2 ounces) chicken broth
1 can (14-1/2 ounces) chicken gravy
2 cups sliced peeled potatoes
1 package (16 ounces) frozen sliced carrots, thawed
1 package (16 ounces) frozen cut green beans, thawed
1 teaspoon pepper
2 tablespoons cornstarch

1/3 cup cold water
1 cup french-fried onions

Place chicken in a 5-qt. slow cooker. Add the broth, gravy, potatoes, carrots, beans and pepper. Cover and cook on low for 5 to 5-1/2 hours or until chicken juices run clear.

In a small bowl, combine cornstarch and water; stir into cooking juices. Sprinkle with onions. Cover and cook on high for 15 minutes or until thickened. **yield:** 4 servings.

SLOW COOKER CACCIATORE

prep 20 minutes | **cook** 4 hours

1/3 cup all-purpose flour
1 broiler/fryer chicken (3 to 4 pounds), cut up
2 tablespoons canola oil
2 medium onions, cut into wedges
1 medium green pepper, cut into strips
1 jar (6 ounces) sliced mushrooms, drained
1 can (14-1/2 ounces) diced tomatoes, undrained
2 garlic cloves, minced
1/2 teaspoon salt
1/2 teaspoon dried oregano
1/4 teaspoon dried basil
1/2 cup shredded Parmesan cheese

Place flour in a large resealable plastic bag. Add chicken, a few pieces at a time, and shake to coat. In a large skillet, brown chicken in oil on all sides. Transfer to a 5-qt. slow cooker.

Top with the onions, green pepper and mushrooms. Combine the tomatoes, garlic, salt, oregano and basil; pour over vegetables. Cover and cook on low for 4-5 hours or until the chicken and vegetables are tender. Serve with Parmesan cheese. **yield:** 6 servings.

nutrition facts: 1 serving (calculated without skin) equals 296 calories, 12 g fat (3 g saturated fat), 78 mg cholesterol, 582 mg sodium, 16 g carbohydrate, 3 g fiber, 29 g protein.

diabetic exchanges: 3 lean meat, 2 vegetable, 1 fat, 1/2 starch.

This chicken recipe is lower in calories, fat or sodium.

denise hollebeke
penhold, alberta

Prep for this Italian classic entree only takes 20 minutes. The chicken comes out tender and flavorful.

LIME CHICKEN TACOS

prep 10 minutes | **cook** 5-1/2 hours

This chicken recipe is lower in calories, fat or sodium.

1-1/2 pounds boneless skinless chicken breasts
3 tablespoons lime juice
1 tablespoon chili powder
1 cup frozen corn
1 cup chunky salsa
12 flour tortillas (6 inches), warmed

Sour cream, shredded cheddar cheese and shredded lettuce, optional

Place the chicken in a 3-qt. slow cooker. Combine the lime juice and chili powder; pour over the chicken. Cover and cook on low for 5-6 hours or until the chicken is tender.

Remove chicken; cool slightly. Shred and return to the slow cooker. Stir in corn and salsa. Cover and cook on low for 30 minutes or until heated through. Serve in tortillas with sour cream, cheese and lettuce if desired. **yield:** 12 tacos.

nutrition facts: 1 taco (prepared with fat-free tortillas; calculated without sour cream and cheese) equals 148 calories, 2 g fat (trace saturated fat), 31 mg cholesterol, 338 mg sodium, 18 g carbohydrate, 1 g fiber, 14 g protein.

diabetic exchanges: 2 very lean meat, 1 starch.

tracy gunter
boise, idaho

This fun recipe is great and simple for a casual dinner with friends or family. Lime adds zest to this easy filling for tortillas, and leftovers make for a refreshing topping to any taco salad.

HEARTY JAMBALAYA

prep 15 minutes | **cook** 6-1/4 hours

jennifer fulk
moreno valley, california

I love anything with Cajun spices, so I came up with this slow cooker jambalaya that's just as good as a restaurant's. I like to serve it with warm corn bread and garnish it with sliced green onions. If you can't find andouille sausage, hot links, smoked sausage or chorizo will also work.

1	can (28 ounces) diced tomatoes, undrained
1	pound fully cooked andouille sausage links, cubed
1/2	pound boneless skinless chicken breasts, cut into 1-inch cubes
1	can (8 ounces) tomato sauce
1	cup diced onion
1	small sweet red pepper, diced
1	small green pepper, diced
1	cup chicken broth
1	celery rib with leaves, chopped
2	tablespoons tomato paste
2	teaspoons dried oregano
2	teaspoons Cajun seasoning
1-1/2	teaspoons minced garlic
2	bay leaves
1	teaspoon Louisiana-style hot sauce
1/2	teaspoon dried thyme
1	pound cooked medium shrimp, peeled and deveined
	Hot cooked rice

In a 5-qt. slow cooker, combine the first 16 ingredients. Cover and cook on low for 6-7 hours or until chicken juices run clear.

Stir in shrimp. Cover and cook 15 minutes longer or until heated through. Discard bay leaves. Serve with rice. **yield:** 8 servings.

SLOW 'N' EASY BARBECUED CHICKEN

prep 20 minutes | **cook** 3 hours

1/4	cup water
3	tablespoons brown sugar
3	tablespoons white vinegar
3	tablespoons ketchup
2	tablespoons butter
2	tablespoons Worcestershire sauce
1	tablespoon lemon juice
1	teaspoon salt
1	teaspoon paprika
1	teaspoon ground mustard
1/2	teaspoon cayenne pepper
1	broiler/fryer chicken (2-1/2 to 3 pounds), cut up and skin removed
4	teaspoons cornstarch
1	tablespoon cold water

dreama hughes
london, kentucky

I rely on this yummy recipe often during the summer and fall when I know I'm going to be out working in the yard all day. After pairing it with a side vegetable and salad, supper is served! It's also delicious with pork or beef and easy to double for a crowd.

In a small saucepan, combine the first 11 ingredients. Bring to a boil. Reduce heat; simmer, uncovered, for 5 minutes. Remove from the heat.

Place the chicken in a 3-qt. slow cooker. Top with the sauce. Cover and cook on low for 3-4 hours or until the chicken juices run clear.

Remove chicken to a serving platter and keep warm. Strain cooking juices and skim fat; transfer to a small saucepan. Combine cornstarch and water until smooth; stir into juices. Bring to a boil; cook and stir for 2 minutes or until thickened. Spoon some of the sauce over chicken and serve the remaining sauce on the side. **yield:** 4 servings.

CHICKEN MERLOT WITH MUSHROOMS

prep 10 minutes | **cook** 5 hours

shelli mcwilliam
salem, oregon

Slow cooked and savory, this dish is perfect for any night of the week. It's sure to become a staple in your home.

5-1/4 cups sliced fresh mushrooms
1 cup chopped onion
2 teaspoons minced garlic
3 pounds boneless skinless chicken thighs
1 can (6 ounces) tomato paste
3/4 cup chicken broth
1/4 cup Merlot wine *or* additional chicken broth
2 tablespoons quick-cooking tapioca
2 teaspoons sugar
1-1/2 teaspoons dried basil
1/2 teaspoon salt
1/4 teaspoon pepper
2 tablespoons grated Parmesan cheese
Hot cooked pasta, optional

Place the mushrooms, onion and garlic in a 5-qt. slow cooker. Top with chicken.

In a small bowl, combine the tomato paste, broth, wine or additional broth, tapioca, sugar, basil, salt and pepper. Pour over the chicken. Cover and cook on low for 5-6 hours or until the chicken is tender.

Sprinkle with Parmesan cheese. Serve with pasta if desired. **yield:** 5 servings.

HERBED SLOW COOKER CHICKEN

prep 5 minutes | **cook** 4 hours

1 tablespoon olive oil
1 teaspoon paprika
1/2 teaspoon garlic powder
1/2 teaspoon seasoned salt
1/2 teaspoon dried thyme
1/2 teaspoon dried basil
1/2 teaspoon pepper
1/2 teaspoon browning sauce, optional

4 bone-in chicken breast halves (6 ounces *each*)
1/2 cup chicken broth

In a small bowl, combine the first eight ingredients; rub over the chicken. Place in a 5-qt. slow cooker; add the broth. Cover and cook on low for 4-5 hours or until a meat thermometer reads 170°. **yield:** 4 servings.

sundra hauck
bogalusa, louisiana

I use my slow cooker to prepare these well-seasoned chicken breasts that cook up moist and tender. My daughter, who has two young sons to keep up with, shared this great recipe with me several years ago. Since then, I've made it many times.

ULTIMATE KITCHEN TIP

Dried herbs don't spoil, but they will lose flavor and potency over time. To maximize the flavor in your cooking, you may want to replace herbs that are over a year old. Dried herbs will stay fresher when stored in airtight containers away from light and any heat source. It's best not to put them in the cupboard above the stove.

COOKING *for* ONE *or* TWO

HONEY LIME CHICKEN, P. 236

CHICKEN CHEESE ROLLS

prep 10 minutes | **bake** 25 minutes

leonora wilkie

bellbrook, ohio

This entree is an elegant dinner for two or for any special occasion. The cheese filling is tasty and combines well with the sweet and spicy flavors from the chutney. It's an uncomplicated recipe that easily impresses.

2 boneless skinless chicken breast halves (6 ounces *each*)
1/4 cup shredded cheddar cheese
2 tablespoons cream cheese, softened
1 tablespoon butter, melted
2 teaspoons chutney

Line a small baking pan with foil and grease the foil. Flatten chicken to 1/4-in. thickness. Combine the cheddar cheese and cream cheese; spread over chicken. Roll up and secure with toothpicks. Place in prepared pan.

Combine the butter and chutney; spoon over the chicken. Bake, uncovered, at 350° for 25-30 minutes or until the juices run clear. Discard toothpicks. **yield**: 2 servings.

BROCCOLI CHICKEN FETTUCCINE

prep/total time 25 minutes

4 ounces uncooked fettuccine
1/2 pound boneless skinless chicken breasts, cut into 1-inch pieces
1 small onion, halved and sliced
4 garlic cloves, minced
2 tablespoons butter
1 can (10-3/4 ounces) condensed cream of chicken soup, undiluted
1 cup chicken broth
1-1/2 cups frozen broccoli florets, thawed
1 can (4 ounces) mushroom stems and pieces, drained

1 teaspoon onion powder
1/2 teaspoon pepper
1/4 cup shredded Parmesan cheese

Cook fettuccine according to package directions. Meanwhile, in a large skillet, saute the chicken, onion and garlic in butter until no longer pink. Stir in the soup, broth, broccoli, mushrooms, onion powder and pepper. Bring to a boil.

Drain fettuccine; add to chicken mixture. Reduce heat; cover and simmer for 5 minutes or until heated through. Sprinkle with Parmesan cheese. **yield**: 2 servings.

elaine mizzles

ben wheeler, texas

I served this comforting pasta dish with garlic bread, and my finicky-eating, 6-year-old grandson absolutely loved it!

CHICKEN ALFREDO STROMBOLI

prep/total time 25 minutes

1	French bread baguette (5 ounces), halved lengthwise
6	ounces boneless skinless chicken breast, cubed
1	teaspoon olive oil
4	teaspoons butter, softened, *divided*
1/3	cup canned mushroom stems and pieces, drained
1/4	teaspoon salt
1/4	teaspoon garlic powder
1/4	teaspoon pepper
1/4	cup sour cream
1/4	cup grated Parmesan cheese
1/2	cup shredded part-skim mozzarella cheese

Place bread, cut side up, on an ungreased baking sheet. Broil 4-6 in. from the heat for 2-3 minutes or until lightly toasted; set aside.

In a small skillet, saute chicken in oil and 1 teaspoon butter until juices run clear; drain. Add the mushrooms, salt, garlic powder and pepper; cook for 1-2 minutes or until heated through.

In a small bowl, combine the sour cream, Parmesan cheese and remaining butter; spread over bread halves. Top each with 2/3 cup chicken mixture. Sprinkle with the mozzarella cheese. Broil for 1-2 minutes or until the cheese is melted. **yield**: 2 servings.

tracy haven
henryville, indiana

After combining my favorite fettuccine Alfredo recipe with a chicken Alfredo pizza from a local restaurant, I came up with this satisfying, open-faced sandwich.

CHICKEN 'N' BISCUIT BAKE

prep 1 hour | **bake** 20 minutes

shireen rancier

killam, alberta

My mother used to make this homey dish years ago, and everyone in the family always enjoyed it.

2 cups chicken broth
1 pound bone-in chicken breast halves
1 medium onion, chopped
1 celery rib, cut into 1/2-inch pieces
1 teaspoon salt
1 bay leaf

CREAM SAUCE

3 tablespoons plus 1-1/2 teaspoons butter, melted
3 tablespoons plus 1-1/2 teaspoons all-purpose flour
Salt and pepper to taste
Dash ground mace
1/3 cup milk
1/8 teaspoon Worcestershire sauce

BISCUITS

2/3 cup plus 1 tablespoon all-purpose flour
1-1/4 teaspoons baking powder
1/8 teaspoon salt
2 tablespoons shortening
1/3 cup milk

In a large saucepan, combine the broth, chicken, onion, celery, salt and bay leaf. Bring to a boil. Reduce heat; cover and simmer for 20 minutes or until chicken juices run clear.

Remove chicken from broth; cool. When cool enough to handle, remove skin and meat from bones. Discard skin and bones. Cut up meat. Strain broth. Reserve vegetables and 1 cup broth; discard bay leaf. (Discard or save remaining broth for another use.) Arrange chicken and vegetables in a greased 3-cup dish.

For the cream sauce, melt the butter in a saucepan. Stir in the flour, salt, pepper and mace until smooth. Gradually add the milk, Worcestershire sauce and reserved broth. Bring to a boil; cook and stir for 2 minutes or until thickened. Pour over the chicken.

For the biscuits, in a small bowl, combine the flour, baking powder and salt; cut in the shortening until the mixture resembles coarse crumbs. Stir in the milk.

On a floured surface, knead 8-10 times. Pat into a 1/2-in.-thick square and cut into quarters. Arrange biscuits over sauce. Bake, uncovered, at 450° for 17-20 minutes or until the biscuits are golden brown. **yield**: 2 servings.

CHICKEN WRAPPED IN BACON

prep 20 minutes | **bake** 35 minutes

6 bacon strips
2 boneless skinless chicken breast halves (5 ounces *each*)
1 package (3 ounces) cream cheese, softened
2 garlic cloves, minced
1/2 teaspoon salt
1 can (4 ounces) chopped green chilies, drained

ladonna reed

ponca city, oklahoma

The taste of smoky bacon over tender chicken breasts is hard to beat. This main dish comes together in a snap and is a huge success with my family.

In a large skillet, cook the bacon over medium heat until cooked but not crisp. Remove to paper towels to drain. Flatten the chicken to 1/8-in. thickness. Spread with cream cheese; sprinkle with garlic and salt. Top with chilies. Roll up from a long side; tuck the ends in.

Wrap three bacon strips around each piece of chicken; secure with toothpicks. Place in a greased 1-qt. baking dish. Bake, uncovered, at 350° for 35-40 minutes or until chicken juices run clear and bacon is crisp. Discard toothpicks before serving. **yield**: 2 servings.

PINEAPPLE MACADAMIA CHICKEN

prep/total time 25 minutes

kimberlie smith
coeur d'alene, idaho

My family enjoys this summertime entree. It's quick, easy and oh-so-good, served with cantaloupe wedges and iced tea. Each spicy-sweet bite reminds us of our trip to Hawaii.

- 2 boneless skinless chicken breast halves
- 3/4 cup finely chopped macadamia nuts
- 1/4 teaspoon seasoned salt
- 1/4 teaspoon Caribbean jerk seasoning
- 1/8 teaspoon dried minced onion
- 1/8 teaspoon onion powder
- 1/8 teaspoon pepper
- 1 egg, lightly beaten
- 2 tablespoons canola oil
- 1/4 cup crushed pineapple
- 1 tablespoon apricot preserves, warmed

Lettuce leaves

Flatten chicken to 1/4-in. thickness. In a shallow bowl, combine the nuts, seasoned salt, jerk seasoning, minced onion, onion powder and pepper. Place egg in another shallow bowl. Dip chicken in egg; coat with nut mixture. Let stand for 5 minutes.

In a large skillet, cook chicken in oil for 3-4 minutes on each side or until chicken juices run clear. In a small bowl, combine pineapple and apricot preserves. Place lettuce on each plate; top with chicken and pineapple mixture. **yield:** 2 servings.

CHICKEN AND DUMPLINGS

prep 10 minutes | **cook** 30 minutes

- 2 boneless skinless chicken breast halves, cut into 1/2-inch cubes
- 1-1/2 cups chicken broth
- 1 medium carrot, sliced
- 1 small potato, peeled and cubed
- 1/4 cup chopped onion
- 2 tablespoons chopped celery
- 1 bay leaf
- 1/4 teaspoon salt
- 1/8 teaspoon pepper

DUMPLINGS

- 1/4 cup all-purpose flour
- 1 teaspoon dried parsley flakes
- 1/2 teaspoon baking powder

Pinch ground cloves

Pinch salt

- 3 tablespoons milk

In a small saucepan, combine the first nine ingredients; bring to a boil. Reduce heat; cover and simmer for 15 minutes or until vegetables are tender. Discard bay leaf.

For the dumplings, in a small bowl, combine the flour, parsley, baking powder, cloves and salt. Stir in milk just until moistened. Drop by heaping teaspoonfuls onto simmering chicken mixture. Cover and simmer for 15 minutes or until a toothpick inserted into a dumpling comes out clean (do not lift the cover while simmering). **yield:** 2 servings.

claire bruno
tucson, arizona

Here, chunks of chicken and vegetables in a warm broth are topped with tender dumplings. What a great treat on a chilly fall or winter day, or on any day for that matter!

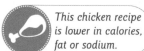

This chicken recipe is lower in calories, fat or sodium.

SPICED CHICKEN WITH MELON SALSA

prep 20 minutes | **grill** 15 minutes

roxanne chan
albany, california

Both sweet and spicy, this summery entree can be grilled or broiled. It's nutritious and delicious. To speed up preparation, I buy a container of mixed melon pieces at the supermarket.

1/4	teaspoon salt
1/4	teaspoon ground ginger
1/4	teaspoon ground nutmeg
1/8	to 1/4 teaspoon crushed red pepper flakes
2	boneless skinless chicken breast halves (5 ounces *each*)

SALSA

1/3	cup *each* diced cantaloupe, honeydew and watermelon
2	tablespoons diced celery
1	green onion, finely chopped
2	teaspoons minced fresh mint *or* 1/4 teaspoon dried mint
2	teaspoons chopped candied ginger

2	teaspoons lime juice
2	teaspoons honey
1/4	teaspoon grated lime peel

In a small bowl, combine the salt, ginger, nutmeg and pepper flakes; rub over the chicken. Grill, covered, over medium heat or broil 6 in. from the heat for 6 minutes on each side or until meat juices run clear. Meanwhile, in a small bowl, combine the ingredients for the salsa. Serve with chicken. **yield:** 2 servings.

nutrition facts: 1 chicken breast half with 1/2 cup salsa equals 225 calories, 4 g fat (1 g saturated fat), 78 mg cholesterol, 380 mg sodium, 18 g carbohydrate, 1 g fiber, 29 g protein.

diabetic exchanges: 4 very lean meat, 1 fruit, 1/2 fat.

DEVILED CHICKEN THIGHS

prep/total time 30 minutes

bernice morris
marshfield, missouri

When I make this dish, I invite my next-door neighbor over for supper. It's just enough for the two of us. This tasty chicken is tender and moist, with a bit of crunch from the cashews.

- 1 teaspoon butter, softened
- 1 teaspoon cider vinegar
- 1 teaspoon prepared mustard
- 1 teaspoon paprika

Dash pepper

- 2 boneless skinless chicken thighs (about 4 ounces *each*)
- 3 tablespoons soft bread crumbs
- 2 tablespoons chopped cashews

In a large bowl, combine the butter, vinegar, mustard, paprika and pepper. Spread over chicken thighs. Place in a greased 11-in. x 7-in. baking dish. Sprinkle with bread crumbs.

Bake, uncovered, at 400° for 15 minutes. Sprinkle with the cashews. Bake 7-12 minutes longer or until the chicken juices run clear and topping is golden brown. **yield:** 2 servings.

CHICKEN PICCATA

prep/total time 25 minutes

- 2 boneless skinless chicken breast halves (4 ounces *each*)
- 2 tablespoons all-purpose flour
- 1/4 teaspoon salt
- 1/8 teaspoon pepper
- 1 tablespoon canola oil
- 2 tablespoons white wine *or* reduced-sodium chicken broth
- 1 garlic clove, minced
- 1/3 cup reduced-sodium chicken broth
- 1 tablespoon lemon juice
- 1-1/2 teaspoons capers
- 1-1/2 teaspoons butter
- 2 thin lemon slices

Flatten chicken to 1/2-in. thickness. In a shallow bowl, combine the flour, salt and pepper. Add chicken, one piece at a time, and turn to coat.

In a small skillet, brown the chicken in oil for 2-3 minutes on each side or until juices run clear. Remove and keep warm.

Add wine or broth and garlic to the pan; cook and stir for 30 seconds. Add broth, lemon juice and capers. Bring to a boil; cook for 1-2 minutes or until slightly thickened. Stir in butter and lemon slices. Return chicken to the pan; heat through. **yield:** 2 servings.

carol cottrill
rumford, maine

This is a flavorful and healthy dish. With the lemon juice, the salt isn't missed. I usually serve this with rice or pasta, but it takes longer to cook either one of these than it does the chicken!

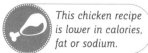
This chicken recipe is lower in calories, fat or sodium.

CHICKEN WITH MANGO SALSA

prep 20 minutes + chilling | **cook** 10 minutes

denise elder
hanover, ontario

I blend tangy tropical flavors to make the fresh and sassy salsa that tops the tender chicken entree. For extra flavor, you can grill the chicken.

1/2	cup chopped peeled mango
1/2	cup chopped tomato
2	tablespoons minced fresh cilantro
1	tablespoon chopped jalapeno pepper
1	tablespoon chopped red onion
1-1/2	teaspoons chopped celery
1-1/2	teaspoons lime juice
1/4	teaspoon grated lime peel
2	boneless skinless chicken breast halves (6 ounces *each*)
1/4	teaspoon salt
1/8	teaspoon pepper
1	tablespoon canola oil

For salsa, in a small bowl, combine the mango, tomato, cilantro, jalapeno, onion, celery, lime juice and peel. Cover and refrigerate for 2-3 hours.

Sprinkle chicken with salt and pepper. In a large skillet, cook chicken in oil over medium-high heat for 5-6 minutes on each side or until juices run clear. Serve with salsa. **yield:** 2 servings.

nutrition facts: 1 chicken breast half with 1/2 cup salsa equals 285 calories, 11 g fat (2 g saturated fat), 94 mg cholesterol, 384 mg sodium, 10 g carbohydrate, 2 g fiber, 35 g protein.

diabetic exchanges: 5 very lean meat, 2 vegetable, 1 fat.

editor's note: When cutting hot peppers, disposable gloves are recommended. Avoid touching your face.

CHICKEN-FETA PHYLLO BUNDLES

prep 20 minutes | **bake** 30 minutes

6	sheets phyllo dough (14 inches x 9 inches)
1/4	cup butter, melted
2	boneless skinless chicken breast halves
	Lemon-pepper seasoning
1/2	cup crumbled feta *or* shredded part-skim mozzarella cheese

Place one sheet phyllo dough on a work surface; brush with melted butter. Repeat with 2 more sheets or phyllo, brushing each layer. (Keep remaining phyllo dough covered with plastic wrap and a damp towel to prevent it from drying out.)

Season chicken with lemon-pepper. Place 1 chicken breast along one short edge of pastry. Top with 1/4 cup cheese. Fold sides over chicken, then roll up. Brush with melted butter.

Place on an ungreased baking sheet. Repeat with remaining ingredients. Bake, uncovered, at 350° for 30-35 minutes or until phyllo dough is golden brown. **yield:** 2 servings.

kathryn acreman
carstairs, alberta

Making these delicious bundles requires just a few ingredients. I put the remaining pastry back in the freezer to use another time.

STUFFED RANCH CHICKEN

prep 15 minutes | **bake** 25 minutes

This chicken recipe is lower in calories, fat or sodium.

- 1 bacon strip, cut in half lengthwise
- 2 boneless skinless chicken breast halves (4 ounces *each*)
- 2 tablespoons prepared fat-free ranch salad dressing
- 3 tablespoons finely chopped fresh mushrooms
- 3 tablespoons finely chopped sweet red pepper
- 3 tablespoons finely chopped green onions
- 2 teaspoons cornstarch
- 6 tablespoons fat-free evaporated milk

In a small nonstick skillet, cook bacon over medium heat until cooked but not crisp. Drain on paper towel. Flatten chicken to 1/4-in. thickness; spread with ranch dressing. Top with mushrooms, red pepper and onions. Roll up and wrap a piece of bacon around each; secure with a toothpick if needed.

Place in a shallow 1-qt. baking dish coated with cooking spray. Bake, uncovered, at 350° for 25-30 minutes or chicken juices run clear. Remove and keep warm. Remove toothpicks.

Strain pan juices. In a small saucepan, combine cornstarch and milk until smooth; stir in pan juices. Bring to a boil; cook and stir for 1 minute or until thickened. Serve with chicken. **yield:** 2 servings.

nutrition facts: 1 chicken breast half with 2 tablespoons sauce equals 220 calories, 5 g fat (1 g saturated fat), 67 mg cholesterol, 339 mg sodium, 15 g carbohydrate, 1 g fiber, 28 g protein.

diabetic exchanges: 3 very lean meat, 1 starch, 1 fat.

ladonna reed
ponca city, oklahoma

My husband and I are trying to eat healthier, so I keep on the lookout for light, flavorful foods that serve two. Stuffed with red pepper, green onion and creamy ranch dressing, this supper is a winner.

FESTIVE CHICKEN

prep/total time 30 minutes

rebecca baird

salt lake city, utah

Here's a special dish that's great for holidays and special get-togethers. I set the chicken on a bed of sauteed spinach and top it with a tangy cranberry, orange and pecan sauce.

- 1/2 cup all-purpose flour
- 1/4 teaspoon salt
- Dash pepper
- 2 boneless skinless chicken breast halves
- 2 teaspoons olive oil

CRANBERRY ORANGE SAUCE
- 1 cup fresh or frozen cranberries
- 1/2 cup orange juice
- 2 tablespoons brown sugar
- 1 teaspoon grated orange peel
- 2 tablespoons chopped pecans
- 1 garlic clove, minced
- 1 tablespoon butter
- 2 cups fresh spinach

In a resealable plastic bag, combine the flour, salt and pepper. Flatten the chicken to 3/8-in. thickness; place in the bag and shake to coat. In a large skillet, cook the chicken in olive oil for 3 minutes on each side or until chicken juices run clear. Remove and keep warm.

For the sauce, add cranberries and orange juice to the skillet. Cover and cook over medium heat for 5 minutes or until the berries begin to pop. Add brown sugar and orange peel; cook 1 minute longer. Stir in pecans; remove from the heat.

In another skillet, saute garlic in butter until tender. Add the spinach; saute for 1 minute or until spinach begins to wilt. Place spinach on serving plates; top with the chicken and cranberry sauce. **yield:** 2 servings.

HONEY LIME CHICKEN

prep/total time 25 minutes

- 1/3 cup all-purpose flour
- 1/4 teaspoon cayenne pepper
- 10 ounces boneless skinless chicken breast, cut into strips
- 1 tablespoon butter
- 2 tablespoons lime juice
- 2 tablespoons honey
- 1 tablespoon brown sugar
- 1 teaspoon Worcestershire sauce

In a large resealable plastic bag, combine flour and cayenne. Add chicken, a few strips at a time, and shake to coat. In a small skillet, brown chicken in butter on all sides.

Combine the lime juice, honey, brown sugar and Worcestershire sauce; pour over chicken. Cook for 1-2 minutes or until juices run clear and sauce is thickened. **yield:** 2 servings.

karen jurgens

terril, iowa

I concocted this tangy dish while trying to come up with some new ways to fix chicken for the two of us. My husband loves it!

ULTIMATE KITCHEN TIP

Look for limes that are firm, feel heavy for their size and have a bright green color. Avoid any with bruises or wrinkles. Store at room temperature for about 3 days or in your refrigerator's crisper drawer for 2 to 3 weeks. For longer storage, freeze whole limes. For lime juice, defrost a single lime in the microwave and juice.

ASPARAGUS-STUFFED CHICKEN BREASTS

prep/total time 25 minutes

renee smith
clinton township,
michigan

This easy microwave recipe has been a family favorite for many years. Chicken breasts drizzled with a luscious lemony sauce and sprinkled with toasted almonds make for restaurant-quality fare.

2 boneless skinless chicken breast halves (6 ounces *each*)
1 tablespoon Dijon mustard
1 green onion, finely chopped
10 asparagus spears, trimmed
3 tablespoons crushed butter-flavored crackers

HOLLANDAISE SAUCE
1/4 cup butter, cubed
2 egg yolks
2 teaspoons lemon juice
1 teaspoon water
1/8 teaspoon salt
1/4 cup sliced almonds, toasted

Flatten chicken to 1/4-in. thickness. Spread with mustard; sprinkle with onion. Place asparagus spears down the center of chicken; fold over and secure with toothpicks if necessary.

Place seam side down in an ungreased 8-in. square microwave-safe dish. Sprinkle with cracker crumbs. Microwave, uncovered, on high for 6-8 minutes or until chicken juices run clear. Keep warm.

For the sauce, in a small microwave-safe bowl, melt the butter. Gradually whisk in the egg yolks, lemon juice, water and salt. Microwave, uncovered, at 30% power for 30 seconds or until mixture reaches 160° and is thickened, stirring once. Spoon over chicken. Sprinkle with almonds. Discard toothpicks. **yield:** 2 servings.

editor's note: This recipe was tested in a 1,100-watt microwave.

GARLIC-CREAM CHICKEN FLORENTINE

prep/total time 20 minutes

1 boneless skinless chicken breast half (4 ounces), cut into 1-inch cubes
1/8 teaspoon salt
1/8 teaspoon pepper
1 shallot, chopped
1 to 2 garlic cloves, minced
1 tablespoon butter
1/2 teaspoon all-purpose flour
1/2 cup half-and-half cream
3/4 cup fresh baby spinach
2 slices French bread baguette, toasted

Sprinkle the chicken with salt and pepper. In a small skillet, saute the chicken, shallot and garlic in the butter until chicken is no longer pink. Remove and keep warm.

In a small bowl, combine the flour and cream until smooth; stir into the skillet. Bring to a boil; cook and stir for 1 minute. Add spinach and chicken; heat through. Serve with toasted baguette. **yield:** 1 serving.

sarah vasques
milford, new hampshire

I love this dish because it's loaded with tender chunks of garlic-seasoned chicken and covered in a creamy, comforting sauce.

PEPPER JACK CHICKEN

prep/total time 20 minutes

dorothy storms
winder, georgia

As a senior citizen who is retired and with a working husband, I have to make easy dinners for two. These grilled chicken breasts topped with zippy cheese and salsa are a favorite.

2 boneless skinless chicken breast halves (5 ounces *each*)
2 teaspoons olive oil
1/2 to 1 teaspoon seasoned pepper
1/4 teaspoon garlic powder
2 slices pepper Jack cheese (3/4 ounce *each*)
1/4 cup salsa
Hot cooked egg noodles, optional

Brush chicken with oil; sprinkle with seasoned pepper and garlic powder. Grill on an indoor grill coated with cooking spray for 4-5 minutes on each side or until juices run clear.

Transfer chicken to serving plates; top with cheese and salsa. Serve with noodles if desired. **yield:** 2 servings.

POPPY SEED CREAMED CHICKEN

prep 10 minutes | **bake** 30 minutes

june sheaffer
fredericksburg,
pennsylvania

A dear friend gave me this recipe. It's been such a hit with family that I'm happy to share it. A few years back, it won a blue ribbon in a chicken recipe contest.

2 cups cubed cooked chicken
1 can (10-3/4 ounces) condensed cream of chicken soup, undiluted
1/2 cup sour cream
1 teaspoon poppy seeds
3/4 cup crushed butter-flavored crackers (about 18 crackers)
2 tablespoons butter
Hot cooked noodles

In a large bowl, combine the chicken, soup, sour cream and poppy seeds. Pour the mixture into a greased shallow 3-cup baking dish. In a small bowl, combine the cracker crumbs and butter; sprinkle over top.

Bake, uncovered, at 350° for 30-35 minutes or until bubbly. Serve over noodles. **yield:** 2 servings.

GREEK CHICKEN DINNER

prep 20 minutes | **bake** 50 minutes

1 to 1-1/4 pounds broiler/fryer chicken, cut up
2 to 3 tablespoons olive oil
2 medium carrots, cut into 1-inch pieces
1 medium potato, cut into 1/2-inch cubes
1 small onion, quartered
1 teaspoon minced fresh parsley
1 teaspoon dried basil
1/4 teaspoon dried oregano
1/8 teaspoon garlic powder
Salt and pepper to taste
1 to 2 tablespoons lemon juice

In a large skillet, brown chicken in 1 tablespoon oil. In a greased 9-in. square baking dish, place the carrots, potato and onion. Drizzle with remaining oil and toss to coat. Top with chicken.

In a small bowl, combine the parsley, basil, oregano, garlic powder, salt and pepper. Sprinkle over the chicken and vegetables; drizzle with the lemon juice.

Cover and bake at 375° for 40 minutes. Uncover; bake 15-20 minutes longer or until the chicken juices run clear and the vegetables are tender. **yield:** 2-3 servings.

mary anne janzen
manitoba, canada

I received this wonderful recipe from our daughter-in-law, who is from Athens, Greece.

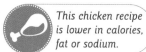
This chicken recipe is lower in calories, fat or sodium.

SIMPLE SALSA CHICKEN

prep 10 minutes | **bake** 25 minutes

jan cooper
troy, alabama

One evening I baked this chicken for my husband, and we liked it so much, it's a regular item on our dinner menu.

2   boneless skinless chicken breast halves (5 ounces *each*)
1/8   teaspoon salt
1/3   cup salsa
2   tablespoons taco sauce
1/3   cup shredded Mexican cheese blend

Place chicken in a shallow 2-qt. baking dish coated with cooking spray. Sprinkle with salt. Combine salsa and taco sauce; drizzle over chicken. Sprinkle with cheese.

Cover and bake at 350° for 25-30 minutes or until chicken juices run clear. **yield:** 2 servings.

nutrition facts: 1 chicken breast half (prepared with reduced-fat cheese) equals 226 calories, 7 g fat (3 g saturated fat), 92 mg cholesterol, 628 mg sodium, 3 g carbohydrate, trace fiber, 34 g protein.

diabetic exchanges: 5 very lean meat, 1 fat.

TANGY GLAZED CHICKEN

prep 15 minutes | **cook** 30 minutes

2   bone-in chicken breast halves
1/4   teaspoon salt, optional
4-1/2   teaspoons butter
1   small onion, thinly sliced
1   celery rib, thinly sliced
1/2   cup chicken broth
1/2   cup apple jelly
3   tablespoons orange juice
1   tablespoon minced fresh parsley
1/4   to 1/2 teaspoon dried thyme

Sprinkle chicken with salt if desired. In a large skillet, melt butter over medium heat; brown chicken on all sides. Remove and keep warm.

In the pan drippings, saute onion and celery until tender. Add the remaining ingredients; cook and stir until jelly is melted. Return chicken to pan. Cook, uncovered, for 30-35 minutes or until meat juices run clear. Remove skin if desired. Top chicken with onion mixture. **yield:** 2 servings.

barbara haney
st. louis, missouri

The finger-licking citrus sauce offers a hint of sweet apple jelly, making it perfect served over bone-in chicken breasts. Potatoes or rice and a salad round out the meal nicely.

GRILLED CHICKEN CLUB PITAS

prep 15 minutes + marinating | **grill** 10 minutes

- 3 tablespoons mayonnaise
- 3 tablespoons honey
- 3 tablespoons spicy brown mustard
- 1/4 teaspoon salt-free garlic seasoning blend
- 2 boneless skinless chicken breast halves (5 ounces *each*)
- 2 whole pita breads
- 1/2 cup shredded lettuce
- 2 bacon strips, cooked and crumbled
- 2 slices Swiss cheese

In a small bowl, combine the mayonnaise, honey, mustard and seasoning blend; set aside 3 tablespoons. Brush remaining mixture over chicken. Place in a large resealable plastic bag; seal and refrigerate for at least I hour. Refrigerate reserved mayonnaise mixture until serving.

Grill chicken, covered, over medium heat or broil 4 in. from the heat for 5-7 minutes on each side or until juices run clear. Cut the chicken into 1-in. strips.

Spread reserved mayonnaise mixture over pita breads; top with lettuce, chicken, bacon and cheese. **yield:** 2 servings.

lynne zeigler
odenton, maryland

Why heat up the kitchen on warm Indian summer evenings? Take dinner in hand with these hearty chicken pitas. I also roll up the chicken strips in flour tortillas and serve as grab-and-go wrap sandwiches.

ROASTED CHICKEN WITH BASIL-RICE STUFFING

prep 25 minutes | **bake** 1 hour + standing

edna hoffman
hebron, indiana

This stuffing, with its pleasant herb flavor, is a nice change of pace from traditional bread stuffing in this meal-in-one. The crunch comes from sunflower kernels.

1/4 cup chopped celery
1-1/2 teaspoons butter
1 cup cooked long grain rice
2 tablespoons minced fresh parsley
1 tablespoon sliced green onion
1 tablespoon minced fresh basil *or* 1 teaspoon dried basil
2-1/4 teaspoons sunflower kernels *or* chopped almonds
1/8 teaspoon salt
Dash pepper
1 broiler/fryer chicken (3 pounds)

In a small skillet, saute celery in butter until crisp-tender. In a large bowl, combine the celery, rice, parsley, green onion, basil, sunflower kernels, salt and pepper. Stuff chicken. Tie drumsticks together with kitchen string if desired. Place breast side up on a rack in a roasting pan.

Bake, uncovered, at 375° for 1-1/4 to 1-1/2 hours or until juices run clear and a meat thermometer reads 180° for chicken and 165° for stuffing. Cover and let stand for 10 minutes before removing stuffing. Remove skin before serving. **yield**: 3-4 servings.

MUSHROOM CHICKEN ALFREDO

prep/total time 30 minutes

This chicken recipe is lower in calories, fat or sodium.

1/2 pound boneless skinless chicken breasts, cut into 2-inch cubes
1 tablespoon butter
1 cup sliced fresh mushrooms
1 small onion, sliced
1-3/4 cups water
1/2 cup 2% milk
1 package (4.4 ounces) quick-cooking noodles and Alfredo sauce mix
Minced fresh parsley, optional

In a large nonstick skillet, cook chicken in butter for 6 minutes or until juices run clear. Remove and keep warm. In the same skillet, saute mushrooms and onion until tender.

Stir in the water and milk; bring to a boil. Stir in the contents of the noodles and sauce mix; boil for 8 minutes or until the noodles are tender.

Return chicken to the pan; heat through. Garnish with parsley if desired. **yield**: 3 servings.

nutrition facts: 1-1/3 cups equals 317 calories, 11 g fat (6 g saturated fat), 105 mg cholesterol, 727 mg sodium, 30 g carbohydrate, 1 g fiber, 24 g protein.

diabetic exchanges: 3 lean meat, 2 starch.

margery bryan
moses lake, washington

All you need is one skillet to make this delicious scaled-down dinner. It's an easy way to dress up packaged noodles and sauce, plus cleanup is a breeze.

ULTIMATE KITCHEN TIP

To effectively clean mushrooms, gently remove dirt by rubbing with a soft brush or wiping with a damp paper towel. You can also rinse them quickly under cold water, drain and pat dry with paper towels. Do not peel mushrooms, but do trim off their stems. Mushrooms can be eaten raw, marinated, sauteed, stir-fried, baked, broiled or grilled.

SANTA FE CHICKEN AND RICE

prep/total time 30 minutes

debra cook

pampa, texas

*Cheesy chicken breasts are
even more scrumptious
served on a bed of tender,
Southwest-style rice. This
effortless meal is ready in
only half an hour.*

1/2	cup chopped onion
2	teaspoons butter
2/3	cup chicken broth
1/2	cup salsa
1/2	cup uncooked long grain rice
1/8	teaspoon garlic powder
2	boneless skinless chicken breast halves (5 ounces *each*)
1/3	cup shredded cheddar cheese

Chopped fresh cilantro, optional

In a skillet, saute onion in butter until tender. Add broth and
salsa; bring to a boil. Stir in the rice and garlic powder. Place
chicken over rice; cover and simmer for 10 minutes.

Turn chicken over; cook 10-15 minutes longer or until chick-
en juices run clear and rice is tender. Remove from the heat.
Sprinkle with cheese; cover and let stand for 5 minutes. Garnish
with cilantro if desired. **yield:** 2 servings.

CHICKEN WITH LEMON SAUCE

prep/total time 20 minutes

2	boneless skinless chicken breast halves (5 ounces *each*)
5	tablespoons all-purpose flour, *divided*
1/4	cup grated Parmesan cheese
3/4	teaspoon salt, *divided*
1/2	teaspoon pepper, *divided*
2	eggs
2	tablespoons butter, *divided*
1	tablespoon olive oil
3/4	cup chicken broth
1/2	cup apple juice
1	tablespoon lemon juice
1	tablespoon minced fresh parsley

Flatten chicken to 1/4-in. thickness. In a shallow
bowl, combine 4 tablespoons flour, Parmesan
cheese, 1/2 teaspoon salt and 1/4 teaspoon pepper. In another shallow bowl, beat the eggs. Dip
chicken into eggs, then coat with flour mixture.

In a large skillet, cook the chicken in 1 tablespoon butter and the olive oil over medium heat for
3-5 minutes on each side or until juices run clear.
Remove and keep warm.

In a small bowl, combine the remaining, salt
and pepper; stir in broth until smooth. Add apple
juice to the skillet, stirring to loosen any browned
bits. Stir broth mixture and add to the pan. Bring
to a boil; cook and stir for 1-2 minutes or until
thickened and bubbly.

Stir in lemon juice; cook for 1 minute. Add parsley and remaining butter; cook and stir until butter
is melted. Serve over chicken. **yield:** 2 servings.

brenda hoffman

stanton, michigan

*This delicious Italian dish is
easy to prepare, but it looks
like you fussed. With crusty
bread and a crisp salad, it's
a meal fit for a king.*

MIDWEST CHICKEN DRUMSTICKS

prep 30 minutes | **cook** 25 minutes

susan bice
litchfield, nebraska

Tender chicken legs are gussied up with barbecue sauce and corn for this lip-smacking entree. It tastes best when I use sweet corn that has been picked fresh from the field.

- 1/4 cup all-purpose flour
- 1/4 teaspoon salt
- 1/4 teaspoon garlic powder

Dash cayenne pepper

- 4 chicken drumsticks (4 ounces each), skin removed
- 2 tablespoons canola oil
- 4 green onions, sliced
- 1 cup fresh *or* frozen corn
- 1/2 cup barbecue sauce

In a large resealable plastic bag, combine the flour, salt, garlic powder and cayenne. Add drumsticks; seal bag and shake to coat. In a large skillet, brown chicken in oil, turning occasionally. Remove and keep warm.

In the same skillet, saute onions until tender. Add corn; cook for 5 minutes. Stir in the barbecue sauce; return chicken to the pan and coat with sauce. Cover and simmer for 25-30 minutes or until juices run clear and chicken is evenly coated. **yield:** 2 servings.

BARBECUED CHICKEN LEGS

prep 10 minutes | **bake** 50 minutes

agnes golian
garfield heights, ohio

On a lazy, sunny summer day, this chicken is the best ever. We enjoy it with baked beans and watermelon. Try the zesty barbecue sauce on other grilled meats, too.

- 2 chicken leg quarters
- 1 tablespoon canola oil
- 1/4 cup ketchup
- 2 tablespoons Worcestershire sauce
- 1 tablespoon sugar
- 1 tablespoon cider vinegar
- 1 tablespoon steak sauce

Dash hot pepper sauce

In a large nonstick skillet, brown the chicken in oil. Transfer to an 8-in. square baking dish coated with cooking spray. In a bowl, combine the ketchup, Worcestershire sauce, sugar, cider vinegar, steak sauce and hot pepper sauce; pour over the chicken.

Bake, uncovered, at 350° for 55-60 minutes or until a meat thermometer reads 180°, basting every 15 minutes with sauce. **yield:** 2 servings.

SPICY CHICKEN ENCHILADAS

prep/total time 30 minutes

- 1 package (6 ounces) ready-to-use Southwestern chicken strips
- 1-1/2 cups (6 ounces) shredded cheddar cheese, *divided*
- 1 can (10 ounces) enchilada sauce, *divided*
- 1 cup refried beans
- 4 flour tortillas (7 inches), warmed
- 1 can (2-1/2 ounces) sliced ripe olives, drained

Chopped tomato and shredded lettuce, optional

In a large bowl, combine the chicken, 1 cup cheese and 1/2 cup enchilada sauce. Spread 1/4 cup refried beans down the center of each tortilla. Top with chicken mixture; roll up.

Place in two ungreased small baking dishes. Top with the remaining enchilada sauce and cheese; sprinkle with olives.

Cover and bake at 400° for 15-20 minutes or until heated through. Garnish with tomato and lettuce if desired. **yield:** 2 servings.

amy dando
apalachin, new york

Cooked chicken strips and canned enchilada sauce hurry along this zesty entree. I came up with it shortly after I got married. It's a delicious dinner for two that's easy to double for company.

This chicken recipe is lower in calories, fat or sodium.

SUNDAY CHICKEN SUPPER

prep 15 minutes | **cook** 6 hours

ruthann martin

louisville, ohio

This convenient slow cooker supper makes a hearty and delicious meal that's special any day of the week.

2 small carrots, cut into 2-inch pieces
1/2 medium onion, chopped
1/2 celery rib, cut into 2-inch pieces
1 cup cut fresh green beans (2-inch pieces)
2 small red potatoes, halved
2 bone-in chicken breast halves (7 ounces *each*), skin removed
2 bacon strips, cooked and crumbled
3/4 cup hot water
1 teaspoon chicken bouillon granules
1/4 teaspoon salt
1/4 teaspoon dried thyme
1/4 teaspoon dried basil
Pinch pepper

In a 3-qt. slow cooker, layer the first seven ingredients in the order listed. Combine the water, bouillon, salt, thyme, basil and pepper; pour over the top. Do not stir. Cover and cook on low for 6-8 hours or until vegetables are tender and meat thermometer reads 170°. Remove chicken and vegetables. Thicken cooking juices for gravy if desired. **yield:** 2 servings.

nutrition facts: 1 serving equals 304 calories, 7 g fat (2 g saturated fat), 94 mg cholesterol, 927 mg sodium, 21 g carbohydrate, 5 g fiber, 37 g protein.

diabetic exchanges: 5 very lean meat, 1 starch, 1 vegetable, 1/2 fat.

CHICKEN WELLINGTON CASSEROLE

prep 20 minutes | **bake** 20 minutes

2 boneless skinless chicken breast halves
2 teaspoons butter
1 package (3 ounces) cream cheese, softened
1/2 cup sliced fresh mushrooms
1 tablespoon chopped green onion
1/8 teaspoon salt
Dash pepper
1 tube (4 ounces) refrigerated crescent rolls

In a large skillet, cook the chicken in butter 3-4 minutes on each side or until meat juices run clear. Place the chicken in a greased 3-cup baking dish. Meanwhile, in a large bowl, combine the cream cheese, mushrooms, onion, salt and pepper. Spoon over the chicken.

Unroll dough into one long rectangle; seal seams and perforations. If necessary, trim dough to fit top of dish and patch together by overlapping edges. Pinch edges to seal. Place over filling. Bake, uncovered, at 350° for 20 minutes or until heated through. **yield:** 2 servings.

jennifer hassen

tecumseh, oklahoma

A friend shared this recipe with me after I got married, and it's been my husband's favorite ever since.

CHICKEN TORTELLINI SKILLET

prep/total time 25 minutes

2 cups frozen cheese tortellini
1/2 pound boneless skinless chicken breast, cubed
1 tablespoon canola oil
1 cup meatless spaghetti sauce
1/2 cup shredded part-skim mozzarella cheese

Cook tortellini according to package directions. Meanwhile, in a large skillet, cook chicken in oil over medium heat until juices run clear.

Drain tortellini; add to skillet. Stir in spaghetti sauce. Sprinkle with cheese. Reduce heat to low. Cover and cook for 3-5 minutes or until cheese is melted. **yield:** 2 servings.

chandra benjamin
eden prairie , minnesota

Dinner's on the table in no time with this tasty chicken and pasta recipe. I'm a graduate student and live alone, so I prefer recipes that are inexpensive and make just a few servings.

CURRY CHICKEN TENDERLOIN WITH SWEET POTATOES

prep 15 minutes | **cook** 25 minutes

gloria bradley
naperville, illinois

What I love about this recipe is the fragrant sauce and the addition of sweet potatoes, which are a favorite of mine.

3/4 pound chicken tenderloins, cut into 1-inch cubes
1 small green pepper, cut into thin strips
2 shallots, thinly sliced
2 teaspoons minced fresh gingerroot
1 teaspoon curry powder
1 garlic clove, minced
1 tablespoon canola oil
1-1/3 cups chicken broth
1 tablespoon lime juice
1/2 teaspoon sugar
1/4 teaspoon crushed red pepper flakes
1 medium sweet potato, peeled and cut into 1-inch pieces

3/4 cup light coconut milk
Chopped peanuts and flaked coconut, optional
Hot cooked rice, optional

In a large skillet, saute the chicken, green pepper, shallots, ginger, curry and garlic in oil until chicken is no longer pink. Stir in the broth, lime juice, sugar and pepper flakes. Bring to a boil. Reduce the heat; simmer, uncovered, for 10 minutes or until thickened.

Add sweet potato and coconut milk; bring to a boil. Reduce heat; cover and simmer for 8-10 minutes or until potato is tender. If desired, sprinkle with peanuts and coconut and serve with rice.
yield: 3 servings.

GOLDEN CHICKEN CORDON BLEU

prep 20 minutes | **bake** 20 minutes

2 boneless skinless chicken breast halves (6 ounces *each*)
2 slices deli ham (3/4 ounce *each*)
2 slices Swiss cheese (3/4 ounce *each*)
1/2 cup all-purpose flour
1/4 teaspoon salt
1/8 teaspoon paprika
1/8 teaspoon pepper
1 egg
2 tablespoons 2% milk
1/2 cup seasoned bread crumbs
1 tablespoon canola oil
1 tablespoon butter, melted

taste of home test kitchen
greendale, wisconsin

For an entree that's as elegant as it is easy, try this moist chicken classic from our Test Kitchen. It's a simple recipe but looks like you really fussed.

Flatten chicken to 1/4-in. thickness; top each with a slice of ham and cheese. Roll up and tuck in ends; secure with toothpicks.

In a shallow bowl, combine the flour, salt, paprika and pepper. In another bowl, whisk egg and milk. Place bread crumbs in a third bowl. Dip chicken in flour mixture, then egg mixture; roll in crumbs.

In a small skillet, brown chicken in oil on all sides. Transfer to an 8-in. square baking dish coated with cooking spray.

Bake, uncovered, at 350° for 20-25 minutes or until chicken juices run clear. Discard toothpicks; drizzle with butter.
yield: 2 servings.

SESAME CHICKEN STIR-FRY

prep/total time 30 minutes

michelle mcwilliams
fort lupton, colorado

When our children were little, my husband frequently worked late. This stir-fry was a satisfying alternative to a big dinner. For more than one serving, increase the recipe accordingly.

1   boneless skinless chicken breast half, cut into thin strips
2   teaspoons canola oil
7   snow peas
1   cup fresh broccoli florets
1/3 cup julienned sweet red pepper
3   medium fresh mushrooms, sliced
3/4 cup chopped onion
1   tablespoon cornstarch
1   teaspoon sugar
1/2 cup cold water
3   to 4 tablespoons soy sauce
Hot cooked rice
1   teaspoon sesame seeds, toasted

In a large skillet or wok, stir-fry chicken in oil for 6-8 minutes or until juices run clear. Remove chicken and set aside. In the same skillet, stir-fry peas, broccoli and red pepper for 2-3 minutes. Add mushrooms and onion; stir-fry for 3-4 minutes.

Combine cornstarch and sugar; stir in water and soy sauce until smooth. Add to the pan. Bring to a boil; cook and stir for 1-2 minutes or until thickened. Return chicken to the pan; cook until mixture is heated through and vegetables are tender. Serve over rice. Sprinkle with sesame seeds. **yield:** 1 serving.

CHICKEN-RICOTTA STUFFED SHELLS

prep 25 minutes | bake 30 minutes

6   uncooked jumbo pasta shells
2/3 cup ricotta cheese
2   ounces cream cheese, softened
1/8 teaspoon chicken bouillon granules
2/3 cup shredded cooked chicken breast
2   tablespoons shredded Parmesan cheese

SAUCE
1/3 cup heavy whipping cream *or* half-and-half cream
1   tablespoon butter
5   tablespoons shredded Parmesan cheese, *divided*
1/2 teaspoon dried parsley flakes

Cook pasta according to package directions. Meanwhile, in a small bowl, beat the ricotta, cream cheese and bouillon until blended. Stir in chicken and Parmesan cheese. Drain shells; stuff with chicken mixture. Place in a shallow 3-cup baking dish coated with cooking spray.

For the sauce, in a small saucepan, bring cream and butter to a boil. Whisk in 3 tablespoons Parmesan cheese and parsley. Stir until cheese is melted. Pour over shells.

Cover and bake at 350° for 25 minutes. Uncover; sprinkle with remaining Parmesan. Bake 5-10 minutes longer or until cheese is melted and filling is heated through. **yield:** 2 servings.

amy hixon
ringgold, georgia

My husband and I don't care for tomato-based pasta sauces, so I came up with this variation on stuffed shells. It tastes like chicken Alfredo, and we really enjoy it.

CHICKEN ADOBO

prep 10 minutes + marinating | **grill** 15 minutes

carma blosser
livermore, colorado

Seasonings and a splash of lime make this chicken something special. It is also really tasty in salads and sandwiches and can also be prepared on an indoor grill.

2 tablespoons lime juice
1 tablespoon minced fresh cilantro
1 tablespoon olive oil
2 garlic cloves, minced
1 green onion, minced
1/4 teaspoon salt
1/4 teaspoon ground cumin
1/4 teaspoon minced fresh thyme
1/4 teaspoon minced fresh oregano
1/4 teaspoon pepper
2 boneless skinless chicken breast halves (6 ounces *each*)

In a large resealable plastic bag, combine the first 10 ingredients; add chicken. Seal bag and turn to coat; refrigerate for at least 4 hours.

Coat the grill rack with cooking spray before starting the grill. Drain and discard marinade. Grill the chicken, covered, over medium heat for 6-8 minutes on each side or until juices run clear. **yield:** 2 servings.

CORDON BLEU BAKE

prep 20 minutes | **bake** 30 minutes

mrs. helen musenbrock
o'fallon, missouri

This comforting casserole is fast and easy to assemble. Plus it's a great way to use up leftovers.

- 1/2 cup water
- 3 tablespoons butter, *divided*
- 1 cup stuffing mix
- 1 cup frozen mixed vegetables, thawed
- 2/3 cup condensed cream of mushroom *or* cream of chicken soup, undiluted, *divided*
- 3/4 cup cubed cooked chicken breast
- 2 ounces thinly sliced lean deli ham, cut into strips
- 1/2 cup shredded Swiss cheese

In a small saucepan, bring the water and 1 tablespoon butter to a boil. Stir in the stuffing mix. Remove from the heat; cover and let stand for 5 minutes.

Meanwhile, in a shallow 1-qt. baking dish coated with cooking spray, combine vegetables with 1/3 cup soup. Combine the chicken with remaining soup; spoon over vegetables. Layer with ham and cheese. Fluff stuffing with a fork; spoon over cheese. Melt remaining butter; drizzle over stuffing. Bake, uncovered, at 350° for 30-35 minutes or until heated through. **yield:** 2 servings.

SPINACH CHICKEN ROLL

prep 20 minutes | **cook** 15 minutes

This chicken recipe is lower in calories, fat or sodium.

- 1 tablespoon finely chopped onion
- 1 teaspoon olive oil
- 3 cups fresh baby spinach
- 1/4 teaspoon dill weed
- 1 boneless skinless chicken breast half (6 ounces)
- 2 tablespoons crumbled feta cheese

In a small nonstick skillet, saute onion in oil over medium heat until tender. Add spinach; cook and stir for 2-3 minutes or just until wilted. Stir in dill. Remove from the heat.

Flatten chicken to 1/4-in. thickness. Place spinach mixture and feta cheese down the center; fold one side over filling and roll up tightly. Secure with a toothpick.

Place seam side down in the skillet. Cover and cook over medium heat for 15-20 minutes or until chicken juices run clear, turning occasionally. Discard toothpick. **yield:** 1 serving.

nutrition facts: 1 serving equals 281 calories, 11 g fat (3 g saturated fat), 101 mg cholesterol, 289 mg sodium, 5 g carbohydrate, 3 g fiber, 40 g protein.

diabetic exchanges: 4 lean meat, 1 vegetable, 1 fat.

ellen fortuna
santa clara, utah

Fresh baby spinach and feta cheese dress up tender chicken in this yummy entree. A touch of dill adds delicious flavor to the dish.

WEEKNIGHT
FAVORITES

ALMOND CRANBERRY CHICKEN, P. 272

CHICKEN STIR-FRY BAKE

prep/total time 30 minutes

carly carter
nashville, tennessee

*One night, I opted to use
frozen vegetables in my
chicken stir-fry. Not wanting
to stand watch over the
stovetop, I baked the entree
in the oven. People say this
tastes like it's hot from
the skillet.*

- 2 cups uncooked instant rice
- 1 can (8 ounces) sliced water chestnuts, drained
- 2 cups cubed cooked chicken
- 1 package (16 ounces) frozen stir-fry vegetables, thawed
- 1 can (14-1/2 ounces) chicken broth
- 1/4 cup soy sauce
- 1 garlic clove, minced
- 1/2 to 3/4 teaspoon ground ginger

Place rice in a greased 11-in. x 7-in. baking dish. Layer with the water chestnuts, chicken and vegetables. Combine remaining ingredients; pour over top. Cover and bake at 375° for 25 minutes or until rice is tender. **yield:** 4 servings.

RANCH CHICKEN 'N' RICE

prep 10 minutes | **bake** 35 minutes

- 2 cups uncooked instant rice
- 1-1/2 cups milk
- 1 cup water
- 1 envelope ranch salad dressing mix
- 1 pound boneless skinless chicken breasts, cut into 1/2-inch strips
- 1/4 cup butter, melted

Paprika

Place rice in a greased shallow 2-qt. baking dish. In a bowl, combine the milk, water and salad dressing mix; set aside 1/4 cup. Pour remaining mixture over rice. Top with chicken strips. Drizzle with butter and reserved milk mixture.

Cover and bake at 350° for 35-40 minutes or until rice is tender and chicken juices run clear. Sprinkle with paprika. **yield:** 4 servings.

erlene crusoe
litchfield, minnesota

*When I clipped this recipe
from a neighborhood
shopper a few years ago, I
couldn't wait to try it. Just
as I expected, it quickly
became a family favorite.*

SAUCY TARRAGON CHICKEN

prep 10 minutes | **cook** 25 minutes

This chicken recipe is lower in calories, fat or sodium.

3 cups uncooked egg noodles
4 boneless skinless chicken breast halves (4 ounces *each*)
3/4 teaspoon dried tarragon
3/4 teaspoon lemon-pepper seasoning
1 tablespoon butter
2 cups sliced fresh mushrooms
4 garlic cloves, minced
1 can (14-1/2 ounces) reduced-sodium chicken broth, *divided*
3 tablespoons sherry *or* additional reduced-sodium chicken broth
3 tablespoons all-purpose flour
1/4 cup reduced-fat sour cream

Cook noodles according to package directions. Meanwhile, sprinkle chicken with tarragon and lemon-pepper. In a large nonstick skillet over medi-um-high heat, brown chicken in butter on both sides. Remove and keep warm.

In the same skillet, saute mushrooms and garlic until tender. Add 1 cup broth and sherry or additional broth, stirring to loosen browned bits from pan. Return chicken to the pan; bring to a boil. Reduce heat; simmer, uncovered, for 7-10 minutes or until a meat thermometer reads 170°. Remove chicken and keep warm.

Combine flour and remaining broth until smooth; stir into pan juices. Bring to a boil; cook and stir for 1-2 minutes or until thickened. Remove from the heat; stir in sour cream. Drain noodles; serve with chicken and sauce. **yield:** 4 servings.

nutrition facts: 1 chicken breast half with 1/4 cup sauce and 3/4 cup noodles equals 379 calories, 9 g fat (4 g saturated fat), 116 mg cholesterol, 454 mg sodium, 39 g carbohydrate, 2 g fiber, 33 g protein.

diabetic exchanges: 3 lean meat, 2-1/2 starch.

mary steiner
west bend, wisconsin

This delightful golden chicken dish boasts plenty of mushroom gravy and a mild, satisfying taste with just a hint of lemon and tarragon.

SESAME CHICKEN

prep 15 minutes + marinating | **bake** 15 minutes

anne wegener
springville, indiana

Soy sauce, garlic, lemon juice and ground ginger give this easy-to-fix dish a delicious Asian flair.

1/4	cup lemon juice
1/4	cup soy sauce
2	tablespoons canola oil
3	garlic cloves, minced
1/2	teaspoon ground ginger
6	boneless skinless chicken breast halves (4 ounces *each*)
4	teaspoons cornstarch
1/2	cup water
1/4	cup chicken broth

Hot cooked rice

1/4	cup sesame seeds, toasted

In a large resealable plastic bag, combine the lemon juice, soy sauce, oil, garlic and ginger. Set aside 1/4 cup for basting, cover and refrigerate. Add chicken to remaining marinade; seal bag and turn to coat. Refrigerate for 8 hours or overnight.

Drain and discard marinade. Broil chicken 4 in. from the heat for 6-7 minutes on each side or until a meat thermometer reads 170°.

Meanwhile, in a large saucepan, combine the cornstarch, water, broth and reserved marinade until smooth. Bring to a boil; cook and stir for 2 minutes or until thickened. Serve chicken and sauce with rice. Sprinkle with sesame seeds. **yield: 6 servings.**

MANDARIN ORANGE CHICKEN

prep/total time 30 minutes

This chicken recipe is lower in calories, fat or sodium.

4	boneless skinless chicken breast halves (4 ounces *each*)
2	tablespoons all-purpose flour
1/4	teaspoon salt
1/4	teaspoon pepper
1	tablespoon canola oil
1/2	cup orange juice
1/4	cup orange marmalade
2	tablespoons honey mustard
1/4	teaspoon dried rosemary, crushed
1	can (11 ounces) mandarin oranges, drained
1	teaspoon grated orange peel

Hot cooked rice, optional

clara coulston
washington court house, ohio

I jazz up a meal with this mouth-watering recipe. Juicy chicken is treated to a tangy sauce with plenty of citrus flavor.

Flatten chicken to 1/4-in. thickness. In a large resealable bag, combine the flour, salt and pepper; add chicken. Seal bag and turn to coat; In a large skillet, brown chicken in oil on both sides.

Combine the orange juice, marmalade, mustard and rosemary; pour over chicken. Bring to a boil. Reduce heat; cook for 5-8 minutes or until chicken juices run clear and sauce is thickened. Stir in oranges and orange peel. Serve with rice if desired. **yield:** 4 servings.

nutrition facts: 1 serving (made with reduced-sugar marmalade; without rice) equals 254 calories, 6 g fat (1 g saturated fat), 66 mg cholesterol, 240 mg sodium, 21 g carbohydrate, 1 g fiber, 0 protein.

diabetic exchanges: 3 lean meat, 1-1/2 fruit.

CHICKEN CHOPPED SALAD

prep/total time 20 minutes

diane halferty
corpus christi, texas

Lime dressing gives lively flavor to this crunchy salad tossed with peaches, peppers and peanuts. The unusual combination is a great way to use up leftover chicken or turkey and packs well for lunches or picnics. It's terrific with grapefruit sections or pineapple.

- 2 cups chopped *or* torn mixed salad greens
- 2 cups chopped cooked chicken
- 1 cup chopped celery
- 1 can (15-1/4 ounces) peaches, drained and chopped
- 1 cup chopped sweet red *or* yellow pepper
- 1/3 cup limeade concentrate
- 1/4 cup canola oil
- 2 tablespoons white vinegar
- 2 to 3 tablespoons minced fresh cilantro
- 1-1/2 teaspoons minced fresh gingerroot
- 1/4 teaspoon salt
- 1/2 cup dry roasted peanuts

In a large salad bowl, combine the first five ingredients. In a jar with a tight-fitting lid, combine the limeade concentrate, oil, vinegar, cilantro, ginger and salt; shake well. Pour over salad and toss to coat. Sprinkle with peanuts. Serve immediately. **yield:** 6 servings.

MUSTARD CHICKEN BREASTS

prep/total time 20 minutes

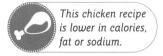
This chicken recipe is lower in calories, fat or sodium.

- 4 bone-in chicken breast halves (6 ounces *each*), skin removed
- 1 teaspoon paprika
- 1 medium lemon, thinly sliced
- 1/3 cup spicy brown mustard
- 1/3 cup honey
- 1 teaspoon dried minced onion
- 1/2 teaspoon curry powder
- 1/2 teaspoon lemon juice

Arrange the chicken breast halves in a 9-in. or 10-in. microwave-safe pie plate, with the thickest side toward the outside of the plate. Sprinkle with paprika; top with the lemon slices. Cover and microwave, on high for 6-8 minutes, rotating the dish a half turn once.

In small microwave-safe bowl, combine the remaining ingredients. Microwave, uncovered, on high 1 to 1-1/2 minutes or until heated through; stir.

Drain chicken; top with sauce. Cover and cook on high for 1-1/2 minutes until a meat thermometer reads 170°. **yield:** 4 servings.

nutrition facts: 1 chicken breast half equals 232 calories, 3 g fat (1 g saturated fat), 63 mg cholesterol, 332 mg sodium, 28 g carbohydrate, 2 g fiber, 27 g protein.

diabetic exchanges: 2-1/2 lean meat, 1-1/2 fruit.

editor's note: This recipe was tested in a 1,100-watt microwave.

tina footen
nampa, idaho

Curry powder, lemon juice, honey and mustard make a lip-smacking sauce for paprika-sprinkled chicken that is cooked in the microwave. The made-in-minutes main dish is a favorite with my family, and I'm sure it will be with yours, too.

ULTIMATE KITCHEN TIP

When a recipe calls for fresh lemon juice, it's okay to use frozen or bottled as well. If lemons are in season or you have extra juice, freeze by measuring 1 or 2 tablespoons of juice into each cube section of an ice cube tray. When frozen, remove the cubes and place in resealable freezer bags. It's great to have fresh lemon juice readily available!

This chicken recipe is lower in calories, fat or sodium.

CHICKEN TOSTADAS WITH MANGO SALSA

prep 30 minutes + marinating | **cook** 20 minutes

erin renouf mylroie
santa clara, utah

The candied ginger adds a pleasant zing to this twist on a traditional tostada. It's so easy to eat healthful foods when good fresh salsa is around.

1/3	cup orange juice
5	tablespoons lime juice, *divided*
1	teaspoon garlic powder
1	teaspoon ground cumin
1	pound boneless skinless chicken breast halves
2	medium mangoes, peeled and diced
1	small red onion, chopped
1/2	cup minced fresh cilantro
1	serrano pepper, seeded and minced
2	tablespoons finely chopped candied ginger
1	tablespoon brown sugar
1/4	teaspoon salt
6	corn tortillas (6 inches)
3	cups coleslaw mix
6	tablespoons fat-free sour cream

In a large resealable plastic bag, combine the orange juice, 3 tablespoons lime juice, garlic powder and cumin; add chicken. Seal bag and turn to coat; refrigerate for at least 20 minutes.

For the salsa, in a small bowl, combine the mangoes, onion, cilantro, serrano pepper, candied ginger, brown sugar, salt and remaining lime juice. Cover and chill until serving.

Drain and discard the marinade. Place the chicken on a broiler pan coated with cooking spray. Broil 4-6 in. from the heat for 5-7 minutes on each side or until a meat thermometer reads 170°. Cut the chicken into thin strips.

In a nonstick skillet, cook tortillas over medium heat for 1-2 minutes on each side or until lightly browned. Top each with coleslaw mix, chicken, mango salsa and sour cream. **yield:** 6 servings.

nutrition facts: 1 chicken breast half equals 238 calories, 3 g fat (1 g saturated fat), 44 mg cholesterol, 203 mg sodium, 35 g carbohydrate, 3 g fiber, 19 g protein.

diabetic exchanges: 2 very lean meat, 1-1/2 starch, 1 fat.

editor's note: When cutting hot peppers, disposable gloves are recommended. Avoid touching your face.

CORNY CHICKEN WRAPS

prep/total time 10 minutes

sue seymour

valatie, new york

Tender chicken is combined with corn and salsa for a fast-to-fix main dish. My girls like these so much, they ask for them every week!

2 cups cubed cooked chicken breast
1 can (11 ounces) whole kernel corn, drained
1 cup salsa
1 cup (4 ounces) shredded cheddar cheese
8 flour tortillas (6 inches), warmed

In a large saucepan, combine the cooked chicken, corn and salsa. Cook over medium heat until heated through.

Sprinkle the cheddar cheese over tortillas. Place about 1/2 cup chicken mixture down the center of each tortilla; roll up. Secure with toothpicks. **yield:** 4 servings.

CHICKEN NOODLE STIR-FRY

prep/total time 25 minutes

1 package (3 ounces) chicken-flavored Ramen noodles
1 pound boneless skinless chicken breasts, cut into strips
1 tablespoon canola oil
1 cup fresh broccoli florets
1 cup fresh cauliflowerets
1 cup sliced celery
1 cup coarsely chopped cabbage
2 medium carrots, thinly sliced
1 medium onion, thinly sliced

1/2 cup canned bean sprouts
1/2 cup teriyaki or soy sauce

Set aside the seasoning packet from the noodles. Cook noodles according to package directions. Meanwhile, in a large skillet or wok, stir-fry the chicken in oil for 5-6 minutes or until no longer pink. Add the vegetables; stir-fry for 3-4 minutes or until crisp-tender.

Drain noodles; add to the pan with contents of seasoning packet and the teriyaki sauce. Stir well. **yield:** 4 servings.

darlene brenden

salem, oregon

I rely on Ramen noodles to stretch this appealing stir-fry. You can use whatever vegetables you happen to have on hand. The dish is deliciously different every time I make it.

ULTIMATE KITCHEN TIP

When using ramen noodles for recipes, you may have extra seasoning packets leftover. To use one up, here's a simple rice dish. Heat 1 tablespoon of oil in a saucepan, then stir in 1/3 cup uncooked long grain rice and the contents of the seasoning packet. Add 2/3 cup of chicken broth, cover and simmer for 15 minutes. Turn off the heat and let it sit until the liquid is absorbed. It makes one serving of seasoned rice.

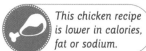
This chicken recipe is lower in calories, fat or sodium.

CHERRY-TOPPED CHICKEN

prep/total time 15 minutes

tabetha moore

new braunfels, texas

This scrumptious four-ingredient entree is simple enough to fix everyday, but special enough to serve for company dinners.

4	boneless skinless chicken breast halves (4 ounces *each*)
1	tablespoon canola oil
1/2	cup cherry preserves
1/4	teaspoon ground allspice

Flatten chicken to I/4-in. thickness. In a large skillet, cook chicken in oil over medium heat for 5 minutes on each side or until juices run clear.

Meanwhile, in a small microwave-safe bowl, combine preserves and allspice until blended. Heat in the microwave until warmed. Serve with chicken. **yield:** 4 servings.

nutrition facts: 1 chicken breast half with 2 tablespoons preserves equals 252 calories, 6 g fat (1 g saturated fat), 63 mg cholesterol, 55 mg sodium, 26 g carbohydrate, trace fiber, 23 g protein.

diabetic exchanges: 3 very lean meat, 2 fruit, 1/2 fat.

PIEROGI CHICKEN SUPPER

prep/total time 30 minutes

1	package (16 ounces) frozen pierogies
1	pound boneless skinless chicken breasts, cut into 2-inch strips
1/2	large sweet onion, thinly sliced
2	tablespoons butter
1/4	teaspoon salt
1/8	teaspoon pepper
1/2	cup shredded cheddar cheese

Cook pierogies according to package directions. Meanwhile, in a large nonstick skillet, saute chicken and onion in butter until chicken juices run clear; remove and keep warm.

Drain pierogies; add to skillet. Cook over medium heat until lightly browned. Return chicken mixture to the pan. Stir in salt and pepper. Sprinkle with cheese. Cover and remove from the heat. Let stand for 5 minutes or until cheese is melted. **yield:** 4 servings.

barbara scott

walkersville, maryland

This change-of-pace dish combines chicken, cheese and onion with frozen pierogies for a complete meal. The satisfying skillet supper takes just 30 minutes to get on the table.

CHICKEN WITH FLORENTINE SAUCE

prep/total time 30 minutes

6   boneless skinless chicken breast halves (4 ounces *each*)
1/2 cup grated Parmesan cheese
1/2 teaspoon dried basil
1/2 teaspoon dried oregano
3   tablespoons butter, *divided*
2   green onions, chopped
1   teaspoon minced garlic
1   tablespoon all-purpose flour
1/4 teaspoon salt
1/2 cup milk
1   tablespoon sherry *or* chicken broth
1   package (10 ounces) frozen chopped spinach, thawed and squeezed dry
2   tablespoons diced pimientos
1/2 cup sour cream
1   cup (4 ounces) shredded part-skim mozzarella cheese

Flatten chicken to 1/2-in. thickness. In a large resealable plastic bag, combine the Parmesan cheese, basil and oregano. Add chicken, a few pieces at a time, and shake to coat.

In a large skillet over medium heat, cook chicken in 2 tablespoons butter for 4-5 minutes on each side or until a meat thermometer reads 170°. Remove and keep warm.

In the same skillet, saute onions and garlic in remaining butter for 2-3 minutes or until tender. Gradually add flour and salt; stir in milk and sherry or broth until blended. Bring to a boil. Reduce heat; cook and stir for 1-2 minutes or until thickened. Stir in spinach and pimientos; heat through.

Remove from the heat. Stir in sour cream until blended. Spoon over chicken; sprinkle with mozzarella cheese. **yield:** 6 servings.

julie fitzgerald
st louis, missouri

Here is my very favorite chicken-and-spinach recipe. A creamy topping and pretty presentation make it elegant, but it's still easy and casual enough for busy weeknights!

SPECIAL SCALLOPS AND CHICKEN

prep 15 minutes | **bake** 20 minutes

sheila vail
long beach, california

I make this easy main course when I want to "wow" company. It tastes heavenly, and guests always love it.

1/2 cup all-purpose flour
1/2 teaspoon salt
1/2 teaspoon pepper
6 boneless skinless chicken breast halves (4 ounces *each*)
1/2 pound bay scallops
1/4 cup olive oil
1-1/2 cups sliced fresh mushrooms
1 medium onion, chopped
1/4 cup white wine *or* chicken broth
2 teaspoons cornstarch
1/2 cup heavy whipping cream
1 teaspoon dried tarragon
1/2 cup shredded Swiss cheese

In a large resealable plastic bag, combine the flour, salt and pepper. Add chicken and scallops in batches; shake to coat. In a large skillet, saute chicken and scallops in oil until lightly browned. Transfer to a greased 13-in. x 9-in. baking dish.

In the pan drippings, saute mushrooms and onion. Add wine or broth. Bring to a boil; cook until liquid is reduced to 2 tablespoons. Combine cornstarch, cream and tarragon until blended; add to skillet. Bring to a boil; cook and stir for 1 minute or until thickened. Spoon over chicken and scallops. Sprinkle with cheese.

Bake, uncovered, at 375° for 18-20 minutes or until chicken juices run clear. **yield:** 6 servings.

CHICKEN FAJITA SPAGHETTI

prep/total time 20 minutes

This chicken recipe is lower in calories, fat or sodium.

8 ounces uncooked spaghetti
1 pound boneless skinless chicken breasts, cut into strips
1 tablespoon canola oil
1 small onion, sliced
1 small sweet red pepper, julienned
1 small sweet yellow pepper, julienned
1 can (4 ounces) chopped green chilies
1/2 cup water
1/2 cup taco sauce
1 envelope fajita seasoning mix

heather brown
frisco, texas

I combine two of my favorite foods in this dish. The taco sauce and fajita seasoning add a wonderful, zesty flavor to the chicken.

Cook the spaghetti according to package directions. Meanwhile, in a large skillet, cook the chicken over medium heat in oil for 4-5 minutes on each side or until the juices run clear; remove and keep warm.

In the same skillet, saute the onion and peppers until tender. Add the chicken, chilies, water, taco sauce and fajita seasoning; heat through. Drain spaghetti; toss with chicken mixture. **yield:** 6 servings.

nutrition facts: 1-1/4 cups equals 282 calories, 5 g fat (1 g saturated fat), 42 mg cholesterol, 722 mg sodium, 37 g carbohydrate, 2 g fiber, 21 g protein.

diabetic exchanges: 2 starch, 2 lean meat, 1 vegetable.

BISCUIT NUGGET CHICKEN BAKE

prep/total time 30 minutes

kayla dempsey
o'fallon, illinois

Topped with seasoned golden biscuits, this yummy casserole will fill up a family in no time. As a beginning cook, I really enjoy trying new recipes, and this is one of my favorites for a weeknight meal.

- 3 cups cubed cooked chicken
- 1 can (10-3/4 ounces) condensed cream of chicken soup, undiluted
- 1 cup milk
- 1 jar (4-1/2 ounces) sliced mushrooms, drained
- 1/2 teaspoon dill weed
- 1/2 teaspoon paprika

BISCUIT TOPPING
- 1/4 cup grated Parmesan cheese
- 1 tablespoon dried minced onion
- 1 teaspoon dried parsley flakes
- 1/2 teaspoon paprika
- 1 tube (12 ounces) refrigerated buttermilk biscuits

In a large saucepan, combine the first six ingredients. Cook and stir over medium heat for 5-7 minutes or until heated through; keep warm.

For the biscuit topping, in a large resealable plastic bag, combine the cheese, onion, parsley and paprika. Separate biscuits and cut into quarters; add to bag and shake to coat. Place on an ungreased baking sheet. Bake at 400° for 5 minutes.

Transfer the chicken mixture to a greased 8-in. square baking dish; top with the biscuits. Bake, uncovered, for 10-13 minutes or until bubbly and the biscuits are golden brown. **yield:** 4-6 servings.

ORANGE CASHEW CHICKEN

prep/total time 25 minutes

- 1 pound boneless skinless chicken breasts, cut into 1-inch cubes
- 2 medium carrots, sliced
- 1/2 cup chopped celery
- 2 tablespoons canola oil
- 2 tablespoons cornstarch
- 1/4 teaspoon ground ginger
- 3/4 cup orange juice
- 1/4 cup honey
- 3 tablespoons soy sauce
- 1/4 to 1/2 cup salted cashews

Hot cooked rice

In a large skillet or wok, stir-fry the chicken, carrots and celery in oil for 8-10 minutes or until chicken juices run clear. Reduce heat.

In a small bowl, combine the cornstarch, ginger, orange juice, honey and soy sauce until blended. Stir into chicken mixture. Bring to a boil; cook and stir for 2 minutes or until thickened. Stir in cashews. Serve with rice. **yield:** 4 servings.

nutrition facts: 3/4-cup serving (prepared with reduced-sodium soy sauce and 1/4 cup cashews; without rice) equals 375 calories, 13 g fat (2 g saturated fat), 66 mg cholesterol, 625 mg sodium, 34 g carbohydrate, 2 g fiber, 29 g protein.

diabetic exchanges: 3-1/2 lean meat, 2 vegetable, 1-1/2 starch.

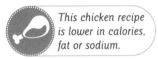

This chicken recipe is lower in calories, fat or sodium.

andrea bolden
unionville, tennessee

This delicious stir-fry is quick to fix yet tasty enough for company. The tender chicken, crunchy cashews and sweet citrus sauce are always a hit.

ORIENT EXPRESS CHICKEN SALAD

prep 25 minutes + marinating | **grill** 10 minutes

sara dziadosz
olathe, kansas

This always-popular salad makes use of lots of convenience items, but it's still healthy and nutritious. I created it one Mother's Day and received rave reviews. It's perfect for a fancy lunch or weeknight dinner, and it comes together in no time flat!

4 boneless skinless chicken breast halves (4 ounces *each*)
1 cup sesame ginger marinade
1/2 cup balsamic vinaigrette
2 tablespoons brown sugar
1 tablespoon reduced-sodium soy sauce
1/2 teaspoon ground ginger
1/4 teaspoon crushed red pepper flakes, optional
1 package (5 ounces) spring mix salad greens
1 cup chow mein noodles
1/2 cup sliced green onions
1/2 cup shredded Parmesan cheese
1/3 cup dried cranberries
1 tablespoon sesame seeds, toasted
1 can (11 ounces) mandarin oranges, drained
1/4 cup slivered almonds, toasted

Place chicken in a large resealable plastic bag; add marinade. Seal bag and turn to coat; refrigerate for at least 30 minutes. For dressing, in a small bowl, whisk the vinaigrette, brown sugar, soy sauce, ginger and red pepper flakes if desired. Cover and refrigerate until serving.

Drain and discard marinade. Grill chicken, covered, over indirect medium heat or broil 4 in. from the heat for 5-6 minutes on each side or until a meat thermometer reads 170°.

In a large bowl, toss the salad greens, noodles, onions, Parmesan cheese, cranberries and sesame seeds. Divide among four plates. Top with oranges and almonds. Cut chicken into diagonal slices; arrange over each salad. Serve with dressing.
yield: 4 servings.

ITALIAN PINEAPPLE CHICKEN

prep/total time 20 minutes

becky lohmiller
monticello, indiana

This yummy chicken is a quick and easy dinner to prepare after a long day at work. Children especially like the sweet tang from the sliced pineapple.

- 4   boneless skinless chicken breast halves (4 ounces *each*)
- 1/2   cup Italian salad dressing
- 2   tablespoons olive oil
- 1   can (8 ounces) sliced pineapple, drained
- 1/3   cup shredded Swiss cheese, optional

Flatten chicken to 1/2-in. thickness. Pour salad dressing into a shallow bowl; dip chicken in dressing. In a large skillet, heat oil. Add chicken; cook over medium-high heat for 5-7 minutes on each side or until juices run clear. Remove and keep warm.

Add pineapple slices to the skillet; cook for 30 seconds on each side or until lightly browned. Place a slice on each chicken breast half. Sprinkle with cheese if desired. **yield:** 4 servings.

CHICKEN IN CREAMY GRAVY

prep/total time 25 minutes

- 4   boneless skinless chicken breast halves (4 ounces *each*)
- 1   tablespoon canola oil
- 1   can (10-3/4 ounces) reduced-fat reduced-sodium condensed cream of chicken and broccoli soup, undiluted
- 1/4   cup fat-free milk
- 2   teaspoons lemon juice
- 1/8   teaspoon pepper
- 4   lemon slices

In a large nonstick skillet, cook chicken in oil 5-6 minutes on both sides or until browned; drain. In a large bowl, combine the soup, milk, lemon juice and pepper. Pour over chicken. Top each chicken breast with a lemon slice. Reduce heat; cover and simmer for about 5 minutes or until a meat thermometer reads 170°. **yield:** 4 servings.

nutrition facts: 1 serving equals 232 calories, 7 g fat (1 g saturated fat), 72 mg cholesterol, 644 mg sodium, 18 g carbohydrate, 5 g fiber, 30 g protein.

diabetic exchanges: 3 lean meat, 1 starch.

This chicken recipe is lower in calories, fat or sodium.

jean little
charlotte, north carolina

You only need a few ingredients and a few minutes to put this tasty main dish on the table. A burst of lemon in every bite makes it a well-received standby at home.

CHICKEN AND BOWS

prep/total time 25 minutes

danette forbes
overland park, kansas

I first made this recipe when I was a professional nanny. I can fix it quickly at dinnertime when the children are hungry.

1 package (16 ounces) bow tie pasta
2 pounds boneless skinless chicken breasts, cut into strips
1 cup chopped sweet red pepper
1/4 cup butter, cubed
2 cans (10-3/4 ounces *each*) condensed cream of chicken soup, undiluted
2 cups frozen peas
1-1/2 cups milk
1 teaspoon garlic powder
1/4 to 1/2 teaspoon salt
1/4 teaspoon pepper
2/3 cup grated Parmesan cheese

Cook pasta according to package directions. Meanwhile, in a Dutch oven, cook chicken and red pepper in butter over medium heat for 5-6 minutes or until chicken juices run clear.

Stir in the soup, peas, milk, garlic powder, salt and pepper. Bring to a boil. Reduce heat; simmer, uncovered, for 1-2 minutes or until heated through. Stir in Parmesan cheese. Drain pasta; add to chicken mixture and toss to coat.

Serve half of the mixture immediately. Cool remaining mixture; transfer to a freezer container. Cover and freeze for up to 3 months.

To use the remaining frozen casserole: Thaw in the refrigerator overnight. Transfer to an ungreased shallow 3-qt. microwave-safe dish. Cover and microwave on high for 8-10 minutes or until heated through, stirring once. **yield:** 2 casseroles (6 servings each).

nutrition facts: 1-1/3 cups equals 357 calories, 12 g fat (5 g saturated fat), 64 mg cholesterol, 636 mg sodium, 37 g carbohydrate, 3 g fiber, 26 g protein.

diabetic exchanges: 3 very lean meat, 2 starch, 2 fat.

editor's note: This recipe was tested in a 1,100-watt microwave.

MEXICAN RICE WITH CHICKEN

prep 5 minutes | **cook** 30 minutes

1 package (6.4 ounces) Mexican-style rice and vermicelli mix
2 tablespoons butter
1-3/4 cups water
1 can (14-1/2 ounces) diced tomatoes with onions, undrained
2 cups cubed cooked chicken
1 jalapeno pepper, seeded and chopped

debra rzodkiewicz
erie, pennsylvania

This skillet supper comes together with leftover cooked chicken and a packaged mix. I serve the extra rice on tortillas with cheese and sour cream the next day. Both meals are a big hit.

In a large skillet, cook and stir rice and pasta mix in butter until lightly browned, about 5 minutes. Add the water, tomatoes and contents of rice seasoning packet. Bring to a boil. Reduce heat; cover and cook for 10 minutes.

Add chicken and jalapeno. Cover and cook for 8-10 minutes or until rice is tender and liquid is absorbed. **yield:** 4 servings.

editor's note: When cutting hot peppers, disposable gloves are recommended. Avoid touching your face.

GUACAMOLE CHICKEN ROLL-UPS

prep/total time 15 minutes

taste of home test kitchen

greendale, wisconsin

Flour tortillas are available in a variety of flavors, including sun-dried tomato, spinach and whole wheat. Leftover guacamole served with chips makes a perfect accompaniment to the tasty sandwiches.

1/4   cup guacamole
4   flavored flour tortillas of your choice (10 inches)
4   large lettuce leaves
1-1/3   cups chopped fresh tomatoes
2   packages (6 ounces *each*) thinly sliced deli smoked chicken breast
2   cups (8 ounces) shredded Mexican cheese blend

Spread 1 tablespoon of guacamole over each tortilla. Layer with lettuce, tomatoes, smoked chicken and cheese. Roll up tightly. **yield:** 4 servings.

PINEAPPLE CHICKEN STIR-FRY

prep/total time 25 minutes

This chicken recipe is lower in calories, fat or sodium.

1   can (20 ounces) unsweetened pineapple tidbits
2   tablespoons cornstarch
1/4   cup cider vinegar
1/4   cup ketchup
2   tablespoons brown sugar
2   tablespoons soy sauce
1/4   teaspoon ground ginger
1-1/2   pounds boneless skinless chicken breasts, cubed
3   tablespoons canola oil, *divided*
1/2   teaspoon garlic salt
2   medium carrots, sliced
1   medium green pepper, julienned
1   medium tomato, cut into wedges
Hot cooked rice

Drain pineapple, reserving the juice; set pineapple aside. In a small bowl, combine the cornstarch and reserved juice until smooth. Stir in the cider vinegar, ketchup, brown sugar, soy sauce and ground ginger; set aside.

In a wok or large skillet, stir-fry the chicken in 2 tablespoons oil for 5-6 minutes or until the juices run clear; sprinkle with garlic salt. Remove and keep warm. Stir-fry the carrots in remaining oil for 4 minutes. Add the green pepper; cook and stir until the vegetables are crisp-tender. Add the chicken and pineapple.

Stir pineapple juice mixture; pour into skillet. Bring to a boil; cook and stir for 1-2 minutes or until thickened. Add the tomato wedges. Serve with rice. **yield:** 6 servings.

nutrition facts: 1 cup stir-fry mixture (made with reduced-sodium soy sauce; calculated without rice) equals 283 calories, 9 g fat (1 g saturated fat), 66 mg cholesterol, 492 mg sodium, 24 g carbohydrate, 2 g fiber, 28 g protein.

diabetic exchanges: 3 lean meat, 1-1/2 fruit, 1 fat.

mel miller

perkins, oklahoma

The brown sugar called for in this recipe, along with the soy sauce and ginger, gives chicken a rich and delicious taste. You wouldn't think such a flavorful dish could be table-ready in less than half an hour!

ULTIMATE KITCHEN TIP

Recipes often call for a particular type of vinegar because each has a different flavor. White vinegar tastes sharp and harsh and is used for pickling or for recipes that desire a clean strong flavor. Cider vinegar, made from apples, is faint, fruity and milder. Store vinegar in a cool, dark place. Unopened, it keeps indefinitely; once opened, it keeps up to 6 months.

BARBECUE CHICKEN BURRITOS

prep/total time 30 minutes

amy dando
apalachin, new york

We always have the ingredients for these on hand. My husband came up with this simple recipe, and it turned out to be a hit!

1/2	pound boneless skinless chicken breasts, cut into 1/2-inch cubes
1-1/2	cups julienned green peppers
1	cup chopped onion
4	tablespoons vegetable oil, *divided*
1/2	cup barbecue sauce
1-1/2	cups (6 ounces) shredded Mexican cheese blend
4	flour tortillas (10 inches), warmed

Lime wedges, sour cream, shredded lettuce and chopped tomatoes, optional

In a large skillet, cook the chicken, green peppers and onion in 2 tablespoons oil over medium heat for 6-8 minutes or until chicken juices run clear. Stir in barbecue sauce. Bring to a boil. Reduce heat; simmer for 1-2 minutes or until heated through.

Sprinkle cheese down the center of each tortilla; top with chicken mixture. Fold sides and ends over filling and roll up.

In a large skillet, brown burritos in remaining oil on all sides over medium heat. Serve with lime wedges, sour cream, lettuce and tomatoes if desired. **yield:** 4 servings.

CHICKEN SALSA PIZZA

prep/total time 20 minutes

1	prebaked Italian bread shell crust (14 ounces)
2	cups (8 ounces) shredded cheddar cheese, *divided*
1	jar (11 ounces) salsa
1	cup cubed cooked chicken

Place bread shell on an ungreased 12-in. pizza pan. Sprinkle with 3/4 cup of shredded cheese. Top with salsa, chicken and remaining cheese. Bake at 450° for 8-10 minutes or until cheese is bubbly. **yield:** 4 servings.

mrs. guy turnbull
arlington, massachusetts

This zippy chicken pizza is sure to become the most requested version in the house. The cooked chicken and a prebaked crust make it quick, easy and oh-so-good.

SAUCY APRICOT CHICKEN

prep/total time 25 minutes

   4   boneless skinless chicken breast
       halves (4 ounces *each*)
1/4 teaspoon salt
1/4 teaspoon pepper
   2   tablespoons butter
   1   can (15 ounces) apricot halves
   3   teaspoons cornstarch
1/4 cup apricot preserves
   2   tablespoons white wine vinegar
   4   green onions, chopped
Hot cooked rice, optional

Sprinkle chicken with salt and pepper. In a large skillet, cook chicken in butter over medium heat for 2-3 minutes on each side. Cover and cook 5 minutes longer or until a meat thermometer reads 170°. Remove and keep warm.

Drain the apricots, reserving juice. Cut apricots into 1/2-in. slices; set aside. In a small bowl, combine cornstarch and reserved juice until smooth. Stir in the apricot preserves and vinegar until combined; pour into skillet.

Bring to a boil over medium heat; cook and stir for 1-2 minutes or until thickened. Add apricots and chicken; heat through. Sprinkle with onions. Serve with rice if desired. **yield:** 4 servings.

**taste of home
test kitchen**
greendale, wisconsin

*Canned apricots add color
and nutrition to a delicious
sauce that is served over
tender chicken breasts.*

CHICKEN RICE DISH

prep/total time 25 minutes

rebecca vandiver

bethany, oklahoma

Fresh early-spring asparagus and a hint of lemon dress up this tasty chicken main dish. To round out the meal, serve with a fresh salad and toasted garlic bread.

2 cups water
2 cups cut fresh asparagus (1-inch diagonal pieces)
1 package (6 ounces) long grain and wild rice mix
1/4 cup butter, *divided*
3/4 pound boneless skinless chicken breasts, cut into 1-inch strips
1 teaspoon minced garlic
1/4 teaspoon salt
1 medium carrot, shredded
2 tablespoons lemon juice
1/2 teaspoon grated lemon peel, optional

In a large saucepan, combine the water, asparagus, rice mix with contents of seasoning packet and 2 tablespoons butter. Bring to a boil; reduce heat. Cover and simmer for 10-15 minutes or until the water is absorbed.

Meanwhile, in a large skillet, saute the chicken, garlic and salt in remaining butter until chicken juices run clear. Add the carrot, lemon juice and lemon peel if desired; cook and stir for 1-2 minutes or until heated through. Stir into rice mixture. **yield:** 4 servings.

nutrition facts: 1-1/4 cups (prepared with reduced-fat butter) equals 247 calories, 7 g fat (4 g saturated fat), 54 mg cholesterol, 668 mg sodium, 29 g carbohydrate, 2 g fiber, 20 g protein.

diabetic exchanges: 2 lean meat, 1-1/2 starch, 1 vegetable.

SOUTHWEST STUFFED CHICKEN

prep 15 minutes | **bake** 25 minutes

6 boneless skinless chicken breast halves (4 ounces *each*)
6 ounces Monterey Jack cheese, cut into 2-in. x 1/2-in. sticks
2 cans (4 ounces *each*) chopped green chilies, drained
1/2 cup dry bread crumbs
1/4 cup grated Parmesan cheese
1 tablespoon chili powder
1/2 teaspoon salt
1/4 teaspoon ground cumin
3/4 cup all-purpose flour
1/2 cup butter, melted

alcy thorne

los molinos, california

Our daughter served the tender chicken rolls to us a long time ago, and we've enjoyed them often since then. A zippy cheese filling gives them special flavor while a golden coating enhances their appearance.

Flatten chicken to 1/8-in. thickness. Place a cheese stick down the middle of each; top with chilies. Roll up and tuck in ends. Secure with a toothpick.

In a shallow bowl, combine the bread crumbs, Parmesan cheese, chili powder, salt and cumin. Place flour in another shallow bowl. Place butter in a third shallow bowl. Coat chicken with flour, then dip in butter and roll in crumb mixture.

Place roll-ups, seam side down, in a greased 13-in. x 9-in. baking dish. Bake, uncovered, at 400° for 25 minutes or until chicken juices run clear. Discard toothpicks. **yield:** 6 servings.

CHICKEN CHILI

prep/total time 30 minutes

yvonne morgan

grand rapids, michigan

My aunt gave me the recipe for this thick "instant" chili. To save time, I usually cook and cube the chicken the night before or use leftovers. The next day, it's simple to simmer the ingredients together on the stovetop. To make it a meal, serve with crunchy corn chips or warm bread.

- 2 cans (15 ounces *each*) great northern beans, rinsed and drained
- 2 jars (16 ounces *each*) picante sauce
- 4 cups cubed cooked chicken
- 1 to 2 teaspoons ground cumin

Shredded Monterey Jack cheese

In a large saucepan, combine the beans, picante sauce, chicken and cumin. Bring to a boil. Reduce heat; cover and simmer for 20 minutes. Sprinkle with cheese. **yield:** 6 servings.

HONEY-DIJON CHICKEN

prep 15 minutes | **bake** 20 minutes

- 12 boneless skinless chicken breast halves (4 ounces *each*)
- 4 garlic cloves, minced
- 2 teaspoons dried thyme

Salt and pepper to taste

- 1 tablespoon canola oil
- 2 tablespoons cornstarch
- 1-1/2 cups pineapple juice
- 1/2 cup water
- 1/2 cup Dijon mustard
- 1/3 cup honey

Hot cooked rice *or* noodles

Rub chicken with garlic and thyme. Sprinkle with salt and pepper. In a large skillet, cook chicken in oil or until a meat thermometer reads 170°. In a small bowl, combine the cornstarch, pineapple juice and water until smooth. Stir in mustard and honey. Add to the skillet. Bring to a boil; cook and stir for 2 minutes or until thickened.

Spoon half of the chicken and sauce into a greased 11-in. x 7-in. baking dish; cool. Cover and freeze for up to 3 months. Serve remaining chicken and sauce with rice or noodles.

To use the frozen chicken: Completely thaw in the refrigerator. Remove from the refrigerator 30 minutes before baking. Cover and bake at 350° for 35 minutes or until heated through. **yield:** 2 casseroles (6 servings per casserole).

barbara leventhal

hauppauge, new york

These moist chicken breasts are nicely browned, then covered in a flavorful sauce that gets its sweetness from honey and pineapple juice. It's delicious served over egg noodles. Even kids are sure to like it.

ULTIMATE KITCHEN TIP

In general, lighter-colored honey is milder in flavor, whereas darker styles of honey are stronger in flavor. If your honey has crystallized, simply place the honey jar in warm water and stir it until the crystals dissolve. Or place the honey in a microwave-safe container and with the lid off, microwave it, stirring every 30 seconds. Be sure not to burn the honey.

ALMOND CRANBERRY CHICKEN

prep/total time 25 minutes

**taste of home
test kitchen**

greendale, wisconsin

Add seasonal flair to everyday chicken with this flavorful sauce that showcases fresh cranberries. It's a snap to prepare on the stovetop. Round out the meal with side dishes of steamed broccoli and buttered couscous.

6	boneless skinless chicken breast halves (4 ounces *each*)
1/2	cup all-purpose flour
1/2	teaspoon salt
1/4	teaspoon cayenne pepper
1/4	cup butter
1	cup fresh *or* frozen cranberries
1	cup water
1/2	cup packed brown sugar
1	tablespoon red wine vinegar
1/4	to 1/2 teaspoon grated orange peel
1/4	cup slivered almonds, toasted

Flatten chicken to 1/4-in. thickness. In a large resealable bag, combine the flour, salt and cayenne; add chicken, a few pieces at a time, and shake to coat. In a large skillet, brown chicken in butter over medium heat for 10-12 minutes or until juices run clear. Remove and keep warm.

In the same skillet, combine the cranberries, water, brown sugar, vinegar and orange peel. Bring to a boil; cook for 10 minutes or until thickened, stirring occasionally. Spoon over chicken; sprinkle with almonds. **yield:** 6 servings.

EASY CHICKEN AND NOODLES

prep/total time 15 minutes

shirley heston

lancaster, ohio

I can prepare this supper in mere minutes. Canned soup makes the sauce a snap to throw together while the noodles boil.

1 can (10-3/4 ounces) condensed cream of chicken soup, undiluted
3/4 cup milk
1/3 cup grated Parmesan cheese
1/8 teaspoon pepper
3 cups cooked wide egg noodles
2 cups cubed cooked chicken

In a large saucepan, combine the soup, milk, Parmesan cheese and pepper. Stir in the noodles and chicken; heat through. **yield:** 4 servings.

CHICKEN DIVINE

prep/total time 25 minutes

6 boneless skinless chicken breast halves (4 ounces *each*)
Dash pepper
3 cups frozen chopped broccoli, thawed
2 medium carrots, julienned
2 tablespoons water
1 jar (16 ounces) Parmesan and mozzarella pasta sauce
2 tablespoons sherry *or* chicken broth
1/8 teaspoon ground nutmeg
Hot cooked noodles

Place chicken in a greased 11-in. x 7-in. microwave-safe dish; sprinkle with pepper. Cover with waxed paper. Microwave on high for 4-6 minutes or until juices run clear.

In a microwave-safe bowl, combine the broccoli, carrots and water. Cover and microwave on high for 2-3 minutes or until crisp-tender; drain. Spoon over chicken.

In a small bowl, combine the pasta sauce, sherry and nutmeg; pour over the chicken and vegetables. Cover and cook on high for 2-3 minutes or until heated through. Serve with the noodles. **yield:** 6 servings.

editor's note: This recipe was tested in a 1,100-watt microwave and with Ragu creamy pasta sauce.

shirley miller

san diego, california

I dress up a jar of creamy white pasta sauce with sherry and nutmeg, then cook it with chicken and vegetables. Served over noodles, the hearty combination is swift and satisfying.

CHICKEN IN LIME BUTTER

prep/total time 20 minutes

denise segura
draper, utah

*A few on-hand ingredients
make this tender chicken
really extraordinary! The
flavor from the buttery
sauce and lime juice has
made it a winner at our
house for 20 years.*

4   boneless skinless chicken breast
     halves (4 ounces *each*)
1/8 teaspoon salt
1/8 teaspoon pepper
2   tablespoons canola oil
1/4 cup butter
1   tablespoon lime juice
1/2 teaspoon dill weed
1/4 teaspoon minced chives

Sprinkle the chicken with salt and pepper. In a large skillet, cook the chicken in oil over medium heat for 5-7 minutes on each side or until a meat thermometer reaches 170°; drain. Remove and keep warm.

Add butter and lime juice to the skillet; cook and stir until butter is melted. Stir in dill and chives. Drizzle over chicken. **yield:** 4 servings.

EASY CHICKEN DIVAN

prep 15 minutes | **bake** 20 minutes

3   cups cubed cooked chicken
1/2 teaspoon salt
1/4 teaspoon pepper
1   package (10 ounces) frozen
     broccoli florets, thawed
2   cans (10-3/4 ounces *each*)
     condensed cream of chicken soup,
     undiluted
1/3 cup mayonnaise
1/4 cup milk
2   cups (8 ounces) shredded taco *or*
     Mexican cheese blend *or* cheddar
     cheese, *divided*

In a greased shallow 2-1/2-qt. baking dish, combine the chicken, salt and pepper. Top with broccoli. In a large bowl, combine the soup, mayonnaise, milk and 1-1/2 cups cheese; pour over broccoli. Sprinkle with remaining cheese.

Bake, uncovered, at 375° for 20-25 minutes or until heated through. **yield:** 4-6 servings.

editor's note: Reduced-fat or fat-free mayonnaise is not recommended for this recipe.

violet engler
leicester, new york

I got this recipe from a co-worker and then made a few changes to it to suit my family's tastes. It's excellent with corn bread.

CHICKEN PESTO PASTA

prep/total time 25 minutes

1 package (16 ounces) bow tie pasta
1 cup cut fresh asparagus (1-inch pieces)
1-1/4 cups sliced fresh mushrooms
1 medium sweet red pepper, sliced
1-1/2 teaspoons minced garlic
2 tablespoons olive oil
2 cups cubed cooked chicken
1 can (14 ounces) water-packed artichoke hearts, rinsed and drained
2 jars (3-1/2 ounces *each*) prepared pesto
1 jar (7 ounces) oil-packed sun-dried tomatoes, drained and chopped
1 teaspoon salt

1/8 teaspoon crushed red pepper flakes
1 cup (4 ounces) shredded Parmesan cheese
2/3 cup pine nuts, toasted

Cook pasta according to package directions, adding asparagus during the last 3 minutes of cooking.

Meanwhile, in a large skillet, saute the mushrooms, red pepper and garlic in oil until tender. Reduce heat; stir in the chicken, artichokes, pesto, tomatoes, salt and pepper flakes. Cook 2-3 minutes longer or until heated through.

Drain pasta; toss with chicken mixture. Sprinkle with cheese and pine nuts. **yield:** 8 servings.

barbara christensen
arvada, colorado

This is one of my favorite recipes because it's so quick and easy, but looks and tastes like I spent all day cooking it. And it includes all of my favorite flavors and ingredients!

COMPANY CHICKEN WITH ARTICHOKES

prep/total time 30 minutes

shirley lough
northglenn, colorado

This recipe from my son is one of our most popular family meals. The speedy chicken and artichoke combination is easy. It's elegant enough for company but casual enough for last-minute guests.

1/4   cup all-purpose flour
1/2   teaspoon salt
1/2   teaspoon rubbed sage
1/4   teaspoon pepper
4   boneless skinless chicken breast halves (4 ounces *each*)
2   tablespoons canola oil
1   can (14 ounces) water-packed artichoke hearts, rinsed and drained
1   jar (4-1/2 ounces) sliced mushrooms, drained
3   tablespoons chicken broth
1/4   cup white wine *or* additional chicken broth
2   tablespoons grated Parmesan cheese
2   tablespoons minced fresh parsley

In a large resealable plastic bag, combine the flour, salt, sage and pepper. Remove I tablespoon to a small bowl and set aside. Add chicken to bag, two pieces at a time, and shake to coat.

In a large skillet, cook chicken in oil over medium heat for 6-7 minutes on each side or until a meat thermometer reads 170°; drain. Remove and keep warm.

In the same skillet, combine the artichokes, mushrooms and broth. Stir wine or additional broth into reserved flour mixture until smooth; gradually add to skillet. Bring to a boil; cook and stir for 2 minutes or until thickened. Serve with the chicken. Sprinkle with Parmesan cheese and parsley. **yield:** 4 servings.

POTATO CHIP CHICKEN

prep/total time 15 minutes

1   cup coarsely crushed potato chips
1   tablespoon minced fresh parsley
1/2   teaspoon salt
1/2   teaspoon paprika
1/4   teaspoon onion powder
1   pound boneless skinless chicken breast halves
2   tablespoons mayonnaise

In a large resealable plastic bag, combine the potato chips, parsley, salt, paprika and onion powder. Brush chicken with mayonnaise; add chicken to the crumb mixture and shake to coat.

Place in an ungreased microwave-safe 11-in. x 7-in. baking dish. Cover with microwave-safe paper towels; cook on high for 6-8 minutes or until a meat thermometer reads 170°. **yield:** 4 servings.

editor's note: This recipe was tested in a 1,100-watt microwave.

jody roberts
hollister, california

This is one of the best recipes I've ever used. Crushed potato chips make the crispy coating for the moist, tender chicken. Not only is it quick and easy, but I think it tastes better than fried chicken.

CHICKEN RICE BOWL

prep/total time 10 minutes

tammy daniels
batavia, ohio

This is so easy to toss together on a busy weeknight, and I usually have the ingredients on hand. I saute the onion and pepper first, then I prepare the instant rice. If you like, top it with shredded cheddar cheese.

1 cup uncooked instant rice
1 cup chicken broth
1/2 cup chopped frozen green pepper, thawed
1/4 cup chopped onion
2 teaspoons olive oil
1 package (9 ounces) ready-to-use grilled chicken breast strips
1/2 cup frozen corn, thawed
1/2 cup frozen peas, thawed
1 teaspoon dried basil
1 teaspoon rubbed sage
1/8 teaspoon salt
1/8 teaspoon pepper

Cook the rice in broth according to package directions. Meanwhile, in a large skillet, saute the green pepper and onion in oil for 2-3 minutes or until crisp-tender. Stir in the chicken, corn, peas, basil and sage. Cook, uncovered, for 4-5 minutes over medium heat or until heated through. Stir in the rice, salt and pepper. **yield:** 4 servings.

CLOCK-WATCHER CHICKEN

prep 20 minutes | **cook** 15 minutes

4 boneless skinless chicken breast halves (4 ounces *each*)
1 medium onion, chopped
2 tablespoons canola oil
1 can (14-1/2 ounces) Italian diced tomatoes, undrained
2 cups chicken broth
1 teaspoon dried basil
1/4 teaspoon pepper
8 ounces uncooked spaghetti, broken into 2-inch pieces
1/4 cup grated Parmesan cheese

In a large skillet, cook the chicken and onion in oil until onion is tender; remove and keep warm. In the same skillet, add the diced tomatoes, broth, basil and pepper to the skillet. Bring to a boil; stir in the spaghetti.

Reduce heat; cover and simmer for 15-20 minutes. Return chicken to pan; cook until a meat thermometer reads 170° and spaghetti is tender. Sprinkle with Parmesan cheese. **yield:** 4 servings.

anne drouin
dunnville, ontario

We have three children and a busy life in the country, so I appreciate not having to dirty extra pots and pans when I make dinner. This one-skillet dish of chicken and pasta in a light tomato sauce easily fits the bill.

ULTIMATE KITCHEN TIP

It's okay to use an equal amount of shredded Parmesan for grated in your favorite recipes. If you decide to buy a chunk of Parmesan cheese and grate your own, be sure to use the finest section on your grating tool. You can also use a blender or food processor. Simply cut the cheese into 1-inch cubes and process 1 cup of cubes at a time on high until finely grated.

BUFFALO CHICKEN PIZZA

prep 20 minutes | **bake** 20 minutes

shari digirolamo
newton, pennsylvania

If your family likes spicy chicken wings, they'll love this pizza made with bottled buffalo wing sauce and refrigerated pizza dough. Serve the blue cheese salad dressing on the side, so you can drizzle it over each slice.

2 tubes (13.8 ounces *each*) refrigerated pizza crust
1 cup buffalo wing sauce, *divided*
1-1/2 cups (6 ounces) shredded cheddar cheese
1-1/2 cups (6 ounces) part-skim shredded mozzarella cheese
2 pounds boneless skinless chicken breasts, cubed
1/2 teaspoon *each* garlic salt, pepper and chili powder
2 tablespoons butter
1/2 teaspoon dried oregano
Celery sticks and blue cheese salad dressing

Unroll pizza crusts into a lightly greased 15-in. x 10-in. x 1-in. baking pan; flatten dough and build up edges slightly. Bake at 400° for 7 minutes. Brush dough with 3 tablespoons buffalo wing sauce. Combine cheddar and mozzarella cheeses; sprinkle a third over the crust. Set aside.

In a large skillet, cook the chicken, garlic salt, pepper and chili powder in butter until chicken is browned. Add the remaining wing sauce; cook and stir over medium heat for about 5 minutes or until the chicken juices run clear. Spoon over cheese. Sprinkle with oregano and remaining cheese.

Bake for 18-20 minutes or until crust is golden brown and cheese is melted. Serve with celery and blue cheese dressing. **yield:** 8 slices, 4 servings.

editor's note: This recipe was tested with Frank's Red Hot Buffalo Wing Sauce.

This chicken recipe is lower in calories, fat or sodium.

CHICKEN SALAD CLUB

prep/total time 15 minutes

nan janecke
kalamazoo, michigan

My sister and I made this wonderfully light chicken salad for our sister-in-law's bridal shower. It's easy to fix for a large crowd, and delicious on croissants or oatmeal bread.

3 cups shredded cooked chicken breast
3/4 cup chopped celery
3 tablespoons chopped green onions
1/3 cup plus 1 tablespoon fat-free mayonnaise
1/3 cup plus 1 tablespoon fat-free plain yogurt
2 tablespoons dried parsley flakes
1 tablespoon lemon juice
1/2 teaspoon salt
1/4 teaspoon pepper
12 slices white bread *or* 6 hard rolls, split
6 cooked bacon strips

In a large bowl, combine the chicken, celery and onions. In a small bowl, combine the mayonnaise, yogurt, parsley, lemon juice, salt and pepper. Pour over chicken mixture and mix well. Serve on bread or rolls with a strip of bacon. **yield:** 6 servings.

nutrition facts: 1 sandwich equals 315 calories, 9 g fat (2 g saturated fat), 67 mg cholesterol, 771 mg sodium, 29 g carbohydrate, 2 g fiber, 29 g protein.

diabetic exchanges: 3-1/2 lean meat, 2 starch, 1 fat.

SUNNY CHICKEN 'N' RICE

prep 15 minutes + marinating | **cook** 15 minutes

1-1/2 cups orange juice
1 cup apricot preserves
1/4 teaspoon ground allspice
1/4 teaspoon salt
1/4 teaspoon pepper
1/8 teaspoon ground ginger
2 cups uncooked instant rice
6 boneless skinless chicken breast halves (4 ounces *each*)

In a small microwave-safe bowl, combine the orange juice, apricot preserves, ground allspice, salt, pepper and ground ginger. Microwave, uncovered, on high for 1 to 1-1/2 minutes or until preserves begin to melt; stir to blend.

Place the rice in a shallow 3-qt. microwave-safe dish; arrange chicken on top. Pour sauce over chicken and rice. Cover and refrigerate for 4 hours.

Cover and microwave at 80% power for 11-15 minutes or until chicken juices run clear and the rice is tender. **yield:** 6 servings.

editor's note: This recipe was tested in a 1,100-watt microwave.

diana duda
glenwood, illinois

A sweet and spicy apricot sauce adds lots of flavor to my tender chicken entree. It's especially fast because it's made with instant rice. Serve it with crusty bread, fresh fruit and a green salad.

A WORLD
of FLAVOR

CHIPOTLE CHICKEN AND BEANS, P. 289

CARIBBEAN CHICKEN

This chicken recipe is lower in calories, fat or sodium.

prep 15 minutes + marinating | **grill** 10 minutes

rusty collins
orlando, florida

You'd be hard-pressed to find a marinade that's this flavorful from any store! It adds a wonderful and zippy flavor to the chicken.

1/2	cup lemon juice
1/3	cup honey
3	tablespoons canola oil
6	green onions, sliced
3	jalapeno peppers, seeded and chopped
3	teaspoons dried thyme
3/4	teaspoon salt
1/4	teaspoon ground allspice
1/4	teaspoon ground nutmeg
6	boneless skinless chicken breast halves (4 ounces *each*)

In a blender, combine the first nine ingredients, cover and process until smooth. Pour 1/2 cup into a small bowl for basting; cover and refrigerate. Pour remaining marinade into a large resealable plastic bag; add chicken. Seal bag and turn to coat; refrigerate for up to 6 hours.

Drain and discard marinade. Coat grill rack with cooking spray before starting the grill. Grill chicken, covered, over medium heat for 4-6 minutes on each side or until juices run clear, basting frequently with the reserved marinade. **yield:** 6 servings.

nutrition facts: 1 chicken breast half equals 205 calories, 6 g fat (1 g saturated fat), 66 mg cholesterol, 272 mg sodium, 11 g carbohydrate, trace fiber, 27 g protein.

diabetic exchanges: 3 lean meat, 1/2 starch.

editor's note: When cutting hot peppers, disposable gloves are recommended. Avoid touching your face.

GERMAN CHICKEN

prep 10 minutes | **bake** 1-1/2 hours

3/4	cup all-purpose flour
1	broiler/fryer chicken (3-1/2 to 4 pounds), cut up
3	tablespoons canola oil
3	tablespoons butter
3/4	teaspoon garlic powder, *divided*
1/2	teaspoon pepper, *divided*
1	large head green cabbage (3 pounds), coarsely chopped
1	large onion, chopped
1	can (29 ounces) sauerkraut, rinsed and drained
1	can (15 ounces) tomato sauce
1/3	cup packed brown sugar
1/4	cup cider vinegar

Place flour in a large resealable plastic bag. Add chicken to bag, a few pieces at a time. Seal bag and toss to coat. In a large skillet, brown chicken in oil and butter on all sides. Transfer to a large Dutch oven or roaster; sprinkle with 1/4 teaspoon garlic powder and 1/8 teaspoon pepper. Top with half of the cabbage and onion.

In a large bowl, combine the sauerkraut, tomato sauce, brown sugar, vinegar and remaining garlic powder and pepper. Pour half over the cabbage and onion. Repeat layers.

Cover and bake at 350° for 1-1/2 hours or until chicken juices run clear and cabbage is tender. **yield:** 4 servings.

grace nelson
lakewood, colorado

I came up with this chicken and cabbage dish on my own. But I owe it all to my two grandmothers, who taught me everything they know about cooking traditional German dishes.

CHICKEN CHORIZO LASAGNA

prep 40 minutes | **bake** 55 minutes + standing

    1   package (15 ounces) chorizo
    1/4 cup chopped seeded jalapeno
        peppers
    1   cooked rotisserie chicken
        (2-1/2 pounds), shredded
    2   eggs, lightly beaten
    1   carton (15 ounces) ricotta cheese
    4   cans (10 ounces *each*) enchilada
        sauce
    12 no-cook lasagna noodles
    4   cups (16 ounces) shredded
        Monterey Jack cheese
    1/2 cup minced fresh cilantro

AVOCADO CREAM SAUCE

    2   medium ripe avocados, peeled,
        pitted and halved
    1/4 cup sour cream
    2   tablespoons lime juice
    1/4 teaspoon salt

In a large skillet, cook chorizo and jalapenos over medium heat until meat is no longer pink; drain. Stir in chicken. In a bowl, combine eggs and ricotta.

Spread 1 cup enchilada sauce in a greased 13-in. x 9-in. baking dish. Top with four lasagna noodles, a third of the ricotta mixture, half of the meat mixture, 1 cup Monterey Jack and 1 cup enchilada sauce. Repeat layers. Top with the remaining noodles, ricotta mixture, enchilada sauce and Monterey Jack.

Cover and bake at 375° for 45-50 minutes. Uncover; bake 10 minutes more or until bubbly. Sprinkle with the minced cilantro. Let stand 15 minutes before serving.

Meanwhile, place sauce ingredients in a food processor; cover and process until smooth. Serve with lasagna. **yield:** 12 servings.

editor's note: When cutting hot peppers, disposable gloves are recommended. Avoid touching your face.

kari wheaton
beloit, wisconsin

The combination of roasted chicken and chorizo is so good, you have to serve this lasagna at your next Mexican-themed meal. The avocado and lime cream adds a bit of coolness to offset the recipe's heat.

MATZO BALL SOUP

prep 25 minutes + chilling | **cook** 2 hours

taste of home
test kitchen
greendale, wisconsin

There's nothing like a warm cup of this soup on a chilly day. For convenience, you can make the soup a day ahead and reheat it just before serving.

10 cups water
12 garlic cloves, peeled
3 medium carrots, cut into chunks
3 small turnips, peeled and cut into chunks
2 medium onions, cut into wedges
2 medium parsnips, peeled and cut into chunks
1 medium leek (white portion only), sliced
1/4 cup minced fresh parsley
2 tablespoons snipped fresh dill
1 teaspoon salt
1 teaspoon pepper
3/4 teaspoon ground turmeric

MATZO BALLS
3 eggs, *separated*
3 tablespoons water *or* chicken broth
3 tablespoons rendered chicken fat
1-1/2 teaspoons salt, *divided*
3/4 cup matzo meal
8 cups water

For broth, in a large soup kettle, combine the first 12 ingredients. Bring to a boil. Reduce heat; cover and simmer for 2 hours. Meanwhile, for matzo balls, in a bowl, beat yolks on high for 2 minutes or until thick and lemon-colored. Add water, fat and 1/2 teaspoon salt. In another bowl, beat egg whites on high until stiff peaks form; fold into yolk mixture. Fold in matzo meal. Cover and refrigerate for 1 hour or until thickened.

In another large soup kettle, bring water to a boil; add remaining salt. Drop eight rounded tablespoonfuls of matzo ball dough into boiling water. Reduce heat; cover and simmer for 20-25 minutes or until a toothpick inserted into a matzo ball comes out clean (do not lift cover while simmering).

Strain broth, discarding vegetables and seasonings. Carefully remove matzo balls from water with a slotted spoon; place one matzo ball in each soup bowl. Add broth. **yield:** 8 servings.

ARTICHOKE CHICKEN FETTUCCINE

prep/total time 30 minutes

8 ounces uncooked fettuccine
1 pound boneless skinless chicken breasts, cut into 1-inch strips
4 bacon strips, diced
1/4 cup chopped onion
2 tablespoons chopped sweet red pepper
2 tablespoons butter
2 tablespoons all-purpose flour
1 cup chicken broth
1/2 cup milk
1 teaspoon Dijon mustard
2 tablespoons grated Parmesan cheese
1 can (14 ounces) water-packed artichoke hearts, rinsed and drained
2 tablespoons mayonnaise

winnie struse
hereford, arizona

My mother-in-law created this recipe after enjoying a similar dish on a trip to Denver. A medley of artichokes, red pepper and chicken creates a lovely entree when paired with pasta and a creamy sauce.

Cook fettuccine according to directions. Meanwhile, in a large skillet, saute chicken, bacon, onion and red pepper until chicken juices run clear and vegetables are tender; drain and keep warm.

In a large saucepan, melt butter; stir in flour until smooth. Gradually add the broth, milk and mustard. Bring to a boil; cook and stir for 2 minutes or until thickened. Stir in Parmesan cheese and artichokes. Remove from the heat; stir in mayonnaise and chicken mixture. Drain fettuccine; serve with chicken mixture. **yield:** 4 servings.

SOUTHERN BARBECUED CHICKEN

prep 25 minutes + marinating | **grill** 40 minutes

revonda stroud

fort worth, texas

Growing up, I traveled the U.S. and abroad as part of a military family. Tasting various cuisines made me adventurous in the kitchen.

2 cups cider vinegar
1 cup canola oil
1 egg, lightly beaten
2 tablespoons hot pepper sauce
1 tablespoon garlic powder
1 tablespoon poultry seasoning
2 teaspoons salt
1 teaspoon pepper
1 broiler/fryer chicken (3 to 4 pounds), cut up

In a large saucepan, combine the first eight ingredients. Bring to a boil, stirring constantly. Reduce heat; simmer, uncovered, for 10 minutes, stirring often. Cool.

Pour 1-2/3 cups marinade into a large resealable plastic bag; add the chicken.

Seal bag and turn to coat; refrigerate overnight, turning occasionally. Cover and refrigerate remaining marinade for basting.

Prepare grill for indirect heat, using a drip pan. Drain and discard marinade from chicken. Place skin side down over pan. Grill, covered, over indirect medium heat for 20 -25 minutes on each side or until juices run clear, basting occasionally with reserved marinade. **yield:** 4 servings.

COUNTRY CASSOULET

prep 65 minutes + standing | **bake** 1-1/2 hours

3/4 pound dried navy beans
3 cups water
1 bay leaf
1 can (14-1/2 ounces) chicken broth
1/4 pound bacon, diced
4 chicken legs *or* thighs
2 medium carrots, quartered
2 medium onions, quartered
1 cup canned diced tomatoes
1/4 cup coarsely chopped celery with leaves
2 garlic cloves, crushed
1 teaspoon salt
1/2 teaspoon dried marjoram leaves
1/2 teaspoon rubbed sage
1/4 teaspoon pepper
1 teaspoon whole cloves
1/2 pound smoked sausage, cut into 2-inch pieces
Minced fresh parsley

Sort beans and rinse with cold water. In a Dutch oven or soup kettle, combine the beans, water and bay leaf. Bring to a boil; boil, uncovered, for 2 minutes. Remove from the heat; cover and let stand for 1 to 4 hours or until beans are softened. Do not drain.

Stir in broth; bring to a boil. Reduce heat; cover and simmer for 1 hour. Meanwhile, in a small skillet, cook bacon over medium heat until crisp. Using a slotted spoon, remove to paper towels; drain, reserving 2 tablespoons drippings. In the same skillet, brown chicken in reserved drippings on all sides; drain and set aside.

In a 3-qt. baking dish or Dutch oven, combine the beans with cooking liquid, bacon, carrots, onion, tomatoes, celery, garlic, salt, marjoram, sage and pepper. Place whole cloves on a double thickness of cheesecloth; bring up corners of cloth and tie with string to form a bag. Add to bean mixture; top with chicken.

Cover and bake at 350° for 1 hour. Uncover; add sausage. Bake 30-35 minutes longer or until beans are tender. Discard bay leaf and spice bag. Garnish with parsley. **yield:** 4 servings.

roberta strohmaier

lebanon, new jersey

Our home is on 2 acres of land, with a vegetable garden plus fruit trees and berry bushes. This dish is one that I make frequently with my garden bounty— my husband's a bean lover!

This chicken recipe is lower in calories, fat or sodium.

STIR-FRIED BASIL CHICKEN

prep 15 minutes + marinating | **cook** 10 minutes

mildred sherrer
fort worth, texas

The pleasant aroma and flavor of fresh basil stands out in this easy-to-make, Thai-inspired entree.

1	tablespoon water
1	tablespoon soy sauce
2	teaspoons sugar
1-3/4	pounds boneless skinless chicken breasts, cut into strips
3	green onions, sliced
6	teaspoons canola oil, *divided*
3	garlic cloves, minced
1/4	teaspoon crushed red pepper flakes
6	cups sliced bok choy
1	cup loosely packed fresh basil leaves, thinly sliced

In a large resealable bag, combine the water, soy sauce and sugar; add chicken. Seal bag and turn to coat. Refrigerate for 30 minutes.

In a wok or skillet, stir-fry the onions in 1 teaspoon oil until crisp-tender. Stir in garlic and pepper flakes; cook and stir for 1 minute. Remove and keep warm.

Drain and discard any marinade from chicken. In the same wok, stir-fry chicken in 3 teaspoons oil for 4-5 minutes or until juices run clear.

Meanwhile, in another skillet, saute the bok choy in remaining oil until crisp-tender. Add onion mixture to chicken. Stir in basil; heat through. Serve with bok choy. **yield:** 4 servings.

nutrition facts: 1 serving (prepared with reduced-sodium soy sauce) equals 317 calories, 12 g fat (2 g saturated fat), 110 mg cholesterol, 307 mg sodium, 8 g carbohydrate, 4 g fiber, 44 g protein.

diabetic exchanges: 6 very lean meat, 2 fat, 1 vegetable.

POLISH POULTRY

prep 10 minutes | **bake** 1 hour

dorothea kampfe
gothenburg, nebraska

Nebraska claims many residents of Polish descent. This tasty recipe is one of my family's favorites, and I'm sure it'll become one of yours, too.

1   medium onion, chopped
1   garlic clove, minced
1   teaspoon caraway seeds
1   can (27 ounces) sauerkraut, undrained
3/4   pound smoked kielbasa *or* Polish sausage, cut into 1-inch pieces
1   broiler/fryer chicken (2 to 3 pounds), cut up
1/2   teaspoon salt
1/4   teaspoon pepper
1/4   to 1/2 teaspoon dried thyme

In a large bowl, combine the first four ingredients. Place on the bottom of a 13-in. x 9-in. baking dish. Top with sausage and chicken. Sprinkle with salt, pepper and thyme.

Bake at 350° for 60-65 minutes or until chicken is tender and juices run clear, basting occasionally with pan juices. **yield:** 6 servings.

FRENCH-STYLE CHICKEN

prep/total time 25 minutes

This chicken recipe is lower in calories, fat or sodium.

6   boneless skinless chicken breast halves (4 ounces *each*)
3/4   teaspoon salt-free lemon-pepper seasoning
1-1/3   cups reduced-sodium chicken broth
3   medium unpeeled apples, cut into wedges
1   medium onion, thinly sliced
4   tablespoons apple cider *or* juice, *divided*
1/4   teaspoon ground cinnamon
1/8   teaspoon ground nutmeg
1   tablespoon cornstarch
Minced fresh parsley

Sprinkle chicken with lemon-pepper. In a large non-stick skillet coated with cooking spray, cook chicken for 5-6 minutes on each side or until juices run clear. Remove and keep warm.

In the same skillet, combine the broth, apples, onion, 3 tablespoons cider, cinnamon and nutmeg. Bring to a boil. Combine cornstarch and remaining cider until smooth; stir into apple mixture. Bring to a boil; cook and stir for 1-2 minutes or until thickened. Top with chicken; sprinkle with parsley. **yield:** 6 servings.

nutrition facts: 1 serving equals 186 calories, 3 g fat (1 g saturated fat), 63 mg cholesterol, 194 mg sodium, 16 g carbohydrate, 2 g fiber, 24 g protein.

diabetic exchanges: 3 lean meat, 1 fruit.

catherine johnston
stafford, new york

When I have friends over, I make this classy light recipe and serve with a tossed salad and crisp French bread. Toasted almond slices sprinkled on top add a crunchy, finishing touch.

ULTIMATE KITCHEN TIP

To turn French-Style Chicken into a complete meal, add a salad and dessert. For an easy vinaigrette, combine 3/4 cup vegetable oil, 1/4 cup red wine or cider vinegar, 2 tablespoons Dijon mustard, 1 minced garlic clove, and salt and pepper to taste in a jar with a tight-fitting lid. For dessert, top fresh fruit salad with low-fat vanilla yogurt.

GORGONZOLA CHICKEN PENNE

prep/total time 30 minutes

c.w. steve stevenson

newfoundland,
pennsylvania

I came up with this recipe in my attempt to re-create a meal at a European restaurant. The hearty Gorgonzola sauce pairs well with the sauteed chicken and pasta.

2   cups uncooked penne pasta
2   cups fresh broccoli florets
1   tablespoon water
1   pound boneless skinless chicken breasts, cut into 1-inch cubes
9   tablespoons butter, *divided*
1   large onion, chopped
6   tablespoons all-purpose flour
2   cups chicken broth
3/4 cup white wine *or* additional chicken broth
1-1/2 cups (6 ounces) crumbled Gorgonzola cheese
Pepper to taste

Cook pasta according to package directions. Meanwhile, place broccoli and water in a small microwave-safe bowl. Cover and microwave on high for 2 to 2-1/2 minutes or until crisp-tender. Set aside.

In a large skillet, saute chicken in 3 tablespoons butter until chicken juices run clear. Remove and keep warm. In the same skillet, saute onion in remaining butter until tender. Stir in flour until blended. Gradually add broth and wine or additional broth. Bring to a boil; cook and stir for 2 minutes or until thickened. Reduce heat to low; stir in cheese until blended.

Drain pasta and broccoli; add to onion mixture. Add chicken; heat through. Season with pepper. **yield:** 6 servings.

INDONESIAN PASTA

prep/total time 20 minutes

1/2 cup chicken broth
2   jalapeno peppers, seeded and chopped
2   tablespoons soy sauce
2   tablespoons peanut butter
1   tablespoon dried minced onion
1   tablespoon lemon juice
1/4 teaspoon brown sugar
18 fresh asparagus spears, trimmed and cut into 1-inch pieces
1/2 medium sweet red pepper, julienned
2   teaspoons olive oil
6   ounces uncooked angel hair pasta
1/2 cup sliced green onions

In a small saucepan, combine the first seven ingredients. Bring to a boil, stirring constantly. Remove from the heat; keep warm.

In a large skillet, saute the asparagus and red pepper in oil for 6-8 minutes. Meanwhile, cook the pasta according to package directions. Add green onions to the asparagus mixture; saute for 2-3 minutes or until vegetables are crisp-tender. Drain pasta; toss with vegetable mixture and reserved sauce. **yield:** 4 servings.

editor's note: When cutting hot peppers, disposable gloves are recommended. Avoid touching your face.

jolene caldwell

council bluffs, iowa

My family really enjoys this delectable asparagus dish. The flavors blend to create an interesting taste.

CHIPOTLE CHICKEN AND BEANS

prep 15 minutes | **cook** 30 minutes

3/4	cup water, *divided*
1/2	cup reduced-sodium chicken broth
1/2	cup uncooked long grain rice
6	boneless skinless chicken breast halves (4 ounces *each*)
1/4	teaspoon salt
3	bacon strips, diced
1	cup chopped onion
3	garlic cloves, minced
1	cup chopped plum tomatoes
1/2	teaspoon ground cumin
1/4	teaspoon ground cinnamon
1/2	cup whole-berry cranberry sauce
4-1/2	teaspoons minced chipotle peppers in adobo sauce
1-1/2	teaspoons lime juice
1	can (15 ounces) black beans, rinsed and drained
1	can (15 ounces) white kidney *or* cannellini beans, rinsed and drained

In a small saucepan, bring 1/2 cup water and broth to a boil. Stir in rice. Reduce heat; cover and simmer for 15-18 minutes or until rice is tender.

Meanwhile, cut each chicken breast half widthwise into six strips. Sprinkle with salt. In a large nonstick skillet coated with cooking spray, cook chicken for 5 minutes on each side or until lightly browned. Remove and keep warm.

In the same skillet, cook bacon over medium heat until crisp. Using a slotted spoon, remove to paper towels; drain, reserving 1/2 teaspoon drippings. In the drippings, saute onion and garlic until tender. Add the tomatoes, cumin and cinnamon; cook for 2 minutes. Stir in the cranberry sauce, chipotle peppers, lime juice and remaining 1/4 cup water. Bring to a boil.

Return chicken to the pan. Reduce heat; cover and simmer for 6-10 minutes or until chicken juices run clear. Remove and keep warm. Add cooked rice and beans to the skillet; heat through. Serve chicken over bean mixture; sprinkle with bacon. **yield:** 6 servings.

jenny kniesly
dover, ohio

I was skeptical about this Southwestern recipe due to its combination of ingredients, but it immediately became one of our all-time favorites.

SPANISH-STYLE PAELLA

prep 10 minutes | **cook** 35 minutes

**taste of home
cooking school**

greendale, wisconsin

*If you enjoy cooking ethnic
foods, this hearty rice dish
will be a favorite. It's
brimming with generous
chunks of sausage, shrimp
and vegetables.*

1/2 pound bulk Italian sausage

1/2 pound boneless skinless chicken
breasts, cubed

1 garlic clove, minced

1 tablespoon olive oil

1 cup uncooked long grain rice

1 cup chopped onion

1-1/2 cups chicken broth

1 can (14-1/2 ounces) stewed
tomatoes, undrained

1/2 teaspoon paprika

1/4 teaspoon ground cayenne pepper

1/4 teaspoon salt

10 strands saffron, crushed *or* 1/8
teaspoon ground saffron

1/2 pound uncooked medium shrimp,
peeled and deveined

1/2 cup sweet red pepper strips

1/2 cup green pepper strips

1/2 cup frozen peas

In a Dutch oven or large saucepan over medium-high heat, cook sausage, chicken and garlic in oil for 5 minutes or until lightly browned, stirring frequently. Drain if necessary. Add rice and onion. Cook until onions are tender and rice is lightly browned, stirring frequently.

Add chicken broth, stewed tomatoes, paprika, cayenne, salt and saffron. Bring to a boil. Reduce heat to low; cover and cook 10 minutes. Stir in shrimp, peppers and peas. Cover and cook 10 minutes or until rice is tender and liquid is absorbed. **yield:** 6-8 servings.

SOUTHERN-STYLE CHICKEN SALAD

prep 20 minutes + chilling

marion greer
ballston lake, new york

A home economics teacher from Virginia gave me the recipe for this popular sweet and tangy salad. It's a big hit at local gatherings.

2 egg yolks
1/4 cup sugar
1/4 cup cider vinegar
2 teaspoons prepared mustard
1/2 teaspoon salt
2 tablespoons butter
2 tablespoons milk
2 tablespoons mayonnaise
4 cups diced cooked chicken
1-1/2 cups diced celery
3 hard-cooked eggs, chopped
2 tablespoons finely chopped onion

In a small saucepan, combine the egg yolks, sugar, vinegar, mustard and salt. Cook and stir over medium heat until mixture reaches 160° or is thick enough to coat the back of a metal spoon. Stir in butter until melted. Cover and chill for 30 minutes.

Stir in milk and mayonnaise. In a large bowl, combine remaining ingredients. Add dressing and toss to coat. Chill until ready to serve. Refrigerate leftovers. **yield:** 8-10 servings.

GRILLED THAI CHICKEN SALAD

prep 20 minutes + marinating | **grill** 10 minutes

1/2 cup hot water
2 tablespoons lime juice
3/4 cup flaked coconut
2 teaspoons curry powder
2 teaspoons minced fresh gingerroot
1 teaspoon salt
4 boneless skinless chicken breast halves (4 ounces *each*)
4 cups torn mixed salad greens
1/2 medium sweet red pepper, julienned
1/2 cup canned bean sprouts, rinsed and drained
1/2 cup fresh sugar snap peas
DRESSING
1/4 cup reduced-sodium soy sauce
2 tablespoons lime juice
2 tablespoons coconut milk

2 tablespoons reduced-fat creamy peanut butter
4 teaspoons sugar

In a blender, combine the first six ingredients; cover and process until blended. Pour into a large resealable plastic bag; add chicken. Seal bag and turn to coat; refrigerate for at least 1 hour.

If grilling the chicken, coat grill rack with cooking spray before starting the grill. Drain and discard marinade. Grill chicken, covered, over medium heat or broil 4 in. from the heat for 4-7 minutes on each side or until juices run clear.

In a large salad bowl, combine the greens, red pepper, bean sprouts and peas. In a small bowl, whisk the dressing ingredients until smooth. Pour over salad and toss to coat. Cut chicken into strips; arrange over salad. **yield:** 4 servings.

grace kunert
salt lake city, utah

My husband and I love to eat Thai and Indian food, but notice that most of these cuisines do not offer fresh salads on their menus. This is a recipe we developed to keep all those ethnic flavors when we needed a light dinner.

YOGURT-MARINATED CHICKEN

prep 5 minutes + marinating | **grill** 30 minutes

 *This chicken recipe is lower in calories, fat or sodium.*

naheed saleem
stamford, connecticut

This tender, marinated chicken gets its zing from ginger, chili powder and cumin. I sometimes add a tablespoon of tomato paste to the marinade or replace the chili powder with chopped green chilies. It's a surefire hit of summer cookouts.

1/2 cup fat-free yogurt
3 garlic cloves, minced
2 tablespoons lemon juice
1 tablespoon canola oil
1 tablespoon minced fresh gingerroot
1 teaspoon sugar
1 teaspoon chili powder
1/2 teaspoon salt
1/2 teaspoon ground cumin
6 bone-in chicken breast halves (6 ounces *each*)

In a large resealable plastic bag, combine the yogurt, garlic, lemon juice, oil, ginger, sugar and seasonings; add the chicken. Seal bag and turn to coat; refrigerate for at least 8 hours or overnight.

Coat grill rack with cooking spray before starting the grill. Prepare the grill for indirect heat. Drain and discard marinade. Grill chicken, covered, bone side down over indirect medium heat for 2 minutes. Turn; grill 25-35 minutes longer or until juices run clear. **yield:** 6 servings.

nutrition facts: 1 chicken breast half equals 149 calories, 4 g fat (1 g saturated fat), 68 mg cholesterol, 163 mg sodium, 2 g carbohydrate, trace fiber, 25 g protein.

diabetic exchanges: 3 lean meat.

HUNGARIAN CHICKEN PAPRIKASH

prep 20 minutes | **bake** 1-1/2 hours

1 large onion, chopped
1/4 cup butter, cubed
4 to 5 pounds broiler/fryer chicken pieces
2 tablespoons paprika
1 teaspoon salt
1/2 teaspoon pepper
1-1/2 cups hot water
2 tablespoons cornstarch
2 tablespoons cold water
1 cup (8 ounces) sour cream

In a large skillet, saute onion in butter until tender. Sprinkle chicken with paprika, salt and pepper; place in an ungreased roasting pan. Spoon onion mixture over chicken. Add hot water. Cover and bake at 350° for 1-1/2 hours or until chicken juices run clear.

Remove the chicken and keep warm. In a small bowl, combine cornstarch and cold water until smooth. Gradually add to pan juices with onion. Bring to a boil over medium heat; cook and stir for 2 minutes or until thickened. Remove from the heat. Stir in sour cream. Serve with the chicken. **yield:** 6 servings.

pamela eaton
lambertville, michigan

My mom learned to make this tender chicken dish when she volunteered to help prepare the dinners served at her church. It's my favorite main dish, and the gravy, seasoned with paprika, sour cream and onions, is the best.

CHICKEN SATAY

prep 15 minutes + marinating | **broil** 5 minutes

- 2 pounds boneless skinless chicken breasts
- 1/3 cup soy sauce
- 1 green onion, sliced
- 2 tablespoons sesame oil
- 1 tablespoon brown sugar
- 1 tablespoon honey
- 2 garlic cloves, minced
- 1/2 teaspoon ground ginger

PEANUT SAUCE
- 1/2 cup salted peanuts
- 1/4 cup chopped green onions
- 1 garlic clove, minced
- 3 tablespoons chicken broth
- 3 tablespoons butter, melted
- 2 tablespoons soy sauce
- 1 tablespoon lemon juice
- 1 tablespoon honey

- 1/2 teaspoon ground ginger
- 1/4 to 1/2 teaspoon crushed red pepper flakes

Flatten the chicken to 1/4-in. thickness; cut lengthwise into 1-in.-wide strips. In a large resealable plastic bag, combine the soy sauce, green onion, sesame oil, brown sugar, honey, garlic and ginger; add the chicken. Seal bag and turn to coat; refrigerate for 4 hours.

In a food processor, combine the peanuts, onions and garlic; cover and process until mixture forms a paste. Add the broth, butter, soy sauce, lemon juice, honey, ginger and pepper flakes; cover and process until smooth. Transfer to a serving bowl. Refrigerate until serving.

Drain and discard marinade. Thread chicken strips onto soaked wooden skewers. Broil 6 in. from the heat for 2-4 minutes on each side or until chicken is no longer pink. Serve with peanut sauce. **yield:** 10-12 servings.

taste of home test kitchen
greendale, wisconsin

This Asian-style dish features a simple-to-prepare peanut sauce. It's a hearty addition to an appetizer buffet.

COQ AU VIN

prep 30 minutes | **cook** 30 minutes

**taste of home
test kitchen**

greendale, wisconsin

*Coq au vin, a classic French
dish, is typically made with
red wine. This wonderful
version calls for white
wine instead.*

4	cups water
1	cup pearl onions
4	bacon strips, cut into 1-inch pieces
2	bone-in chicken breast halves (8 ounces *each*)
1/4	teaspoon salt
1/8	teaspoon pepper
3/4	cup sliced fresh mushrooms
2	garlic cloves, minced
4-1/2	teaspoons all-purpose flour
3/4	cup chicken broth
3/4	cup white wine *or* additional chicken broth
1	bay leaf
1/2	teaspoon dried thyme

Hot cooked noodles

In a large saucepan, bring water to a boil. Add onions; boil for 3 minutes. Drain and rinse in cold water; peel and set aside.

In a large skillet, cook bacon over medium heat until crisp. Using a slotted spoon, remove to paper towels. Sprinkle chicken with salt and pepper. Brown chicken in the drippings; remove and keep warm. Add onions to drippings; saute until crisp-tender. Add mushrooms and garlic; saute 3-4 minutes longer or until almost tender.

Combine flour and broth; stir into onion mixture. Add wine or additional broth, bay leaf and thyme; bring to a boil. Return chicken and bacon to the pan. Reduce heat; cover and simmer for 25-30 minutes or until a meat thermometer reads 170°.

Remove chicken and keep warm. Continue to cook sauce over medium heat until slightly thickened. Discard bay leaf. Serve chicken and sauce with noodles. **yield:** 2 servings.

GREEK ROASTED CHICKEN AND POTATOES

prep 10 minutes | **bake** 2 hours

pella visnick
dallas, texas

I've served this dish many times—you'll find this roast is a nice one to serve company or to your family for Sunday supper. All you need for a complete meal is a tossed salad and some crusty French bread.

1   roasting chicken (about 6 pounds)
Salt and pepper to taste
2   to 3 teaspoons dried oregano, *divided*
4   to 6 baking potatoes, peeled and quartered
1/4 cup butter, melted
3   tablespoons fresh lemon juice
3/4 cup chicken broth

Place chicken breast side up on a rack in a roasting pan. Sprinkle with salt and pepper and half the oregano. Arrange potatoes around the chicken; sprinkle with salt and pepper and the remaining oregano. Pour butter and lemon juice over chicken and potatoes. Add chicken broth to pan.

Bake uncovered at 350° for 2 to 2-1/2 hours or until the juices run clear and a meat thermometer inserted into thigh reads 180°, basting frequently. Cover and let stand for 10 minutes before carving. If desired, thicken the pan drippings for gravy. **yield:** about 8-10 servings.

SPINACH-FETA CHICKEN ROLLS

prep 25 minutes | **bake** 45 minutes

1/2 cup sun-dried tomatoes (not packed in oil)
1   cup boiling water
1   package (10 ounces) frozen chopped spinach, thawed and squeezed dry
1   cup (4 ounces) crumbled feta cheese
4   green onions, thinly sliced
1/4 cup Greek olives, chopped
1   garlic clove, minced
6   boneless skinless chicken breast halves (6 ounces *each*)
1/4 teaspoon salt
1/4 teaspoon pepper

Place tomatoes in a small bowl; add boiling water. Let stand for 5 minutes. In another bowl, combine the spinach, feta cheese, onions, olives and garlic. Drain and chop tomatoes; add to spinach mixture.

Flatten the chicken to 1/4-in. thickness; sprinkle with salt and pepper. Spread the spinach mixture over the flattened chicken. Roll up and secure with toothpicks. Place in a 13-in. x 9-in. baking dish coated with cooking spray.

Cover and bake at 350° for 30 minutes. Uncover; bake 15-20 minutes longer or until a meat thermometer reads 170°. Discard toothpicks. **yield:** 6 servings.

nutrition facts: 1 stuffed chicken breast half equals 272 calories, 9 g fat (3 g saturated fat), 104 mg cholesterol, 583 mg sodium, 7 g carbohydrate, 3 g fiber, 40 g protein.

diabetic exchanges: 5 very lean meat, 1 vegetable, 1 fat.

This chicken recipe is lower in calories, fat or sodium.

linda gregg
spartanburg, south carolina

This dish was inspired from a favorite Greek appetizer. It may take a bit of extra work, but it's worth it!

CHICKEN MILAN

prep/total time 20 minutes

lara priest
gansevoort, new york

This restaurant-style dish comes together in under half an hour. But it tastes as if you cooked for hours.

8   ounces uncooked linguine
1   tablespoon minced garlic
3   tablespoons olive oil, *divided*
1/2 teaspoon dried parsley flakes
1/2 teaspoon pepper, *divided*
1/4 cup all-purpose flour
1   teaspoon dried basil
1/2 teaspoon salt
2   eggs
1-1/2 pounds boneless skinless chicken breasts, cut into strips

Cook linguine according to package directions. Meanwhile, in a large skillet, saute garlic in 1 tablespoon oil for 2-3 minutes or until tender; stir in parsley and 1/4 teaspoon pepper. Remove to a small bowl and set aside.

In a shallow bowl, combine the flour, basil, salt and remaining pepper. In another shallow bowl, whisk the eggs. Dredge chicken strips in flour mixture, then dip in eggs.

In the same skillet, cook the chicken in the remaining oil over medium-high heat for 8-10 minutes or until juices run clear. Drain linguine and place on a serving platter. Pour reserved garlic mixture over linguine and toss to coat; top with chicken. **yield:** 6 servings.

KUNG PAO WINGS

prep/total time 30 minutes

8   whole chicken wings (about 1-1/2 pounds)
2   tablespoons sugar
2   teaspoons cornstarch
1/4 cup water
1/4 cup soy sauce
2   tablespoons lemon juice
1/4 teaspoon crushed red pepper flakes
1   tablespoon canola oil
1   small sweet red pepper, diced
1/2 cup diced onion
1   to 2 garlic cloves, minced
1/3 cup peanuts
Hot cooked rice

Cut the chicken wings into three sections; discard wing tip section. Set the wings aside. In a small bowl, combine the sugar, cornstarch, water, soy sauce, lemon juice and pepper flakes until blended; set aside.

In a large skillet, cook chicken wings, uncovered, over medium-high heat for 10-15 minutes or until chicken juices run clear, turning occasionally.

Add the red pepper, onion and garlic; cook, uncovered, for 3-5 minutes or until vegetables are crisp-tender. Stir cornstarch mixture; gradually add to skillet. Bring to a boil; cook and stir for 2 minutes or until sauce is thickened and vegetables are tender. Sprinkle with peanuts. Serve with rice. **yield:** 4 servings.

editor's note: Uncooked chicken wing sections (wingettes) may be substituted for whole chicken wings.

kathy evans
lacey, washington

Served as an entree over hot cooked rice, these delicious drummettes have plenty of personality—with sweet red pepper for color, red pepper flakes for zip and peanuts for crunch. They're quick and easy to prepare, too.

CHICKEN POTSTICKERS

prep 50 minutes | **cook** 10 minutes

1 pound boneless skinless chicken thighs, cut into chunks
1-1/2 cups sliced fresh mushrooms
1 small onion, cut into wedges
2 tablespoons hoisin sauce
2 tablespoons prepared mustard
2 tablespoons sriracha Asian hot chili sauce *or* 1 tablespoon hot pepper sauce
1 package (14 ounces) potsticker dumpling wrappers
1 egg, lightly beaten

SAUCE

1 cup soy sauce
1 green onion, chopped
1 teaspoon ground ginger

In a food processor, combine the uncooked chicken, mushrooms, onion, hoisin sauce, mustard and chili sauce; cover and process until blended.

Place 1 tablespoon of chicken mixture in the center of each wrapper. (Until ready to use, keep wrappers covered with a damp towel to prevent them from drying out.) Moisten edges with egg. Bring opposite sides together to form a semicircle; pinch to seal.

Place the potstickers in a single layer on a large greased steamer basket rack; place in a Dutch oven over 1 in. of water. Bring to a boil; cover and steam for 8-10 minutes or until the filling juices run clear.

Meanwhile, in a small bowl, combine sauce ingredients. Serve with potstickers. Refrigerate leftovers. **yield:** 4 dozen.

jacquelynne stine
las vegas, nevada

Chicken and mushrooms make up the filling in these potstickers, a traditional Chinese dumpling. Greasing the steamer rack makes it easier to remove them once they're steamed.

CHICKEN AND OKRA GUMBO

prep 40 minutes | **cook** 2 hours

catherine bouis
palm harbor, florida

We used to live in New Orleans, but our stomachs don't know we moved yet. I still make many Creole dishes, and this gumbo is one of our favorites.

1   broiler/fryer chicken (2-1/2 to 3 pounds), cut up
2   quarts water
1/4   cup canola oil *or* bacon drippings
2   tablespoons all-purpose flour
2   medium onions, chopped
2   celery ribs, chopped
1   medium green pepper, chopped
3   garlic cloves, minced
1   can (28 ounces) tomatoes, drained
2   cups fresh *or* frozen sliced okra
2   bay leaves
1   teaspoon dried basil
1   teaspoon salt
1/2   teaspoon pepper
1   to 2 teaspoons hot pepper sauce
2   tablespoons sliced green onions
Minced fresh parsley
Hot cooked rice

Place chicken and water in a large kettle. Cover and bring to a boil. Reduce heat; cover and simmer for 30-45 minutes or until chicken is tender.

Remove the chicken; reserve broth. Set the chicken aside until cool enough to handle. Remove the chicken from bones; discard bones and cut meat into cubes; set aside.

In a soup kettle, combine oil or drippings and flour until smooth. Cook over medium-high heat for 5 minutes, stirring constantly. Reduce heat to medium. Cook and stir about 5 minutes more or until mixture is reddish-brown (the color of a penny). Turn the heat to high. Stir in 2 cups reserved broth. Bring to a boil; cook and stir for 2 minutes or until thickened.

Add the onions, celery, green pepper and garlic; cook and stir for 5 minutes. Add the tomatoes, okra, bay leaves, basil, salt, pepper and pepper sauce. Cover and simmer for 1-1/2 to 2 hours.

Discard bay leaves. Garnish with green onions and parsley. Serve with rice. **yield:** 8-10 servings.

OREGANO OLIVE CHICKEN

prep 15 minutes | **cook** 30 minutes

This chicken recipe is lower in calories, fat or sodium.

consuelo lewter
murfreesboro, tennessee

Folks won't believe a recipe that tastes so savory and special could be so light! Full of fresh-herb flavor, this chicken boasts a wonderful fragrance as it cooks.

1   broiler/fryer chicken (4 pounds), cut up and skin removed
1/4   teaspoon pepper
2   tablespoons olive oil
1/2   cup white wine *or* reduced-sodium chicken broth
1/2   cup chopped pimiento-stuffed olives
1/4   cup capers, drained
2   tablespoons minced fresh oregano
1   tablespoon minced fresh mint
1   tablespoon cider vinegar
2   garlic cloves, minced
1   teaspoon minced fresh thyme

Sprinkle chicken with pepper. In a large nonstick skillet coated with cooking spray, brown chicken on all sides in oil. Remove and keep warm. Drain drippings from skillet.

Combine the remaining ingredients; pour into skillet, stirring to loosen browned bits. Bring to a boil. Carefully return chicken to the pan. Reduce heat; cover and simmer for 20-25 minutes or until chicken juices run clear. **yield:** 8 servings.

nutrition facts: 3 ounces cooked chicken with 2 tablespoons olive mixture equals 217 calories, 11 g fat (2 g saturated fat), 73 mg cholesterol, 370 mg sodium, 2 g carbohydrate, trace fiber, 24 g protein.

diabetic exchanges: 3 lean meat, 1 fat.

ITALIAN CHICKEN ROLL-UPS

prep 20 minutes | **bake** 25 minutes

barbara wobser
sandusky, ohio

Because I have a busy schedule, I like to keep a batch of these tender chicken rolls in the freezer. Coated with golden crumbs, they seem fancy enough for company.

8   boneless skinless chicken breast halves (4 ounces *each*)
8   thin slices (4 ounces) deli ham
4   slices provolone cheese, halved
2/3   cup seasoned bread crumbs
1/2   cup grated Romano *or* Parmesan cheese
1/4   cup minced fresh parsley
1/2   cup milk
Cooking spray

Flatten chicken to 1/4-in. thickness. Place a slice of ham and half slice of cheese on each piece of chicken. Roll up from a short side and tuck in ends; secure with a toothpick.

In a shallow bowl, combine crumbs, Romano cheese and parsley. Pour milk into another bowl. Dip chicken rolls in milk, then roll in crumb mixture.

Wrap each of four chicken roll-ups in plastic wrap; place in a large freezer bag. Seal and freeze for up to 2 months. Place the remaining roll-ups, seam side down, on a greased baking sheet. Spritz chicken with cooking spray. Bake, uncovered, at 425° for 25 minutes or until juices run clear. Remove toothpicks.

To use frozen chicken: Completely thaw in the refrigerator. Unwrap roll-ups and place on a greased baking sheet. Spritz with cooking spray. Bake, uncovered, at 425° for 30 minutes or until juices run clear. **yield:** 8 servings.

CHICKEN CACCIATORE

prep 10 minutes | **cook** 50 minutes

6   boneless skinless chicken breast halves (4 ounces *each*)
1   teaspoon salt, *divided*
1/8   teaspoon pepper
2   tablespoons olive oil, *divided*
1   medium green pepper, chopped
1/2   pound fresh mushrooms, sliced
4   garlic cloves, minced
1   can (15 ounces) tomato puree
1   can (14-1/2 ounces) stewed tomatoes, cut up
1   tablespoon balsamic vinegar
2   teaspoons sugar
1-1/2   teaspoons dried basil
1-1/2   teaspoons dried oregano
1/4   teaspoon crushed red pepper flakes
1/4   cup minced fresh parsley
Hot cooked spaghetti, optional

Sprinkle chicken with 1/4 teaspoon salt and pepper. In a large nonstick skillet, brown chicken in 1 tablespoon oil. Remove and set aside. In the same skillet, saute the green pepper, mushrooms and garlic in remaining oil until vegetables are tender.

Add the tomato puree, stewed tomatoes, vinegar, sugar, basil, oregano, red pepper flakes, remaining salt and reserved chicken. Bring to a boil. Reduce heat; cover and simmer for 30 minutes.

Stir in parsley. Simmer, uncovered, 15 minutes longer or until sauce is thickened. Serve over spaghetti if desired. **yield:** 6 servings.

nutrition facts: 1 chicken breast half with 1/2 cup sauce (calculated without spaghetti) equals 248 calories, 8 g fat (1 g saturated fat), 67 mg cholesterol, 857 mg sodium, 18 g carbohydrate, 3 g fiber, 29 g protein.

diabetic exchanges: 3 lean meat, 3 vegetable.

taste of home test kitchen
greendale, wisconsin

For an entree with Italian flair, try these tender chicken breasts simmered in a nicely seasoned tomato sauce. The sauce has chunks of green pepper and mushrooms, and gets a little zip from balsamic vinegar and red pepper flakes.

SANTA FE CHICKEN

prep/total time 30 minutes

jon carole gilbreath
tyler, texas

Chicken and rice are dressed up with a zippy sauce for a complete meal that's ready in a dash. Garnished with fresh cilantro, it's a festive weeknight supper or special occasion menu.

1   large onion, chopped
1   to 2 tablespoons chopped seeded jalapeno pepper
1   garlic clove, minced
1   tablespoon olive oil
1-1/4   cups reduced-sodium chicken broth
1   can (10 ounces) diced tomatoes and green chilies, undrained
1   cup uncooked long grain rice
4   boneless skinless chicken breast halves (4 ounces *each*)
1/2   teaspoon salt
1/4   teaspoon pepper
1/4   teaspoon ground cumin

3/4   cup shredded reduced-fat cheddar cheese

Minced fresh cilantro, optional

In a large skillet, saute the onion, jalapeno and garlic in oil until tender. Add broth and tomatoes; bring to a boil. Stir in rice.

Sprinkle the chicken with salt, pepper and cumin; place over rice mixture. Cover and simmer for 10-15 minutes on each side or until the chicken juices run clear.

Remove from the heat. Sprinkle with cheese; cover and let stand for 5 minutes. Garnish with cilantro if desired. **yield:** 4 servings.

editor's note: When cutting hot peppers, disposable gloves are recommended. Avoid touching your face.

TUSCAN CHICKEN BREASTS

prep/total time 30 minutes

erin renouf mylroie
santa clara, utah

I teach a college humanities class one night a week and rely on quick recipes to make dinner for my family before I race out the door. This has been a favorite that everyone adores.

1 cup chopped onion
1 cup *each* chopped sweet yellow and red peppers
1 tablespoon olive oil
1 tablespoon minced garlic
4 boneless skinless chicken breast halves (4 to 6 ounces *each*)
1 can (14-1/2 ounces) Italian diced tomatoes, drained
2/3 cup chicken broth
1 tablespoon balsamic vinegar
3/4 teaspoon salt
1/4 teaspoon sugar
1/8 teaspoon crushed red pepper flakes
1/8 teaspoon pepper
Hot cooked pasta
1/4 cup shredded Parmesan cheese

In a large skillet, saute the onion and peppers in oil for 4-5 minutes or until crisp-tender. Stir in the minced garlic; cook 1-2 minutes longer or until the vegetables are tender.

Flatten chicken to 1/2-in. thickness; place over vegetables. Add the tomatoes, broth, vinegar, salt, sugar, pepper flakes and pepper. Bring to a boil. Reduce heat; simmer, uncovered, for 20-25 minutes or until chicken juices run clear and sauce is thickened. Serve with pasta. Sprinkle with Parmesan cheese. **yield:** 4 servings.

CHICKEN GYROS

prep 20 minutes + marinating | **cook** 10 minutes

1/4 cup lemon juice
2 tablespoons olive oil
3/4 teaspoon minced garlic, *divided*
1/2 teaspoon ground mustard
1/2 teaspoon dried oregano
1/2 pound boneless skinless chicken breasts, cut into 1/2-inch strips
1/2 cup chopped peeled cucumber
1/3 cup plain yogurt
1/4 teaspoon dill weed
2 whole gyro-style pitas (6 inches)
1/2 small red onion, thinly sliced

In a large resealable plastic bag, combine the lemon juice, oil, 1/2 teaspoon garlic, mustard and oregano; add chicken. Seal bag and turn to coat; refrigerate for at least 1 hour. In a small bowl, combine the cucumber, yogurt, dill and remaining garlic; cover and refrigerate until serving.

Drain and discard marinade. In a large non-stick skillet, saute the chicken for 7-8 minutes or until juices run clear. Spoon onto each pita bread. Top with yogurt mixture and onion; fold in half. **yield:** 2 servings.

taste of home test kitchen
greendale, wisconsin

These yummy Greek specialties are a cinch to prepare at home. Just take cooked chicken, coat it in a creamy cucumber-yogurt sauce, then tuck it into pita pockets. If you like, top the gyros with lettuce and diced tomato.

PINEAPPLE PEPPER CHICKEN

prep 30 minutes | **bake** 1 hour

phyllis minter
wakefield, kansas

I came up with this recipe years ago by combining a couple of family favorites. Easy and versatile, it's great for potlucks. I can make the sauce ahead and use all wings or leg quarters when they're on sale.

4 cups unsweetened pineapple juice
2-1/2 cups sugar
2 cups white vinegar
1-1/2 cups water
1 cup packed brown sugar
2/3 cup cornstarch
1/2 cup ketchup
6 tablespoons soy sauce
2 teaspoon chicken bouillon granules
3/4 teaspoon ground ginger
2 broiler/fryer chickens (3 to 3-1/2 pounds *each*), cut up
3 tablespoons canola oil
1 can (8 ounces) pineapple chunks, drained
1 medium green pepper, julienned

In a large saucepan, combine the first 10 ingredients; stir until smooth. Bring to a boil; cook and stir for 2 minutes or until thickened. Set aside. In a large skillet over medium-high heat, brown the chicken in oil on all sides.

Place chicken in two greased 13-in. x 9-in. baking dishes. Pour reserved sauce over chicken. Bake, uncovered, at 350° for 45 minutes or until chicken juices run clear. Add pineapple and green pepper. Bake 15 minutes longer or until heated through. **yield:** 12 servings.

JAMBALAYA

prep 20 minutes | **cook** 20 minutes

1 pound smoked kielbasa *or* smoked Polish sausage, cut into 1/4-inch slices
1 pound boneless skinless chicken breasts, cut into 1-inch cubes
2 celery ribs, thinly sliced
1 large onion, chopped
1 medium green pepper, chopped
2 garlic cloves, minced
1 can (28 ounces) diced tomatoes, undrained
2 cups uncooked rice
2 cups water
1/2 pound fresh *or* frozen uncooked medium shrimp, peeled and deveined
3 tablespoons minced fresh parsley
2 tablespoons Worcestershire sauce
1 teaspoon salt
1/2 teaspoon dried thyme
1/4 to 1/2 teaspoon cayenne pepper

In a Dutch oven, saute sausage for 1 minute. Add chicken; saute 2 minutes longer. Add the celery, onion, green pepper and garlic; saute for 2 minutes or until vegetables are crisp-tender. Stir in the remaining ingredients. Bring to a boil.

Reduce heat; cover and simmer for 20 minutes or until chicken juices run clear. Stir to fluff the rice. Let stand for 5 minutes to absorb any remaining liquid before serving. **yield:** 8 servings.

glada marie st. clair
crossville, tennessee

I first tasted this dish at a church potluck. I got the original recipe from my daughter's godfather and adapted it to suit my family's tastes.

ARROZ CON POLLO

prep 10 minutes | **cook** 50 minutes

1	can (14-1/2 ounces) diced tomatoes, drained
1/2	cup chopped onion
4	garlic cloves, peeled
1	teaspoon salt, *divided*
1/2	teaspoon dried Mexican oregano
1/2	teaspoon chili powder
1/2	teaspoon pepper, *divided*
1	broiler/fryer chicken (3 to 4 pounds), cut up
3	tablespoons canola oil, *divided*
1-1/2	cups uncooked long grain rice
3	cups chicken broth
1	cup frozen peas

In a blender, combine the tomatoes, onion, whole garlic cloves, 1/2 teaspoon salt, oregano, chili powder and 1/4 teaspoon pepper; cover and process until smooth. Set aside.

Sprinkle chicken with remaining salt and pepper. In a large skillet over medium heat, cook the chicken in batches in 2 tablespoons oil for 10 minutes or until lightly browned. Remove and keep warm. In the same skillet, saute the rice for 2 minutes or until lightly browned. Stir in broth.

In a Dutch oven, heat the remaining oil; add tomato mixture. Bring to a boil; cook and stir for 4 minutes. Stir in rice mixture; bring to a boil.

Arrange chicken in pan. Reduce heat to medium; cover and cook for 25-30 minutes or until rice is tender and chicken juices run clear. Stir in peas; cover and let stand for 4 minutes or until peas are heated through. **yield:** 5-6 servings.

taste of home test kitchen
greendale, wisconsin

If comfort food is what you crave, then Chicken with Rice is the dish for you. It has a little bit of everything: heartiness, ease of preparation and great flavor.

MULLIGATAWNY SOUP

prep 20 minutes | **cook** 45 minutes

esther nafziger

la junta, colorado

One taste of this traditional curry-flavored soup that originated in India, and folks will know it didn't come from a can! This soup fills the kitchen with a wonderful aroma while it's simmering.

1	medium tart apple, peeled and diced
1/4	cup *each* chopped carrot, celery and onion
1/4	cup butter, cubed
1/3	cup all-purpose flour
1	teaspoon curry powder
1/2	teaspoon sugar
1/2	teaspoon salt
1/8	teaspoon pepper
1/8	teaspoon ground mace
6	cups chicken *or* turkey broth
1	cup cubed cooked chicken *or* turkey
1	medium tomato, peeled, seeded and chopped
1/2	cup chopped green pepper
2	whole cloves
1	tablespoon minced fresh parsley
1	cup cooked rice

In a Dutch oven or soup kettle, saute the apple, carrot, celery and onion in butter for 5 minutes or until tender. Stir in the flour, curry powder, sugar, salt, pepper and ground mace until blended. Gradually add the broth.

Bring to a boil. Cook and stir for 2 minutes or until thickened. Add the chicken, tomato, green pepper, cloves and parsley; return to a boil. Reduce heat; cover and simmer for 20-30 minutes. Add rice; heat through. Discard cloves before serving. **yield:** 8 servings (about 2 quarts).

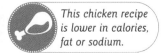

This chicken recipe is lower in calories, fat or sodium.

ISLAND JERK CHICKEN

prep 15 minutes + marinating | **grill** 10 minutes

lynn davis
st. louis park, minnesota

My husband is crazy about hot sauce and I'm not. But to my surprise, I absolutely loved this chicken!

- 3/4 cup water
- 4 green onions, chopped
- 2 tablespoons canola oil
- 1 tablespoon hot pepper sauce
- 4 teaspoons ground allspice
- 3 garlic cloves, minced
- 2 teaspoons ground cinnamon
- 1 teaspoon salt
- 1 teaspoon ground nutmeg
- 4 boneless skinless chicken breast halves (4 ounces *each*)

In a small saucepan, combine the first nine ingredients; bring to a boil. Reduce heat; simmer, uncovered, for 10 minutes. Cool to room temperature.

Pour 1/2 cup marinade into a large resealable plastic bag; add the chicken. Seal the bag and turn to coat the chicken; refrigerate overnight. Transfer the remaining marinade to a small bowl; cover and refrigerate for basting.

Coat grill rack with cooking spray before starting the grill. Drain and discard marinade. Grill chicken, covered, over medium heat for 4-7 minutes on each side or until juices run clear, basting occasionally with reserved marinade. **yield:** 4 servings.

nutrition facts: 1 chicken breast half equals 168 calories, 7 g fat (1 g saturated fat), 63 mg cholesterol, 437 mg sodium, 2 g carbohydrate, 1 g fiber, 23 g protein.

diabetic exchanges: 3 very lean meat, 1 fat.

SZECHUAN CHICKEN NOODLE TOSS

prep/total time 20 minutes

- 4 quarts water
- 6 ounces uncooked thin spaghetti
- 1 package (16 ounces) frozen stir-fry vegetable blend
- 1 tablespoon reduced-fat stick margarine
- 1 pound boneless skinless chicken breasts, cut into 2-inch strips
- 2 garlic cloves, minced
- 1/8 teaspoon crushed red pepper flakes
- 1 tablespoon canola oil
- 1/3 cup stir-fry sauce
- 3 green onions, chopped

In a Dutch oven, bring water to a boil. Add spaghetti; cook for 4 minutes. Add vegetables; cook 3-4 minutes longer or until spaghetti and vegetables are tender. Drain. Toss with margarine; set aside and keep warm.

In a nonstick skillet, stir-fry the chicken, garlic and red pepper flakes in oil until the chicken is no longer pink. Add the stir-fry sauce; heat through. Add the onions and spaghetti mixture; toss to coat. **yield:** 4 servings.

editor's note: This recipe was tested with Parkay Light stick margarine.

carol roane
sarasota, florida

My family loves Chinese food, so I came up with this quick and easy recipe to use up leftover chicken, pork or beef. It's so good, you won't order out again.

SOUTHWEST SMOTHERED CHICKEN

prep/total time 30 minutes

debbie schaefer
durand, michigan

*Wow! There's a fiesta in
every bite of this tasty
chicken dish. Let it spice up
dinner tonight! If you're
worried about the heat,
simply reduce the amount
of jalapenos.*

4 boneless skinless chicken breast
halves (6 ounces *each*)
1/2 teaspoon ground cumin
1/2 teaspoon cayenne pepper
1 tablespoon canola oil
1 cup fresh *or* frozen corn
1 cup salsa
1 cup (4 ounces) shredded pepper
Jack cheese
1/4 cup pickled jalapeno slices
1/4 cup sour cream

Flatten chicken to 1/2-in. thickness. Sprinkle both
sides with cumin and cayenne. In a large skillet,
cook chicken in oil over medium heat for 4-5 minutes on each side or until juices run clear.

Meanwhile, combine corn and salsa; spoon over
chicken. Top with cheese and jalapenos. Cover
and cook for 3-5 minutes or until heated through
and cheese is melted. Top each chicken breast
with a dollop of sour cream. **yield:** 4 servings.

THAI RESTAURANT CHICKEN

prep/total time 30 minutes

2 tablespoons cornstarch
1 tablespoon brown sugar
1/4 teaspoon pepper
1 can (14-1/2 ounces)
reduced-sodium chicken broth
2 tablespoons rice vinegar
2 tablespoons reduced-sodium soy
sauce
2 tablespoons reduced-fat peanut
butter
1 pound boneless skinless chicken
breasts, cut into 1-inch cubes
2 teaspoons sesame oil, *divided*
1 large onion, halved and sliced
1 medium sweet red pepper,
julienned
1 cup sliced fresh mushrooms
2 garlic cloves, minced
2 cups hot cooked rice

In a large bowl, combine cornstarch, brown sugar
and pepper. Add broth; stir until smooth. Stir in the
vinegar, soy sauce and peanut butter; set aside.

In a large nonstick skillet or wok, stir-fry the
chicken in 1 teaspoon sesame oil until no longer
pink. Remove and keep warm.

Stir-fry the onion and red pepper in remaining
oil for 2 minutes. Add mushrooms and garlic; stir-
fry 2-3 minutes longer or until crisp-tender.

Stir cornstarch mixture and add to the pan.
Bring to a boil; cook and stir for 1-2 minutes or
until thickened. Add chicken; heat through. Serve
with rice. **yield:** 4 servings.

nutrition facts: 1 cup stir-fry with 1/2 cup rice equals
359 calories, 8 g fat (2 g saturated fat), 63 mg cholesterol, 704 mg sodium, 40 g carbohydrate, 2 g fiber, 31 g
protein.

diabetic exchanges: 3 very lean meat, 2 starch,
1 vegetable, 1 fat.

*This chicken recipe
is lower in calories,
fat or sodium.*

trisha kruse
eagle, idaho

*Additional veggies can be
added to make your own
version of this Thai
restaurant specialty.*

GREEN TEA TERIYAKI CHICKEN

prep/total time 25 minutes

This chicken recipe is lower in calories, fat or sodium.

3-1/2 teaspoons green tea leaves, *divided*
    1 cup boiling water
    4 green onions, chopped, *divided*
    3 tablespoons honey
    2 tablespoons cider vinegar
    2 tablespoons reduced-sodium soy sauce
    4 garlic cloves, minced
  1/2 teaspoon minced fresh gingerroot
  1/8 teaspoon sesame oil
    4 boneless skinless chicken breast halves (4 ounces *each*)

Place 2-1/2 teaspoons tea leaves in a small bowl; add boiling water. Cover and steep for 5-6 minutes.

Strain and discard leaves; pour tea into a large skillet. Add half of the onions. Stir in the honey, vinegar, soy sauce, garlic, ginger and sesame oil. Bring to a boil. Reduce heat; simmer, uncovered, until sauce is reduced to about 3/4 cup.

Add chicken and remaining tea leaves; cover and cook over medium heat for 4-5 minutes on each side or until chicken juices run clear. Cut chicken into thin slices; serve with sauce. Garnish with remaining onions. **yield:** 4 servings.

nutrition facts: 1 chicken breast half with 3 table-spoons sauce equals 184 calories, 3 g fat (1 g saturated fat), 63 mg cholesterol, 359 mg sodium, 16 g carbohy-drate, trace fiber, 24 g protein.

diabetic exchanges: 3 very lean meat, 1 starch.

taste of home test kitchen
greendale, wisconsin

Tender chicken is treated to an Asian-inspired sauce with green tea for a low-fat entree that really stands out. Serve it with fragrant rice, like jasmine, for a restaurant-quality meal.

EASY CHICKEN ENCHILADAS

prep 20 minutes | **bake** 25 minutes

kristi black
harrison township,
michigan

This recipe is so quick and easy, and I always receive a ton of compliments when I serve it. It quickly becomes a favorite of friends whenever I share the recipe.

1 can (10 ounces) enchilada sauce, *divided*
4 ounces cream cheese, cubed
1-1/2 cups salsa
2 cups cubed cooked chicken
1 can (15-1/2 ounces) pinto beans, rinsed and drained
1 can (4 ounces) chopped green chilies
10 flour tortillas (6 inches)
1 cup (4 ounces) shredded Mexican cheese blend
Shredded lettuce, chopped tomato, sour cream and sliced ripe olives, optional

Spoon 1/2 cup of the enchilada sauce into a greased 13-in. x 9-in. baking dish. In a large saucepan, cook and stir the cream cheese and salsa over medium heat for 2-3 minutes or until blended. Stir in the chicken, beans and chilies.

Place about 6 tablespoons of chicken mixture down the center of each tortilla. Roll up and place seam side down over sauce. Top with remaining enchilada sauce; sprinkle with cheese.

Cover and bake at 350° for 25-30 minutes or until heated through. Serve with shredded lettuce, tomato, sour cream and olives if desired. **yield:** 5 servings.

MANGO CHICKEN CURRY

prep/total time 30 minutes

taste of home test kitchen
greendale, wisconsin

Be sure not to confuse coconut milk with cream of coconut, a thick sweet product often used to make drinks. Coconut milk can be found in the Asian section of your grocery store.

1/2 cup chopped onion
1 medium sweet red pepper, julienned
2 teaspoons canola oil
1-1/2 pounds boneless skinless chicken breasts, cut into thin strips
1 tablespoon curry powder
2 teaspoons minced fresh gingerroot
1 teaspoon minced garlic
1/2 teaspoon salt
1/8 teaspoon cayenne pepper
1 cup chopped peeled mango
3/4 cup coconut milk
2 tablespoons tomato paste
Hot cooked rice, optional

In a large skillet, saute onion and red pepper in oil for 2-4 minutes or until crisp-tender. Add the chicken, curry, ginger, garlic, salt and cayenne. Cook and stir for 5 minutes.

Stir in the mango, coconut milk and tomato paste; bring to a boil. Reduce heat; cover and simmer for 10 minutes or until chicken juices run clear. Serve with rice if desired. **yield:** 4 servings.

CREOLE CHICKEN

prep 15 minutes | **cook** 25 minutes

This chicken recipe is lower in calories, fat or sodium.

2 boneless skinless chicken breast halves (4 ounces *each*)
1 teaspoon canola oil
1 can (14-1/2 ounces) stewed tomatoes, cut up
1/3 cup julienned green pepper
1/4 cup chopped celery
1/4 cup sliced onion
1/2 to 1 teaspoon chili powder
1/2 teaspoon dried thyme
1/8 teaspoon pepper
1 cup hot cooked rice

In a small nonstick skillet coated with cooking spray, cook the chicken in oil over medium heat for 5-6 minutes on each side or until juices run clear. Remove and keep warm.

In the same skillet, combine the tomatoes, green pepper, celery, onion, chili powder, thyme and pepper. Bring to a boil. Reduce heat; cover and simmer for 10 minutes or until vegetables are crisp-tender. Return chicken to pan; heat through. Serve with rice. **yield:** 2 servings.

nutrition facts: 1 chicken breast half with 2/3 cup sauce and 1/2 cup rice equals 320 calories, 5 g fat (1 g saturated fat), 63 mg cholesterol, 447 mg sodium, 41 g carbohydrate, 3 g fiber, 27 g protein.

diabetic exchanges: 3 very lean meat, 3 vegetable, 1-1/2 starch, 1/2 fat.

susan shields
arcadia, florida

Chili powder lends just a hint of heat to this full-flavored and oh-so-easy chicken entree.

General Recipe Index

• recipe includes nutrition facts

• recipe includes nutrition facts

• recipe includes nutrition facts

• recipe includes nutrition facts

• recipe includes nutrition facts

• recipe includes nutrition facts

• recipe includes nutrition facts

Alphabetical Recipe Index

• recipe includes nutrition facts

• recipe includes nutrition facts

• recipe includes nutrition facts